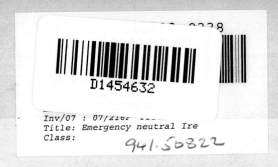

Inv/07 : 07/216F
Title: Emergency neutral Ire
Class: 941.50322

THE EMERGENCY

Brian Girvin is Professor of Comparative Politics at the
University of Glasgow. He is the author of many books, most notably
Between Two Worlds: Politics and Economy in Independent Ireland,
The Right in the Twentieth Century and *Union to Union:
Nationalism, Democracy and Religion in Ireland*.

WITHDRAWN FROM FINGAL
COUNTY LIBRARY STOCK

BRIAN GIRVIN

THE EMERGENCY

NEUTRAL IRELAND 1939–45

PAN BOOKS

First published 2006 by Macmillan

First published in paperback 2007 by Pan Books
an imprint of Pan Macmillan Ltd
Pan Macmillan, 20 New Wharf Road, London N1 9RR
Basingstoke and Oxford
Associated companies throughout the world
www.panmacmillan.com

ISBN 978-0-330-49329-1

Copyright © Brian Girvin 2006

The right of Brian Girvin to be identified as the
author of this work has been asserted by him in accordance
with the Copyright, Designs and Patents Act 1988.

Picture credits can be found on page 387.

All rights reserved. No part of this publication may be
reproduced, stored in or introduced into a retrieval system, or
transmitted, in any form, or by any means (electronic, mechanical,
photocopying, recording or otherwise) without the prior written
permission of the publisher. Any person who does any unauthorized
act in relation to this publication may be liable to criminal
prosecution and civil claims for damages.

1 3 5 7 9 8 6 4 2

A CIP catalogue record for this book is available from
the British Library.

Typeset by SetSystems Ltd, Saffron Walden, Essex
Printed and bound in Great Britain by
Mackays of Chatham plc, Chatham, Kent

This book is sold subject to the condition that it shall not,
by way of trade or otherwise, be lent, re-sold, hired out,
or otherwise circulated without the publisher's prior consent
in any form of binding or cover other than that in which
it is published and without a similar condition including this
condition being imposed on the subsequent purchaser.

Visit **www.panmacmillan.com** to read more about all our books
and to buy them. You will also find features, author interviews and
news of any author events, and you can sign up for e-newsletters
so that you're always first to hear about our new releases.

To

RONA

with all my love

and to the memory of my father
BRENDAN GIRVIN
1924–98

Contents

Preface

My original interest in Ireland, the Emergency and the Second World War was sparked by a conversation nearly twenty years ago with a research student. We were discussing Irish migration to Britain during the war and I mentioned those Irish citizens who had joined the British armed forces between 1939 and 1945. She replied that they had been forced to do so because of unemployment in Ireland. This seemed unconvincing to me, as they could just as easily have travelled to Britain and worked in the war industries, as many indeed did. Moreover they would have also been paid a lot more and not placed themselves in immediate danger.

The issue intrigued me and I raised the question with others when the occasion allowed. The most common response was similar to that of my research student, but others argued that those Irish who joined up were simply mercenaries fighting for another country in a struggle that was no business of Ireland's. These two standpoints fascinated me and I began to look more closely at the war and how it had affected Ireland. Reading Robert Fisk's excellent *In Time of War* (1983) I discovered that the issue of Irish citizens fighting in the Second World War had been highly contentious and the cause of some controversy between Britain and Ireland at the end of the war. Nationalists and Unionists had vied with one another in using the volunteers to promote their points of view. More seriously, although various figures existed for the number of those who had volunteered for the British forces, there was no certainty about them. Estimates ranged from 40,000 to over 200,000, but the basis of these figures was not at all certain. However, the excellent work of Richard Doherty and Yvonne McEwen has now provided accurate assessments of the numbers from Ireland north and south that fought in the war. There is still work to be done on this issue, but at least we now have some strong figures on which to work.

Finding out how many individuals had volunteered was important but did not explain why they had done so. The opportunity to explore this question occurred when my friend and colleague Geoff Roberts suggested that we apply for a grant to interview surviving volunteers. The President's Fund of University College Cork generously awarded us a grant to pursue this objective. The interviews put a human face on the statistics, as the personal histories of those who enlisted make fascinating reading. In every case the reasons for volunteering were complex, but in virtually no instance were financial or mercenary reasons the key explanation. Most volunteers respected Ireland's decision to remain neutral during the war, though some certainly believed that their country might have played a more active role on the Allied side. What we did find was considerable regret that their contribution was ignored in Ireland after the war and that they were often marginalized if they returned home. Indeed, in so far as a conclusion can be drawn from the existing evidence, most of those who volunteered returned to an Ireland that was uneasy with them and often unwelcoming. It is perhaps not surprising that most of those who volunteered chose to live elsewhere after the war.

The other stimulus to my research came from the ongoing debate on Irish neutrality and its significance for the future of Ireland in the European Union. I was an active proponent of European integration, believing that Ireland should join NATO as part of its commitment to European defence, but the debate raised more questions than it answered. I discovered that neutrality was not about the best policy option for the Irish state and people, but was linked to defending Irish identity and hostility to Britain. In my book *From Union to Union* (2002) I addressed the issue of Irish identity and its distinctive character in a fashion that I believe emphasized the long-term stability of Irish identity. However, studying these themes raised the question of what Irish neutrality was and how it has been used by the Irish state. If neutrality was not a policy position that could be changed when conditions merited it but an expression of some deeper emotional need on the part of Irish nationalism, how did such a stance emerge? This drove me more and more to look at Irish neutrality in the Second World War and the consequences for Ireland and its neighbours of the decisions taken at that time.

What is recounted in this book is the deeply ambiguous nature of Ireland's relationship with the Allies during the war and the morally dubious stance taken by the Irish government on certain occasions and issues. The clearest example of this is discussed in Chapter One, which assesses the reasons and the consequences of Eamon de Valera's decision to offer his condolences on Hitler's death in May 1945. But this was not an isolated incident, as the narrative shows in some detail. What this incident highlights is that opinion in Ireland was seriously divided during the war and, notwithstanding later denials, there was widespread support for Hitler and the Axis. The most explicit expression of this was the active cooperation of the Irish republican movement with Nazi Germany, but sympathy for the Axis cause extended well beyond the IRA.

There was another related issue that spurred me to write this book. Most studies of Irish policy during the Second World War conclude that there was no alternative to neutrality. This is a widespread if not altogether persuasive assessment which presupposes that the choice was between all-out involvement in the war or complete neutrality to the extent that the Irish state was indifferent to its outcome. Yet, as certain chapters here suggest, other options were available at various times and some of these would have involved Ireland giving the Allies much-needed support without actually going to war. Ireland could also have joined the war at any time after 1943 with relatively little cost but considerable benefit. That the Irish government decided not to pursue any of these options suggests to me that the policymakers (a fairly small group around de Valera) were neutral as to the war's outcome. This seems a morally questionable position at best, but it is one that the Irish state has in effect asserted ever since. Ireland might maintain that it was both neutral and in favour of democracy and protecting human rights, but there is very little evidence that it was prepared to risk neutrality if that was what was required to support democracy.

I have been deeply influenced in considering these issues by Michael Walzer and his writing on the notion of the just war. In *Just and Unjust Wars* (originally published in 1977) there is an important, if neglected, discussion on the rights and responsibilities attendant on a state being neutral in wartime. Walzer asks, 'How can any state stand and watch the destruction of a neighbour? How can the rest of us respect its right to stand and watch if, by violating that right, we might avert the destruction?' These are stark questions and ones that have particular importance in considering the Second World War. Every state has the right to be neutral, but has it the right to be indifferent to outcome?

The Second World War was obviously more morally complex at the time than appears in retrospect. Europeans favoured fascism, communism or liberal democracy for complex reasons and sometimes out of desperation. That democratic Finland fought alongside the Axis powers against the Soviet Union is understandable, even if strategically and politically it provided much-needed support to Nazi Germany. After May 1940 Britain stood alone in defence of democracy, decency and human rights, though this was not a view shared by Gandhi or the Indian National Congress. Notwithstanding this, the moral position was not ambiguous; if Britain were defeated democracy would have been extinguished. Irish democracy was protected throughout the Second World War by British defiance, its navy and its air force. At crucial times Ireland could have aided Britain in its hour of need but chose not to. It was the Irish state's right to act in this way, but in doing so its government evaded a moral responsibility and may also have weakened the national interest. Ireland was not the worst neutral in this respect, though this may have had more to do with its fortuitous geographical position and its relationships with the United Kingdom and the United States than any stance adopted by the government. Sweden and Switzerland were in more invidious positions and neither state emerged unblemished. Swiss neutrality has been the focus of increasingly bitter criticism in recent years, especially because of its treatment of Jews, and its self-interestedness seems to have gone well beyond acceptable limits for a democracy. Sweden adapted its neutrality as the war progressed. When occupied Denmark could no longer protect its Jewish citizens, Sweden agreed to accept them and they were ferried out of the country by the Danish resistance. This occurred in October 1943, and it is questionable if Sweden would have been as willing to accept the Jews a year earlier. Ireland had more choices available to it by 1943, yet what became apparent from my research is that its neutrality became more inflexible as the war progressed.

My continuing fascination with Fianna Fáil and its leader Eamon de Valera was another factor which prompted me to write this book. De Valera remains the most important political figure in twentieth-century Irish history and Fianna Fáil has been the most successful political party in the Irish state. I was interested in how neutrality, national interest and domestic politics intersected. As this book reveals, de Valera and Fianna Fáil quite consciously used the Emergency to consolidate the party's political power and extend its ideological influence into every sphere of Irish political life. I also conclude that though de Valera successfully defended Irish sovereignty, the cost was extremely high. Neutrality consolidated the border between north and south, while deepening divisions within Northern Ireland. It isolated Ireland from the victorious Allies for nearly two decades and, even more seriously, prevented Ireland from appreciating the advantages to it of participating in the expanding Europe of the 1950s. Isolation also reinforced trends which had an overwhelmingly negative impact on post-war Ireland. Emigration, population decline, economic stagnancy, Catholic intolerance and nationalist extremism were all sustained by the Irish experience of the Emergency. It is only when de Valera leaves the scene in 1959 that Ireland awakens from the slumber that set in during the Emergency. Only then could the state and its citizens rejoin Europe and begin the slow and difficult task of cooperating with its neighbours and improving the lot of those who lived in Ireland.

*

This book would definitely not have been written if Catherine Clarke had not persuaded me to do so. I am delighted that she did and would like to thank her for her support during the process. Likewise George Morley, my editor at Pan Macmillan, was supportive and patient with me, while encouraging me to meet my deadlines (not always successfully). This book has been helped immeasurably by the advice and help provided by many people. Not all of them will agree with what I have written or with the conclusions that I have drawn. I am ultimately responsible for everything written here, though some of my debts will be clear from the text. The most important single influence is Geoff Roberts, a friend with whom I worked after he joined the History Department at University College Cork ten years ago. The impact of the Second World War on Ireland has been a recurring focus of our discussions. Since I left Cork Geoff has been central in forcing me to think through the issues and has provided material support for visits. His support, intellectual and personal, places me in his debt. A special word of thanks is due to those Irish men and women who agreed to be interviewed for the Volunteers Project. Their reflections and thoughts on many subjects illuminated my research and provided me with insights that only those who have lived through an event can possess. Tina Neylon interviewed the volunteers in a thoughtful and sensitive fashion and provided me with summaries of the extensive oral archive. Tina has played a central role in this project and I am grateful to her for her involvement. Fiona Bell typed a considerable amount of the text at a crucial moment, allowing me to concentrate on refining the work. Her application and skill are appreciated. Other scholars have been generous with their help. I have gained in particular from Eunan O'Halpin's work, but Eunan has also been generous with his research and pointed me in the direction of material that I needed. Yvonne McEwen has generously shared her path-breaking work on the volunteers and I am grateful to her for letting me have a copy of her unpublished research.

The Department of Politics at Glasgow University has helped in numerous ways over the years, while the departmental travel fund has aided research trips on various occasions. Andrew Lockyer, the head of department, supported my application for a period of leave without which this book would not have been completed when it was. The British Academy awarded me a research grant to visit archives to search for documents central to this study. Seamus Helferty and his hard-working staff at the Archives Department, University College Dublin, provided an environment conducive to research on key personal papers. The general secretary of Fianna Fáil kindly granted me permission to consult the party papers. Commandant Victor Laing at the Military Archives in Dublin identified a number of important sources for me and he and his staff were helpful on all occasions. Likewise the staff at the National Archives of Ireland and the National Library of Ireland provided much-needed advice and support for my many requests and queries. In London the Public Records Office at Kew has been an important source of material on British attitudes and policy. In the United States staff at the Roosevelt Presidential Library at Hyde Park were unfailingly attentive to my requests for material, and in the small and intimate surroundings of the former Roosevelt residence it was possible to see some of the characters come to life. The National Archives of the United States at College Park Maryland was the main source for US State Department and intelligence and security material. I would like to thank Blythe E. Roveland-Brenton at St John's University New York for her help in accessing the archives of the American Friends of Irish Neutrality.

*

Rona Fitzgerald, with whom I have lived for over ten years, has supported me in my research and writing in unhesitating fashion, even when she was engaged on difficult and engaging work herself. Authors often thank their partners for support while writing a book; in my case this is absolutely appropriate. Without Rona I might never have finished this book. She provided emotional and logistical support without complaint, but her most important contribution was intellectual. She read various versions of the text and commented in her usual incisive and intelligent fashion while also embarking on a demanding job herself. Those who deny that women are the stronger sex have not had the fortune to see Rona in action. We live in an impermanent world, but her companionship makes it all worthwhile. This book is dedicated with love and affection to her, but I hope she also sees it as an encouragement to complete her own creative purposes in the near future. It is also dedicated to the memory of my father Brendan Girvin, who died in 1998. Our relationship was never untroubled, but we had become easier with our differences during the last decade of his life. While he probably would have disagreed with some of this book, I do hope he would have enjoyed it.

Brian Girvin

Time Line

1800   Act of Union between Britain and Ireland agreed by both Irish and British parliaments. This ended the formal parliamentary independence conceded in 1782, though Ireland had had a separate parliament since 1295. Daniel O'Connell (1775–1847) opposed the Union and in a series of campaigns organized Catholic opinion in opposition. His campaign led to Catholic emancipation in 1829, but he failed in his ultimate ambition to repeal the Union itself.

1845–1849   The Great Famine decimated Irish society, leaving one million dead and leading many more to emigrate. Nationalists blamed the British government for negligence in the face of this tragedy.

1882   Eamon de Valera born in New York (d. 1975), but raised and educated in County Limerick.

1886–1914   Home Rule Bills introduced 1886, 1893 and 1912. The first two were rejected, while the third was enacted in 1914 but suspended for the duration of the First World War. Designed to meet Irish nationalist demands for reform of the Union, but British and Unionist opposition alienated some sections of the nationalist movement.

1916   *24 April to 1 May.* Easter Rising (also known as the Irish Rebellion). Radical nationalists occupied much of central Dublin and fought crown forces until forced to surrender. Fifteen of the leaders were executed, but de Valera's death sentence was commuted in part due to his American birth.

1917   Jailed nationalists released. De Valera was elected president of a reorganized Sinn Fin in October and of the paramilitary Irish Volunteers two days later.

1918   *17–18 May.* Leaders of Sinn Féin arrested in 'German plot' and deported to Britain.

1918   In December general election, Sinn Féin becomes the dominant party in nationalist Ireland; winning seventy-three of the Irish seats. Sinn Féin adopts a policy of abstention from Westminster.

1919   *21 June.* Sinn Féin deputies meet in Dublin as Dáil (Irish parliament). Dáil declares independence, publishes a provisional constitution, an address to the free nations of the world and a democratic programme. On the same day Irish Volunteers in Tipperary attack a consignment of explosives and kill two policemen, often considered the first engagement of the Irish War of Independence.

   1 April. De Valera elected president of Dáil Eireann after escaping from jail in Britain on 3 February.

   28 June. Treaty of Versailles signed.

   12 September. Dáil Eireann declared illegal by British government.

1920   Violence escalates within Ireland as Irish Volunteers (IRA) and British government forces vie for control. Atrocities on both sides radicalize opinion. June local elections confirm continuing wide support for Sinn Féin.

   In December the Government of Ireland Act is enacted, providing two parliaments in Ireland. This legislative recognition of partition is rejected by nationalist opinion.

1921   *13 May.* In elections under the terms of the Government of Ireland Act, one hundred and twenty-four Sinn Féin and four independent candidates returned unopposed for Southern Ireland.

   9 July. Truce signed by IRA and British army.

   11 October. Anglo-Irish negotiations begin in London.

   6 December. Treaty between Irish and British governments signed in London.

   14 December. Dáil Eireann debates the terms of the Treaty (continues until 7 January 1922).

1922   *7 January.* Treaty approved by Dáil.

   9 January. De Valera resigns as president of Dáil in opposition to Treaty and is succeeded by Arthur Griffith.

16 June. Irish Free State general election: pro Treaty parties win 92 seats while those opposed win 36.

28 July. Irish civil war begins with government attack on paramilitary forces in Four Courts in Dublin. Continues until 27 April 1923 when de Valera and Frank Aiken order end of military activities by anti-Government forces.

1923 *27 August.* General Election: Cumann na nGaedheal 63; Republican 44; Labour 14; farmers 15; Independent and others 17.

10 September. Irish Free State becomes member of League of Nations.

1926 *16 May.* Fianna Fáil party launched by de Valera at La Scala Theatre, Dublin.

19 November. Imperial conference in London agrees that Dominions are 'autonomous communities within the British empire'.

1927 *9 June.* General Election: Cumann na nGaedheal 47; Fianna Fáil 44; Labour 22; farmers 11; National League 8; Sinn Féin 5; Independents and others 16.

10 July. Kevin O'Higgins, Minister for Justice, murdered by IRA.

20 July. Government introduces three bills to address crisis. The Electoral (Amendment No. 2) Act 1927 would exclude candidates who did not agree to take the oath of allegiance once elected.

16 August. Fianna Fáil members take oath of allegiance and take their seats in Dáil.

15 September. In second general election, Cumann na nGaedheal 62; Fianna Fáil 57; Labour 13; Farmers 6; National League 2; Independent and others 13.

1931 *Irish Press* newspaper published for first time. Controlled by the de Valera family, it is the propaganda voice of Fianna Fáil.

12 December. The Statute of Westminster extends effective sovereignty of Dominions by providing them with legal autonomy. In effect British law is no longer dominant in the Dominions.

1932 *16 February.* General Election. Fianna Fáil wins 72 seats but does not gain a majority. However, de Valera forms minority government with Labour support.

30 June. Beginning of economic war with Britain, which lasts until Anglo-Irish Agreements in 1938.

1933 *24 January.* De Valera calls snap general elections, which provides Fianna Fáil with majority. This provides de Valera with a mandate to introduce radical reforms that restructure the Irish state over the next five years.

2 September. New Fine Gael party established as counter to Fianna Fáil. Includes Cumann na nGaedheal, the Centre Party and the National Guard.

1937 New Constitution introduced by de Valera.

1 July. In general election Fianna Fáil loses its majority but the new Constitution is approved by a narrow majority.

29 December. Constitution comes into operation.

1938 *25 April.* Anglo-Irish agreement ends economic war, resolves outstanding financial issues and agrees the return of Treaty ports to Irish sovereignty.

17 June. Snap general election provides Fianna Fáil with working majority in Dáil.

1939 *12 January.* IRA demands Britain withdraw from Northern Ireland.

16 January. IRA bomb targets in British mainland.

4 May. UK government decides not to extend conscription to Northern Ireland due to opposition from de Valera and nationalist opinion.

25 August. Coventry bombing by IRA kills five. Barnes and McCormack executed on 7 February 1940.

1 September. Germany invades Poland.

2 September. De Valera addresses Dáil and receives overwhelming support for declaration of Irish neutrality in the event of war.

3 September. Britain and France declare war on Germany. Emergency Powers Act, 1939 enacted in Eire.

22 September. Chamberlain and de Valera agree that Sir John Maffey be appointed the UK Minister in Eire.

23 December. IRA raid on the Magazine Fort in the Phoenix Park – over one million rounds of ammunition taken.

1940   *3 January.* Irish government introduces new legislation to combat IRA.

25 February. IRA prisoners begin hunger strike. Government refuses concession and two prisoners die.

9 April. Germany invades Norway and Denmark.

5 May. German secret agent Hermann Görtz parachutes into Eire (remains free until November 1941).

10 May. Germany invades the Netherlands, Belgium and Luxembourg. Winston Churchill becomes prime minister.

29 May to 3 June. British evacuate from Dunkirk after collapse of the French forces.

10 June. Italy declares war on Britain and France.

17–27 June. British Minister for Health, Malcolm MacDonald, in Dublin negotiating with de Valera in attempt to bring Eire into war. Irish government refuses to abandon neutrality.

22 June. France surrenders to Germany.

5–7 November. Churchill criticizes Irish neutrality, while de Valera insists that the ports will not be leased or handed over to Britain.

1941   *1–3 January.* German bombing attacks on Eire.

2 January. Britain restricts supplies to Eire, leading to rationing and shortages during the year.

April/May. German bombing attacks on Belfast result in substantial loss of life and widespread destruction.

31 May. German bombing attack on Dublin leave thirty-four dead and ninety injured in North Strand.

22 June. Germany invades Soviet Union.

7 December. The United States enters the war after Japanese attack on Pearl Harbor.

1942   *January/February.* US troops arrive in Northern Ireland. Irish government complains to Americans.

19 February. James Dillon resigns from Fine Gael after advocating entering the war in support of US.

19 August. In local elections Fianna Fáil and Fine Gael do badly, while Labour, farmers' candidates and independents do well.

1943   *22 June.* In general election Fianna Fáil loses majority and Labour increases its share of vote. The new farmers' party Clann na Talmhan wins 10 seats. De Valera forms minority government.

10 July. Allies invade Sicily.

1944   *14 January.* Split in Labour Party and formation of National Labour Party.

18 January. W. T. Cosgrave resigns as leader of Fine Gael, succeeded by Richard Mulcahy.

21 February. American Minister David Gray delivers note requesting removal of German and Japanese diplomats from Dublin. De Valera refuses request. The Allies impose a blockade on communication and travel into and out of Eire in the run up to D-Day.

10 May. De Valera calls snap election after Dáil defeat.

30 May. Fianna Fáil wins comfortable majority in general election.

6 June. D-Day.

1945   *30 April.* Hitler commits suicide.

2 May. De Valera meets German minister to extend condolences on Hitler's death. The President's secretary also does so.

7–8 May. Anti-Allied demonstrations and riots after flag incident at Trinity College, Dublin.

8 May. End of war in Europe.

13 May. Churchill criticizes Irish neutrality in victory speech.

16 May. De Valera replies to Churchill.

14 August. Japan surrenders; end of war.

IRELAND, 1939

Lough Swilly

ANTRIM

DONEGAL

Derry

DERRY

Ballymena

Donegal

TYRONE

Omagh

Belfast

Lisburn

DOWN

FERMANAGH

Enniskillen

Sligo

Monaghan

ARMAGH

Newry

SLIGO

LEITRIM

MONAGHAN

MAYO

Castlebar

Carrick-on-Shannon

Cavan

CAVAN

Dundalk

LOUTH

ROSCOMMON

Longford

LONGFORD

Navan

MEATH

Roscommon

WESTMEATH

Mullingar

GALWAY

Galway

OFFALY
(KING'S)

Tullamore

Dublin

KILDARE

DUBLIN

Kildare

Portlaoise

LAOIS
(QUEEN'S)

Wicklow

WICKLOW

CLARE

Ennis

Carlow

CARLOW

Limerick

Kilkenny

Tralee

LIMERICK

TIPPERARY

KILKENNY

WEXFORD

Clonmel

Wexford

KERRY

Waterford

WATERFORD

Dungarvan

CORK

Cork

Cobh

Berehaven

| 0 | 25 | 50 | 75 | 100 kilometres |

| 0 | 10 | 20 | 30 | 40 | 50 miles |

OCCUPIED WESTERN EUROPE, 1942

0 100 200 300 400 500 kilometres

0   100   200   300 miles

- Greater Germany
- Powers co-operating with the Axis
- Territories under German occupation
- Italy and its territories
- Neutral countries

Atlantic Ocean

NORWAY

SWEDEN

Oslo

Stockholm

Gothenburg

IRELAND

Dublin

UNITED KINGDOM

DENMARK

Copenhagen

Hamburg

London

NETHERLANDS

The Hague

Berlin

GERMANY

BELGIUM

Brussels

Channel Islands

Frankfurt

Dresden

Paris

Prague

Rennes

FRANCE

Munich

Vienna

SLO.

Bern

Bratislava

Vichy

SWITZ.

AUSTRIA

HUNGARY

VICHY FRANCE

Bilbao

Zagreb

YUGOSLAVIA

ITALY

Sarajevo

PORTUGAL

Lisbon

Madrid

Barcelona

Corsica

Rome

SPAIN

Seville

Balearic Islands

Sardinia

Naples

Gibraltar

Mediterranean Sea

Palermo

Sicily

Rabat

Casablanca

Algiers

Tunis

MALTA

MOROCCO

ALGERIA

TUNISIA

1. CONDOLENCES ON HITLER'S DEATH

I acted correctly, and, I feel certain, wisely

Eamon de Valera, May 1945

When Hitler committed suicide at the end of April 1945, there were not many places where his death was mourned. For most in those countries newly liberated by the Allies Hitler's passing promised an end to the destruction he had unleashed on the world, although there was considerable unease among those in Europe, including the leaders of Spain and Portugal, who had hoped for a German victory. In Ireland, Taoiseach Eamon de Valera had been worried about the outcome of the war and its consequences.[1] In a conversation in late 1941 with Frank Gallagher, a close friend and adviser, he remarked, 'I wish there was some way of knowing who will win the war. It would make decisions much easier.' If de Valera was uncertain about the future in 1941, any doubts about the war had gone as Russian forces closed in on Berlin in April 1945.[2] Yet he dramatically signalled his distance from democratic Europe in a most uncompromising fashion when, on 2 May 1945, he paid a courtesy visit to the German minister in Ireland, Dr Eduard Hempel, offering his condolences on behalf of the Irish government on the death of Hitler. De Valera's formal and very public call was followed by a visit from the secretary of Douglas Hyde, the President of Ireland, who conveyed the head of state's condolences to Hempel.

Dan Breen, an influential member of de Valera's governing Fianna Fáil party, is reported to have cried all day when he heard the news of Hitler's death. Breen was a militant nationalist all his life who during the Irish War of Independence had had a £1,000 reward on his head. He had been close to the Nazis during the war and the British believed

Leabharlanna Fhine Gall

him to be a paid intelligence officer of the German legation. Breen considered Hitler the greatest man that Europe had produced in the recent past.[3] Likewise, Breen's fellow Fianna Fáil member and chairman of Bord na Mona (a semi-state body for harvesting turf) Todd Andrews recalls in his memoirs frequent visits to the German legation during the war. Andrews asserts that he and his wife 'always made a point of attending' functions and that Dr Hempel welcomed them because Andrews and those who came 'were genuinely neutral in our attitude to the war'. While there is no evidence that Andrews was a paid agent of the Germans – indeed he voices disquiet at anti-Semitism in Germany at one place in his memoirs – his actions confirm the view of historian Eunan O'Halpin that 'Many people of a nationalist outlook hoped that Germany would win, and thereby bring about the destruction of the British Empire. Some thought this would be the prelude to Irish unity.'[4]

De Valera's visit to Hempel provoked outrage on the part of the Allies, and Britain and the United States discussed the possibility of a coordinated withdrawal of diplomats from Dublin. While this did not happen, Sir John Maffey, Britain's representative in Dublin, condemned the visit as an 'unwise step', a view echoed by other Allied representatives.[5] Robert Brennan, the Irish minister in Washington, DC and a close personal friend of de Valera, reported to Dublin that American reaction, including radio and newspaper comment, was universally hostile. The *New York Times*, in a measured editorial more in sorrow than anger, expressed bewilderment that a democratic leader could show such indifference to international opinion and questioned de Valera's use of protocol and Ireland's commitment to neutrality. Other news reports and editorials were less restrained; the *New York Herald Tribune* thought that Irish neutrality had 'gone mad' as it could not distinguish between good and evil.[6] This indifference continued to be a feature of Irish opinion for some time after the war. J. J. Walsh, a 1916 Rising veteran, former government minister and successful businessman, wrote to the mass circulation *Sunday Independent* in 1946 praising Ireland's lack of involvement:

> In the late war we had the common sense to take a back seat and watch other fellows kill each other. All the world over we are now being applauded on our neutrality. We are still a partitioned

country. It will be soon enough for us to decide on matters concerning other people when our own troubles are finished with. In any case why should we worry ourselves about the ills of mankind. We stood on our own legs and won, and we can do so again.

Walsh's view may not have been representative of everyone in Ireland in 1946, but many nationalists who continued to admire Hitler and Germany shared it, and long after the event there are those in Ireland who continue to defend the action as statesmanlike.[7] As late as 1988 the Fianna Fáil Minister for Foreign Affairs Brian Lenihan not only defended de Valera, but also asserted that his visit could be judged farsighted.[8]

It is true the war had been a close-run affair until the end of 1942 and even then the outcome remained uncertain, as de Valera had hinted to Gallagher. The future of Europe was still unclear in April 1945, but the outcome of the war no longer so. De Valera's attitude in May 1945 is quite puzzling in the circumstances. President Franklin D. Roosevelt and Prime Minister Winston Churchill were committed to establishing democracy wherever possible, a policy maintained by their successors Truman and Attlee. The war had been primarily fought by the Allies in defence of democracy and freedom and now also provided an opportunity to actively promote these values in Europe, an opportunity, however, frequently limited by the need to maintain the alliance with Stalin. Although public opinion in Britain and the United States demanded a complete victory for democracy in Western Europe, the realities of geopolitics often intruded.

European stability after 1945 presumed not only the death of Nazism but also a refusal to endorse the nationalism that had prevailed since the late nineteenth century. This environment had provoked a war that resulted in fifty million deaths in the conflagration that National Socialism had set alight. Not only had nationalism caused the war, but in many cases it had also provided a popular basis for expansionism, irredentism and genocide. One of the consequences of Hitlerism was a 'revolt against nationalism', David Ellwood has argued, a reaction widely shared across Europe. In some cases (for example in France, Germany and Italy) new constitutions aimed to limit sovereignty in the interests of the greater

European good. The new post-war order was created to eliminate nationalist conflict. To a greater or lesser extent this was achieved in Western Europe, though in different ways. Democratization in Germany, the Common Market and NATO were important aspects of this process. A new institutional form was created, one that was democratic, liberal and stable. Some parts of Europe were left out of this benign environment. Eastern European states under Soviet control were forcibly incorporated into a multinational empire, though one that was as anti-nationalist as the new political elites in Germany and Italy. Also excluded were the increasingly unrepresentative dictatorships in Spain and Portugal. Over the next thirty years these states were to retain the political institutions and characteristics most closely associated with inter-war Europe, whereas the rest of Europe not only institutionalized democracy but also came to grips with nationalism by introducing innovative reforms to prevent a return to the instability of the 1920s and '30s.[9] Perhaps most surprising of all, Ireland also maintained institutional arrangements reflective of old-style nationalism for at least a quarter of a century after the end of the war. Unlike Spain or Portugal, Ireland was a successful democracy. However, in the decades immediately following the Second World War it became less comparable with say Denmark or the Netherlands and in some respects, especially in its economy and in social life, is better compared with Spain and Portugal.[10] These failures came to be closely associated with the leadership, ideology and personality of de Valera, who had been head of the irish government since 1932.[11]

Why did de Valera offer his condolences for the death of Hitler? Was it a lack of knowledge, indifference to international opinion or strict impartiality in time of war? For most people outside Ireland it was an act hostile to the nations about to win the war and attempting to re-establish a benign political order in Europe. That it was protocol has been the consistent defence of de Valera's apologists ever since 1945, though as editorials and correspondence at the time insisted it was a fundamental error to equate Hitler with any other leader. De Valera himself invoked protocol as part of his explanation for the visit. He pointed to the Irish government's response to the death of President Roosevelt on 12 April 1945: de Valera had adjourned the Dáil, called on David Gray, the American minister in Dublin, to offer his sympathy and sent a message to President Truman. In the Dáil immediately after Roosevelt's death was announced, de Valera offered a positive appreciation of the late president. According to de Valera's official biographers, these measures were 'more than a formal gesture', but they also admit that 'there was a sense of balance which annoyed the victors'. It is this equivalence between the democrat Roosevelt and the genocidal Hitler that infuriated the British and American public, not to mention the small Jewish community in Ireland. De Valera's action in May 1945, whatever the intention, placed the Allies and the Axis on the same moral plane, a view implicitly maintained by Lenihan forty years later. In this context it is interesting that the memoirs written by Robert Brennan on his time as Irish minister in Washington, DC do not mention the visit. As they were written to justify the Irish position in the Second World War, the omission is an important reminder that de Valera and one of his friends thought it impolitic to mention the controversy just over a decade after the events.[12]

However the key point with the protocol issue is that de Valera presented his action as normal, a courtesy that would be extended to any leader who died in office. Circumstances could not intrude on such diplomatic niceties, as Irish sovereignty was to be affirmed even in the most questionable circumstances. Nor was the visit a spontaneous gesture on de Valera's part, one that might have been regretted subsequently. Officials in the Department of External Affairs tried to persuade him not to visit Hempel, though the secretary of the department, Joseph Walshe, who accompanied him, did support the action. Walshe was a friend of the German minister and David Gray claimed that Walshe had spent his holidays with Hempel during the summer of 1940.[13] Some of de Valera's closest colleagues also supported the visit; Frank Aiken, perhaps the most militant defender of neutrality among this group, continued to justify the visit long after the event. Seán T. O'Kelly also recommended de Valera to go. We have no evidence for the views of other senior members of the government, though given the strength of Fianna Fáil loyalty these would not have surfaced even if there had been disquiet. Furthermore, the decision to permit McDunphy, the president's secretary, to visit the German minister and offer condolences is unlikely to have been taken without consultation, suggesting a degree of premeditation on de Valera's part. In some ways McDunphy's visit was more serious than that of de Valera as he had not visited the American legation when Roosevelt died. David Gray raised this issue with the Department of External Affairs, asking for a letter of clarification rather than an apology. However, despite a number of telephone calls to McDunphy and the promise of a letter of explanation, nothing was forwarded to Gray. As a result Gray reported the matter to the State Department and drafted a note to the new president of Ireland, Seán T. O'Kelly, who had succeeded Hyde in 1945. Gray decided not to send the letter to O'Kelly as the State Department advised that the incident occurred during Hyde's presidency and therefore should not be pursued with the new head of state.[14]

In defence of the protocol argument it might be said that de Valera was unaware of the Holocaust or the depravity of German rule in Europe. This is unlikely to have been the case, despite the censorship so pervasive in Ireland at the time. Frank Aiken used censorship to shield the Irish public from some aspects of the war and this included the mounting evidence for the Holocaust. However, de Valera had foreign newspapers available to him in uncensored form and Walshe provided him with summaries and cuttings from newspapers throughout the war. Even if this had not been the case, the American legation circulated an information bulletin, which included reports and photographs of German atrocities. Thus, the issue published on 22 September 1944 provided a detailed account of the Lublin concentration camp with photographs of the cremation ovens and the ashes of victims. This bulletin had a circulation of 30,000 by the end of the war and is believed to have been widely available within the country. It is inconceivable that his officials would not have alerted de Valera to such a piece, even if his antipathy to the American minister might have made him disinclined to believe what it contained.

More damning is the correspondence between de Valera and Isaac Herzog, chief rabbi of Palestine, who had previously been chief rabbi of Eire and had been consulted by de Valera concerning the religious articles in the 1937 Irish constitution. Though he left Ireland in 1937 Herzog continued writing to de Valera. As historian Dermot Keogh has shown, de Valera received numerous telegrams during the war from Herzog pleading for help to prevent the destruction of European Jewry. One telegram read: 'Revered friend pray leave no stone unturned to save tormented remnant of Israel doomed alas to utter annihilation in Nazi Europe Greetings Zions Blessings.' A longer telegram sent on 30 January 1943 made more explicit claims, warning that two million Jews were now threatened with extinction in occupied Europe. It is unlikely that de Valera could have done much to save European Jews from the Nazis, yet he was certainly not unaware of the threat to them. Keogh has described Irish policy towards the Jews as 'reactive rather than proactive throughout the war', though this might be an overgenerous assessment.[15] De Valera was not insensitive to the plight of the Jews and there is evidence of concern in the archives and in the behaviour of individuals in Ireland at the time. However, as he noted in his reply to Herzog early in 1943, all Irish actions in respect of the Jews would have to conform to its position on neutrality. This of course limited Irish options, as any initiative would involve publicity which could be perceived as pro-Allied and anti-German. Consequently de Valera's sense of what neutrality entailed took priority over opposition to genocide. Ireland was not alone in the indifference it showed to the plight of the Jews, but this indifference was not based on ignorance as is sometimes hinted.[16]

From this evidence it is clear that de Valera knew that the Holocaust was taking place when he went to see Hempel on that day in May. But the visit never became an issue for him or for his party in the decades after 1945. In a Dáil statement defending his actions, de Valera claimed that Hempel was the representative of the German nation not of Nazism and added that the visit 'implied no question of approval or disapproval or judgement of any kind on the German people or the state represented here'.[17] Given the nature of the German state under Hitler it was naive of de Valera to make this claim, yet his reasons for doing so are evident from a letter written to Robert Brennan in Washington. De Valera writes that his visit to Hempel had been criticized: 'I have noted that my call on the German Minister on the announcement of Hitler's death was played up to the utmost.' He is clear that the decision to visit was neither spontaneous nor mistaken: 'I expected this. I could have had a diplomatic illness but, as you know, I would scorn that sort of thing.' Despite this, de Valera and his supporters could have 'diplomatic illnesses' when it suited them. When Daniel Cohalan, bishop of Cork, died in 1952 neither de Valera nor President O'Kelly attended the funeral, an unusual departure from protocol in Ireland. Cohalan had threatened to excommunicate the IRA in Cork during the War of Independence and had been hostile to republicans during the Civil War. De Valera was conveniently in hospital in the Netherlands, while O'Kelly attended the funeral of a priest who had been sympathetic to the IRA to avoid having to be present at Cohalan's funeral.[18] Nevertheless, while de Valera implies that the 1945 decision was as much to do with his hostility to the American minister, there is also considerable sympathy for Hempel:

> So long as we retained our diplomatic relations with Germany, to have failed to call upon the German representative would have been an act of unpardonable discourtesy to the German nation and to Dr Hempel himself. During the whole of the war, Dr Hempel's conduct was irreproachable. He was always friendly and invariably correct – in marked contrast with Gray. I certainly was not going to add to his humiliation in the hour of defeat.

At the heart of de Valera's visit was irritation with the American minister, who had been a thorn in the side of the Irish government for much of the war. Most recently Gray had pressurized the Irish government to give the Allies access to the German legation before the minister or his staff had time to destroy documents. There is also considerable evidence, as Mark Hull has shown, that Hempel was not as innocent as de Valera claimed. Hull has documented a darker side to Hempel's activities in Ireland, one that was known to the Irish intelligence agencies.[19] While diplomatic niceties were an important aspect of de Valera's decision, so too may have been residual hostility to the United States, if not to the United Kingdom. Moreover, Hempel did what de Valera considered he should do, whereas Gray did not. De Valera insisted on the maintenance of neutrality under any circumstances:

> It would establish a bad precedent. It is of considerable importance that the formal acts of courtesy paid on such occasions as the death of a head of a State should not have attached to them any further special significance, such as connoting approval or disapproval of the policies of the State in question, or of its head. It is important that it should never be inferred that these formal acts imply the passing of any judgements, good or bad.

Nor was de Valera prepared to defend his actions in public because 'an explanation would have been interpreted as an excuse, and an excuse as a consciousness of having acted wrongly. I acted correctly, and, I feel certain, wisely.'[20] This was de Valera's considered view of the situation at the time and one he maintained subsequently. It is contained in his official biography, written by Lord Longford and T. P. O'Neill, a book de Valera took great care to influence. More generally, de Valera was obsessed with his place in history, insisting that his position at each stage of his career had been the only correct one. A writer who met him during the 1950s was left with the impression that de Valera considered himself infallible and everybody else wrong. So involved was de Valera in the Longford and O'Neill biography that Patrick Murray has suggested that the book cannot be considered a biography in the normal sense but a 'disguised autobiography'.[21]

Senior members of the British government and news media refused to accept de Valera's view of events, emphasizing his moral failure in visiting Hempel,[22] while Churchill also challenged de Valera's public view of Ireland's role in the war. Coming less than two weeks after de Valera's condolences on Hitler's death, it was not surprising that the prime minister would challenge Irish self-satisfaction. Although his 13 May broadcast included other matters, it was the comments on Ireland that caused most controversy. Churchill opened the broadcast by reminding his listeners that it was just over five years since he had been appointed prime minister and went on to praise the Soviet Union, the United States and France for their role in the war against Germany. It was a speech to the British people and one that looked forward to the post-war world. On Ireland his comments were harsh and stark, contrasting the thousands of Irish who had volunteered to fight against Germany with Dublin's indifference to the outcome of the war. Most cutting were Churchill's remarks about neutrality and the resources denied Britain in its hour of need. Churchill continued that his government had shown great forbearance in not occupying Irish ports during the war, but had simply 'left the Dublin Government to frolic with the Germans'.[23] This was not what the Irish government wanted to hear; indeed de Valera did not wish to hear anything critical from any source at that time. Censorship in Ireland had been pervasive and used for overt political purposes so de Valera and his government had been well placed throughout the war to block any critical views on its policies. As a consequence opinion in Ireland was outraged at Churchill's 'insult' to Irish neutrality and the questioning of its honour. Frank Gallagher invested considerable efforts among diplomats in Dublin after the war in Europe had ended in asserting that Irish neutrality had no impact on the outcome of the war and that not a single life had been lost as a result.[24]

Irish sensibilities had been offended by a number of aspects of Churchill's speech. The emphasis on Northern Ireland grated on nationalist sensibilities, but also forced them to recognize that the political situation was now less than favourable to any prospect of a united Ireland. Likewise, singling out the large numbers of Irish men and women who had volunteered to join the Allied cause highlighted the fact that not all Irish citizens had been prepared to accept the limited version of neutrality espoused by de Valera. The most irritating aspect of the speech was Churchill's almost casual dismissal of Irish neutrality and the hint that had circumstances been different the Allies would have had no other option but to intervene in Ireland. What was to be ignored was Churchill's emphasis on the British government's self-restraint in this respect. He was saying that the British might have been justified in intervening but actually had not done so, even when the situation was desperate, as it was in 1940 and 1941.

In Ireland de Valera's response was awaited with considerable apprehension and excitement, a mood heightened by the government-dominated media. In his reply on 16 May de Valera invoked images originally presented in his famous St Patrick's Day broadcast to the United States, when he had outlined his vision of a future Ireland. On both occasions the Gaelic language was presented as a bulwark against the materialistic outside world, although unfortunately most of de Valera's listeners in Ireland in 1945 did not understand his opening remarks precisely because they were in Gaelic. Members of his own party had complained about the failure to promote Gaelic usage more widely under Fianna Fáil. Though his government was committed to the revival of Gaelic as a working language and had placed it in a superior constitutional position to English, the reality was that English was the vernacular language for the vast majority of Irish citizens in 1945. Gaelic was used for nationalist purposes by Fianna Fáil and by sections of the middle classes to secure advancement in public service or education. It also fostered isolationism, a sense of superiority and fanaticism in some language activists that worked to Fianna Fáil's advantage in times of crisis, a point rather surprisingly made by the archbishop of Dublin later in the year to Maffey. When de Valera turned to the substance of his remarks these were made in English and here he defended the policy of neutrality under all circumstances. There was a hint that de Valera recognized that international public opinion was not completely sympathetic to him or his views and his points were extremely moderate at first. He recalled his speech at the beginning of the war and reasserted his view that neutrality was the only possible policy available to the Irish state at that time. He invoked partition and Ireland's experience of the First World War as reasons why participation was impossible for his government. He then went on to praise the national solidarity shown during the war and the support received by the government from the majority of people. While warning that dangers continued to exist and shortages would continue, he welcomed the end of the war in Europe as an opportunity for Ireland to make a contribution to reconstruction and to aid those European states in need of help after the devastation. American diplomats were subsequently puzzled at Irish officials' insistence that they had a spiritual contribution to make to post-war reconstruction.[25]

De Valera's reply was intelligent and considered. He chose his ground carefully and defended his position with vigour. He at first played the injured statesman rather than the wounded nationalist, more sorrowful than angry, although he said that his reply to such a challenge twenty-five years ago would have been very different. He acknowledged that many in Ireland wanted a vigorous and aggressive response to Churchill but he would not provide one. He then presented himself as the temperate statesman when compared with Churchill, whose remarks he described as 'unworthy'. He, de Valera, would not lower himself to this level; his remarks would be dispassionate as he did not wish to 'fuel the flames of hatred and passion' which had just caused so much hardship and devastation. De Valera portrayed himself as having been wronged by Churchill and as one who now had to explain the facts to the world as well as his own people. He concentrated on the more general issue of whether a large state ever had the right to violate the sovereignty of another country. By doing so he evaded any discussion of the rights and wrongs of Britain's war with Germany or the possible consequences had Britain been defeated in 1940 or 1941. For him it was enough to insist that Ireland's sovereignty had to be sustained even when its neighbour was under severe threat. There is a fundamental point at issue in de Valera's claim. Most sensible people would agree that a country should not be invaded just because a stronger state decides it is in its interests to do so. But they would also probably agree that there might be extreme circumstances when a state's sovereignty should take second place to a more immediate concern, in this case the survival of European democracy. What de Valera did not consider here or elsewhere is that there may be circumstances when it is right for a state to enter a war even though it could avoid doing so.[26]

What de Valera's reply also ignored was that Churchill had placed considerable emphasis on the fact that Britain had not invaded or violated Irish sovereignty despite the threat to its existence. De Valera is at one point quite gracious in acknowledging that Churchill and Britain did not invade and links this to the possibility of improved relations between the two states. However, he rather spoils the effect by invoking the memory of Neville Chamberlain, whom de Valera not only praises but also believes will 'find the honoured place in British history which is due to him, as certainly he will find in any fair record of the relations between Britain and ourselves'. De Valera spoke favourably of Chamberlain on many occasions, and that Ireland had benefited from Chamberlain's premiership there can be no doubt, but to praise an individual often seen as responsible for Britain's difficulties in 1940 was misplaced in 1945. De Valera concluded his broadcast in far more emotive terms than those promised at the outset. He reiterated the view that neutrality was a consequence of partition, though again he was not willing to consider means to overcome the mistrust in Ireland. He recognized that the war had introduced 'blinding hates and rancours' into European politics and was thankful that such a situation did not exist in Ireland. This had some validity in Eire but not on the island of Ireland. At the end of the Second World War Ireland was the one place in Europe where 'blinding hates and rancours' continued to be at the centre of political debate and more seriously of political behaviour. Unionists and nationalists in Northern Ireland and many nationalists in the south shared in this animosity, though the worst of it had been neutralized in the south outside Fianna Fáil and extremist republican ranks.[27]

De Valera's broadcast reflected the worst aspects of nationalism. He recalled the centuries of animosity between Britain and Ireland, ignoring any positive aspects to the relationship. He focused on massacres, famines and aggression and exaggerated their place in the relationship. Accordingly, de Valera declared, 'we have pledged ourselves to the dead generations who have preserved intact for us this glorious heritage [of resistance], that we too will strive to be faithful to the end, and pass on this tradition unblemished'.[28] If war-torn Europe paid any attention to de Valera in May 1945 it must have been to recoil from this rhetoric, which shared much with the militant nationalism of Nazism and fascism; such sentiments had brought Hitler to power and given him the means to destroy the continent and his own nation. Of course de Valera was directing his comments at an Irish audience, and most Europeans including the British did not listen to his broadcast. Whether Churchill heard it or not is a moot point, but the satirical journal *Dublin Opinion* unintentionally captured the self-satisfied atmosphere in Ireland at the time when it published a cartoon of Churchill listening to de Valera's broadcast. He is despondent and the caption underneath is 'Listen and learn'. Of course if *Dublin Opinion* had attempted to publish a cartoon critical of de Valera's speech it would not have been permitted to do so by Frank Aiken. In the broadcast de Valera had been insistent that Ireland's sovereignty should be respected under all circumstances, yet that sovereignty was always dependent on the goodwill of Britain, a point brought home to the Irish authorities by the fact that they needed to apply to Britain to rebroadcast the speech to the United States. Churchill was asked if he favoured permitting the transmission of the Irish broadcast and raised no objections even though the speech was clearly critical. The prime minister and British officials agreed that given their censorship powers they could prevent the broadcast but that 'it would be undesirable to utilise this prohibition in the case of a speech by the Prime Minister of Eire'.[29]

De Valera did not forget the criticism of his visit. In July he had a meeting with Maffey in which he complained about the British reaction. He again insisted that the issue was about formalities and protocols, adding that Maffey 'knew as well as he did how opposed he was personally to the Nazi regime'. De Valera expressed surprise that reaction to his visit had been so violent and claimed that relations between Britain and Ireland had deteriorated seriously as a result. Maffey countered that de Valera was behind the times and that Ireland's sovereignty was both recognized and accepted. The issue of neutrality during the war rested on the Allied belief that 'when a tiger was loose in Europe, Irishmen were thought to be the kind of people who would lend a hand'; when this was not forthcoming there was shock and disappointment. Maffey believed that it would take a long time for opinion to recover from this. De Valera responded that British disappointment was linked to their view that the Irish should be loyal to them and this could not be the case. He then stated that Ireland wanted better relations with Britain but that he could initiate no move in this direction, as this 'would look like an admission that their neutrality had been wrong and they had been sorry for it'. He stated that if a gesture came from Britain he would be prepared to respond favourably. Maffey seems to have considered this window dressing, concluding that there was growing unease among Irish diplomats and within the government that the state's foreign policy during the war had not been successful and that they must mend fences.[30]

De Valera defended his visit to the German minister in the Dáil on 19 July. He reiterated the diplomatic case, arguing that protocol demanded his action and adding that critics only wanted to malign the state. He then drew an invidious comparison between his visit and the state's response to Roosevelt's death in April. While he may have viewed that response as acceptable and indeed the American State Department conceded its generosity, de Valera's argument did not win much sympathy in the United States or Britain in May 1945.

> But I want to say this, that I did what I did as my duty, and I am going to do my duty, and I was quite aware when I was doing it that it was capable of being misrepresented. I am going to do my duty, and pay the necessary courtesies as Minister for External Affairs, even though I have to face the misrepresentation, and our country has to face the misrepresentation, that it causes. Anything else would bring us into contempt.

Unfortunately for de Valera his visit inspired the contempt it was supposed to deflect.

While de Valera may have wished to improve relations with the United Kingdom, he wanted any improvement to be on his terms. In his public statements and in his private papers there is no evidence that he wished to respond positively to Britain or indeed to the Allies generally. This can be seen in a number of ways. Although Ireland was still officially a dominion within the British commonwealth, it acted as if it was not. Speaking in the Dáil on 18 July in a debate on the constitutional position of the state he was dismissive of the dominions, asserting the republican nature of the Irish state. He continued, 'We want to be friends with Canada, Australia and New Zealand, but we cannot do that so long as our nation is partitioned, and we cannot accept a status beneath the dignity of this ancient nation.' Perhaps this acknowledged inadvertently that the dominions would not help de Valera in his pursuit of a united Ireland. He then went on to make it very clear how he perceived the dominions and Ireland:

> The constitutional forms which have grown up naturally express our position. Canada and Australia grew up as British colonies, where their constitutional forms represent their loyalties. We have not these loyalties. We cannot accept these forms. We are not a British colony grown up. We are ourselves a Mother Country, and will accept no status lower than that.

In the same speech he delivered another rebuff to the British on the question of Northern Ireland. There could be no compromise on this issue, he exclaimed, and quoted the Unionist slogan 'Not an inch' to give force to his determination to unite the island under his rule. All else except the continuation of national sovereignty, he continued, should be subordinated to this aim.[31] What de Valera was engaged in here was not diplomacy but generating national unity and support for his own party. While he could complain that in some parts of Northern Ireland there was a nationalist majority and if a referendum was held in these areas they were likely to express a wish to join the south, this was not as certain as de Valera maintained and his government never used this as a realistic tactic to persuade the British government to move on the issue of partition. In addition de Valera was behind the times as Maffey maintained, especially on questions of border revision, referenda on population changes and irredentism generally. Such was the reaction against nationalist expansionism at the end of the war that the Allies agreed informally that most existing borders of Europe would be maintained.[32]

Although Germany's borders were altered and the country partitioned into Allied zones of occupation there was no prospect of the territory of the nation that had held out longest against the Nazi threat being reduced. De Valera's remarks also smacked of the rhetoric that Hitler had used in his irredentist campaigns during the second half of the 1930s, especially over the Sudetenland. Nor was was this parallel lost on de Valera, who hinted to British officials in 1938 that he had his own Sudetenland in Northern Ireland.[33] In effect de Valera was rejecting not only dominion status but also the efforts made by the previous Cumann na nGaedheal government to improve relations with the United Kingdom and with Northern Ireland especially. Cumann na nGaedheal had attempted to develop a realistic approach to Northern Ireland – in effect recognizing the Unionist regime and attempting to establish conditions for dialogue. This was always going to be difficult, but de Valera's strategy ignored Unionist sentiment, simply insisting that the British turn the area over to his jurisdiction. Although de Valera was never to know this, his counterpart in Northern Ireland Sir Basil Brooke was deeply concerned that the status of the north would be changed by the British government. In a private talk between Brooke and Herbert Morrison in September 1946, Brooke insisted that if the question of partition was reopened there would 'be a storm' in Northern Ireland. Tellingly, he added that in the hypothetical context of such a discussion, Unionists would insist on Eire remaining in the commonwealth, that the position of the monarchy be recognized in some form and that certain military undertakings be given. Brooke also pointed to what he considered to be the excessive influence of the Catholic Church on public life in Eire, but considered that if this was controlled in some way the same could be done for Protestant preachers in the north. Brooke's conclusions were, to say the least, accommodating: 'If a United Ireland was granted independence before these things were secured, there would certainly be strong opposition from Ulster. These observations in no way minimise the opposition of Northern Ireland to discussions about partition being opened.'[34] This raises the question of how realistic de Valera's policy (or more accurately non-policy) in respect of Northern Ireland was in the post-war years. It also suggests that if the Irish government had worked actively within the commonwealth for a change in Northern Ireland policy, the British would have found it difficult not to make concessions on the issue. This was especially true after the Labour victory in the general election in 1945, and there would also have been considerable pressure on the Unionists to make concessions.[35]

Yet, Fianna Fáil seemed committed to its uncompromising course. Little was heard from those within the cabinet most associated with pro-Allied views. Among these might be included Seán Lemass, Seán MacEntee and possibly also Gerald Boland, none of whom seem to have been consulted by de Valera prior to the visit to Hempel. The voices heard at the end of the war are the most nationalistic and those associated with strict neutrality. The most prominent of these was Frank Aiken, who often acted as de Valera's second-in-command and was officially minister of coordination of defensive measures and chairman of the Defence Conference but was also in effect the political censor for the duration of the war. Aiken was rewarded for his services to de Valera when he was appointed minister for finance on 19 July 1945 after O'Kelly had been elected president. His change of office had little impact on Aiken's narrow conception of nationalism or his anti-British sentiments. When Sir John Keane argued in the senate that Ireland should be more interdependent with other states, Aiken rejected this as an ideal in international life. Instead he reiterated the conventional Fianna Fáil commitment to economic nationalism amounting to autarky. He went further and asserted that he 'wanted to see that as far as possible in the shortest time, this country would become so economically independent that it would be able to carry on its normal life, and keep its people in a healthy standard of comfort without being dependent on foreigners for vital necessities of life'. Senator Johnston provided Aiken with the opportunity to comment on the war when he asked what would have happened to Ireland if the Nazis had won the war. The suggestion here and among those favourable to the British was that the Allies were fighting for Ireland as much as for their own cause. Aiken would have none of that and the language of his response is of particular note:

> There has been a war in Europe and one of the contestants has been eliminated, but I do not agree that the British people were fighting for our liberty. If they had been fighting the war for liberty, they did not have to lose a single soldier to give the Irish people the liberty that was their due in getting freedom for the thirty-two counties. I do not want to be making propaganda against the British, but if people are going to make propaganda here at the expense of the Irish people I am going to contest it all along the line.

Aiken was obviously deeply annoyed by the pro-British sentiment that had been expressed in certain quarters once censorship had been removed. He argued that those who had voiced such views should not have been so 'outspoken' and described them as the 'spiritual fathers of the young men who burned the Irish flag at Trinity College'. Johnston protested at the accusation that he and others were the spiritual fathers of the flag-burners, loudly asserting, 'I claim to be an Irish citizen.' While Aiken did not deny Johnston's citizenship he countered by saying that if Johnston 'claimed the British victory in this war was his victory' then he should have been involved directly in the war. Although not saying so directly, Aiken implied that any Irish citizen who expressed support for the Allies (especially the British) but had not actually volunteered in some capacity was hypocritical and should be treated with contempt.[36]

*

Official Irish attitudes implied that there was no real difference between the Allies and the Axis. If de Valera's visit to Hempel was the most controversial example of this, there were others both before and after that particular incident. In late 1944, just a few months after D-Day and with the end of the war in sight, the United States sought assurances from Ireland and from other neutrals that Nazi war criminals would not be given political asylum if they were able to make their way to a non-belligerent state. The British were at first reluctant to pursue this issue as vigorously as the United States, recognizing that in the past the Irish government had not been prepared to extradite to Britain members of the IRA suspected of involvement in bombing campaigns; the Irish authorities were very uneasy about extradition when it involved what could be described as political crimes. However, as there was public concern about the prospect of neutrals providing asylum for war criminals, the British quickly associated themselves with the United States on an approach to Ireland. De Valera responded evasively. He stated that Ireland would not act in a manner detrimental to the interests of friendly states, but would not give the commitments required. This was clearly unsatisfactory and the US and UK representatives in Dublin, David Gray and Sir John Maffey, concluded that de Valera's refusal should be considered unfriendly. The British expressed the view that if Ireland provided asylum for war criminals, this would prove detrimental to its interests. De Valera responded that 'the right to grant asylum is not in question', adding that the Irish government 'can give no assurances which would preclude them from exercising that right should justice, charity or the honour or interest of the nation so require'. The United States was deeply disturbed and Gray was instructed to protest to Joseph Walshe, the secretary at the Department of External Affairs. Walshe in turn complained at the United States's attitude to Ireland, while countering that defining a war criminal was in fact quite difficult. He added that while the Irish government might not grant asylum to any Nazi it would probably do so in the case of the leader of Vichy France, Marshal Pétain. Once the issue became public, the United States expressed the view that the Irish position 'did not go as far as we would have liked in all particulars'.[37]

Critics of Irish neutrality were quick to take advantage of Irish ambiguity in this matter. In December 1944 Lord Vansittart put down a motion in the House of Lords calling attention 'to the refusal of the government of Eire to guarantee not to give asylum to Axis war criminals'. A little later, Professor Savory, Unionist MP for Queen's University in Belfast, criticized Irish neutrality and its refusal to give clear assurances on the war criminal issue in the House of Commons. Matters became somewhat murky at this stage when it emerged that the British Special Operations Executive (SOE) was involved in a black propaganda scheme to undermine morale among the German elite in the later stages of the war by spreading rumours that leading Nazi

officials were attempting to gain asylum in Ireland. There is some
evidence that the SOE planted the question with Savory, though just
prior to the House of Commons debate the SOE decided to discard
Ireland as the supposed destination and use Argentina instead for
those Nazis fleeing the Allies. Ironically, the plans were codenamed
Casement, an allusion to Roger Casement, who had travelled to
Ireland from Germany during the First World War in a submarine just
prior to the 1916 rebellion.[38]

The Dominions Office in London was concerned that the issue of
asylum would create difficulties between Britain and Ireland. Maffey
was instructed to explore further the Irish position and see if he
could get assurances from de Valera. When originally approached by
the Americans, de Valera had adopted the form of words used by the
Swiss government when it replied to the same United States request
in August 1943. However, the United States then pressurized the
Swiss, who subsequently provided an oral assurance that Switzerland
would not be used as a refuge for fleeing Nazi officials. This allowed
the Allies to publicly confirm that satisfactory assurances had been
received from the Swiss government, though no additional written
documentation was required. The British Foreign Office also noted
that similar assurances had been received from the majority of neutrals, not only pro-Nazi states such as Portugal, Spain and Argentina
but also from democratic Sweden. In all cases these assurances went
beyond the original Swiss formula that de Valera insisted on using. De
Valera was unwilling to go further and the Dominions Office pointed
out that if he maintained this position, the government's response to
Vansittart's motion would be less favourable to Ireland than might be
the case. As the Dominions Office noted in its comment on de Valera,
'clearly if the Eire Government saw fit to make some further statement
on these lines, this would have a direct bearing on the reply which the
Secretary of State would be able to give'. As a minimum, de Valera
was asked to adopt the Portuguese position by providing an informal
undertaking that could be used in a public statement, while formally
the original statement would remain in place.[39]

The Irish government was not prepared to offer an additional
informal assurance and in the House of Commons and the House of
Lords its neutrality was the object of fierce criticism. The British
government was not especially critical of the Irish stance, though it

did regret the equivocal position taken. In the House of Lords the Lord Chancellor agreed that the Irish position was an unhappy one, but warned that criticism of Ireland in the House would not persuade the Irish government to change its mind on the issue. British officials sought to play down the most serious criticism, but there was evident disquiet at de Valera's stand. De Valera was using the opportunity to assert his independence of the Allies, although whether this policy was genuinely in Ireland's interest is open to serious doubt. The asylum question did not go away, moreover. At the end of the war the Allies insisted that de Valera repatriate Germans interned in Ireland to their control in Germany. De Valera resisted for some time, but under considerable pressure finally agreed to return the individuals to Allied control, but only after receiving assurances that they would not be placed under Soviet control or tried for crimes for which they might be executed. These assurances did not help one of those affected, who committed suicide before his extradition could take place. This raises the question of what the Irish government would have done if a Nazi official facing the death penalty had arrived in Ireland and claimed political asylum. In terms of the Irish constitution, such an official could have made a good case for asylum.[40]

This issue was not an academic one. De Valera was clearly uneasy at the end of the war and uncertain about what the future would hold. The world he was looking at was not the one he had expected. He expressed some of his anxieties in a letter he wrote to Malcolm MacDonald, who was then British high commissioner in Canada. De Valera concluded that 'Europe however is in a terrible state,' adding, 'I do hope the victors will consider the future in all their actions.' While he did not spell out what he meant by this, he went on, 'They can sow the seeds of friendship or of hate. Which will it be?' The Nuremberg trials convinced de Valera that the seeds of hate were being planted. In September 1946 he expressed his dislike of the trials to Herbert Morrison, who visited him at this time. Shortly after, he received a letter from Hempel – who had been given asylum in Ireland – urging him to intervene on behalf of those German officials who had been sentenced to death by the court. Hempel was opposed to the death sentences at the 'so called Nürnberg trials' apparently on principle, implying that the victors should have tried no one. He emphasized the damage that would occur if the sentences were carried out. The German population would be outraged, he claimed, and he appealed to de Valera 'to take any other appropriate measures in case you should see any possibility of help to avert a disaster'. De Valera was galvanized by this letter in a way he was not by Hertzog's appeal for the Jews and called in Maffey to express his concern. Echoing Hempel, he told Maffey that the executions would be a 'tragic mistake', and he asked for British assistance in contacting the South African prime minister, Field Marshal Smuts, though he recognized that Smuts actually favoured the executions. The British government was unwilling to entertain de Valera's concerns, replying tartly that the trials had their complete support.[41]

Immediately after the receipt of Hempel's letter, de Valera set the Department of External Affairs the task of assessing the legitimacy of the proposed executions. Two days later an initial draft was submitted by officials, which argued that no one should be tried 'under a law which did not exist at the date of his crime'. According to this view, Articles 38 and 40 of the Irish constitution would conflict with the Nuremberg trials, and the draft paper suggests that the court was 'simply the instrument of the victorious Allies established to punish individuals, citizens of a defeated Axis state, Germany', for actions committed during the war, which three months after the cessation of hostilities had been defined as 'crimes against the peace'. In a revised and more elaborate statement of the Irish case circulated some days later the position of the papacy was awaited eagerly. It was reported that the pope had pleaded for clemency for some of those condemned, that opposition to the trials and verdicts was increasing daily and that in Ireland in particular there was considerable opposition to them. The constitution was again cited against the verdicts, as was the view that this was a victors' law rather than an acceptable one. There is an implication in the supporting argument that any executions would be murder, while the paper compares Nuremberg with the use of judicial execution by the British in Ireland. In addition it was claimed that, 'being a Christian people we are probably more inclined than most other peoples – even than those which make a constant profession of Christianity in their daily propaganda – to favour mercy, whether or not justice has been done'. Nor was opposition to the executions limited to the circle around de Valera; Irish diplomats seemed to share the views expressed in the paper. Brennan wrote to Joseph Walshe from Washington in early 1947 recounting a conversation his wife Una had had with the wife of Justice Robert H. Jackson, one of the judges, who asked her opinion on the trials. Una Brennan refused to answer on the grounds that her answer would 'hurt you very much', which, as Brennan added to his own letter, 'of course was saying a mouthful'.[42]

It is likely that de Valera genuinely considered the Nuremberg trials illegitimate. He continued to view the combatants in the war as morally equivalent and the trials as an instrument of the victors. If this is so, then de Valera was continuing to apply traditional criteria to the rights and obligations of states in wartime, criteria largely overtaken by the Holocaust and German aggression. State sovereignty had a special place in de Valera's world view and on this occasion seemed to result in acts committed by the state being seen differently from those committed by individuals. In taking the view that the trials were at least suspect, de Valera identified closely with German opinion, which opposed them.[43] In his response to the outrage at his visit to Hempel, de Valera emphasized his respect for the German people and distinguished the nation from the regime. His belief in national sovereignty overrode any concerns he might have had about the crimes committed during the war by representatives of the German state and nation. But the distinction between rulers, state and nation is never as clear-cut as de Valera claimed. He frequently insisted that state, people and party in Ireland were closely associated if not identical, and if he held this view about Ireland why should it not also be applied to Germany? This standpoint could lead, as it seems to have done in the case of de Valera and his closest colleagues, to a public attitude amounting almost to disdain for the Holocaust and indifference to the actions of the Nazis. One does not have to share completely the thesis proposed by Daniel Goldhagen that the Germans were Hitler's willing executioners to recognize that culpability and compliance with the Holocaust were widespread in Nazi Germany.[44]

De Valera's concerns over Nuremberg, his unwillingness to give guarantees in respect of war criminals and his visit to Hempel consistently subordinated morality to state sovereignty and as a result placed Irish foreign policy in a difficult position after the war. In one response to de Valera, a United States State Department official wrote that the

Hempel visit would not quickly be forgotten. Though this version of
the letter was not sent, it certainly reflected widespread revulsion at
de Valera's actions. While the world was moving on in 1945, de Valera
and his government were not. In a tense meeting with Maffey in July
1945 de Valera blamed Churchill for the deterioration of relations
between Britain and Ireland. Maffey noted in his report to London
that de Valera's touchiness indicated a recognition that his foreign
policy had failed and that Irish diplomats and public opinion were
uneasy about the future. Two days before this meeting Maffey had
paid a visit to the most influential member of the Irish Catholic
hierarchy, John Charles McQuaid. The archbishop condemned militant nationalism and de Valera's policy for reviving the Irish language,
and complained about the impact of Ireland's isolation on the
country. Maffey concluded, 'It is interesting to find that the Catholic
hierarchy, having cashed in heavily on nationalism, extremism, neutrality etc, now find that things are not quite so good for them as they
were in the "Good Old Days".' Maffey may have been hearing what he
wanted to on this occasion, yet he was an experienced diplomat and
it is not unrealistic to accept that he was noticing a degree of unease
at the changes in the international system among the Irish elite. It
remains questionable whether McQuaid's expressed views were genuine or merely reflected his acceptance of the need to come to terms
with the victorious Allies. As Mrs Cameron (the novelist Elizabeth
Bowen), noted in another report to the Dominions Office, the apparent desire to improve relations with Britain on McQuaid's part rested
uneasily with the traditional behaviour of the Irish Catholic Church,
which 'fosters anti-British feeling and cultivates isolation as a safe-
guard against the contagion of non-Catholic culture'.[45]

A little over a year later Herbert Morrison found de Valera in a
much more pessimistic mood. Morrison had become lord president
of the council in the post-war Labour government, having been home
secretary in the wartime coalition. While on holiday in Cork he agreed
to visit de Valera when Maffey arranged a meeting. The two men
discussed foreign affairs and de Valera expressed concern at Soviet
policy in Europe. Morrison found de Valera dismissive about Ireland's
failure to gain membership of the United Nations, though he did
speculate that the rejection had offended his dignity. There is little
doubt that the UN rejection rankled, as a conversation with the British

ambassador, W. C. Hankinson, in 1953 illustrated. De Valera said that he no longer had any interest in the UN or in Irish membership of the body. He added petulantly that if Ireland had been accepted in 1946 he would probably have 'walked out by now'. As might be expected, most of the conversation with Morrison concentrated on Northern Ireland and partition, and it was in respect of this issue that de Valera was clearly behind the times, as Maffey had previously suggested. Morrison observed the diplomatic niceties in his conversation, emphasizing in his notes that he was gentle with de Valera's sensibilities when it came to the Irish role in the war. Though Morrison may have pulled his punches, there was no disguising the point he was making. Coming from a Labour politician, it marked a departure in attitudes on the part of a section of British political opinion that previously had been sympathetic to the Irish position. Morrison placed the rights of Northern Ireland on an equal if not superior footing to those of Ireland. He highlighted the strong ties between Northern Ireland and Britain, while noting that the war had deepened the differences between north and south:

> Eire, exercising the rights she claimed, either according to his views about the status of Ireland or under the Statute of Westminster and dominion status, had remained neutral in the war. As a purely practical matter, British public opinion noted that the Northern Ireland ports and airfields were of the greatest value to our war effort; and, on the other hand, that the absence of such facilities in Eire had necessarily involved increased Allied casualties in the Battle of the Atlantic.

De Valera countered this argument vigorously, arguing that Ireland's lack of involvement was actually a benefit to the United Kingdom. However Morrison reiterated that:

> There was, therefore, a strong feeling that it would be dangerous to run the risk that in any future war the whole of Ireland might be neutral and we should be denied any military facilities in so vital an area. This was altogether apart from the great loyalty of the British people and of Ulster to the Crown.

This placed de Valera in a decidedly defensive frame of mind and he returned to his traditional positions on the war, partition and unity.

He refused to accept that Irish neutrality had caused any problems for the Allies, denying also that Ireland was a dominion in the same way that Canada or Australia was. De Valera continued to believe that the relationship between the dominions and Britain was one of British dominance, refusing to accept that the relationship between Ireland and Britain could be one of equality within the commonwealth, though he did not actually leave the organization.

One is left with the impression of two politicians talking past one another. Yet Morrison held the high ground, not only dismissing de Valera's claim to Northern Ireland but clearly stating that the Labour government would not coerce the north into a united Ireland. De Valera and Morrison focused on different areas. For de Valera the crux was the British government, whereas for Morrison it was the people of Northern Ireland and especially the Unionists. It is ironic that the British government should have stressed the importance of people over territory while the veteran nationalist remained bound up in an old-fashioned obsession with territory. Morrison recognized that little could be achieved with de Valera, warning Prime Minister Attlee and his cabinet colleagues in a memorandum that it was doubtful if the Irish leader would 'concede anything in practice until a declaration of all-Ireland independence had been made'. As this was not practical politics, Morrison recommended that in any future negotiations with de Valera, the government should make it 'clear that he has to give as well as take, and that the giving cannot be a vague anticipation of the future'. Although the memorandum was written in the careful style common to ministerial papers, it had steel in it. Morrison had seen through de Valera, recognizing, as Maffey had, that de Valera would hold out various possibilities on the prospect of obtaining a particular objective but with no commitment of substance. Morrison also recommended that the British government take account of the diplomatic reality that de Valera had made Ireland a foreign country in most respects. Given the pro-Unionist sentiments expressed to de Valera and the assertion that Northern Ireland would continue to play a key role in Britain's strategic judgements, the Irish government's policy in respect of the north was in tatters by 1946.[46]

Just under a decade later President O'Kelly confided to the author Shane Leslie that he was puzzled by Northern Ireland and confessed that he would not know where to begin if given the opportunity to

solve the partition problem.[47] Such honesty was not matched in
Fianna Fáil circles for the most part, though Seán Lemass was
attempting to devise a new policy at this time. Matters might have
been different though. Unionists were deeply concerned in 1945 that
the Labour government would destabilize the existing institutional
arrangements between Britain and Northern Ireland as well as
between north and south. There was a fear that the British government would force Northern Ireland to engage in discussions with de
Valera's government to achieve unity. There was also some distaste
in Westminster over the Unionists' authoritarian rule. British Home
Secretary Chuter Ede described the Unionists as 'remnants of the old
ascendancy class, very frightened of the Catholics and the general
world trend to the left'. Sir Basil Brooke, the Northern Ireland prime
minister, speculated candidly about the future; none of the options
were especially attractive for him: 'stay as we are with possible chaos;
join Eire – unthinkable; back to Westminster – dangerous; Dominion
status, might lower living standards'. Historian Brian Barton has
shown that these fears were exaggerated and not realized. There was
only one serious Labour backbench revolt during the debate on the
Northern Ireland Bill in 1947, but this was an isolated incident and
Northern Ireland secured its position within the United Kingdom
between 1945 and 1951. Shared wartime experience cemented a
relationship which had been weak prior to 1939, while Irish neutrality
and nationalist agitation alienated all but the most dedicated pro-
nationalist sections of British opinion. Irish diplomatic efforts 1945–51
to revive the anti-partition campaign and the decision to declare a
republic in 1949 further undermined any remaining goodwill. By 1951,
Unionists were positive about the impact of the Labour government
on Northern Ireland, secure in their political dominance within the
region and optimistic about the future.[48]

In a cutting though not unsympathetic analysis of the state of
Anglo-Irish relations as a consequence of Irish neutrality, Maffey
emphasized that Britain 'came through [the war] and we came
through without any help from Eire'. He recognized that the consequences had not been entirely negative and that there were some
advantages for Britain in having Ireland neutral. But his most important observation was that the position taken by de Valera during the
war had changed, perhaps irrevocably, the close-knit relationship

between the nations and peoples of the two islands and had done so for the foreseeable future. In less diplomatic fashion, the poet Louis MacNeice gave voice to much of the frustration that British opinion felt towards neutral Ireland. In his frequently quoted and deeply resented poem 'Neutrality', written in September 1942 not long after his friend Graham Sheppard had lost his life in the North Atlantic, he asks his Irish readers to think again about the war:

> But then look eastward from your heart, there bulks
> A continent, close, dark, as archetypical sin,
> While to the west off your own shores the mackerel
> Are fat – on the flesh of your kin.

MacNeice's appeal did not move de Valera, though many Irish men and women answered the call to fight 'archetypical sin'. Perhaps what hurt British sensibility most was that the Irish did not consider them kin any more. This may not now seem surprising, but it supports Morrison's view in 1946 that Ireland had become a foreign country. In many respects the war and Irish neutrality made it so.[49]

2. THE MAKING OF
DE VALERA'S IRELAND 1916–38

When Australian Prime Minister Robert Menzies arrived in Dublin on Friday 4 April 1941, he described it as a 'distressful country'. He had come, as others had before him, to persuade de Valera that playing a more active role in the war would benefit his national ambitions. Once again the prospects of reconciliation and an end to partition were raised, but to no avail. To de Valera and his cabinet colleagues Ireland was no 'distressful country' but a sovereign independent democratic state, with its own constitution and a unique political culture. The Fianna Fáil government, which had been in office since 1932, agreed unanimously to remain neutral in September 1939. That same cabinet was still in office in May 1945 when de Valera visited Hempel to offer his condolences on the death of Hitler.[1] The decision to remain neutral in 1939 had been out of step with the dominions, though by then Eire's political behaviour appeared unusual to many in Europe and the United States. Against all the odds, predictions and considerable pressure, Ireland remained outside the war, independent and partitioned between 1939 and 1945. It is one of the many paradoxes of Irish history that while the experience of the Second World War enhanced Irish sovereignty and confidence in its independent institutions, it also consolidated partition and sectarian divisions on the island. The American minister in Dublin in 1939, John Cudahy, writing to President Roosevelt, remarked positively on de Valera's decision to remain neutral, but warned that defending this position would not be easy for the Fianna Fáil government.[2]

Irish neutrality had its origins in the First World War, when militant nationalists opposed John Redmond's support for Britain against Germany.[3] Most of those sitting around the cabinet table between

1939 and 1945 had been radicalized by the First World War. In this they were not unlike many others in Britain, Germany or Italy at the time, driven by memories and experience of that other great conflict. Most Irish ministers had literally been blooded by that experience which had had a profound influence on them. Whether individuals learn from the past is an unanswerable question, but they are certainly influenced by it, especially if, as young men or women, they participate in great events. The badge of honour for active participation in Irish political life for over thirty years had been involvement in the independence struggle. As late as 1948 over 40 per cent of Dáil members had participated in either the 1916 Rising or the War of Independence, while many more had family members who had done so.[4] A typical example was Donnchadh O'Briain, who was Fianna Fáil TD (Member of the Dáil) for Limerick from 1933 to 1969. O'Briain eventually achieved ministerial office, but spent his early career as a backbencher. As Seán Fitzpatrick has shown, O'Briain had fought in the War of Independence, opposed the Treaty establishing the Irish Free State in 1922 and was for a period general secretary of the Gaelic League, as well as later the first general secretary of Fianna Fáil. O'Briain, like many others in his party, was contemptuous of TDs who had not participated in the independence struggle. People like him believed they held the moral high ground and used this position ruthlessly against their opponents. These men and women (but mainly men) made up the core of de Valera's political support in 1939. They accepted his leadership uncritically, at least in public, and were dogmatic in asserting what they believed were the core values of the party and Irish nationalism. They were parochial, especially if they represented rural constituencies in the west of Ireland, and frequently isolationist in respect of the rest of the world. At the centre of their understanding of the world was suspicion of Britain and hostility to those in Ireland they associated with British interests.[5]

For Fianna Fáil members like O'Briain, Eamon de Valera symbolized an unbroken tradition of honesty, selflessness and integrity. His every action represented the forward march of Irish nationalism in its historic journey to a prosperous, independent and sovereign Ireland. De Valera was the dominant figure in Irish politics by 1939 and remained so for many years. In many respects an unlikely charismatic figure, he has been loved and hated in equal measure. His loyal supporters thought him infallible; his opponents rarely, and then only grudgingly, acknowledged when he was right. His real enemies always thought him wrong. The passions he aroused seem strange at this historical distance, yet they were a key feature of Irish politics for most of the twentieth century. For many, he embodied the very essence of Irish nationality, though born in New York of Spanish–Irish parentage. His origins gave rise to racial slurs and questions about his legitimacy, accusations he angrily rejected. His strength was his fortitude in the face of adversity, whether during the 1916 Rising, when he assumed the leadership in prison after his surrender, or later in life leading the country when he was effectively blind.

Robert Brennan, a lifelong friend, has described his first encounter with de Valera in jail in 1916. He was immediately struck by his height and the presence that this gave him and by de Valera's quiet dignity and the grave nature of his countenance. However, it was de Valera's steely determination and leadership qualities, whether in prison then or on the political platform later, that impressed Brennan and many others the most. These characteristics repelled others, who saw a narrow and dogmatic mind framed by the most insular aspects of Irish nationalism. James Dillon described de Valera as cobra-like, while others considered him fundamentally authoritarian in his political style.[6]

There is a danger of seeing de Valera as a 'unique dictator', in Desmond Ryan's telling phrase, attributing to him everything that went right or wrong in Ireland between 1916 and 1959. But, notwithstanding his power, de Valera was not surrounded by yes-men in 1939 or 1945. He had indeed a unique position as chief of the cabinet and party, but his position was unlike that of authoritarian rulers such as Franco or Salazar. A better comparison might be made with the American Democratic party under President Roosevelt or Charles de Gaulle's leadership of the Fifth Republic in France. These leaders represented the party, but were not the sum of the party. What all three leaders achieved in their lifetimes was to associate the party in an intimate fashion with the nation and state, providing their successors with a powerful symbolic tool for political competition.

The composition of the Fianna Fáil cabinet in 1939 reinforces this view. It contained mercurial individuals who in terms of ability were de Valera's equal while in organizational capacity were often superior. It was a cabinet that not only shared a loyalty to the leader and party, but a common experience in war and death. The youngest member was Seán Lemass, who at forty represented many of the ambiguities of nationalist politics. A man of the left in some respects, he would have been a social democrat in Britain or Sweden. Since 1932 he had guided Ireland through a minor industrial revolution as minister for industry and commerce and now took over as minister for supplies, the effective coordinator of the economy for the duration of the war. Though the youngest, his political credentials as a nationalist were among the strongest. He had fought in 1916 at the age of sixteen, his youth sparing him jail after the Rising. He was an IRA 'hard man' during the War of Independence, and may have been a member of the Michael Collins assassination squad in Dublin in 1919 and 1920. He opposed the Treaty and was interned for a period at the end of the Civil War, while Free State forces murdered his brother in 1923. Although a militant he does not seem to have been uncompromising; indeed, his intellectual interests provided the basis for him to convert to mainstream political action later in the 1920s.[7]

Frank Aiken was just two years older than Lemass, yet a very different type of politician. Born in Northern Ireland, Aiken had a difficult upbringing. Orphaned early, he took over the family farm as a teenager, while at the same time involving himself in nationalist politics. He led IRA operations in Armagh between 1919 and 1921, in what was often a hostile environment for nationalists. While Lemass and others faced the British, those who fought in Northern Ireland were as likely to face those they considered fellow Irishmen, the Unionist and Protestant community there. Aiken was another hard man, becoming IRA chief of staff in 1923 during the Civil War. He issued the ceasefire order that marked the end of the Civil War, though it might be suggested that for him the war never ended; he always gave the impression of one at war, especially during the period up to 1945. Despite his lack of formal education, Aiken was deeply interested in economic and scientific matters. The comparison between Aiken and Lemass is striking. Lemass had a subtle mind open to nuance and the possibility of negotiation and reconciliation, whereas Aiken had a blunt uncompromising nature in terms of ideas and policymaking. Aiken was described by a friendly observer as 'usually a hard hitter, and as obstinate as a young colt', adding that 'anything in the nature of compromise, on fundamental issues, he detests by instinct'.

Nor were Aiken or Lemass untypical of the men who served with de Valera in 1939. Seán T. O'Kelly, who was tánaiste (deputy prime minister), had followed a political path similar to his colleagues. All were in their forties or early fifties, but probably none of them would have been as prominent as they were if it had not been for 1916 and the War of Independence. James Ryan, minister for agriculture, had been a medical doctor who gave up his practice for health and political reasons. Seán MacEntee from Belfast had been an engineer with the prospect of a good life ahead but took part in the 1916 rebellion and was sentenced to death. Others might have stayed on the family farm or worked in local government or as teachers. Yet all were attracted by militant Irish nationalism, breaking with the Home Rule consensus between 1914 and 1916. They challenged the dominance of the Home Rule party in 1917 and 1918, contributing to the political success of Sinn Fein in 1918 in what was a landslide election victory for the extremists. Nor did Fianna Fáil have a monopoly of republican virtue. Many in the opposition parties, the trade unions and in the general population had participated in the War of Independence and remained committed to the ideals of an independent, united and sovereign Ireland. The new elite was much wider than Fianna Fáil, but by 1939 it was the government party's robust nationalism that had captured the political high ground.[8]

In 1939 independent Ireland was unusual because it was a functioning democracy. By that time Ireland and Finland were the only recently established states that remained democratic. Authoritarian government had become the norm outside democracy's heartland in north-west Europe and even there the future was uncertain. Moreover, all the indications were that Ireland too might soon become authoritarian. No Catholic agrarian state with a strong nationalistic culture had remained independent and democratic for very long during the inter-war period; most existing democratic states were Protestant or liberal republican. Political scientist Tom Garvin has shown that many of those who participated in the struggle for Irish independence were 'unenthusiastic democrats' attracted by authoritarian and militaristic alternatives to representative government. However, Bill Kissane has countered this, arguing that representative institutions were already deeply embedded in Irish nationalist political culture in the nineteenth century. Some of this was a result of British influence, but the evidence suggests that by 1914 Ireland had internalized democracy as the appropriate method of resolving disputes within the national community. Kissane is persuasive but he does not adequately address Garvin's challenge that within Irish nationalism there were militaristic and authoritarian strains. What happened after 1914 and contributed to the violence of that period was that democracy and nationalism came into conflict over the future of Irish sovereignty.[9]

Ireland's democratic political culture was seriously challenged between 1914 and 1924. This challenge took various forms, but the driving force for it was nationalism. Up to 1914 Irish nationalism had expressed itself primarily in constitutional terms. Though demanding Home Rule from Britain, moderate Irish nationalists had worked within the British political system to achieve a major reform of the constitution. John Redmond and his colleagues in the Home Rule party worked to convince a majority in Westminster that devolved government should be conceded to Ireland, and they were not prepared to work outside the constitutional structure to achieve this end. This was almost achieved when the third Home Rule Bill was passed in 1914. However, Irish nationalists were agreed that any Home Rule settlement should apply to the entire island of Ireland, and Ulster Unionists rejected nationalist claims to the north. Ulster Unionism asserted Northern Ireland's right to be considered as an autonomous community with sovereign rights. This dispute has been central to the political conflict in Ireland ever since, and has an echo in virtually every religious and ethnic conflict within states during the twentieth century. The question was determining which majority was acceptable for deciding major political change. Irish nationalists argued that it was the majority on the island which should decide, whereas Ulster Unionists favoured either the majority within the British state or the majority within the north. The core of Ulster Unionism's case was that Unionists were not part of the Irish nation and that the same consideration should be given to them as to Irish nationalists. The British parliament had acknowledged the justice of the Unionist case by 1914, but the right of the north to remain with the United Kingdom was rejected by Irish nationalists, even the most moderate. Both sides armed to defend their claims, leading to the ethnic–religious confrontation that was to characterize Irish political life for the rest of the century. The First World War postponed this conflict, but as a result the commitment to democracy by both nationalists and unionists had weakened.[10]

For Irish nationalists the notion of partition was outrageous, and in common with many nationalists, de Valera was radicalized by this threat. It also drew him to the centre of an anti-democratic conspiracy against not only the British state, but majority opinion within the nationalist community. De Valera shared with the leaders of the 1916 rebellion a contempt for the complex compromises and negotiations at the heart of constitutional politics. In its place these radicals emphasized the will to power, which was in turn based on an unchallengeable utopian republican vision. The radicals distinguished between the will of the people as an ideal represented by themselves and the actual existing will as expressed in elections and through public opinion. This provided the justification for the 1916 Rising, but what in fact occurred was an unrepresentative coup d'état by an unelected group in a political system that remained open to change. That this was the case was demonstrated over the next two years, when Sinn Féin challenged the Home Rule party for the leadership of the nationalist community. Sinn Féin was a radical nationalist party originally founded in 1905. Reorganized in 1917, it became the political vehicle for all those nationalists opposed to the moderate Home Rule party. Sinn Féin's challenge was successful, but the leadership remained unenthusiastic democrats. The ballot box was used to radicalize opinion, promote republican utopianism and justify the 1916 coup, not to consolidate democracy. As a result constitutional politicians were swept aside at the 1918 election, nationalist representatives seceded from Westminster and confrontation between Irish nationalism and the British state became central to Irish political life. Nor did this end violence. In 1917 de Valera was elected president of Sinn Féin, but was also appointed leader of the paramilitary volunteers. The volunteer executive was given the authority to declare war on Britain if the need arose. This is a version of the 'Armalite and ballot-box' strategy favoured by the later Sinn Féin, but also provides evidence for de Valera and Sinn Féin's reluctance to embrace democratic elections.[11]

Sinn Féin certainly received a mandate at the 1918 elections, but it was not a mandate for armed revolt. There were two powerful constraints on nationalist violence. The first of these was the Roman Catholic Church, which opposed the use of violence to achieve political objectives. Throughout the War of Independence, the Catholic Church remained uneasy about the use of violence by the IRA, though more frequently criticizing British repression. Sinn Féin and the IRA had to justify the use of violence and did so by emphasizing its defensive character. The other constraint was public opinion itself. Nationalist opinion was never homogeneous, despite what Sinn Féin claimed in its propaganda. Most nationalists in 1918 had voted for a change of leadership not for a declaration of war on Britain. Like the Church, opinion remained uneasy about violence though more ready to condemn the state than the nation. Nevertheless, the complex nature of Irish public opinion meant that Sinn Féin and the IRA had to continue to take account of the deeply rooted commitment to democracy on the part of many Irish nationalists while pursuing what was a radical and utopian political strategy. The contradiction in this was obscured during the War of Independence, when Britain was successfully characterized as the aggressor in Ireland, but the influence of representative politics did not disappear.[12]

Despite these constraints Ireland's democratic tradition was seriously threatened by the use of violence during the War of Independence and thereafter. IRA volunteers developed a militaristic mindset which was frequently impatient with the slow processes of democratic participation. Many believed they had a duty to fallen comrades to pursue the principle of an Irish republic by all means available. It is not surprising to find Seán O'Hegarthy, the IRA leader in Cork, ordering the local TD J. J. Walsh to vote against the Treaty on the grounds that any other action would be treason to the republic.[13] IRA militants intimidated opponents during the War of Independence, but also during the crucial debates surrounding the Treaty. Michael Collins warned that these actions would lead to civil war: 'the result of that will really mean the destruction of all our hopes and the return of the English'.[14] De Valera shared the IRA's lack of enthusiasm for democracy. His political stance was to blame Britain for every problem and to insist on simple solutions. In respect of Unionism, he declared in 1917, 'if Ulster stood in the way of Irish freedom Ulster would have to be coerced'. On another occasion Unionists were described as a 'foreign garrison' and 'not Irish people'; 'they would have to go under' if they did not accept a united Ireland. Nor was this mere rhetoric, as Peter Hart's description of the pogrom against West Cork Protestants demonstrates.[15]

De Valera's uncompromising nature gave him credibility among the most militant republicans, but made it difficult for him to compromise. Unlike Collins, who remained in Ireland throughout the War of Independence, de Valera went to the United States and remained there until the end of 1921. De Valera's stance mirrored that of the militaristic wing of the IRA during the Treaty debates: he consistently refused to accept the majority view in the Dáil, in the country or among his colleagues. The so-called Pact-Election held on 16 June 1922 was effectively a referendum on the Treaty and was a resounding victory for those who supported a moderate solution to the conflict. Approximately 75 per cent of those who voted supported candidates or parties that endorsed the Treaty to establish the Irish Free State. However, neither de Valera nor the militarists would accept the verdict of the electorate, but established an alternative government which openly defied the legitimate government. This led directly to civil war, threatening the democratic viability of the new state. De Valera provided a political justification for going to war against the new state while other militants such as Seán O'Hegarthy chose to remain neutral in the conflict.[16] On one occasion de Valera incited his listeners to violence:

> If they accepted the Treaty, and if the Volunteers of the future tried to complete the work the Volunteers of the last few years had been attempting, they would have to complete it, not over the bodies of foreign soldiers, but over the dead bodies of their own countrymen. They would have to wade through, perhaps, the blood of some of the members of the Government in order to get Irish freedom.[17]

He frequently asserted the superiority of the republic over democracy, elections or the will of the population, arguing that 'the people had never a right to do wrong'. 'Republicans maintain that there are rights which a minority may justly uphold, even by arms, against a majority.' It was not that de Valera did not see the alternatives; it was that he chose the anti-democratic one. In a letter to J. J. McGarrity in September 1922 he identified the choice for republicans between democracy and nationalist ideals and chose the latter. Even when the Civil War ended in defeat for the republicans, de Valera refused to accept the surrender but promoted it as a ceasefire – a dangerous legacy for a young democratic state.[18]

*

The major test for Irish democracy came during and immediately after the Civil War. During the conflict, the government applied draconian sanctions to its republican opponents. This coercion was remarkably successful in ending the war, but it did not result in the government losing legitimacy with the public then or later. It confirms the insight formulated by Albert Hirschman that democratic and accountable governments can deal more harshly with internal subversion than authoritarian regimes and still retain their political legitimacy. The anti-Treaty republicans lost their legitimacy because they decided to ignore the 1922 election verdict and were defeated politically and militarily as a result. Furthermore, the government may have been ruthless in the face of the republican threat but it continued to maintain its commitment to democratic norms and values. It did not attempt to maintain emergency legislation after the Civil War, but sought a new mandate by calling an election for August 1923. At this election the republicans received 27 per cent of the vote, but those parties that supported the state and the Treaty received over 70 per cent. In addition, the Catholic Church, the trade unions and most civic organizations openly supported the Treaty settlement, if with varying degrees of enthusiasm.[19]

Irish democracy was saved in 1923 by the ruthlessness of W. T. Cosgrave (whom de Valera dismissed as a 'ninny'), Kevin O'Higgins and Richard Mulcahy, who insisted that majority rule and law and order would be preserved and respected. O'Higgins demanded complete victory over the republicans, insisting, 'this is not going to be a draw, with a replay in the autumn'. Despite this, victory was not assured. De Valera and the republicans refused to accept defeat, ignoring the clearly stated wishes of the electorate in 1922 and 1923.[20] Cosgrave and O'Higgins failed to appreciate the superior claims that nationalism made on the republicans, who hated the new state and worked to destroy it. De Valera and his supporters became a disloyal opposition, with a private army and access to weapons; the IRA remained intact and committed to insurrectionary politics. What Cosgrave and O'Higgins did next was audacious. They ignored the republican abstentionists, who refused to participate in the Dáil, and began a process of state-building which stabilized a liberal democratic and constitutional order over the next four years. Cumann na nGaedheal imposed order on a divided state and effectively countered the lawless legacy of the Civil War. An unarmed police force was put in place and civilian rule asserted over the army, now much reduced in size. Policymaking progressed rapidly on the economy, education and foreign affairs.[21] The restoration of order, the rule of law and the stabilization of the political system had been largely accomplished by the beginning of 1926. The republicans were left out of this, much to their frustration and indignation. Despite this a very real danger continued to stalk the state, as 25 per cent of the electorate remained committed to an anti-system party. De Valera insisted that 'the Free State Constitution made them a state subject to England'. Lemass declared that 'Ireland today is ruled by a British garrison, organised by the Masonic lodges, speaking through the Free State Parliament, and playing the cards of England all the time. If this nation is to get a chance to live we must sweep the Free State and all that it stands for out of existence.'[22]

Cumann na nGaedheal's success, however, forced de Valera to reassess his opposition to the new state, though he did so with great distaste and reluctance. He recommended that Sinn Féin take their seats in the Dáil if the oath of allegiance to the crown was abolished. When he lost this vote, he and his supporters resigned and established Fianna Fáil in 1926. In leaving Sinn Féin de Valera was not making a new commitment to democracy but seeking to preserve nationalism from the sordidness of ordinary politics. As he told McGarrity:

You perhaps will wonder why I did not wait longer. It is vital that the Free State be shaken at the next General Election, for if an opportunity be given it to consolidate itself as an institution – if the present Free State members are replaced by Farmers and Labourers and other class interests, the national interest as a whole will be submerged in the clashing of the rival economic groups. It seems to me a case of now or never – at least in our time.[23]

At the inaugural meeting of Fianna Fáil, held at the La Scala theatre in Dublin on 16 May 1926, de Valera continued to employ gunman imagery to general acclaim. Fianna Fáil remained close to the IRA; indeed for a period there was considerable overlap in membership. They shared a common enemy in the state and its police force, they were both opposed to the emergency legislation used against them and they agreed on the need to remove Cumann na nGaedheal from government. If the two organizations diverged on tactics – Dáil versus armed struggle – this was not enough to divide them between 1926 and 1932. The Fianna Fáil leadership maintained some distance from the IRA, but this was not the case with the rank and file. The IRA prohibited its members from standing as Dáil candidates and many left the organization to fight the 1927 election with Fianna Fáil. Patrick Smith left to stand in County Cavan but did not give up his commitment to militancy. Smith justified this: 'if our present attempt (politically) should be doomed to failure, I hope my action will not prevent me in future taking a line of action in which I have not lost faith'. Smith went on to a successful parliamentary and ministerial career, but his views illustrate the continuing overlap between Fianna Fáil and the IRA at this time.[24]

The decision to form Fianna Fáil was not a decisive break with the past. At most, it was a recognition that a military strategy would not defeat the new state, at least that a more active political strategy had to be pursued. Fianna Fáil maintained right up to 1932 that its republican principles were more important than elections. De Valera continued to defend the use of force, while Lemass described Fianna Fáil as a 'slightly constitutional party'. Lemass argued that parliamentary politics was necessary because it served their purposes, but threatened that other methods might be used if these failed. Nor did the party ever accept the Treaty; as late as 1931 de Valera was describing it as a coup d'état while continuing to assert that 'a majority does not give a right to do wrong'. Fianna Fáil simply refused to accept the verdict of the electorate unless it coincided with their view of what was right or wrong.[25] These views made Fianna Fáil's commitment to democracy contingent for at least a decade, if not longer. Nor did the party participate willingly in Free State politics, but had to be forced to do so by the government. When Kevin O'Higgins was brutally murdered on 10 July 1927 Cosgrave introduced legislation to force Dáil candidates to take their seats if elected. This involved taking the oath of allegiance, which de Valera was loath to do. This was a highly risky strategy on the government's part as it risked pushing Fianna Fáil back into alliance with the IRA. Cosgrave however had taken the measure of Fianna Fáil and de Valera in particular and the crisis provoked by the murder provided the opportunity to force the issue once and for all. After considerable agonizing, the Fianna Fáil parliamentary party agreed to take the oath, though de Valera, humiliated, refused to acknowledge that he had actually done so or that the party had in effect reversed its policy.[26]

De Valera's intention prior to O'Higgins's murder was to force a referendum on the issue, confident that he would win it. With this avenue closed off his anger and frustration was barely contained when he went to the Dáil to sign the oath. In theatrical fashion he read out a statement in Irish that he was not taking the oath, denied that by signing it he was doing so and personally removed a Bible sitting on the book to be signed. His humiliation boiled over as he left the room, when he told a senior clerk in the Dáil that he would personally burn the book one day. This was an inauspicious start to parliamentary participation by Fianna Fáil.[27] De Valera's attitude to the oath was echoed by his followers' attitude to the Dáil itself. The party remained uneasy at the compromises that parliamentary politics required, insisting that its members did not associate with anyone in the government. Party discipline was tight, with very little opportunity for individual conscience or opinion to be expressed.[28]

When O'Higgins was murdered, de Valera assured the public that no republican was involved, while in his memoirs Todd Andrews betrays Fianna Fáil's concern that 'the assassination was worse than a crime, it was a mistake'. Andrews admitted fifty years later that republicans did not mourn O'Higgins's death.[29] We now know who murdered O'Higgins: three members of the IRA, Archie Doyle, Bill Gannon and Timothy Coughlan. Doyle remained a key member of the IRA for the next twenty years, organizing the murder of Detective Sergeant Dennis O'Brien in 1942. Gannon became a communist and we have his later recollections for one version of what happened. According to him, the three men simply came upon O'Higgins and killed him in a rage, although there are a number of inconsistencies in the account that raise serious questions about its accuracy. De Vere

White provides a different version of the story, one that suggests a carefully planned ambush. Earlier in the day O'Higgins's wife had noticed some men loitering at the end of the road, while another witness reported that a boy on a bicycle gave a signal to some men in a car who then jumped out and killed O'Higgins.[30] At the very least there is a strong case that the assassination was not a spontaneous act of rage, but part of the IRA assault on the Irish state. Rather than a maverick operation it had the hallmarks of an IRA plan, one that they regretted subsequently. That it rebounded on them and on Fianna Fáil was an unintended consequence, but unintended consequences are of vital importance in politics. The third killer is of interest here. Tim Coughlan was not only a member of the IRA but also of Fianna Fáil. Nor did he ever give up his commitment to violence, as can be seen in January 1928 when he and others attacked Seán Harling, a police informer, outside his home in Dublin. Harling was armed and in the gun battle Coughlan was killed. There was uproar after this incident. Large numbers of Fianna Fáil deputies attended Coughlan's funeral, a party branch was named after him and Seán MacEntee proclaimed that 'the murder of Timothy Coughlan would not go unpunished'.[31]

Fianna Fáil's ambiguous position in respect of the Free State and democracy can be clearly seen in its attitude towards the police force and emergency legislation. Fianna Fáil deputies were critical of the police for their activities against republicans, some of whom were members of the party. Furthermore, Fianna Fáil consistently opposed the emergency legislation introduced to counter the violent campaign against the state promoted by the IRA. Between 1926 and 1932 the IRA resumed its activities and its members were involved in murder plots against government ministers, the police force and members of the public. Attacks on the judicial system proved especially effective and the Garda – the unarmed police force – and the judicial authorities faced an impossible task getting verdicts in so-called 'political' crimes.[32] By 1930 the jury system had effectively collapsed due to intimidation. Finally in 1931 the government introduced the Public Safety Act after a series of murders, including the 'authorized execution' of a Garda superintendent in County Tipperary.

Conor Brady has persuasively argued that the IRA decided to wage war against the state and the evidence available suggests that this was indeed the case. While Fianna Fáil was not involved directly in this war, its sympathies lay with the IRA. The party leadership might condemn an IRA murder, but it reserved its fiercest criticism for the government, the Garda and the judicial system. This attitude towards the IRA was maintained and applied to similar killings in Northern Ireland and Britain for long after. An important illustration of this was de Valera's speech opposing the Juries Protection Bill in the Dáil in May 1929, when he condemned the legislation as unnecessary and offered tacit support for the IRA campaign of violence.[33] Fianna Fáil members also played an active role in violent demonstrations against Armistice Day celebrations every year up to 1932. This is not to claim that Fianna Fáil and the IRA were the same organization. There were tactical differences, but what drew them together was a shared belief in the illegitimate nature of the Irish Free State. Thus, Fianna Fáil and the IRA were closer to one another up to 1932 than Fianna Fáil was to Cumann na nGaedheal or the other parties in the Dáil. The IRA was critical of Fianna Fáil's decision to enter the Dáil, but did not see them in the same light as the other parties. In 1932 the IRA decided to reverse its previous position and take an active part in the upcoming election, permitting its members to campaign and vote. In consequence IRA members were at the centre of the Fianna Fáil campaign in that election, believing that a Fianna Fáil government would be sympathetic to the organization. This was borne out when de Valera was elected president of the Executive Council on 9 March 1932. One of the first acts of new Minister for Defence Frank Aiken (former officer commanding the IRA) was to visit IRA prisoners in Arbour Hill military barracks. After what was reported to have been a cordial conversation between Aiken and George Gilmore, the IRA leader in the prison, the organization's members were released the following day. A week later the Public Safety Act was suspended, and large numbers of Fianna Fáil TDs and supporters attended the annual IRA Easter Rising commemoration in April.[34]

The year 1932 was a dangerous time in European politics and for Irish democracy. All over Europe democratic governments were under pressure, and in Germany Hitler was soon to become chancellor. Hitler showed how anti-system parties could use the framework of democracy to undermine the foundations of liberal constitutionalism. One of the major challenges in sustaining any democracy is during a change of government, especially if the incoming administration is more radical than its predecessor. Does the existing government pass over its authority or does it retain power by using emergency legislation, invoking a crisis or calling for military intervention? In Ireland there was no guarantee that Cumann na nGaedheal would give up power and no assurance that Fianna Fáil would maintain democracy once it controlled the levers of the state. There were those, such as Eoin O'Duffy the Garda commissioner, who favoured overruling the electorate and installing a military dictatorship rather than let Fianna Fáil come to power. In Fianna Fáil and in the IRA many wanted revenge for the Civil War and were prepared to exact it if given the opportunity.

*

The most remarkable event in the short life of the Irish Free State took place in March 1932. After an eventful but relatively peaceful election campaign, de Valera was poised to take over the despised Free State government. His party had won 72 seats, an increase of 15 over the 1927 election. What is remarkable is how easy the transition proved. Fianna Fáil did not engage in a vendetta against its opponents, although it did remove O'Duffy from his post as Garda commissioner. Nor, except for a brief moment in 1933, did the outgoing governing party challenge the legitimacy of the new government, even when it fundamentally disagreed with it. What happened between 1932 and 1938 was that successive Fianna Fáil governments consolidated Irish democracy. What Fianna Fáil did after 1932 confirmed Collins's assertion that the Free State would be a stepping stone to full independence. De Valera never acknowledged this, but his actions demonstrated that the Free State had achieved much under Cumann na nGaedheal. Without these achievements Fianna Fáil could not have so radically changed the Irish political and institutional environment in such a short time. Cumann na nGaedheal had enhanced Irish sovereignty over the preceding decade, increasing the state's status as well as securing an institutional framework which allowed for further developments. It is not too strong a claim to make that without the changes that Cumann na nGaedheal had introduced, de Valera's position in respect of the British would have been much more difficult.[35]

Fianna Fáil certainly had its authoritarian moments but overall the Irish Free State was safe for democracy by 1938. There are a number of factors that explain this. The first is the peaceful transfer of power in 1932. 'Our opponents accepted the verdict of the electorate notwithstanding, and surrendered power to the representatives of the majority. In doing so, they, to my mind, finally established the principle of majority rule here,' Seán MacEntee acknowledged in 1936.[36] The second is that Fianna Fáil introduced significant political, economic and social changes between 1932 and 1938, without either destabilizing the state or using authoritarian methods to impose them. All these changes achieved majority support in the Dáil or, in the case of the 1937 constitution, was ratified by referendum. The 1933 general election is important here, as Peter Mair has recently pointed out. De Valera did not have a majority after the 1932 election, but depended on the support of the Labour party to govern. He called a snap election in January 1933 and gained an overall majority. He went back to the electorate to seek a further mandate, as he was to do in similar circumstances in 1938 and again in 1944. A third consideration is that Fianna Fáil was prepared to act decisively against paramilitary and anti-system threats, especially if they challenged the state. In the case of the threatened Blueshirt march on the Dáil on 13 August 1933, this may be explained by Fianna Fáil hostility to the right, but in time the activities of the IRA were also outlawed when it refused to accept democratic rule and the legitimacy of the state, especially after the introduction of the new constitution. The fourth factor is the refusal of the conservative elite to support any anti-system challenge led by a demagogue, as in the case of O'Duffy and the Blueshirt movement. The Blueshirts had many of the characteristics of continental fascist movements, including contempt for the government and liberal democracy. The Blueshirts were part of Fine Gael, a political party established in 1933 as a response by the opposition to Fianna Fáil's electoral success. The new party amalgamated Cumann na nGaedheal, the National Centre party and the National Guard, but its leadership was drawn overwhelmingly from the former government party. Despite the short-term prominence of the Blueshirts, Cosgrave effectively neutralized O'Duffy, forcing him out of Fine Gael on the grounds that democratic institutions and practices must be protected. It is telling that in the two cases where democracy remained intact in new states by 1939, in Ireland and Finland, conservative elites overwhelmingly supported the democratic order against possible right-wing takeovers. Where the authoritarian right succeeded, conservatives either threw in their lot with the radicals or were seriously divided and lost their support to the anti-system party.[37]

A further consideration in 1932 and possibly even after the 1933 election is that if Fianna Fáil had attempted to encroach on political rights and liberties the Dáil would have voted them out of power. It is also possible that the army and the Garda would have intervened to protect the constitution. At the very least Fianna Fáil had to be circumspect to avoid a challenge from either of these sources. Also relevant is the democratic nature of Irish political culture itself in the 1930s. Society had become more democratic and participative, not less so; nor was there disengagement from the system. The franchise was universal, unlike in a number of European states where women were excluded from the vote, while participation in elections was widespread and lively. There was an extensive newspaper and magazine culture, appealing to a wide readership, and Irish literacy rates were among the highest in Europe. After the establishment of the *Irish Press* as the organ of Fianna Fáil and de Valera's personal propaganda tool, it is likely that every home in the country received at least one newspaper every day. Political competition might have been vigorous and at times violent, but debate was informed by an independent media and the public was well informed if partisan. This political culture can trace its origins back to the second half of the nineteenth century, and was reinforced by the events of the 1920s and '30s. What this suggests is that the period between 1914 and 1924 was a break with the previous fifty years, while the trends associated with the Irish Free State represent a return to the earlier democratic and parliamentary culture. A major factor in this stabilization was the Roman Catholic Church. Even though the Church held authoritarian views on many matters, this did not translate into support for political authoritarianism. Irish democracy was majoritarian (the 51 per cent principle) and under Fianna Fáil less liberal than under Cumann na nGaedheal, but it was nevertheless still democratic in form and content. That Catholic bishops supported this consciously and consistently is one of the unique features of Irish democracy during the inter-war period.

Paradoxically, the final factor that contributed to the success of

Irish democracy was nationalism. Nationalism had divided the island of Ireland along ethnic lines in the nineteenth century and continued to do so within Northern Ireland after 1920. In addition, as previously discussed, it was used to justify the behaviour of anti-democratic forces in Ireland. However, after 1922 the population of the Irish Free State was fairly homogeneous and had become more so by the 1930s. The non-Catholic population of the state fell from 327,000 in 1911 to 194,500 by 1936, making it one of the most religiously uniform parts of Europe. Political instability is more likely in ethnically or religiously divided societies, as can be seen from comparing north and south since 1920. Moreover, nationalism in Ireland placed a high premium on reconciling conflicts democratically, placing de Valera and the republican movement in a difficult position. If, as they had argued, freedom and democracy within the context of the Irish Free State were illusory then clearly elections would have no real meaning. However, whatever reservations existed were set aside after 1932 when Fianna Fáil pursued an active domestic policy and a revisionist foreign policy. De Valera's government used its democratic mandate to undermine the 1922 Treaty settlement, but did so without destroying Irish democracy. The final achievement in this area was the introduction of the 1937 constitution to replace that agreed with Britain in 1922. In contrast to the 1922 constitution, which was part of the Treaty settlement, the new constitution was ratified in a referendum. It provided that further constitutional changes needed the same form of ratification. While the 1937 constitution had a number of illiberal aspects to it, especially in respect of Northern Ireland, women and the Church, it was accepted quickly by the majority of the population. The important point to note is that the 1937 constitution was not authoritarian or semi-authoritarian like those in contemporary Russia or China. It reinforced democracy and in some respects advanced beyond 1922, providing for example a Supreme Court along the lines established in the United States. De Valera did not have enough confidence in an upper house to provide an independent senate (Seanad) and this limited the liberal character of the new constitution, but it is one of the earliest attempts I know of to reconcile democracy, nationalism and religion within a non-secular institutional framework, and has been a successful one. Its anti-liberal aspects notwithstanding, this is a model that might have relevance for the prospects of democratic governance in predominantly Islamic societies, most especially Turkey, which may soon join the European Union.[38]

While many factors contributed to this consolidation of democracy in Ireland, it was not an entirely smooth process. Fianna Fáil did not simply accept the existing framework, but modified it considerably. If it had not, its opposition to the Free State and its expressed contempt for the 1922 constitution, the state institutions and for Cumann na nGaedheal could rightly have been condemned as hypocrisy. Fianna Fáil wanted the republicanization of Irish society and used the political and institutional resources available to it to achieve this. At the heart of their programme was the desire to make the country's institutions reflect more closely the Catholic and nationalist attributes associated with Irish identity. The Cork writer Daniel Corkery identified nationalism, the land and religion as the three main forces contributing to the emotional make-up of Ireland, an emotional make-up that distinguished the Irish 'national being' from that of England or any other nation. Corkery was a supporter of Fianna Fáil and the party sought to redefine these three crucial elements to give force to their specific interpretation of Irish nationality.[39] Central to this reformulation was Fianna Fáil's exaggerated nationalism deriving from a sense of grievance in respect of partition and resentment at Ireland's place within the commonwealth. De Valera was committed to righting these wrongs, like his predecessors, but his tactics and objectives were quite different. De Valera eschewed any compromise with Britain over Northern Ireland, insisting that Irish unity was a right and that Britain had a responsibility to unify the island. The Fianna Fáil government confronted the Unionists, refusing to accept them as a legitimate government in Northern Ireland or as a party to negotiations. This policy inflamed the situation in the north, providing hope for the nationalist minority that unity could be achieved when there was little likelihood of this occurring. Fianna Fáil also denied the Unionists the right to determine their own future based on majority opinion within Northern Ireland. Cumann na nGaedheal had attempted to build bridges between north and south, though not always successfully, but Fianna Fáil alienated Unionist opinion by refusing to negotiate on any issues for fear this would stabilize the northern government.[40]

Essentially, de Valera and Fianna Fáil insisted that a united Ireland was the only possible outcome and ignored those moderates and liberal Unionists in Northern Ireland who might have been prepared to accept a closer relationship between north and south but not the irredentist politics of militant nationalism. The 1937 constitution provided an institutional basis for irredentism. In Articles 2 and 3 Dublin asserted its jurisdiction over Northern Ireland, declaring that all those who lived on the island were Irish citizens, and in Article 9.2 stated, 'fidelity to the nation and loyalty to the state are fundamental political duties of all citizens'. The insistence that all those living in the north were Irish citizens was politically explosive. Northern Unionists considered themselves subjects of the crown and not Eire, as the Irish Free State was called under the new constitution. It is possible to argue that Fianna Fáil and the 1937 constitution provided a political basis for the entrenchment of the most conservative elements of Unionism as a protection against what was seen as nationalist aggression.[41] The new constitution reinforced division in Ireland in other ways. The preamble emphasized religion and the nationalist aspects of the political community, while the constitution's social principles largely reflected the teachings of the dominant Catholic Church. The priority given to the Gaelic language and the introduction of archaic terms such as taoiseach and tánaiste stressed traditional concerns often hostile to liberalism and modernity.[42] In large and small ways the Ireland that Fianna Fáil created in the course of the 1930s was less liberal, less tolerant and less secular than that inherited from Cumann na nGaedheal, though it was politically more democratic and inclusive. Protestants were pushed to the margins of public life, though not actively discriminated against. Those who identified with the British connection were marginalized in numerous ways, as Fianna Fáil restrictions on Armistice Day commemoration marches attest. Catholicism was given greater prominence and celebrated throughout this period. Instances of this range from the trivial, as when Cardinal MacRory demanded and received special privileges on entering the state from Northern Ireland, to the more serious including recognizing the special position of the Catholic Church in the constitution and the introduction of legislation reflecting its moral concerns.[43]

There was also some controversy over the position of women under the new constitution. De Valera rejected criticism by women's groups on this matter, arguing that it was not his intention to exclude women from political rights. Yet this was not the issue; what was implied in the draft constitution was a limitation of women's social rights and the presumption that a woman's place was normally in the home with her children. Considered together with legislation restricting their involvement in the workplace which may have contributed to reducing the numbers of women at work, Fianna Fáil's vision of the role of women seems decidedly limited. It is possible to argue that what de Valera did in the constitution was popular or at least had widespread support, even among women. This may be so, but it is also necessary to take seriously the extensive criticism from women's organizations and feminists largely ignored by de Valera.[44] The *Irish Press* clearly sensed a challenge to de Valera when it questioned the credentials of those criticizing the constitution, while replying to them in intemperate fashion. Even one of de Valera's closest collaborators, Dorothy Macardle, challenged him personally on what he proposed to put in the constitution. Writing to him on 21 May 1937, she suggested that some of the criticism could be met by amending the draft. As the constitution was then worded, Macardle questioned how she and other progressive people could support it. More congenial to de Valera was probably the letter he received from businessman J. J. Walsh, who recommended sending all women back to the 'home where they belong'. Progressive opinion such as that expressed by Macardle failed to impress de Valera and the original articles in respect of women remained in the constitution ratified by the electorate.[45]

It is probable that the Ireland of 1938, with its legislative changes and constitutional innovations, was more congenial to the majority of Irish citizens than the country created by the Treaty. However, even if this was the case, there was a danger that those who did not fully share the prevailing view or dissented from the strictly Catholic–nationalist nature of the culture would be stigmatized as disloyal or dismissed as British allies. Fianna Fáil was quick to make such accusations when criticized, as was the *Irish Press*. There were serious tensions within the new republican dispensation, tensions that would emerge again after September 1939. Despite this, the 1938 general election confirmed Fianna Fáil's political dominance and assured de Valera of a commanding presence in Irish politics. It was a remarkable achievement by an individual whose political career had appeared finished in 1923, who revived it in 1926 but who continued to reject the existing state until he effectively had control of it. Yet, when Fianna Fáil gained the reins of power, their use of them was judicious if at times intemperate. By building on the foundations already established, de Valera and Fianna Fáil were able to face an uncertain future with some confidence after the 1938 election.

That year should have been a year of triumph for de Valera. His new constitution came into force on 29 December 1937, after being narrowly ratified in a referendum on 1 July. The constitution emphasized the democratic, republican and Catholic nature of Irish nationalism, but it also challenged Eire's position as a dominion. This was not a challenge Britain was prepared to face. In a series of unilateral moves between 1932 and 1937 de Valera's government had extended Ireland's sovereignty to an extent that questioned its continuing membership of the commonwealth. The gradualist nature of these changes disguised de Valera's radical intentions and the British government concluded that the new constitution did not alter the relationship in a fundamental way, yet this was to misunderstand what de Valera intended to do. He warned Lord Devonshire early in 1939 not to assume that Eire would be confined by the British conception of the commonwealth, adding acidly, 'anyone who supposes that any form of Dominion status, with no matter how much internal autonomy, could satisfy the aspirations of the generation of Irish people now growing up, was profoundly mistaken'. At every turn de Valera sought to disengage from the commonwealth, though the British authorities continued to ignore the signs.[46] For Britain, Ireland's evolution since 1922 was part of a complex process within the commonwealth that recognized the diverse identity shared by the white dominions. But for Fianna Fáil the end point of this evolution was an independent republic outside the commonwealth. The two views were incompatible, though in the short term de Valera was prepared to formally remain in the organization while hoping to benefit from Chamberlain's appeasement policy and the ongoing changes within the commonwealth. De Valera was constrained by a number of factors, but he believed that in the longer term there were no real obstacles to his objective of achieving a republic.[47]

In pursuit of this, de Valera agreed to negotiations with Chamberlain early in 1938 to settle the outstanding conflicts between the two states. Britain and Ireland had been engaged in a low-level economic war since 1932, a dispute that had had disastrous consequences for the Irish economy. Despite these very real problems, de Valera told a British visitor in 1939 that he cared little for trade or economic matters; the negotiations provided an opportunity to secure control of the three Irish ports retained by Britain under the 1922 Treaty. Chamberlain was bitterly disappointed by the negotiations, as the Irish leader largely ignored the financial and trade aspects of the discussions, returning repeatedly to the issue of partition. While some progress was made by officials on detail, political agreement was not forthcoming due to de Valera's intransigence. It may be that de Valera was using partition to achieve other objectives, but if he was not primarily concerned with economic issues, many of his colleagues were. Seán MacEntee threatened to resign from the government in protest against de Valera's refusal to accept a deal with Britain. MacEntee believed that the proposed agreement was the best possible and criticized de Valera and fellow cabinet members Frank Aiken and Oscar Traynor for obstructing it. De Valera's objections were eventually overridden by the more moderate majority in the cabinet, though we do not have an extensive record of this discussion. The Anglo-Irish Agreement was actually a triumph for the Irish government, yet it was one that de Valera was not prepared to acknowledge. In the Dáil he was dismissive of the deal, complaining that the main advantages were gained by Britain not Ireland.[48]

Whereas MacEntee, Chamberlain and Dominions Secretary Malcolm MacDonald believed the 1938 agreement provided the basis for a new relationship between the two states, de Valera quickly returned to anti-partitionism. In July 1938 he told Lord Gowrie that he had little interest in Eire's continuing membership of the commonwealth, while in October he gave an ill-judged and bad-tempered interview to the London *Evening Standard*. De Valera insisted that the British had created 'this ghastly mess' and it was up to them to resolve it. He used the Munich agreement to press his own demands on Northern Ireland, but admitted to British officials that he knew very little about central Europe or its politics. De Valera's public comments on Northern Ireland dismayed Chamberlain and other British officials, who complained that his hard-line approach not only alienated Unionists but made it virtually impossible for the British government to respond to him on the issue of partition.[49]

Despite de Valera's complaints, his achievements in 1938 were considerable. Irish sovereignty was extended to all of Eire's territory and acquiring the Treaty Ports reduced the possibility of conflict in the event of war. The end of the trade dispute was also popular, though it did not solve the state's economic problems. The constitution also proved acceptable to most sections of Irish opinion, both as a reflection of a more 'authentic' nationalism and because it was a document of Irish design rather than one imposed by Britain. This success was recognized by the electorate at the snap election called for 17 June 1938. The result was a particularly strong endorsement of de Valera and his government. Fianna Fáil received 52 per cent of the vote and 56 per cent of the seats. Fianna Fáil was now not only dominant; it was also a national as well as a nationalist party. It drew support from across the state, from every region and every social class. Even in Dublin, where Fianna Fáil had traditionally been weak, it received 49 per cent of the vote. This support was not evenly spread, but it demonstrated the national and cross-class appeal of the party. Its political ideology was nationalist, but it had successfully translated this into specific and popular policies now endorsed by the electorate. At the heart of its policies was a commitment to national development, the robust defence of sovereignty and independence, and the promotion of a distinctive national culture. Fianna Fáil self-consciously emphasized both the national character of the party and the importance of nationalism in its policies, rejecting allegations that it promoted class hatred or special interests. At the 1937 general election Fianna Fáil had boasted that 'bit-by-bit the British connection has been broken and the new Constitution heralds the final advance on the road to freedom'. At the 1938 election, Fianna Fáil successfully claimed that this had been largely achieved, promising that the other objectives of Irish nationalism could also be gained.[50]

Despite this, de Valera remained dissatisfied with progress towards Irish unity, insisting that solving the partition question should be a British imperative. For de Valera, solving the Northern Ireland problem entailed incorporating the region into the Irish state and applying the new constitution to all those living there. He never acknowledged Unionist resistance or attempted to meet their objections. When de Valera met Chamberlain and Sir Thomas Inskip in London in March 1939 he dismissed British concerns about Unionist opposition to Irish unity. He rejected the view that Unionists would revolt if the British army was withdrawn from Northern Ireland. According to de Valera there would be a revolt against what he described as the 'ascendancy party' and Unionists would 'before long, reconcile themselves to the position and make terms'. In response to a suggestion that de Valera might 'court' Unionist opinion, he replied in uncompromising fashion that 'very often the best way to court a lady was to turn your back on her'. There is little evidence here or elsewhere that de Valera was entertaining a negotiated settlement of the partition issue. He refused to accept, as did his party, that Ulster Unionism was an authentic expression of a national community within Ireland; Unionism would collapse once British support was withdrawn and a united Ireland would inevitably follow. Consequently there was no need to conciliate Unionists or to consider seriously how to address their concerns.[51]

As war threatened in Europe, de Valera's gamble that appeasement would deliver Northern Ireland to him failed. The IRA decided on a more robust response and in January 1939 declared war on Britain. For the IRA, Britain's difficulties provided an opportunity for Ireland to strike. 'The present crisis caused by the intervention of Germany and Italy, and the success of their campaign makes our job easier. The enemies of England are, by that fact, the friends of Ireland.' When the British government ignored the IRA's ultimatum, the organization initiated an extensive bombing campaign in Britain. After six months there had been over one hundred attacks, leaving one person dead, some fifty-five injured and significant destruction to public property. The prime minister's son Frank Chamberlain was the target of an attack early in the campaign while on a shooting holiday in County Kerry, but escaped injury when a bomb exploded close to his hotel. Others were not so lucky when tube stations, cinemas and busy streets were indiscriminately bombed in what became an increasingly vicious campaign. By June the British government was concerned that the IRA was deliberately targeting civilians as a means of escalating the terror, though the IRA claimed that the bombs were not aimed at them. The pattern of attacks however had all the hallmarks of a terror campaign to intimidate the civilian population in the hope of influencing the government. An attack in Piccadilly Circus on 24 June caused particular concern as the area was crowded with civilians when the bombs went off.[52]

Seamus O'Donovan, an engineer with the Electricity Supply Board in Dublin, had planned the bombing campaign, while its driving force was the ascetic and fanatical Seán Russell, who was appointed IRA chief of staff in April 1938. The campaign was funded by Joe Mc-Garrity, leader of Clan na Gael, the main Irish-American republican organization in the United States. McGarrity not only supported the attacks on British cities, but was in close contact with and sympathetic to Germany. Russell welcomed German interest in the campaign and wrote to McGarrity alerting him to a meeting between members of the IRA and German intelligence to discuss cooperation. This established the basis for wartime liaison between the IRA and Nazi Germany. Not everyone in the IRA leadership was in favour of the bombing campaign. The most hostile was Moss Twomey, a former chief of staff, who predicted the destruction of the IRA and the failure of its objectives if the campaign took place. Twomey was no pacifist and had been a particularly ruthless leader of the IRA, yet he recognized that changing political circumstances in Ireland and the unrealistic nature of the plan doomed it to failure. Twomey's view was that the IRA should wait until war broke out and then hit the British hard to disrupt their war effort, a view ignored by the new leadership.[53]

Twomey's prediction was quickly confirmed and successive waves of IRA volunteers were arrested and sentenced to lengthy spells in British prisons. Despite these successes, the British authorities remained anxious to obtain information from the Irish government about the movements of IRA activists in Ireland and those travelling to England. Substantial Irish communities had been established in a number of British cities and these provided cover for IRA volunteers. The Irish government consistently refused to cooperate with the British in countering the IRA on the grounds that this would compromise the effectiveness of the Garda in dealing with the public. Despite being a member of the commonwealth, the Irish were not prepared to extradite any IRA member, as their crimes were considered political. In a remarkable exchange between the Irish high commissioner in London and Sir Thomas Inskip, the Irish diplomat effectively justified the bombing campaign and praised the bombers. He admitted to knowing at least one of those involved, describing him and his colleagues as 'decent people and good citizens'. All were, he insisted, 'law-abiding and respectable in every way' but frustrated at lack of progress on partition and Northern Ireland. Inskip warned that British public opinion would be outraged if it became known that the Irish authorities were not prepared to track down known bombers who had returned to Ireland.[54] As the situation deteriorated, a senior British official, Percival Liesching, visited Dublin secretly to impress on the Irish government the need to improve security cooperation between the two states. He told Joseph Walshe, the secretary at the Department of External Affairs, that the Garda were not prepared to cooperate with British police on political crimes; nor did the British believe that the IRA campaign was aimed at non-civilian targets. On the contrary, security officials had concluded that the IRA 'might be turning at any moment to deliberate attempts on human life as part of the campaign'. Liesching warned that such an escalation would endanger relations between the two governments and postpone indefinitely any hope of movement on Northern Ireland. Walshe insisted that de Valera and the Irish government deplored the campaign, but offered little more than platitudes on cooperation. While Liesching subsequently expressed some optimism that the Irish authorities would review their position on cooperation, he was mistaken. Britain never received the level of cooperation it expected from the Irish authorities. John Leydon, the secretary at the Department of Industry and Commerce and an official considered fairly friendly to Britain, warned Liesching that most Irish people were very reluctant to provide evidence to the police on matters considered political. As a result, if an IRA member planted a bomb in Britain and successfully returned to Ireland, he would be protected by the Irish state from facing a British court.[55]

Not all IRA volunteers in Britain returned to Ireland. When Brendan Behan was charged with possession of explosives in December 1939 his response was defiant: 'I came to England to carry on a fight for a full and free life for my fellow countrymen north and south, and to remove the baneful influence of British imperialism.'[56] On the very day that Behan was sentenced, a more dramatic trial opened. Five persons of Irish origin were charged with the murder of Elsie Ansell, one of five people killed in Coventry on 25 August 1939. Although overshadowed by the outbreak of war just over a week later, this attack was the most devastating of the entire IRA campaign. The bomb that killed Ansell and the others had been placed in a bicycle carrier, which exploded in the centre of Coventry in the middle of the day. The bomb had a delayed-action mechanism that permitted the IRA operative to leave prior to the explosion, which was of such ferocity that Ansell was only identified by her engagement ring and shoes. The actual bomber returned immediately to Ireland, getting the last boat out before Special Branch closed off the ports in an attempt to locate the killers. The two key operatives charged with the explosion, Barnes and McCormick, were deeply involved in the bombing campaign, more so even than the prosecution claimed.[57] A letter produced in court, allegedly written by Barnes to another Irishman, Jim Kelly, read, 'I go from one place to the other and bring the S. Believe me it is hard, but I get away swell so far.' The prosecution claimed that the letter 'S' referred to 'stuff', meaning explosives. The letter also said that war now looked likely and 'it may be good for us'. McCormick accepted responsibility for keeping and supplying bomb-making equipment, as well as distributing it when required for an attack. He also acknowledged that he and another man had visited a shop to buy a bicycle, though he refused to give the name of the other individual. He told the court that the other person involved was not Peter Barnes and that he was no longer in Britain. McCormick also said that his understanding was that no one should have been hurt by the bombs and that they should not have exploded in the middle of the day. One witness, Brigid O'Hara, recounted how she had shown McCormick a newspaper report on the bomb explosion and that he had said, 'That's the bomb we made in the front bedroom and it went off in time.' Nor did he show much remorse in court. When asked if he was sorry for distributing the materials for the bombs he replied, 'No!' After the two men were sentenced to death, Richards addressed the court in defiant vein: 'I wish to state that the part I took in these explosions since I came to England I have done in a just cause.'[58]

The Irish response to the death sentences reflected greater concern for their countrymen than for those murdered in the attack. De Valera told Maffey that an aircraft accidentally dropping a bomb might have caused the explosion in Coventry. By December there was little doubt in the minds of Irish officials that the two charged had been involved in the campaign, though neither man seemed to have actually planted the bomb. Officials conceded that an appeal was unlikely

to succeed on the basis of a legal challenge to the verdict. Barnes and
McCormick's guilt was tacitly acknowledged by the Irish authorities
but was never admitted to the British. Indeed the Irish government
had information on the two men which would have damaged them
further if it had been revealed at the appeal.[59] The Garda reported that
Barnes had been closely involved with the IRA for most of his life and
had been an officer in the organization in County Offaly. He was
thought to have received bomb training in Dublin between 12 and 18
May 1939, prior to leaving for Britain in July 1939. McCormick was
considered 'an active and dangerous member' of the IRA, and commanded the Mullingar company of the organization between 1937
and 1939. It was alleged that McCormick had held up two Garda
during the funeral of IRA activist Jimmy Joe Reynolds in County
Leitrim, for which the IRA provided a firing party. He was also alleged
to have shot at members of the Garda when the authorities attempted
to arrest those firing the salute at the graveside. McCormick left for
England early in June 1939.[60] Nor did the IRA help Barnes and
McCormick's appeal, attacking a number of targets across Britain
after the verdict was announced.

The Coventry bomb was the last major attack by the IRA on the
British mainland during the war, and while it can be seen as an act of
defiance, emphasizing the continuing existence of the IRA in England,
it was also a provocation to the British authorities and to hard-line
anti-Irish sentiment in the Home Office and elsewhere. The bombing
campaign was already a failure by July 1939 and Coventry escalated
the terror not in the hope of forcing the British to come to terms, but
to create martyrs for the cause.[61] The former IRA leader Tom Barry
wrote to the *Irish Times* on 1 February 1940 claiming he had evidence
that Barnes and McCormick were innocent, but 'for obvious reasons
I cannot go into any court and prove their innocence, nor can I
broadcast the evidence'. Barry approached various people in Cork city
to try to influence the outcome, but to no avail. The bomber was
from Cork and returned there after arriving back in Ireland. While
the IRA did not always trust Barry, he retained contact with them
during this period and would have had knowledge of the small talk
and rumours in republican circles.[62]

A campaign to secure pardons for Barnes and McCormick quickly
grew and many public bodies passed motions in favour of it. Only

Fine Gael distanced itself from this, while government censorship powers were used to direct the agitation. The government itself intervened energetically in an attempt to have the sentences commuted. Walshe prepared very specific instructions for John Dulanty, Irish high comissioner in London, which in effect pleaded political extenuation for the acts committed. Whether intended or not, this amounted to an apologia for the IRA's use of violence, or at least an exhortation to excuse it. Indeed, the Irish case continued in a fashion not dissimilar to that put forward by the IRA itself:

> it is perfectly clear that they do not intend to kill or even to injure. Their object in causing material destruction is to bring to the notice of the British government in that forceful way the continuing dismemberment of Ireland.

This was disingenuous to say the least and played right into the hands of the IRA, who could and did insist that Barnes and McCormick were martyrs to the cause of Ireland. De Valera wrote to Anthony Eden in January 1940, asking him to consider the 'exclusively political character' of the crime, insisting that 'neither of the men was of the criminal type' and recommending that they be imprisoned rather than executed.[63] The Irish government argued that actions that would be criminal in any other set of circumstances or jurisdiction, and would warrant the death penalty, should not be treated as such if these actions occurred in Northern Ireland or in Britain. When the American minister in Dublin, John Cudahy, expressed surprise at de Valera's attitude, Joseph Walshe retorted that the sentences were 'too severe and unjustified'. He expressed 'a certain admiration for the courage and stoicism displayed by the prisoners during the trial', while insisting that there was some justification in the IRA's behaviour:

> in the case of the Ulster authorities they were acting against a minority which was fighting for a just cause, the unity of the country. The Irish government on the other hand was merely preventing a small illegal organization from endangering the safety of the state.

Although de Valera told Cudahy that the IRA was not a threat to Irish security, the latter was not convinced: 'the Government knows from previous and personal experience that any body of fanatically patriotic Irishmen cannot be easily suppressed and are always dangerous'.[64]

*

Fianna Fáil's anti-partition campaigns in the run-up to the Second World War contributed to a political climate that allowed many Irish nationalists to distinguish between IRA actions in Eire on the one hand, and in Northern Ireland and mainland Britain on the other. Despite the IRA's claim to be the legitimate government of Ireland, there were also many Fianna Fáil activists who sympathized with its actions.[65] The heat generated by partition was real and all the more intense because little could be done to damp it down. At a meeting of the Literary and Historical Society at University College Dublin in mid-January 1940, the bishop of Galway, Dr Browne, received the most enthusiastic response of the evening when he said that although he detested dictators, democracy could also be tyrannical, pointing to Northern Ireland as his key piece of evidence for this.[66] While there were humanitarian reasons for not hanging Barnes and McCormick, de Valera and his government were making a special case on nationalist grounds. On one occasion de Valera wrote, 'it will matter little that Barnes and Richards have been found guilty of murder. With the background of our history and the existence of partition many will refuse to regard their action in that light.'[67] Churchill's cousin, the Catholic writer Sir Shane Leslie, opposed the death penalty but was uneasy about the individuals involved: 'I have done my utmost, I do not regard these two men as Irish martyrs of Emmet's type.' Maffey recognized the volatile situation in Eire and recommended penal servitude for life rather than death. He warned that the executions would weaken de Valera, and he was the only one capable of defeating the IRA. President Roosevelt also became involved 'informally and quite unofficially', telling Lord Lothian, the British ambassador in Washington, through Sumner Welles that perhaps it would help if the sentences were deferred for six months and reconsidered after that time depending on the circumstances.[68]

Not surprisingly, when Barnes and McCormick were hanged, Irish opinion was outraged. The lord mayor of Dublin presided over a meeting condemning the executions, while sports fixtures and meetings were cancelled as a mark of respect for the dead. Although the

Irish government avoided direct criticism of Britain, Maffey feared that de Valera intended to stir up anti-English hatred. Concerned that de Valera was allowing unrest over partition to disrupt the relationship between the two countries and weaken his ability to govern Ireland, he wrote to Eden that it was time to view the Irish situation with an eye to the future. This warning was apt, for at the very time that Maffey wrote, the IRA was engaged in a deadly and escalating struggle with the Irish government. By the early months of 1940 relations between Britain and Eire were tense, but the main problem facing de Valera and his government was the nature of the internal threat to its rule and the extent of German collusion with the IRA.[69]

3. NEUTRALITY IN THE PHONEY WAR

By the time Barnes and McCormick were executed, Britain was at war and Eire had declared its neutrality. For Eire what became known as the Emergency began on 2 September 1939 when the Dáil agreed that a national crisis existed. The declaration of an emergency when Eire was not itself at war required an amendment to the constitution. This allowed the government to use powers not otherwise available to it under existing constitutional provisions. The period from September 1939 to the end of the war is referred to as the Emergency, both to emphasize Irish neutrality and to highlight Ireland's special relationship to the war and to Britain. The declaration of war by Britain created anxiety in Eire, but the Irish government retained some advantages in the short term at least. Chamberlain remained prime minister and was not prepared to pressurize the Irish on neutrality, despite Churchill's urging to the contrary. Anthony Eden became secretary of state for the dominions and was sympathetic to Eire's neutral status. There was widespread support for neutrality within Eire, if for various reasons. Practically every newspaper, including the pro-British *Irish Times* and the *Church of Ireland Gazette*, concluded that neutrality was the best policy for the country.[1] When de Valera addressed a concerned and attentive Dáil on 2 September 1939, this feeling was also evident. De Valera was conciliatory, appealing to the assembled deputies to provide the government with the support requested. He repeated his view that neutrality was the only possible policy available to the government, but he also asked the Dáil to appreciate how difficult it might be to maintain such a status:

> In a sense, it brings up for the government of a nation that proposes to be neutral in a war of this sort problems much more

delicate and much more difficult of solution even than the problems that arise for a belligerent.

It would be absolutely necessary, he added, that none of the belligerent states should have cause to complain about the operation of Irish neutrality. The real challenge for the government was how to mediate the strong emotions that would emerge in Ireland as a result of the war.

De Valera recognized that Irish citizens would take sides and hold strong views on the war, but for the security of the state neutrality had to be maintained under all circumstances. He asked the TDs to look to the needs of their own country first and to decide what was in its interest.[2] The government was concerned that it could not declare an emergency when the state was not at war as the constitution used the phrase 'in time of war' in respect of an emergency. Yet de Valera warned:

> We should have war all around us. We may not be participating ourselves in the war, but we shall have conditions here almost the same, so far as the question of supplying the material needs of our people is concerned, as the condition we would have if we were actually a belligerent.

The Dáil was asked to support an amendment to the constitution to allow the government to declare an emergency when there was a war in the region but when Eire was not involved. De Valera received all-party backing for his government's position. Representing Fine Gael, James Dillon, later to be a fierce critic of Irish neutrality, acknowledged that circumstances required that Ireland be neutral, 'if it is humanely possible'. He affirmed however that neutrality was not the same as indifference, making the forceful claim that most Irish people supported the democracies against the totalitarian states. Dillon's warning that Fine Gael's support was not unconditional was ignored by government supporters, who now claimed that backing for neutrality was universal. What the support did show, however, was the extent of the change in Irish politics and the wide-ranging consensus that Fianna Fáil had secured after seven years in government.[3]

While Fine Gael remained suspicious of some aspects of Fianna Fáil policy, the constitution cemented the consensus along republican lines. This was evident in the narrowing of policy options at the 1938 general election and was symbolized by Fianna Fáil and Fine Gael supporting Douglas Hyde as an agreed candidate for the presidency in 1938.[4] In September 1939 Fine Gael effectively abandoned its identification with the commonwealth when it accepted neutrality. Fianna Fáil members had been concerned that Fine Gael would oppose neutrality because of the consequences for commonwealth membership. Dillon recalled later that the party had been divided throughout the war on this issue but in 1939 'avoided final decision among themselves as to the attitude which should be adopted'. Michael Hayes, Fine Gael senator and former speaker of the Dáil, believed, 'even if Mr Cosgrave had been in office we would not, I think, have gone to war. An All-Ireland Dominion might have, a twenty-six-county one, no.' By supporting neutrality in 1939, Fine Gael not only acknowledged Fianna Fáil's dominance in Irish politics but also undercut its own broader and more generous version of nationalism. As historian James Hogan wrote at the end of the war, 'once it ceased to stand for a commonwealth policy, no simple and fundamental issue would remain to distinguish the Fine Gael party from its former rival'.[5]

Fine Gael leaders insisted that commonwealth membership was compatible with a policy of neutrality, a position reluctantly accepted by the British government by late 1939.[6] By supporting neutrality in September 1939, Fine Gael most likely prevented serious political conflict over the issue, as opposition to government policy would have divided the parties and public opinion into pro-British and pro-German camps. Instability on this issue could in turn have led to a more authoritarian response to the situation from Fianna Fáil. In the short term at least, neutrality could satisfy most sections of Irish opinion, whether isolationist or favouring either side. But it was a delicate balancing act because for some neutrality was a contingent necessity, whereas for others, especially in Fianna Fáil, it became an ideological necessity. If neutrality was contingent, then changing circumstances might open the possibility of another option. If not, then neutrality would cease to be a policy and would become an imperative, one that could not be changed whatever the circumstances. In September 1939 these differences were reconcilable, thus providing the political basis for maintaining the consensus demanded by de Valera.

If the decision to declare neutrality was broadly acceptable, there was greater criticism of the Emergency Powers Act 1939, the second stage of which was introduced by Seán Lemass, minister for industry and commerce. The bill provided the government with extensive controls over most aspects of Irish life, including strong censorship powers. It also gave the government the right to arrest and detain individuals who had committed or were about to commit a crime whether that person was an Irish citizen or not. It was a fairly loose piece of legislation and its draconian nature raised the spectre of abuse of power by the government.[7] William Norton, the Labour party leader, conceded that they were living through difficult times, but was concerned that members were giving the government 'very wide and very drastic powers'. He warned that rights guaranteed under the new constitution had now been abrogated. He worried that the ordinary individual 'must depend on the good sense and the discretion of the Government' with regard to his rights, though he did not doubt that these rights would be protected. Fine Gael Deputy T. F. O'Higgins was also very uneasy, but as a senior member of a party that had adopted a law and order platform, he was faced with a dilemma. O'Higgins claimed that he had always been prepared to give any Irish government the powers it asked for when 'the Government itself said that these powers were necessary'. This remained his view, he added, but he was sceptical and dissatisfied with the case made by the government for the new legislation.

The most surprising intervention came from Major James Myles, an independent deputy representing Donegal. Donegal had then and still has a significant number of non-Catholics, both Church of Ireland and Presbyterian – indeed Donegal has the largest number of Presbyterians in any county of the twenty-six. Myles was a retired British army officer, having served with the Royal Inniskilling Fusiliers, who might have been expected to be sceptical of the government and perhaps of neutrality itself. Yet he endorsed the government and its emergency legislation, assuring the Dáil that not only were the powers necessary but that they would be properly used, a view supported by another independent, Patrick Cogan from Wicklow. Patrick

Belton, the Fine Gael deputy for Dublin County, warned that notwith-standing the declaration of neutrality there remained a danger that Ireland's dependence on supplies from Britain would be used against the state. He suggested that the country might be asked to give up neutrality or starve. De Valera reminded the Dáil that democratic government could not work in the ordinary sense when an emergency existed. The government would have to act with speed in response to threats and this meant that the normal constraints of democratic politics could not operate.[8]

The broad consensus on neutrality disguised differences within Ireland, where there was support for both sides in the war. Percival Liesching had noted after his visit to Dublin in July that Irish opinion was largely unsympathetic to Britain:

> My general impression was that it would not cause pain to anybody in Eire if, by entering into war of which Danzig was the immediate cause, or by refusing substantial concessions in the colonial field, the United Kingdom should suffer, and should suffer to an extent which should teach her lessons which she has not learnt during a time of almost unchallenged ascendancy.[9]

De Valera had identified closely with appeasement, but when war did start his government could ill afford to indulge such senti-ments. As the only dominion not declaring war on Germany, Eire was in a difficult position. Proximity to Britain and the presence of a German legation in Dublin complicated matters further, while the German submarine threat and the issue of the Treaty Ports were obvious points of tension. Immediately before the war, the Irish government made it clear to the German minister, Hempel, that it would have to be attentive to British concerns, though at the same time even-handed in its neutrality. Joseph Walshe told Hempel that Irish neutrality could not have 'all the characteristics of those neutral states which have had a long existence as separate states', asking the Germans to respect that situation. Walshe wanted a guarantee that the German legation would not be used for espionage against Britain, warning also that an attack on Irish trade with Britain would constitute a breach of neutrality. He urged Hempel to inform Berlin that special circumstances prevailed, suggesting that if Germany could not accept this then the best policy would be for both states to withdraw their representatives for the duration of the war. Walshe gave an undertaking that Eire would not become involved 'in an active form' in the war against Germany, emphasizing that 'she wishes to remain outside the quarrels of the great ruling countries of the world and to rebuild her own civilisation undisturbed by world rivalries'. In his correspondence with Berlin, Hempel noted that Irish neutrality 'strengthened Irish national self-consciousness'. He advised Ribbentrop to respect Eire's position as this would have a positive impact on opinion in the United States and India.[10]

Notwithstanding Walshe's view that Eire wanted nothing to do with the conflict, the country was immediately affected by the war. Recognizing the importance of the British connection, Walshe travelled to London on Wednesday 6 September for three days of discussions with Anthony Eden and officials at the Dominions Office. Though Eden welcomed Walshe in a friendly and cheerful fashion, Walshe was highly critical of the senior officials at the Dominions Office. He complained that Sir Edward Harding, the permanent under-secretary, had adopted 'an unbelievable narrow-mindedness and rigidity of outlook' by not accepting the special nature of Irish independence or the reality of its sovereignty. Despite this reservation, he passed on de Valera's 'very real sympathy for the British government and people in this hour of trial', and his commitment 'to go as far as possible to assist Great Britain while maintaining the essentials of neutrality'. Walshe wanted Eden to recognize that there would be difficulties in relations between the two states and that Britain should find ways 'of helping us to be friendly'. He held out the prospect of greater cooperation in return for Irish unity, though this would not result in Eire's entry to the war. What de Valera asked was that Britain actively support Irish unity and then guarantee Ireland's neutrality in agreement with the United States. If this was wishful thinking, even more fanciful was the notion that Eire could exercise considerable influence in the 'English speaking Catholic world, and the possibility of her playing a friendly role in the relations between the British and American peoples'.

Throughout the meeting Walshe remained uneasy at the presence of Harding and sought a private interview with Eden to outline the Irish position in some detail. Harding's position was in fact weakening at this time and on one occasion Eden waved him aside saying 'No, no' when he attempted to intervene. Before he left London Walshe was gratified to learn that Harding was to be replaced by Sir Eric Machtig, who was more sympathetic to Eire. In his private meeting with Eden, Walshe urged him to accept that Ireland should be treated as a special case within the commonwealth. At the heart of Walshe's critique of the Dominions Office was the Irish quest for respect, and he hoped that a new framework could be established in response to Irish neutrality. The appointment of a senior diplomat to Dublin would help this, but Walshe warned that the British would have to treat Eire as a 'mother country with a history as venerable as that of Britain' or the opportunity would be lost. According to Walshe, the Irish 'were a proud people, and we refuse to shorten our memories to suit them'. Walshe's visit to London was an important one as it provided an opportunity for de Valera to sound out the British on their intentions but also allowed Eden to test the extent of Irish neutrality. The British were disappointed at Irish inflexibility, but Eden remained conciliatory, defending Irish neutrality to his cabinet colleagues during the following months.[11]

While Eire had a high commissioner in London, the United Kingdom did not have a senior official in Dublin. Chamberlain wrote to de Valera that there could be misunderstandings between the two states over the operation of neutrality. What was needed was a British representative in Dublin to smooth the difficulties that war would bring; to have someone on the spot would reduce the possibility of misunderstanding and provide up-to-date reports on Irish attitudes. De Valera wanted Britain to appoint a minister or ambassador as if Eire was not a dominion. This was a step too far for Chamberlain, who refused, as this would 'raise most contentious issues for us here and it is one which it would not be possible for me to accept'. Walshe told British officials in London early in September that the Irish reluctance to have a British representative in Dublin was due to a fear that this would be taken as a British attempt to restore colonial rule in Ireland and undermine Irish neutrality. Walshe cited Egypt, where the high commissioner was the effective ruler of the country. Despite this, both sides agreed that a satisfactory arrangement needed to be made. De Valera recognized the value of having a local conduit to the British who could provide the Irish view on neutrality in a direct fashion. Chamberlain was anxious to achieve agreement, but was also willing to meet some of de Valera's concerns. While the prime minister anticipated that 'the need for closer contact would grow more and more pressing' as the war progressed, he also wanted to assure de Valera that the British government would operate any arrangement in a way 'as to cause you as little difficulty as possible'.[12]

The compromise agreed on was that Sir John Maffey would be appointed United Kingdom representative in Eire. This proved to be an inspired decision. There was considerable scope for conflict between Eire and the United Kingdom in the early months of the war. Churchill for example wanted to ignore Irish neutrality, while the Irish view of the country's rights under neutrality was often seen in White-hall as overly rigid. However, with Maffey in Dublin, Britain could be assured that information would come directly from its own represent-ative and not via unreliable sources. Moreover, Maffey quickly realized that while Eire would not join in the war on Britain's side, it was prepared to fulfil its responsibilities, at least as it saw them. Maffey was thus able to assure London in October that the Irish authorities were alert to those responsibilities and were careful to keep him informed when German submarines were sighted.[13]

*

The war posed many dilemmas for individual Irish citizens. Samuel Beckett, though in Dublin when the war started, decided to return to France, declaring that 'if there is a war, as I fear there must be soon, I shall place myself at the disposition of this country [France]'. Beckett intended to return to France via England but was refused exit by the British. He persuaded the officials that the relevant regulations did not apply to him, as he was an Irish citizen. His fellow author Patrick Kavanagh had also returned to Ireland for a brief visit when he saw the newspaper posters announcing the war. He made his mind up to remain in Eire while hostilities lasted. In January 1940, author Francis Stuart travelled to Germany on behalf of the IRA to re-establish links with the German intelligence community. Stuart, though born in Aus-tralia, had been a member of the IRA, had fought against the Treaty and had been interned for a period. He married Iseult Gonne, the daughter of Maud Gonne MacBride and sister of Seán MacBride, former IRA leader and later minister for external affairs in the inter-party government of 1948–51. MacBride was close to Hempel and sympathetic to the Nazi regime. Stuart remained in Germany for the rest of the war, broadcasting on a regular basis to Ireland on behalf of the Nazis. In later life Stuart denied he was pro-Nazi, yet his broadcasts do not sustain this retrospective self-defence. Those with less literary ambitions also made similar decisions, some to travel to Britain to back the war effort there; others remained in Ireland and supported the IRA or the Germans. For many the situation was confusing. Government minister Seán MacEntee confessed early in 1940 that it was difficult for him 'to reconcile all the incompatibilities in international politics'.[14]

The tiny Communist Party of Ireland responded to the situation by adopting the Soviet line that the war was imperialist. For once, Irish communism was in step with Irish nationalism and it embarked on a vigorous anti-British campaign, while defending Irish neutrality and supporting the IRA. Perhaps more significantly many Irish women and children, as well as some men avoiding conscription, returned to Ireland immediately after war was declared. One estimate suggests that some 70,000 people arrived in Eire during these early months of the war.[15] However, the movement was not all one way. Shane Leslie has provided a first-hand account of this period in his diaries. He returned in August to his family home at Castle Leslie in County Monaghan, noting, 'Ireland quieter and more peaceful than ever', adding that 'neutrality is promised from Dublin even if Belfast goes to war'. After attending mass on 3 September the family heard that war had been declared. Within twenty-four hours, men from the district were crossing the border to volunteer or rejoin their regiments. Shortly after this, Leslie visited Armagh, where tanks were now in position. The war, he wrote, 'comes right up to the border but not further'. Leslie was pessimistic about the impact of the war on his tightly knit rural society: 'the country is slowly dying. All the young and romantic and adventurous continuously leave, the little cottages contain old people and photos and medals of those who have gone.' Leslie had also decided to return to London to play a part in the war, yet was refused an Irish passport, confiding to his diary, 'this comes of living in No Mans Land'. Leslie recounts some incongruous aspects of life on the border in 1939. A blackout was in force in Northern Ireland but was optional in the south. The town of Pettigo, which straddled the border, had light and dark in equal measure.

Despite the war the north–south border remained porous. Leslie

could cycle to Armagh to have tea with Cardinal MacRory one afternoon, while a visitor could cycle to Castle Leslie from the north to
bring news of a death. However, MacRory's claim that Catholics were
now being stopped and harassed by armed B-Specials in the north
was worrying. This would alienate moderates in the Catholic community, the cardinal predicted, and make them sympathetic to the
IRA. Leslie returned to London in October, leaving his wife and
parents safely in County Monaghan. While visiting the papal nuncio
in Dublin, he also spoke to Dr Hempel, who Leslie described as 'very
nervous to be cut off by England and France from Hitler'. On the boat
to Holyhead that same night, Leslie's travelling companions were Lord
Fingall and his dog. Leslie's thoughts turned to the demise of the
Catholic aristocracy. 'We sat on a soaking mass of lifeboats in pitch
darkness. He (Fingall) is the last of his line. He and Castlerosse will be
our last Catholic Earls of the old stock.' Leslie then added, 'of course
we were not torpedoed. The Germans cannot decide whether the Irish
Mail is neutral or not.' There is a lovely ambiguity in this: two Catholic
aristocrats crossing the Irish Sea to support in their own way the
British war effort. Both Leslie's sons and his daughter actively participated in the war, a reflection once again of the complex nature of
conviction and identity. Leslie joined the Home Guard, working with
another Irishman, General Sir Hubert Gough.[16] Not long after the war
started, Gough wrote to de Valera, offering his services to the Irish
leader. Gough stressed that he was 'Irish born and bred. All my youth
was spent in the country.' Gough wanted de Valera to grasp the
opportunity that the war offered to improve relations between Britain
and Ireland, and especially to work towards 'that very desirable
object', Irish unity. Though not stated, the implication of Gough's
letter was that if Eire played an active role in the war significant
changes could be obtained. Leslie wrote at the end of the war that
Irish unity could have been achieved if Eire had fought as an independent and equal ally of Britain. De Valera replied formally to Gough,
but was unwilling to adopt his suggestions, concluding that any action
would lead to 'misunderstanding'.[17]

*

De Valera reorganized his cabinet to meet the challenges of war and
neutrality. Frank Aiken became coordinator of defensive measures,

with wide-ranging responsibilities for censorship, internal security and neutrality policy. This was a key political appointment which was to determine policy for the remainder of the war. Lemass moved to the new Department of Supplies, where he gained control over most of the Irish economy. MacEntee was demoted and moved to Industry and Commerce, while the more pliable Seán T. O'Kelly became minister for finance. De Valera remained the most important figure throughout the emergency; he was both taoiseach and minister for external affairs, and not a single important decision was taken without his knowledge. While Fine Gael generally supported the government, its leadership criticized army mobilization in September on the grounds of cost and its impact on the economy. During these early months of the war, Fine Gael regularly expressed scepticism in private concerning the government's defence measures. However, when Richard Mulcahy met de Valera and O'Kelly on 13 September, the taoiseach warned the Fine Gael leader that he had agreed to expand the size of the army. The army chiefs wanted an even bigger force than that proposed by the government, but de Valera urged Fine Gael support for expansion 'as a necessary insurance' against future developments. Dominating this meeting as he dominated all meetings with the opposition, he argued that the public would be rightly critical if, in the future, the state's security measures proved inadequate to deal with any threat. Mulcahy concluded that defence policy was formulated by de Valera rather than the army chiefs or the government ministers responsible.

De Valera insisted in September that Eire faced a number of threats, but he conceded that Britain had not objected to neutrality and that trade discussions were continuing. Although not willing to divulge his intelligence sources, he expected cooperation from Fine Gael. Mulcahy confirmed that his party would support the government on 'essential matters', but this 'made the way freer for the Opposition to criticise very strongly on major matters of public importance'.[18] Yet Fine Gael did not have a clear view on how neutrality would operate and its criticisms were fairly muted for the most part. When the government decided to amend the Emergency Powers Act in January 1940 to allow the internment of both nationals and non-nationals, Fine Gael readily supported the government. There were some reservations in the party, but Mulcahy accepted that objections that might have had some force in 'normal times' could no longer be entertained. There were also serious divisions within Fine Gael on how much support to give. 'Quite a number of our supporters have represented that we ought to let them have all the necessary powers – others have represented that they are not fit to be given more power.'[19]

Despite the war, life in neutral Ireland was generally tranquil until May 1940; the Winter War between the Soviet Union and Finland was of greater interest than the 'phoney' war of France and Britain with Germany. A number of Irish citizens made their way to Finland to fight in defence of this small nation.[20] Finland, however, was far away and censorship ensured that Irish knowledge was carefully screened. Colonel Dan Bryan, who played the leading role in Irish military intelligence during the war, noted that as late as April 1940 the general population of the country remained largely unconscious of the threat to Ireland from espionage or the war itself. Bryan cited the case of a parachutist landing in County Meath, but 'no attention seems to have been paid to the incident locally'. This is not to suggest that the government was inattentive to the challenges posed by the war and neutrality, but that most Irish people suffered little inconvenience.

Maffey proved invaluable to the British government throughout this time, providing London with detailed information on events, opinion and policy in Ireland. His careful assessments of the Irish situation did much to deflect the belligerent Churchill, who continued to deny robustly the reality of Irish neutrality. Maffey was not uncritical of Ireland, but when the crisis did occur he had established his position as the key interlocutor between Ireland and Britain and was largely trusted by both sides.[21]

The Irish government was fortunate that the war progressed in such a leisurely fashion until the spring of 1940, because it was ill prepared for what eventually occurred. The army chief of staff, General Dan McKenna, admitted that Eire was 'almost defenceless' between 1939 and May 1940. As a result:

> The defence forces when mobilised were inadequate in size and neither trained or equipped for war. The nation as a whole had no realisation of the problems arising from the adoption of neutrality nor the imminence of a threat of invasion.[22]

Most politicians believed either that there was no threat to Ireland's neutral status or that the war would not come close to the island. The Department of Finance opposed increases in defence expenditure on the grounds that if Ireland were attacked Britain would provide protection, and if the attack came from Britain, defence could only be temporary. Nor was it thought possible that there was any danger of air attack.[23] Defence had been neglected by successive Irish government, partly for reasons of cost and partly due to fear of a large military establishment. McKenna complained that the government exercised 'undue control over the military that prevented developments of a positive kind'. When the cabinet agreed to increase expenditure in early 1939, it was too little too late, and when Britain went to war, the government remained largely complacent and more concerned with issues of cost. It had concluded that the public would not accept the increased expenditure that expanding the army would involve.[24] Although the Department of Defence won some of its institutional battles, it could not persuade the government that Ireland was threatened. In May 1940 the country had effectively no navy, though it was an island – the general assumption was that the British navy would protect it. The army's strength stood at 14,000, well below what army chiefs considered adequate to meet an external attack. Air defences were especially weak, with only a limited number of serviceable warplanes available. Moreover, these aircraft were appropriate for internal policing activities, but wholly inadequate for modern war. In contrast, neutral Sweden and Switzerland had recognized the dangers a good deal earlier than Ireland.[25]

The Irish government had also been negligent over armaments; Ireland was poorly equipped with anti-tank and anti-aircraft weapons. This is not to say that the Department of Defence or army chiefs were unaware of the need for adequate modern equipment, but it is to assert that they failed to convince de Valera and the majority of the cabinet of this need. This is particularly true for the period 1938 to early 1939, when the army asked for £10 million to modernize. The government failed to address this request, though early in 1939, when it was too late, orders were placed with the War Office in London for additional materials. In addition, Colonel M. J. Costello went to the United States on an arms buying mission, but discovered that any purchase would have to be acceptable to Britain, a condition

which the Irish government failed to appreciate even after the war
began. Overall, the attempts to adequately arm the Irish military prior
to May 1940 were largely a failure. This can be attributed to bureau-
cratic obstruction by the Department of Finance, strategic ignorance
particularly on the part of politicians and to a naive belief that Britain
would protect Ireland. Nor were the military innocent of blame.
When Costello visited the United States, he encountered serious
obstacles to the purchase of armaments but discovered that military
aircraft were readily available for purchase. Nevertheless, the Irish air
force turned the aircraft down, on the grounds that Britain would
provide them with adequate supplies of aeroplanes.[26] Army chief of
staff General McKenna painted a stark picture of Irish weakness in
1940:

> Because of the general weakness of the army, there were no striking
> forces available capable of offering prolonged and organised resist-
> ance. Furthermore, the necessity for disposing our small force
> throughout the state for reasons of internal security and of provid-
> ing some elements for coast defence resulted in our being weak
> everywhere.[27]

Complacency was not confined to the governing party. Fine Gael
continued to be opposed to a larger army, favouring a small professional force. In March 1940 most Fine Gael contributions in the
Dáil were critical of the government's request for additional funding
for the military. However, responsibility for the country's defence
rested with the government, and its actions between September 1939
and May 1940 were clearly inadequate when compared with those of
Sweden or Switzerland, and closer to the inaction of other neutrals
such as Denmark and the Netherlands.[28]

The real threat to Irish neutrality and sovereignty between September 1939 and May 1940 came from the IRA, rather than from
Britain or Germany, with the most explosive expression of this occurring just before Christmas 1939, when most people in Ireland were
preparing for the festivities. As Christmas Day fell on a Monday,
Saturday 23 December was the last opportunity to stock up for the
holidays. It was also a day for going out and celebrating with friends
and colleagues. Early that evening a messenger arrived with a parcel
at the Magazine Fort in Phoenix Park, where the Irish army stored

most of its ammunition. When the guard on duty went out to collect the parcel, he was confronted by an armed IRA man who took over the entrance, permitting a detachment of the IRA to occupy the fort. The object of this daring raid was simple: to gain possession of the stored ammunition. In a well planned and executed operation, a dozen lorries were used to ferry over one million rounds of ammunition out of the fort in just over two hours. This was a devastating blow to the Irish army, the police and ultimately to the government itself. It was also the culmination of a disastrous month for Fianna Fáil, challenging their view that they had the IRA under control and could defend Irish neutrality against all threats.

De Valera admitted to Cudahy that the government had been humiliated by the IRA raid but did not consider it a prelude to a more serious attack on the state. De Valera blamed McGarrity and Clan na Gael in America who, he claimed, had sent large sums of money to Ireland for IRA use – in this he was entirely correct. What he did not reveal was that the Irish authorities had been indirectly complicit, as much of this funding was raised through the illegal sale of government-backed Irish Sweepstake tickets in the United States. These tickets were smuggled into the United States by the IRA and Clan na Gael and some of the receipts returned to Ireland to support Irish hospitals. Asked by Cudahy what the IRA wanted, de Valera responded, apparently without irony, that the IRA's total focus was on the republic. He described them as 'vindictive, vehement, venomous, violent Irishmen' who believed that he (de Valera) was under British control.[29] Though the IRA raid was audacious and in the short run successful, its longer-term impact was disastrous on the organization. All state resources were now brought to bear on the IRA and in a few weeks most of the ammunition was recovered. Garda raids netted more ammunition than had been originally taken, but also guns and ammunition hidden in arms dumps by the organization.[30]

In isolation the raid on the Magazine Fort would have been an embarrassment; in the wider context it was much more dangerous. The government had prepared extensive emergency legislation in advance of September 1939 to provide it with the means to meet both internal and external threats. Despite this, Stephen Roche, the secretary at the Department of Justice, warned:

A small country cannot afford to invite attacks from without by a seeming inability to keep order within its own territory. The danger in this case becomes acute when the unlawful organisations extend their activities into other states, while using this country as a base.[31]

The IRA had not only successfully if temporarily deprived the army of most of its ammunition, but was also in close contact with German intelligence. O'Donovan, the author of the English bombing campaign, had visited Germany on a number of occasions prior to September 1939 and this contact was maintained. This was especially dangerous, though in January 1940 not known to the Irish authorities. The Irish government believed that it had the means to control the IRA with what was on paper draconian legislation. Individual rights were no longer protected by the constitution, and the legislation enabled the Irish authorities to intern and jail IRA members and their associates.[32] This legislation was however undermined in December 1939, when Seán MacBride obtained a writ of habeas corpus in the High Court for one of those interned. At the same time, jailed IRA men went on hunger strike. One of those on hunger strike was Patrick McGrath, who had fought in 1916 and had remained a dedicated terrorist.[33] Within the government, Roche was critical of the judicial system, arguing, possibly correctly, that the normal court system was inappropriate to meet the challenge of well-armed and highly motivated terrorists. Roche believed that Ireland was 'living in a permanent state of emergency as regards the administration of justice'. After the High Court decision, most of the prisoners were freed, while McGrath was moved to hospital and quietly released. It was even alleged that some of those who had attacked the Magazine Fort had were among those released as a consequence of the court decision.

To strengthen its powers the government initially considered that an amendment to the constitution might be necessary, but eventually decided to amend the Offences Against the State Act, legislation which was quickly passed by the Dáil and Seanad. The president, as he was empowered to do, sent the legislation to the Supreme Court to test its constitutionality. The Supreme Court decided in favour of the government on the grounds that the state had to protect social order. In effect the individual's rights were deemed subordinate to those of the community, with the state through legislation giving effect to the community's will. The legislation was considered a form of 'preventative justice' rather than punishment.[34]

Thus, in January 1940, the IRA and the government were openly confronting each other and some observers questioned whether the government was strong enough to deal with the situation. The challenge was real enough and led to pitched battles for control of the streets. Between 1935 and 1945, the IRA was linked directly to a series of deadly attacks on the state, most of which occurred between late 1939 and early 1941 and which included ten murders, including those of a number of policemen. Two events were particularly significant for the government. The first was the murder on 3 January 1940 of Detective Officer John Roche by Tomás MacCurtain in Patrick Street, Cork city. At MacCurtain's trial, one Garda witness described how he struggled with MacCurtain after he had killed Roche. MacCurtain had tried to shoot him too but the officer managed to push the gun away and after a further exhausting struggle to subdue the IRA man. MacCurtain was searched at gunpoint and when one of the gardai told him that it was a cowardly thing to shoot a fellow Irishman, he responded, 'I don't know why you think it cowardly. Wasn't it three armed men against one armed man?' When the officer replied that they had not drawn their weapons, MacCurtain retorted, 'I am surprised at you that you did not know before now that we are armed and that we are bound to use them.'[35] The Special Criminal Court sentenced MacCurtain to death in June. The second incident occurred in August, when two policemen were shot dead while raiding a shop in Rathgar, Dublin. Patrick McGrath and Tony Harte were arrested for the murders and also sentenced to death.

The contrast between what happened to MacCurtain and the treatment of McGrath and Harte demonstrates the deteriorating situation in Ireland at the time. MacCurtain was the son of the republican martyr Tomás MacCurtain, who had been murdered in 1920. He benefited from some residual sympathy for the son of a martyr not only in the country but also within the Irish cabinet. Tánaiste Seán T. O'Kelly colluded with MacCurtain's defence counsel Seán MacBride, advising him on the best way to appeal the death sentence. MacBride was able to mount an appeal, which postponed the execution, permitting the cabinet to further debate the issue and allowing public pressure to build. MacCurtain's execution was originally scheduled to take place on 5 July, but the sentence was commuted on 10 July. The secretary to the government at the time, Maurice Moynihan, has been quoted as saying that there was agreement in cabinet that the murderers of gardai would be executed, but this incident suggests that there were serious divisions, a state of affairs confirmed by Lemass's reported unease at executions carried out during the war.[36]

Maffey considered the reprieve a sign of continuing weakness on the part of de Valera and the decision certainly worried the British for some time after.[37] Yet, this was the last major concession made by the cabinet. When the government started arresting and interning IRA activists in January 1940, they were faced once again by a hunger strike to obtain political status. In this vicious conflict between the state and the IRA, prisoners were treated with considerable violence by the police and army. On this occasion the government refused to give in and the hunger strike collapsed after the deaths of Tony D'Arcy and Jack McNeela. Maffey sensed a different mood in Dublin after this. At the funeral for the two men he noticed little anger at the government on the part of the general population while the cabinet was now resolutely opposed to conceding political status to IRA prisoners. The Irish high commissioner in London was asked to approach discreetly the Howard League for Penal Reform to obtain information on how people who demanded political status should be treated. The government was gratified to have its view of political status largely sustained by the reform group, although some officials favoured Franco's attitude to political prisoners, which was to treat them more harshly than ordinary criminals.[38]

On 25 April, in retaliation for the deaths on hunger strike, the IRA successfully planted a bomb in Dublin Castle, the headquarters of the Irish Special Branch. The explosion caused considerable damage to the building and injured five police officers and one civilian. Not only was this a direct attack on the police force, but it was organized by a member of the Special Branch, Jim Crofton, who was an agent for the IRA. The bomb was apparently left in the wrong place, so it is difficult to judge if the intention was to kill. The following month two gardai were seriously injured in a gun battle in Dublin, when an IRA group attempted to intercept mail for the British representative. Crofton also seems to have been instrumental in the murder of Michael Devereux, an IRA leader in Tipperary who he suspected of being an informer. George Plant and others murdered Devereux, probably in September 1940, a particularly dangerous year for the state. In County Cork alone between 1 January and 5 June 1940 nineteen serious incidents were recorded, including MacCurtain's murder of Roche.[39]

The IRA claimed to be the legitimate government of Ireland and denounced de Valera as a tool of British imperialism. There was little room for compromise and Fianna Fáil's attitude hardened in response. The TD Erskine Childers warned that democracy was in danger, claiming that 'already the two principal parties of this state, supported by responsible men, have played with all the stage elements of a dictatorship'. De Valera dismissed the campaign of the IRA as anti-national, insisting that only a democratically elected government could declare war. Government ministers described IRA actions as 'treasonable' and 'dishonourable', while Minister for Defence Oscar Traynor warned that its actions could impair Irish neutrality and sovereignty.[40] There was also mounting evidence of an alliance between the Germans and the IRA, and a number of Nazi agents arrived in the country. The most important of these was Herman Görtz, who parachuted in on 5 May but whose existence was only discovered after a raid on the house of Stephen Held in Dublin on 22 May. Intriguingly, Görtz remained free for well over a year, not only protected by the IRA but possibly also by some government supporters.[41]

As we have seen, the decision to commute MacCurtain's sentence was seen by some as weakness, but a tougher attitude now prevailed. McGrath and Harte were executed on 6 September, just three weeks after their arrest. The state had draconian powers and was prepared to use them. Some years later, in a dramatic Dáil intervention, de Valera admitted that his decision to allow Patrick McGrath's release in December 1939 had been something that he deeply regretted. On one of the few occasions that he publicly apologized, he accepted responsibility for 'one of the biggest mistakes that I have made in my life'. He openly admitted that if McGrath had been allowed to die in December 1939, this would have prevented five further deaths.[42] De Valera defended the use of internment and other emergency measures on the grounds that Eire had avoided civil war as a result. These powers would be retained for as long as required and used when necessary.

The government's decision to hold firm is all the more remarkable when the geopolitical position in September 1940 is considered. If the Germans did invade, their local collaborators would be the IRA who would then seek revenge for the executions of their colleagues. There is some evidence that the IRA, or sections of it at least, were prepared to enter into an arrangement with the Irish government if the executions did not go ahead. The American minister David Gray was approached in late August to intervene on behalf of McGrath and Harte. He wrote to de Valera, informing him that a truce might be possible if the executions were stopped. Gray was not prepared to intervene beyond this, replying to his republican correspondents that he disapproved of armed actions against the state. De Valera had also been approached directly by republican intermediaries to secure a truce if the executions were not carried out. De Valera was not prepared to entertain these proposals, sending only a verbal reply that 'he had no comment to make'. The Czech consul in Dublin, Kostal, who seems to have been well informed about many issues, noted on 13 September that prior to the executions IRA representatives had discussed the possibility of a truce. According to Kostal, and this has a ring of truth about it, the negotiations collapsed because the government could not get assurances that the IRA would actually fulfil the agreement.[43] The cabinet was probably wise on this occasion, as the evidence from IRA activity and its publications at the time is of unrelenting hostility to Fianna Fáil. The IRA's *War News* headlined its July issue, 'The final treachery. De Valera's open sell-out', condemning what it described as 'Mr Churchill's government in the 26 Counties'.

Meanwhile, in May and June 1940, the all-party Defence Conference had discussed internment at its first two meetings. There was agreement not only to intern, but also to restrict the internee's right to appeal.[44] With the government's effective use of internment, the breaking of the hunger strikes and a willingness to execute, the IRA was on the defensive by the end of 1940. Its only hope was a German attack on Ireland. This was not forthcoming, and by the spring of 1941 Hitler was more concerned with the Soviet Union. As the state closed in, the IRA both in and out of prison grew desperate. Funding was closed off from the United States and during 1941 the organization turned to bank robberies to fund its activities. In response, the government on a number of occasions used flogging as a punishment and deterrent.

The case of Pat Shannon from County Galway, who was initially arrested in February 1940 but not released from custody until May 1945, is not untypical of the fate of internees. He was originally sentenced to four months in prison, but actually served five years and three months. The government was prepared to release IRA prisoners interned under the Emergency Powers Orders if they signed an undertaking to break their connection with the IRA and repudiate any organization engaged in violence against the Irish state. Shannon and most internees would not give this guarantee, and even when given, it was sometimes broken. When Sergeant Dennis O'Brien was murdered in September 1942 the Garda believed that at least one of those involved had given this undertaking to the state and been released. Shannon describes the tense and occasionally violent relations between the IRA and the prison authorities in Mountjoy Prison in Dublin, which led to riots and then retaliation against the prisoners. When Shannon was released from Mountjoy he was immediately rearrested and detained in the Curragh internment camp. As a result of a continuing confrontation between the IRA and the governor of the Curragh, on 14 December the IRA burnt the camp to the ground. The Irish army surrounded the camp and opened fire, seriously wounding two prisoners. A more serious incident occurred on the 16th, when military police fired on prisoners attempting to march in military formation to breakfast. One prisoner was killed and others wounded. Shannon claims that the treatment which followed was extremely brutal, with prisoners attacked by military police acting under the protection of the emergency legislation. Shannon also describes how he was released and rearrested throughout the Emergency. His description of the treatment meted out to him has a contemporary resonance:

I was then put in a cell and I was told I must stand up when an officer came in and salute him and obey all orders. I refused to salute or recognise him in any way. When I did refuse the officer concerned walked outside the door and held it open whilst a number of his Military Policemen again beat me. I was then dragged out and put in another cell called 'the dungeon' where there was two inches of water on the floor, and I remained there for three days and three nights. I could neither sit nor lie down. There was no seat or bed in the cell. The only ventilation was a hole in the wall and the only sanitary accommodation was a hole in the ground. I was dragged each day to my breakfast, dinner and tea which consisted of bread and water. This I refused to take and I went on hunger and thirst strike for eight days as a protest against my treatment.[45]

When criticized over conditions at the Curragh or at Portlaoise Prison, the government rejected claims of ill treatment. It argued that the conditions were largely due to the prisoners refusing to accept prison discipline.

By early 1941 the IRA was almost a spent force in Eire, though it still could be deadly when confronted by the police. The organization fared somewhat better in Northern Ireland, though pressed closely by the RUC and British military intelligence. The northern leadership suspected that all was not right and Seán McCaughey and his associates decided that the IRA leader in the south, Stephen Hayes, was a spy. His former associates tortured Hayes until he confessed to working with members of the Irish government to subvert the IRA. Every IRA failure since the late 1930s was attributed to this plot, with Fianna Fáil ministers deeply involved. Hayes was found guilty as charged by the IRA and sentenced to death, but agreed to give a full account of his misdeeds. This gave him a breathing space, which he used to write and rewrite his 'confession'. He was then able to exploit lax IRA security to evade his captors and give himself up to the Garda, proof for many in the IRA that he was indeed guilty. Hayes always insisted he was innocent of the charges and in an attempt to clear his name with republicans he wrote a letter. This was intercepted and used against him as evidence in court and he received five years' imprisonment as a result.[46] The Irish government also issued a statement denying any plot. The British considered that there was little in his 'confession' to support the claim of Irish government collusion with Hayes. Colonel Dan Bryan also investigated the claim and concluded that there was no truth in it.[47] In contrast, Gray was inclined to believe that Hayes might have had some connection with government agencies, though much of what he reported was rumour rather than fact. Gray suggested that the intercepted letter may have been produced specifically for this purpose and was an attempt to protect Hayes from the IRA.[48]

The organization did not disappear from Irish political life in 1942, but after this it was more of a nuisance than a threat. Its leadership was either on the run from Special Branch or more often interned. During the Emergency itself, 1,130 individuals were interned, 1,013 were brought before the Special Criminal Court and of these 914 were convicted. The IRA had lost most of its support in Eire by this time, though it could gain some sympathy for those interned or imprisoned under harsh conditions. Censorship, active repression and the collective Irish commitment to neutrality undermined the IRA's limited appeal.[49]

*

If the Irish government was militarily unprepared for war or underestimated the threat from the IRA, its control over the media and public discussion was overwhelming. Irish censorship has been described by the most authoritative writer on the subject as 'more rigid and wide ranging than that imposed in most other countries, particularly other neutrals'. Although wartime censorship was pervasive, it built on an existing framework of literary surveillance that had resulted in some 1,700 books being banned over a ten-year period. In addition, radio broadcasting was in government hands, and more generally the 1930s had been characterized by state intrusion and control at all levels of Irish society.[50]

Planning for wartime censorship began in late 1938, well before military preparations were considered. Thomas Coyne, a senior Department of Justice official, was given responsibility for establishing the institutional framework. Coyne was to remain a central figure in the application of censorship throughout the war in cooperation with Aiken and Michael Knightly, the chief press censor. The stated policy aim was to use censorship to protect Irish neutrality so that no belligerent would have cause to complain that Eire was favouring one side or the other. However, there was also an appreciation that censorship could be applied to internal matters and would have an impact on the state's own conditions. This suggests that censorship was anticipated as being both extensive and intensive. It was also anticipated, however, that because Eire would be neutral it would not be necessary to apply censorship 'as widely or to the same degree as if Ireland were directly affected'. This proved not to be the case. Once censorship came into operation it operated in an increasingly coercive fashion, extending into virtually every aspect of Irish life.[51]

Coyne became assistant controller of censorship in September 1939, but in late August he wrote, 'it will almost certainly be necessary to stop all communications which appear to be likely to endanger the safety of Great Britain and, of course, to do what we can to prevent this country from being used for the purpose of international espionage'. Coyne was uncertain how to deal with diplomatic correspondence, but it was eventually agreed not to attempt to censor diplomats. It was also recognized that telegrams and cables would have to be effectively policed to prevent information of value to a belligerent getting out of the state.[52] Once neutrality became policy Joseph Walshe demanded that censorship be used to promote the virtues of neutrality as well as controlling what was said in the newspapers:

> Public opinion must be built up on a neutral basis, a neutral-mindedness must be created. A list of the states which are neutral should be frequently and prominently displayed in the Press. The advantages of being neutral should be stressed. The losses and suffering of all kinds, including famine and poverty, which come upon countries at war should be expressed.

This view was quickly adopted by the censor, with Knightly reporting in October that 'we have kept in mind the formation of public opinion both at home and abroad favourable to our policy and to our ultimate aim of national unity'. Walshe not only defended Irish neutrality, he argued that by adopting this policy Eire could influence the belligerents. Ireland's position as a 'Christian state' placed it in a favourable position to cooperate with other small states and 'the Vatican in particular' to shape the peace process and 'take a very real part in bringing about a cessation of hostilities'. Walsh contended, because the Irish state was not an heir 'either on the positive or the negative side, of the Treaty of Versailles', that its concerns were different from those states that had been involved in the First World War, but additionally that there was a good material reason for non-involvement: 'the cost of neutrality is nothing like the cost of war. The amount of suffering we should have to endure is part and parcel of the universal readjustment which any great war imposes.'

Walshe took the view that censorship should be all-embracing. He contended that a number of newspapers, most prominently the *Irish Times*, were overtly supporting one side in the conflict. This could not be permitted to continue, he complained, as it threatened the state: 'there is no question about the vital necessity of neutrality for the preservation of this State'. Accordingly 'the clique which run the anti-Government press have no moral right whatever to oppose that policy'. He warned that newspaper comment and reports could undermine confidence in neutrality at home and abroad, leading to air attacks on Dublin for which the editors would be responsible. Walshe detested the *Irish Times* and was especially scathing about its view of the relationship that existed between Britain and Ireland:

> The greatest danger, in my view, to our neutrality, and conceivably to our continued existence as a State, is the subtle propaganda of an ascendancy clique which will undoubtedly use this occasion to promote their dearest wish which is to bring the British back. When a certain paper says, for instance, that the Irishmen who joined the British Army in 1914 were the real Irish patriots and the cream of our people, it is essentially a principle completely opposed to the continued existence of an Irish State. Such views should be ruthlessly suppressed.

What was required, he concluded, was an effective press agency to promote Ireland's view abroad, a view endorsed by the controller of censorship, Joseph Connolly.[53]

De Valera requested a detailed report, and this was provided by Connolly on 23 September. Censorship was not fully operational due to staff shortages, but the intention was to have it fully in place in the near future. The censors were only doing spot checks on certain mail – for example only 10–15 per cent of United States correspondence was being examined – but all post to continental Europe was being checked. Correspondence between Britain and Ireland at this stage seems to have been exempt in general, though facilities were available to act if necessary. Connolly invoked three criteria to be applied when censoring. Censorship would be imposed on matter that might tend to impair Irish neutrality, on material which would give offence to outside governments or the people of an external state, or if the matter was prejudicial to public safety or the preservation of the Irish state or the maintenance of Irish public order. The criteria were extremely broad, providing the means to control most if not all aspects of the media, if the censorship office so wished. A licensing system was also in operation in respect of foreign (mainly British) printed media, while on 16 September specific guidelines were issued to the newspapers on what could not be published. Banned was any reference to foreign military forces within the state or nearby, any reference to the disposition of the Irish armed forces or items that might cause dissatisfaction, plus anything relating to weather reports, commercial shipping and aircraft. In addition, newspapers were prohibited from publishing 'disquieting news' in respect of supplies, the economy or the financial situation. Perhaps the most significant prohibition was discussion of neutrality itself: 'all matters which might endanger our neutrality or casting doubts on the policy of neutrality or the wisdom or practicality of maintaining it'. On 19 September the remit was extended to include any arrest or detention under the Offences Against the State Act or the Emergency Powers Act. Any relevant photographs, maps or similar items were also prohibited. All matters could be submitted to the censors, who would then authorize or prohibit publication. The censors also had the authority to demand that a newspaper or magazine be submitted in full prior to publication. This was a powerful tool and had already been invoked against a number of publications. Connolly did not wish to have the details of censored publications mentioned, to prevent debate about the issue. In effect a newspaper could not publicize the fact that another newspaper or itself had been censored.

Connolly was upbeat about the cooperation he was receiving from most Irish newspapers, though recognizing that there were real difficulties for the editors in negotiating with his office. He also affirmed that both editors and reporters appreciated the need to preserve neutrality and to eliminate 'all references that could in any way either impair our neutrality or cause offence to outside friendly states whether they are belligerents or not'. There was a very thin line between Connolly's view that 'we simply cannot afford to have our neutrality jeopardised or the safety of the state endangered by what appears in the Press' and a very real curtailment of freedom of the Irish press. Censorship was somewhat easier when it came to foreign newspapers: they could be prohibited, refused a licence or stopped at the point of entry. Already, some newspapers had been warned about content and the possibility of prohibition. Connolly was particularly critical in his report of Patrick McGilligan, a senior member of Fine Gael and former cabinet minister. According to Connolly, McGilligan publicly supported neutrality while at the same time insisting that the policy should be openly and freely discussed in the newspapers. Connolly thought this an impossible position, as 'propaganda from every quarter would be let loose with the most disturbing effect on the population'. He questioned whether McGilligan was truly in favour of neutrality, suggesting he should come out into the open on the issue. Yet McGilligan had shown up a real problem by arguing that news that was already widely known should not be censored. Connolly retorted that if this were accepted, then it would be better not to have censorship at all. His was a particularly narrow conception of free speech within Eire, and reflected the dominant Fianna Fáil position on neutrality.[54]

By early October 1939 the lines of conflict between the censors and the press had become clear. The main focus for the censors' attention was the *Irish Times*. Michael Knightly noted that numerous complaints had been received concerning the content of this newspaper. He believed that 'it seemed to be the studied policy of this paper to undermine our neutrality'. According to Knightly, its editorial policy challenged neutrality by charging that it was either temporary or not a real policy at all. The censorship office was now working a sixteen-hour day, while Knightly had had a telephone installed at his home so that editors could contact him directly over matters of concern. British newspapers with special telephone facilities at Leinster House, the Irish parliament building, had agreed that anything that might be open to censorship should first be submitted to him. Knightly was pleased with the overall content of British reporting at this time, although an early Irish casualty of censorship as the republican journal *The Wolfe Tone Weekly* which ceased publication rather than accept the constraints imposed on it. The censors also threatened the *Catholic Standard* over its failure to 'submit matter of a doubtful nature'. The *Irish Times* refused to accept that freedom of the press should be restricted to the extent demanded by Walshe. There had been a battle of wills between the editor R. M. Smyllie and the censors' office since September 1939. Smyllie seemed anxious to explore the limits of censorship and to extend his leeway if possible, but in January 1940 the censors demanded that the *Irish Times* submit all matter for publication in advance. The *Irish Times* capitulated, agreeing to comply more closely with the guidelines, and as a result, there was effectively no independent media for the duration of the Emergency. Knightly reported in February that the newspaper was now more careful to submit questionable items than before.[55]

Although Knightly was clear that the function of censorship was primarily to preserve Irish neutrality, he admitted that he manipulated the newspapers depending on the issue. When the Soviet Union invaded Poland, Irish Catholic opinion was outraged. Knightly was thus prepared to allow pieces sympathetic to the Polish cause to be published, even though these might break official guidelines.[56] Connolly wrote to Aiken in October setting out how the system was operating. He admitted that the government was using information collected by the censors, adding, 'the less said about it the better'. He advised Aiken to acknowledge publicly that some information was acquired in this way but to defend the practice on the grounds 'that without any abuse of Censorship the Government can hardly be expected not to notice any information of vital interest to it however it may become known to it'. Connolly informed Aiken that the work of the censors' office in respect of the press had 'gone with surprising smoothness'.[57] At this stage Aiken appears to have been taking an even tougher line towards the reporting in British newspapers than the censors. Connolly wrote to him later in October pointing out that 'all the British papers are full of propaganda and if we start prohibiting them where are we going to stop?'[58]

An early example of the difficulties encountered by the censors concerned a sermon by the Roman Catholic bishop of Killaloe, The Most Reverend Doctor Fogarty, which they described as un-neutral and a 'serious problem'. The sermon condemned the German and Soviet attacks on Poland and the bishop had taken the precaution of

sending a copy to a news agency prior to its delivery. The censors
decided to let publication go ahead on the grounds of expediency, but
were deeply concerned at possible consequences. The *Irish Times*
cited the publication of the Fogarty sermon when it was taken to task
for publishing a British White Paper on the mistreatment of internees
in German concentration camps. Smyllie justified publication on the
grounds that the White Paper could not be considered propaganda
because it was an official publication, a point not entertained by the
censors.[59]

As the censorship became more effective, it also became more
intrusive and its application more questionable. It was invoked in
November when farmers' organizations announced that, in pursuit of
a price increase for their products, milk and other agricultural supplies
would be withheld from Dublin. The censors were minded to allow
publication, but the minister for agriculture wanted all statements
prohibited. Connolly went to Aiken, who allowed publication. The
minister for agriculture continued to oppose publication and received
de Valera's support. Censorship was applied to all matters relating to
the strike for three days, but then reluctantly withdrawn. According
to Connolly, the rationale behind this was that:

> Publication of such matter as would imply that the Farmers'
> Federation had any authority to forbid supplies of essential com-
> modities to the public or to issue permits for the provision of such
> supplies was prohibited and a check was kept on the activities of
> strike propagandists. Otherwise strike news was permitted.

In the Dáil, despite his earlier position Aiken defended the decision
on the grounds that the strike was prejudicial to public safety, as
withdrawal of milk interfered with essential supplies. Censoring the
Irish Times was one matter, though the rationale behind the decision
might be questioned; to censor what was a conflict between the
Farmers' Federation and the Department of Agriculture (who decided
the milk price) had much more serious implications. Indeed, the
government not only used censorship, but also applied the Offences
Against the State Act against the striking farmers. There may have
been good reasons for the government's actions but it was difficult for
the average citizen to evaluate the merits of the case. This was the
first instance of censorship being used for matters not directly con-

cerned with neutrality, sovereignty or the progress of the war. It was a warning that the government's definition of what might be covered by the emergency legislation could be quite wide. It also confirmed the fears expressed in September in the Dáil about how the emergency legislation might be used.[60]

When the IRA organized hunger strikes in Mountjoy Prison in November, publicity was severely restricted. The censors were careful to sanitize the news, distinguishing between general reporting about the situation at the jail and statements written to gain sympathy for the hunger strikers. When IRA sympathizers disrupted an address by de Valera at a public meeting at the Mansion House on 14 November, Knightly considered that the circumstances warranted publication of the details. Even at this early stage of the war, at a time when there was little evidence that Irish neutrality was threatened, the censors were taking sensitive political decisions, albeit in conformity with the government's legislation.[61] Three other aspects of the situation proved important in November 1939. The first of these was an increase in anti-Irish articles in British newspapers, though Knightly attributed these to Irish citizens critical of their own country. A second concerned advertisements asking for donations to funds for those injured or otherwise affected by the war. The third matter was the effective prohibition of reports on the arrival, departure and cargoes of all shipping into the state. This was imposed at the request of John Leydon, the powerful secretary of the new Department of Supplies. He requested that any reference to specific cargoes arriving in Irish ports or to transhipment facilities be prohibited.[62]

By the end of 1939 the censorship office was implementing a tough policy for cables and telegrams. Connolly wrote to Aiken to explain how these were treated. One problem was ambiguous or obscure wording in telegrams. Connolly attributed much of this to price-conscious individuals or obscurity as a result of the specialist nature of a particular business. But even when all this was taken into consideration, the censors still had to pay close attention. In the case of suspicious messages or those sent by aliens, the telegrams were very carefully scrutinized before being forwarded, and 'doubtful tele-grams, apparently unnecessary messages or messages with cryptic text, particularly when passed between persons whose bona fides may be suspect are held back for enquiry'. In some cases investigations by

G2 army intelligence or the Garda would satisfy the censors, in others individuals would be asked to explain the nature of a message. If a suspicious telegram arrived in Ireland, particular care was taken to avoid giving the intended recipient knowledge of its content, and an in-depth investigation was then undertaken. All telegrams going to or from Ireland were assessed in this fashion, although telegrams within the country could not be controlled in the same way and censorship was operated only in specific and doubtful cases.[63]

The censors were now also applying severe restrictions on British newspapers circulating in Eire. Knightly was gratified by the cooperation between Eason's, the main newspaper distributors in the country, and the censors' office. The censors also tried unsuccessfully to control information on the Magazine Fort raid at the end of December, while *Irish Golf* was directed to submit all copy for future editions after the Christmas edition proved particularly objectionable for promoting a pro-British line. The *Catholic Standard* was censored for stating, 'the probable scarcity of food in England in the months or years to come is thus the great hope of every Irishman'; the censor described this as unchristian and thought it 'might be made use of by enemies of the country'. In other respects also censorship was tightened: Direction 13 to the newspapers prohibited the publication of items picked up by wireless transmitters from ships or aircraft, though broadcasts intended for public reception could be published. Likewise, when the French army purchased 3,000 horses in Eire, it was decided to issue another direction that no matter could be published in respect of the purchase, sale or movement of livestock out of Ireland to any state. Along the same lines, it was decided that no letters, statements or reports would be permitted referring to Irish citizens in the forces of any of the belligerents without prior submission to the censors. In January the *Irish Times* was forced to remove the column heading 'Role of Honour' above its list of Irish citizens killed in fighting. This was replaced by 'Killed while serving with His Britannic Majesty's forces', which proved more acceptable for a time.[64]

The execution of Barnes and McCormick in Britain in February 1940 placed considerable strain on the censors' office. Prior to the executions the censors took the position that statements or reports that might compromise an appeal for clemency should be prohibited. After the executions, careful control was exercised over the publication of reports and statements. It is clear from the censors' own reports and from the media that censorship was used to temper the worst examples of agitation, though many inflammatory statements were made by Fianna Fáil politicians. Martin Corry TD was censored for hoping that Hitler would blow the British to hell, while P. J. Fogarty TD was banned for saying that the executions were a result of British blood lust. Not all the hostility to Britain came from Fianna Fáil; Richard Corish of the Labour party was censored for praising the bravery of Barnes and McCormick. All appeals to recall Dulanty from London or expel Maffey were excised from the newspapers. The sanitized reports outraged the IRA and their supporters, but also raised questions about the limits of free expression in Ireland. To what extent was censorship protecting the Fianna Fáil government and to what extent was a real national interest being protected? At this early stage of the war when little was happening in Ireland that would have affected its neutrality was the extent of censorship justified? Did the government have any ulterior motives? For his part, Knightly summarized the censors' attitude to the media:

> Our policy has been to deal leniently with newspapers which show
> a ready willingness to co-operate with us. We have not hesitated,
> however, to assert our authority where occasion demanded it.[65]

By early 1940 official censorship not only controlled what went into the newspapers, but it was also manipulating content. At the end of January Aiken produced an extensive defence of censorship for the cabinet, arguing that democratic rights and freedoms could be subordinated to the defence of neutrality. On each occasion that censorship seemed likely to be tested or challenged, the government introduced legislation to extend its operation. Nor were the censors prepared to allow this legislation to be tested in the courts. 'It might be argued,' one official wrote, 'that the state cannot afford to stand aside and allow dangerous publications to be put in circulation while nice points of law are being argued at length by learned counsel in a leisurely court proceeding.' In addition, such a situation could be compounded, as the case 'may not even end in favour of the state'.[66] When the IRA again organized hunger strikes in early 1940 to test the government's will, the censors controlled the media response. One letter from prominent republicans supporting the hunger strikers was permitted, but published alongside a statement by the minister for justice. Other letters were prohibited, as Knightly notes, 'after consultation'. Virtually all publicity, reports and resolutions in favour of the hunger strikers were stopped, as were resolutions from county councils and political parties. The censors were also highly sensitive to any published claims that intelligence was leaking out of Eire. They claimed that these reports had their origin in Northern Ireland and were designed to hurt Eire's neutrality. All obituary notices for personnel in the British forces were now prohibited. Newspapers could no longer provide battalion or other details as this information allegedly could be used for military purposes, but the real reason was to prevent the public from knowing that there were large numbers of Irishmen in the British army.[67]

Once the hunger strike escalated, 'a severe censorship was imposed'. In one respect the censors' task was easier than when Barnes and McCormick were executed, as the IRA was losing widespread support for its campaign. While some Fianna Fáil members and organizations opposed the government, the cabinet and the parliamentary party provided solid support for the strong position taken. Furthermore, censorship was being used for specifically political ends. When the minister for justice addressed the issue in a speech on 7 April, his remarks were widely publicized but the various replies prohibited. After the deaths of D'Arcy and McNeela in April, criticism of the government was closely controlled.[68]

Up until May 1940 the main focus of censorship remained on domestic matters. German military success changed this however and the task became more complex and intensive. Newspapers were permitted to publish stories on Irish preparedness against attacks, but stories of possible threats were suppressed and no debate was permitted on what policy should be pursued in respect of the changing situation.[69] The government decided to take further action when a sensational report was published which was subsequently found to have been fabricated. De Valera's view was that publication of such material should be prohibited until the Government Information Service had provided an official statement. In effect, Frank Gallagher, the director of the service, became the conduit between the government department(s) responsible in the first instance and the censors' office. Gallagher could decide to issue a statement or not as the case might be, but no publication could occur until he had made that decision. The definition of what constituted a sensational report included not only raids and attacks on the Irish armed forces, but also strikes and demonstrations 'when sufficiently grave', a term not clearly defined by the censors or the government. This decision extended the reach of the censors into nearly every aspect of public and political life in Ireland. It applied to 'all matter which is likely to cause public alarm or to bring the armed forces of the state or the police into ridicule'. Judgement in these matters was now left in the hands of a partisan politician, who worked in close cooperation with the censors as well as the taoiseach's office.[70]

This was now news management on a grand scale and it was to continue for the remainder of the war. Assistant Controller of Censorship Coyne recognized that journalists would oppose news management and that the public wanted immediate news. However, the government would not allow anything to be published until it decided whether it was accurate or appropriate. The problem with this was that the censors and the Government Information Service sanitized the news to such a degree that most Irish newspapers became unreadable. The absence of public debate and discussion limited further the news available to the average citizen. By July 1940 the editor of the *Cork Examiner* was complaining that the media was no longer free, especially in respect to Irish matters.[71]

4. AN OFFER THAT COULD BE REFUSED: JUNE 1940

Ireland's complacency was shattered at 11.30 on the night of 22 May 1940 when the Garda raided Stephen Held's home in Dublin. Held was an IRA agent, who had travelled to Berlin in April to discuss cooperation against the British. German agent Herman Görtz had parachuted into the country on 5 May and after various adventures was now staying at the Held family home. Görtz escaped on this occasion, but Held was arrested when gardai discovered a radio transmitter, a uniform, coded messages and $20,000. It was clear that a Nazi agent was in the country and had links with the IRA. De Valera and his government panicked. According to MI5, de Valera assured Maffey on 23 May that the government was in control of the internal situation, but by the following day Maffey had learnt that 'Government Departments were burning secret papers on a large scale'. De Valera held a crisis meeting with Fine Gael leaders on the 24th, asking for their support in the crisis. He offered to include them in consultations and promised to set up a defence council which would include members of the opposition. Mulcahy complained that it was a bit late to appeal for support when they had been ignored since the beginning of the war. De Valera responded that divisions over the Civil War had prevented any serious cooperation between Fianna Fáil and Fine Gael before this but added that an appeal for unity was now appropriate.[1]

Military setbacks in Europe had focused British attention on the possibility that Germany might use Ireland as a back door for an attack on Britain. In April Anthony Eden wrote to Maffey concerning the situation in Eire. Maffey sought to assure his superiors that most of the reporting in Britain on Eire was either malicious or exaggerated, but he also took the opportunity to make the case that Eire's independence and neutrality could work to Britain's advantage. He contrasted the response of the Irish public to the execution of Barnes and McCormick with their reaction to the death on hunger strike in Dublin of two IRA prisoners. Maffey suggested that the Irish had been largely indifferent to the hunger strikers' deaths, and asked his colleagues in London to consider the response if Britain had still been in control. 'To-Day there was no sea of angry faces, no problem for Downing Street. *Do we realise the blessedness of this?'*[2] British policy, he continued, should be based on the assumption that Irish independence was real and inevitable. Maffey argued powerfully that England and Ireland were very different and only sentiment or imperial nostalgia led to other views. Eire has a 'foreign aspect' he insisted, which 'to the Englishman and the Scotsman . . . is alien'. Britain should accept this, Maffey maintained, but should not despair about cooperation. He noted goodwill and sympathy for Britain, drawing attention to the extent of recruiting from independent Ireland. To maintain Irish goodwill, Maffey recommended that action be taken on partition. While critical of de Valera's narrow-mindedness, he recognized that partition was of deep concern to Irish nationalists. It was also the only real cause of conflict between Britain and Ireland.[3]

On the day that Churchill became prime minister, Maffey called on de Valera on his own initiative. While Maffey wanted Ireland's cooperation in the war, de Valera reverted to the partition issue exclaiming, 'I cannot understand why Mr Chamberlain does not tell Craigavon [prime minister of Northern Ireland] to fix up his difficulties with us and come in. That would solve the problem.' Maffey then tried to get to grips with partition, asking de Valera if Ireland would 'automatically be our ally' if the problem was resolved. Maffey reported de Valera's reply in the following words, the only record that we have of this conversation: 'I feel convinced that that would probably be the consequence.' Maffey then told de Valera that a change in the status quo was unlikely during the war, and reported de Valera's view that he had no wish to exploit Britain's difficulties. This was disingenuous, as de Valera immediately used these difficulties to press Maffey again on partition, hinting that Ireland might change its policy under new circumstances. Maffey can be forgiven for believing that de Valera was genuinely concerned to resolve the issue, given his persistent references to it in conversation. On one occasion he responded to Maffey's plea to join the war with 'It was no use asking the people in Ireland to fight on behalf of freedom when freedom was denied in a portion of Ireland owing to the influence of an uncompromising minority.' De Valera held out the prospect that if action was taken on partition, the British might expect a more active role by Ireland in the war, though he did not commit himself. This influenced Maffey: 'I record his rejoinder as an indication of Mr de Valera's line of thought,' but he added, 'his attitude remained the same in all conditions.'⁴

Maffey drew the conclusion that if something was done about partition, this could change opinion in Ireland about cooperation with Britain. De Valera had been impressed by the speed and ruthlessness of the German advance. Two days after the conversation with Maffey, he referred to the threat to Ireland during a speech to Fianna Fáil members in Galway. He criticized the German invasion of Belgium and the Netherlands in a brief comment:

> Today these two small nations are fighting for their lives, and I think I would be unworthy of this small nation if, on an occasion like this, I did not utter our protest against the cruel wrong which has been done them.

De Valera had not protested against the invasions of Denmark or Norway, but the westward expansion of German power offered a more direct threat to Ireland's interests, especially as French and British forces could no longer guarantee Ireland's security. De Valera's comment was not appreciated by the German minister in Dublin, who protested to the Irish government and received what the Germans considered an apology from Frederick Boland, the assistant secretary of external affairs. The Irish representative in Berlin is cited by German sources as being extremely apologetic, but going further and rather enigmatically telling the Germans that Ireland wished to remain neutral and in the First World War 'had struck too early' against England. This, he added, was a mistake that 'would not be repeated'. De Valera had also emphasised that Ireland would fight if invaded, reinforcing the public view of the minister for defence, Oscar Traynor, that Ireland would not give up as easily as Denmark, which had not defended its borders from German invasion. De Valera also used this speech to reassure Britain of Ireland's good intentions, though once again he raised the issue of partition.⁵

As the war went from bad to worse, a number of reports on Eire circulated at the highest levels in Whitehall and Downing Street. Some were ridiculous; one for example confidently asserted that the younger Catholic clergy were becoming communist. Another was more dangerous as it detailed German infiltration into Eire. MI5 tended to be dismissive of these reports, as was Maffey when he had the opportunity to respond to specific queries, yet they could not always control their circulation or impact. Churchill in particular was prone to burst into excited action on reading one of them.[6] Indeed, de Valera might have been particularly concerned if he had learnt of the secret correspondence that had been going on between Churchill and President Roosevelt. The US president had initiated the correspondence in September 1939, though Churchill subsequently became the prime mover in the exchange.[7] A few days after becoming prime minister in May 1940, Churchill wrote to Roosevelt, expressing the hope that his new appointment would not end their letters. Churchill also took the opportunity to admit that the outlook for Britain was bleak, expressing concern at the strength of the Germans on land and in the air. He appealed to Roosevelt to act on grounds of self-interest and to preserve civilization: 'I trust you realize, Mr President, that the voice and force of the United States may count for nothing if they are withheld too long. You may have a completely subjugated, Nazified Europe established with astonishing swiftness, and the weight may be more than we can bear.' He claimed that he was receiving reports of 'possible German parachute or airborne descents into Ireland'; nor were the Irish ports far from his mind. He encouraged Roosevelt to send an American naval squadron to Ireland for a visit that 'might well be prolonged'. This, Churchill added, would be 'invaluable'. Despite his personal support for Churchill, Roosevelt was unable to deliver very much at this stage. His reply the following day was cautious and hedged with qualifications. He promised to expedite the sale of aircraft and anti-aircraft equipment, but could not give any assurances on destroyers. In respect of Ireland, Roosevelt would only offer to give further consideration to Churchill's suggestion on the American navy visiting for an extended period.[8]

On the day Roosevelt wrote this letter to Churchill, he addressed Congress appealing for the resources to defend American liberty. In effect, if not openly, Roosevelt was asking the American public to support his pro-British stance by providing him with the means to expand the military. Almost immediately after the speech, Joseph Kennedy Jr wrote to his father Joseph Kennedy, the United States ambassador to the United Kingdom, reporting that there had been a significant change in public opinion in the United States. 'Overnight,' he claimed, 'the people turned strongly sympathetic to the allies, and now many people are saying that they would just as soon go to war, and that they will have to go anyway and why not now.' This change in public opinion gave Roosevelt the opportunity to press for changes in the US neutrality law, a change required if he was going to actively help the British. Around this time de Valera appealed to the United States to declare Ireland a vital interest for American security and to protect its neutrality, though he does not appear to have been aware of any shift in American opinion.[9]

Both de Valera and the British government were fortunate that there already was a close working relationship between MI5 and Irish intelligence. This link had been established with de Valera's approval in 1938 and the key Irish figure was Colonel Liam Archer, head of G2 Irish military intelligence; Archer had met British officials in London prior to the Held arrest. The link was highly valued by British intelligence, who also recognized its limits. Nevertheless, MI5's own assessment is worth noting:

> The Dublin link was, therefore, established at the request of the Eire Government and operated with the full knowledge and approval of the British and Eire governments. From the outset the personal relations between the British and Irish intelligence officers immediately concerned were extremely friendly and this mutual confidence was, it is believed, maintained and developed during the war.

Irish intelligence was prepared to keep a close watch on individuals in Ireland who concerned the British. More important, when British intelligence passed reports on to the Irish they were quickly dealt with to MI5's satisfaction. Furthermore, the reliability of Irish intelligence reports increasingly undermined the credibility of the exaggerated and unreliable reports of Unionist and disaffected Anglo-Irish sources such as Lord Londonderry and enhanced the value of the link.[10]

Britain and Ireland decided that closer cooperation was now an imperative, though the two governments had rather different views on what form it should take. On the very day that Held's home was raided by the Garda, Archer and Walshe travelled to London to discuss how best to respond to the situation. On the British side Sir Eric Machtig from the Dominions Office was the most experienced official in Irish matters. They were joined by Commander Creswell representing the Admiralty, Major Heyman of the War Office and Squadron Leader Vintras from the Air Ministry. The muted tone of the official minutes cannot, even after sixty years, disguise the crisis facing the two countries. Most remarkably, less than twenty years after fighting a bitter war of independence against the British, two senior Irish officials were now discussing the possibility of military cooperation with them. The British continued to believe that the Irish remained complacent about the German threat, one that recent German successes had demonstrated to be very real. They urged the Irish to consider the evidence that the Germans had a clear interest in Ireland.[11]

Though there may have been a crisis, the Irish were extremely cautious about the commitments they were prepared to give. Archer and Walshe made it clear that the Irish government was not prepared to invite the British in prior to an actual attack by the Germans. The British military representatives complained that this would be too late to counter any attack, as had been shown in other cases. Archer made it clear that Irish forces would have to be 'blooded' before an invitation to intervene could be made:

> *the political situation in Ireland was such that the Irish must take the first brunt of the attack.* It would be quite impossible to call for assistance, even air assistance alone, until Irish public opinion had fully realised that the attack had taken place and that Irish troops were engaged. This realisation might be a matter only of hours, although it might, in the event, be a matter of a day or two.

The British were concerned that a German force of up to 15,000 troops could establish itself in Ireland, and might be difficult to defeat if British forces did not intervene quickly enough. There was also a fear, never openly expressed by the British, that sections of the Irish military might defect to the Germans or would quickly surrender if attacked. The Irish were not in a position to give a clear answer to the

British question as to when any intervention could take place. Archer was so vague as to undermine any forward planning on the part of the British. The primary focus for the Irish officials was sovereignty, while that of the British was strategic; the latter failed to appreciate the Irish need to demonstrate that they were independent and that a spirited defence of their country against a superior force could show this. This seemed foolish to the British representatives, given the extent of the threat, but they failed to fully appreciate Irish sensitivities. The Irish also drew a distinction between giving a warning and asking for assistance. Walshe thought the British could cut off a German second wave by the use of air power, without committing ground troops. He was confident that the Irish army could defeat the first wave of German parachutists, while the RAF and Royal Navy protected Irish territory from further attack. The Irish military clearly had an unduly optimistic view of their capacity to intercept and defeat an invading force and may have misinformed him. This plan was unacceptable to the British and Squadron Leader Vintras emphasized that the RAF could not guarantee the successful interception of a second German wave without facilities in Ireland or an advance invitation to intervene. What the British required was a clear call for assistance at the earliest point in time and one that included an invitation for the military to cross the border into Ireland. The Irish officials, following de Valera's instructions, were reluctant to accept the need to provide such a clear call, believing that the Irish military was capable of holding off an initial German attack.[12]

While this thorny issue was not resolved, the two sides did agree on the need for effective communication between the two states in the event of any attack, also agreeing that the Irish government should review its military preparedness. The British undertook to fully inform the Irish on German tactics during the recent campaign in France.[13] The talks resumed at 11.30 the following morning. Wing Commander Cadell from the Air Ministry and Major Hoysted and Lieutenant Colonel Dudley Clarke of the War Office joined the British team. Clarke had been invited to join the discussions as he had served in the Norwegian campaign and was familiar with German tactics. Both sides reported back on matters arising from the previous day's discussion. Clarke then seems to have taken the lead. He insisted that the real talks had to take place in Ireland and announced his intention of travelling to Northern Ireland to consult with the British GOC there. It was agreed that Archer and Walshe would accompany Clarke and travel on to Dublin from there. Talks in Dublin could take place within two days at most. Walshe insisted that these arrangements were provisional, as he would have to consult with de Valera before any meeting could take place in Dublin.[14]

Clarke duly travelled to Northern Ireland by aeroplane and on to Dublin by train. In Dublin, Walshe was obsessed with protecting the secrecy of the meeting and Clarke understandably travelled in civilian clothes. Clarke's description of his visit, which was censored by the British authorities after the war, reads like a Graham Greene novel, though perhaps Flann O'Brien would have provided a more surreal description. Having collected Clarke from the Shelbourne Hotel on Stephen's Green, Walshe led him through a series of underground passages to a meeting in Government Buildings, even though the hotel was just a few minutes' walk away. Despite all the secrecy, Clarke did meet the army chief of staff, General Dan McKenna, and some of his senior officers. He also met Frank Aiken for dinner, who seemed anxious to expound his views on how the war should be conducted. Clarke did not achieve the purpose of his visit to Dublin: Irish military and political leaders continued to resist any commitments that would allow British forces into Eire prior to a German attack.[15] After his return from Dublin Clarke reported to his colleagues that the Irish had 'sought our advice as to what they should do and left it to us to suggest what help should be provided'. However, he was concerned that they were not taking the issue seriously enough on the grounds that a successful attack was only remotely possible. In particular, he had been unable to convince them that the prospect of an IRA–German alliance continued to be a danger to Irish security. Clarke reported further that in his view the military authorities he had spoken to 'were inclined to view somewhat light-heartedly the possible scale of a German attack'. He hoped that in the light of his visit and discussions the Irish were now more aware of the possibility of a landing on the west coast of Ireland.[16]

The next day, Major General Hastings Ismay, secretary to the war cabinet, wrote to Churchill claiming to have 'information from secret sources' which indicated that the 'Germans have concerted plans with the IRA and that everything is now ready for an immediate descent on the country'. Ismay wrote again the following day, reporting Clarke's conclusions on his meetings with the Irish. He confirmed that the Irish government would only invite British forces into Eire if an actual attack took place. However, while there could be no formal alliance prior to an attack, the two governments were actively cooperating on developing the means to communicate effectively in the event of such an attack. Both parties agreed that assistance could be best directed from Northern Ireland and discussions between Northern Ireland staff officers and their Irish counterparts had already taken place. Given Churchill's interest in Ireland and his suspicion of de Valera, it is improbable that such a limited course of action would have mollified him. However we do not have any direct evidence that he was particularly concerned with Irish matters at this stage.[17]

What we do know is that Ireland had moved up the political agenda in Britain. Immediately after the meeting with Archer and Walshe in London, Foreign Secretary Lord Halifax wrote to Churchill highlighting the need to make a positive approach to the Irish government. Lord Lothian, ambassador to the United States, supported such an initiative as, increasingly, did Chamberlain.[18] Although Churchill remained hostile to Irish neutrality, he seemed inclined to respect its status unless something dramatic happened. Nevertheless, he and others believed that Britain was vulnerable to attack through neutral Ireland and military officials were still sceptical that the Irish could provide effective resistance to a German attack. Maffey sent an urgent note to Chamberlain on 3 June recommending that a substantial offer be made to de Valera. He asked if Britain required Eire's assistance on moral or strategic grounds, describing the internal political situation as 'explosive' and easily exploited. The IRA with German support could use Irish instability decisively, especially if the British strategic situation deteriorated further, he added. The novelist Elizabeth Bowen suggested that in a crisis the IRA might receive support from a larger section of the population than would otherwise be the case, while Maffey pointed out that simply occupying Irish ports would drive local opinion in the opposite direction to that desired. He also ruled out simply giving de Valera a warning and some time to reflect on the position. In Maffey's view this would put de Valera 'in an impossible position unless at the same time we give him a card to play'. For Maffey the card to be played was Northern Ireland – the solution to partition. If this were accomplished, then changes favourable to Britain might occur. At the heart of any proposal, Maffey insisted, should be a clear warning to de Valera that Britain needed Berehaven, one of the three Treaty Ports returned in 1938, and if facilities could not be obtained in Ireland the much-needed military equipment from America would be placed further at risk by the longer sea journey required. This could not be an ultimatum, but should be accompanied by an agreement to refer the partition question to a board of arbitration, which could be chaired by an American. This proposal was surrounded by caveats, but there is no reason to doubt the radical nature of the case being made.

Maffey's view on Ulster Unionism illustrates the evolving position. 'This plan,' he recommended, 'needs an ultimatum for Craigavon. It needs maximum speed as the situation may deteriorate rapidly.' The government should accept two essential facts:

> We no longer want to govern or administer Eire. We have had enough of that and are well quit of it. What we need is to restore the strategic unity of our island group. Nothing else matters.

If this was accepted then Northern Ireland may have to be sacrificed to the greater good of saving Britain and Ireland:

> The fatal results of allowing Ulster to control our inter-state policy on Ireland. This is the last occasion on which she can bring us to ruin with her short sightedness for her own true interests and with her false and sectarian 'loyalty'.

Maffey's tone reflects the deteriorating situation for Britain in early June 1940. He was confident that an agreement on partition would provide de Valera with the political leverage to secure nationalist support for handing over control of the ports. The impact on American and commonwealth opinion would be uniformly positive, but an agreement would also resolve the last outstanding issue between Britain and Ireland. Maffey's proposal was an important departure from previous British establishment opinion on partition, which had emphasized the need for agreement between north and south. Maffey wanted a more forceful and interventionist approach from the British government, one that essentially promoted Irish unity. He nevertheless worried that it was too late to tempt de Valera with an offer on

unity while also recognizing that the gap between de Valera's conception of a united Ireland and what would be acceptable to both Ulster
Unionists and British opinion was still wide. In a somewhat resigned
fashion he concluded his assessment:

> If things go ill we shall have done well to face up to the Partition
> issue now as otherwise its later solution will involve us in a
> humiliation and in the embarrassment of a hostile foreign Catholic
> Republic established on our Western flank.

Maffey's note was important, as it was one of a number of British
suggestions on how to deal with Eire. Not all of them were favourable
to de Valera or to Ireland, but the most influential were judicious and
supportive of Irish interests.[19]

Maffey returned to London for discussions and was somewhat
taken aback by the views circulating among his colleagues on Ireland.
He informed them that the Germans were waiting for the British to
make a false move in relation to the ports, that a German invasion
was unlikely and that the IRA was largely a spent force. Maffey did
think that the Germans might invade Northern Ireland, as this would
pose insuperable difficulties for all involved:

> It is not clear what the attitude of Eire would be if Ulster were
> subject to German invasion. It is a pity that the relationship
> between the two countries do [*sic*] not permit of a combined plan
> of action. But a joint scheme of defence between a country at war
> and a neutral neighbour is not easy to achieve in any event and
> certainly not when a de Valera and a Craigavon have to agree.

Maffey also observed that Eire could not remain unaffected by
instability in Northern Ireland, which would spread to the south with
some sections of the population supporting their fellow nationalists in
the north. If this did happen Maffey concluded that 'de Valera and his
Government would be swept away like chaff before the wind and
Ireland would find itself under the Gauleiter.'[20]

On 16 June the British war cabinet dismissed a recommendation
from General Smuts, the prime minister of South Africa, that the ports
be occupied in defiance of Irish opinion. The cabinet decided on a
very different approach:

The Prime Minister welcomed Mr MacDonald's proposed visit to Mr de Valera and agreed that, although as a last resort we should not hesitate to secure the ports by force, it would be unwise at this moment to take any action that might compromise our position with the USA, in view of the present delicate developments.

Ireland had clearly moved up the political agenda, though understandably France remained the most important focus for Churchill at this time.[21] On the same day the cabinet approved MacDonald's visit to de Valera, it also discussed the radical proposal for a union between France and Britain to continue the war.

The British position was grim when Churchill addressed the House of Commons on 18 June. He described the events in France and Belgium as a 'colossal military disaster', attributing most of the blame to the French. Despite the successful withdrawal from Dunkirk, British military capabilities had been considerably weakened and Churchill recognized the challenge before him. After recounting the advantages that Britain continued to have – the navy and the dominions – he acknowledged that real disaster threatened the island. The 'battle of France' was over, he conceded, but 'the battle of Britain is about to begin. Upon this battle depends the survival of Christian civilization. Upon it depends our own British life and the long continuity of our institutions and our Empire.' He warned that 'if we fail then the whole world, including the United States, and all that we know and care for, will sink into the abyss of a new dark age'. Even though Churchill declared that the struggle would be 'their finest hour' there was no disguising the desperate straits the British were in.[22] Later that same day, Churchill wrote to Ernest Bevin, Labour leader and now member of the cabinet, on the Irish situation, 'I certainly sh'd welcome any approach to Irish unity; but I have forty years experience of its difficulties. I c'd never be a party to the coercion of Ulster to join the Southern counties; but I am in favour of their being persuaded. The key to this is de Valera showing some loyalty to Crown and Empire.' If this was so, then MacDonald's visit to Dublin was already doomed to failure, but Churchill was not as dominant in the cabinet as might be assumed. Chamberlain was still powerful in the Conservative party – it was, in part at least, his initiative – and Bevin's influence in the Labour party was considerable. If these two could agree on a strategy

Leabharlanna Fhine Gall

in respect of Ireland, it would be difficult for Churchill to ignore them, especially if there was some real prospect of additional resources being made available to beleaguered Britain from Ireland.[23]

Bevin wrote to Churchill proposing a new constitution which would provide 'the basis of a united Ireland at the end of the hostilities'. Recognizing the importance of the United States, Bevin also recommended that President Roosevelt appoint the chairman for the constitutional negotiations leading to unity. Chamberlain told the war cabinet on 20 June that he had just seen a preliminary draft of an aide-memoire from the chiefs of staff, 'which included the statement that there could be no security for Eire or the United Kingdom unless proper arrangements were made which included the presence of British or dominion troops and air forces in Eire, and His Majesty's ships in Irish ports'. Most tellingly the chiefs of staff maintained that 'the main, and perhaps the sole, obstacle to such collaboration was the partition question'. Chamberlain concluded that action by Britain after a German invasion of Ireland 'might well come too late'. This being so, he recommended the government to consider 'the question of entering the Irish ports by force'. It is ironic that the prime minister who agreed to hand over the ports to de Valera was now suggesting that they be reoccupied by force, and on this occasion it was Churchill who adopted a moderate course in respect of Ireland. While the prime minister was not prepared to put 'undue pressure on the loyal province of Ulster', he also was not in favour of military action against de Valera at that point. He added significantly that 'he was in favour of allowing the enemy to make the first move; if they succeeded in establishing themselves in Ireland our forces should then be ready to pounce upon them. The whole of Ireland, including Mr de Valera, would in those circumstances be on our side.' Churchill reiterated this view at the secret session of the House of Commons later the same day, concluding, 'Germans in Ireland would fight under great disadvantages' and that he would 'much rather they break Irish neutrality than we'. What is very clear from the cabinet discussion is that Churchill was no friend of de Valera or nationalist Ireland, but at the same time he had an acute sense of what was politically practicable on any specific occasion.[24]

At the defence committee meeting on 21 June Churchill accepted that there was a real chance that the Germans could invade Ireland, but that the British could then apply overwhelming force to defeat them and do so as quickly as possible:

> In view of Mr de Valera's intransigent attitude we should not accede to any requests from the Eire government to be supplied with munitions, which we wanted for our own use. We should continue our pressure upon him to allow us to send in troops before the Germans made a move.

Churchill took up a suggestion that de Valera might accept a brigade of the London Irish in Ireland. He also recommended that troops be placed on the highest state of readiness so that immediate intervention could take place. Of primary importance was the appointment of a commander for those forces to be dispatched to Ireland should the need arise. The commander could then acquaint himself with the challenges of the task before him. What is perhaps surprising is Churchill's rather measured approach to the situation. He was clearly concerned at events in Ireland and the possibility that the Germans would use it as the base for an assault on Britain itself, and on this the cabinet and the chiefs of staff were agreed. Despite his hostility to de Valera he did not pursue what might in the circumstances have seemed reasonable: the occupation of the ports. This was not due to a lack of ruthlessness on his part; after all he was prepared to order the Royal Navy to destroy the French fleet at Oran rather than let it fall into the hands of the Germans, or indeed the Vichy regime. Furthermore, in a note to Halifax – probably the one person who continued to believe that some sort of accommodation with Germany was possible – Churchill insisted that all members of the government must be 'resolved to fight to the death' in the event of a German invasion.[25] On 30 June, as MacDonald's mission to Ireland was coming to an end, Churchill wrote to General Ismay that 'nothing that can happen in Ireland can be immediately decisive', reflecting his clear understanding of the difficulties of a landing in Ireland for the Germans. In consequence he refused to allow two divisions to be sent to Northern Ireland, believing that they would be deployed more effectively in Britain itself. Churchill considered that two or three lightly equipped brigades could move quickly into Ireland at short notice if an invasion did occur.[26]

*

By June 1940, Britain was cut off from the continent and the only obstacle to Hitler's complete dominance of Europe. Successive reverses had brought Churchill to power and changed the balance of British politics. The Labour party joined the government with Clement Attlee and Ernest Bevin becoming key figures in the war cabinet. Churchill was more popular with Labour MPs than among Conservatives, though Chamberlain provided important support for the new prime minister until his death later in the year. The American writer Samuel Beer in his classic study of British politics identified 1940 as a hugely significant year. Total war enhanced Labour's position, as it was indispensable to the war effort. Bevin's inclusion in the war cabinet exemplifies this shift in power. Churchill was prepared to do anything to win the battle for Britain. Radical departures could become realistic politics in these circumstances and it is telling that despite increasing concerns, the cabinet resisted pressure to seize the Irish ports.[27] Reflecting the new politics of Churchill's coalition government, Minister for Health Malcolm MacDonald travelled to Dublin to negotiate with de Valera on the future relationship between the two states in the face of war. By the middle of June 1940 Churchill had in effect adopted a policy of moderation towards Ireland, despite the serious challenges elsewhere.[28]

The original intention had been for a conference to take place in London between de Valera and Craigavon. However, both leaders declined to come, especially Craigavon, who feared that Northern Ireland might be sacrificed for Britain's interests. On Wednesday 12 June Chamberlain wrote to de Valera reminding him of the continuing threat by sea and air to Ireland. Additional information had come to Chamberlain's attention that persuaded him that the situation could only be dealt with by personal negotiation and he wanted to meet de Valera along with Craigavon and the secretary of state for the dominions. The object of the meeting would be to develop close collaboration between north and south to deal with the possibility of an invasion.[29] As de Valera was not prepared to meet in London, the cabinet agreed to send MacDonald to Dublin to open discussions. He initially met de Valera at six in the evening and the talks continued for two hours. After a break of just over two hours the discussion resumed and continued until nearly midnight. When MacDonald arrived in Dublin, France had just surrendered; George Orwell recorded in his diary that fighting to the death and killing someone was the only way to go now that this had happened. He also noted what he described as 'expressions of quiet patriotism' among passengers on the London underground.[30] MacDonald had the advantage of knowing de Valera from the successful negotiations leading to the Anglo-Irish agreements in 1938. The taoiseach was courteous and friendly, as he normally was with visitors, though MacDonald noted that 'his mind is still set in the same hard, confined mould of yore'. However, MacDonald noticed important changes since he had last seen de Valera: the Irish leader seemed tired and depressed and whereas MacDonald had been used to long speeches from him he now engaged in 'a sustained conversation between two people'.

After a general discussion on France, MacDonald turned to the reason for his visit. He emphasized the moral dimension of the war in Europe, insisting that Ireland could not stand aside in the crisis or expect to be unaffected by Germany's conduct of the war. MacDonald also asserted that the United Kingdom had come to the 'definite conclusion' that the Germans would land in Ireland either as part of an invasion of Britain or prior to such an invasion. This was based on British intelligence but also on the documents found when Held was apprehended in Dublin. The staff talks between the Irish and British military were to be welcomed, he continued, thanking the taoiseach for permitting them. Evidence pointed to a German–IRA link. He urged de Valera to accept that Germany would not respect neutrality, as had been demonstrated in the Netherlands and elsewhere. Mac-Donald seemed rattled by the German successes; he thought they could act 'like a stroke of lightning' as they had done elsewhere. From the French coast they could send troops by ship or submarine to Ireland. The Royal Navy would do its best, but could not guarantee preventing a landing. This led to the Irish ports, the denial of which disadvantaged not only the British but Ireland itself. This situation could be further compounded by German parachutists linking up with the Irish fifth column, the IRA.

This was apocalyptic stuff and it is difficult to judge whether MacDonald actually believed it, or if he was just attempting to frighten de Valera. Most likely it was a bit of both. MacDonald wanted de Valera to see the seriousness of the situation and to change policy. He suggested that the Irish military were unlikely to be able to hold off a

German invasion: 'Eire might be effectively overpowered, Dublin captured and an IRA government established within a few hours.' Consequently, MacDonald argued that existing arrangements were not adequate to meet this crisis.

Surprisingly, MacDonald seemed resigned to de Valera's insistence on maintaining neutrality. While he continued to believe that the 'wisest' decision would be for Ireland to join the war he accepted that he could not influence him in this direction. MacDonald however wanted to highlight Irish vulnerability in the face of an attack: 'We were quite capable of dealing with an invasion of Great Britain. It was true that the over-running of Eire would embarrass us, but it would not be decisive against us; it would only be decisive against Eire.' Notwithstanding this view, MacDonald asked de Valera if he and his government were prepared to consider action short of abandoning neutrality and invite British forces into Ireland. As MacDonald presented it, this would not be a violation of Irish territory:

> Our ships and troops would not be there for the purpose of taking offensive action from Irish waters or territory. They would simply be there to defend Irish neutrality, and would only act offensively if that neutrality were violated by Germany.

MacDonald's anxiety is evident throughout the discussion. His fears of a German assault on Ireland were genuine and he sincerely believed that this offer could meet both British defence requirements and Irish sensitivities in respect of neutrality. Nevertheless, de Valera was not tempted by this suggestion. He reasserted that Irish national opinion supported neutrality and it would only be abandoned if Ireland were attacked. He does not seem to have been attracted by the distinction between defensive and offensive intervention by Britain and seriously questioned if Germany would attack the south. He added that an attack was more likely to come through Northern Ireland, where the Germans could operate with nationalist support, adding rather ominously from the British viewpoint, 'In that case they would try to make out that they had come to end partition in Ireland.' MacDonald thought this unlikely, pointing out the probability of the Germans wishing to occupy both parts of the island.

What de Valera wanted was military supplies from Britain to defend the country. He had troops but not enough equipment for them, and this disadvantaged the Irish defence, although de Valera 'thought his men would fight magnificently. The Germans would not find things easy, for the Irish were very skilful at guerrilla warfare.' This is unlikely to have impressed the Germans or MacDonald. Most neutrals thought themselves prepared for an attack, yet German tactics had proved effective in rapidly overcoming resistance.[31] MacDonald pointed this out to de Valera, emphasizing the German use of tanks and other mobile forces to neutralize such tactics.

De Valera then engaged in 'teasing ambiguity', using terms in a highly qualified fashion so that later he could justly claim that the hearer had read more into his position than intended at the time:

> If there had been a United Ireland he might have been able to invite us in now. He wished that such a political change had been accomplished before the war. A United Ireland would have been a great strength to us. It is true that the country would (if he had had his way) have remained neutral at the outset of the war, but by now it might have been a belligerent. He merely told me this because it was his definite view that things would have been different if the country had been one.

De Valera quickly added that he was not suggesting that the British could do anything about partition at this stage. The important message in this was not the reference to a united Ireland, but the emphasis placed on neutrality. The partition issue was being used by de Valera to provide tactical support for continuing neutrality. The hint that Ireland 'might' do otherwise was a smokescreen; the reality was his commitment to neutral status. Invoking partition allowed de Valera to emphasize the potentially hostile nature of Irish public opinion: 'Many of his supporters were inclined to say that Ireland had already been invaded by the British in the North. This feeling prejudiced many who would otherwise have been our friends.' This is a view closely identified with Frank Aiken. The hint here was that neutrality contained all these antagonisms within acceptable limits: 'the best service that he could render to this country and to us was to maintain that unity against the day when Germany struck'. De Valera could not invite the British in ahead of this, he declared. He would be criticized by his own people and the Germans would use the invitation as an excuse for invading, while de Valera would have been deprived of the national

unity that neutrality had brought. He reiterated that 'he was ready
to go as far as he could in co-operation with us at present, short of
publicly compromising the country's neutrality'.

While MacDonald acknowledged de Valera's commitment to neutrality, he hinted that de Valera did not fully appreciate the seriousness
of the situation. In fact, it is likely that de Valera did appreciate the
threat to Britain and this was precisely why he was not prepared to
sacrifice neutrality. It is possible that de Valera hoped that the Germans would not invade Ireland but that Britain would be weakened.
He maintained that while he understood the seriousness of the
situation, most Irish people did not. There was, he continued, little
information available to the public on the fate of neutral states –
though one of the reasons for this was de Valera's zealous use of
censorship. De Valera also claimed that opinion in Ireland was more
likely to conclude 'that the Germans would make them more free' and
would fight more fiercely against Britain than Germany if neutrality
were violated.

The discussion reached an impasse at this stage and MacDonald
now moved into uncharted waters. He asked if de Valera would
change his view on the defence issue if Britain worked for a united
Ireland. Admitting that a united Ireland was not immediately possible,
he held out the prospect that if all-Ireland institutional arrangements
were agreed this would bring Unionists and nationalists together in a
single body for the first time since the Treaty. MacDonald wanted to
see a defence council established along the lines suggested to Craigavon by Gray, but also endorsed by MacEntee in 1938. MacDonald
continued in optimistic form, 'It might be only a first step, to be
followed by others. If the habit of cooperation on matters of common
concern were once established, it would be difficult afterwards to
break it down.' It is not clear if MacDonald had discussed this
particular initiative with Chamberlain, but he assured de Valera that
the British government would be willing to establish a defence council
and hoped that de Valera's supporters would view it positively.[32] Not
unexpectedly, de Valera rejected the proposal out of hand. He agreed
that a defence council would be necessary if there was an invasion,
but only then. Even in the face of a German landing, he added, such a
joint effort between north and south would 'present certain difficulties
between old enemies'. He also stressed that Fianna Fáil supporters

would consider it a threat to neutrality and therefore bring Ireland into the war. De Valera countered MacDonald's suggestion by proposing that the British government immediately declare a united Ireland under a single government which would impose neutrality on the entire island. MacDonald rejected this on the grounds that the majority in Northern Ireland would oppose it and that it would undermine resistance to Hitler. There were also strategic considerations: Northern Ireland protected Glasgow and the Clyde.

MacDonald then pushed the discussion a step forward by arguing that the best chance for Ireland ever being united would come if de Valera joined with Britain in the war. This would have a powerful impact on British opinion, especially on politicians of MacDonald's generation who, he claimed, would not welcome a return to 'old barren controversies' at the end of the war. He also warned that if de Valera did not act, 'then the differences between the twenty-six and the six counties would certainly be aggravated and enlarged, and we politicians at Westminster who had gone through the fight would never agree to handing Ulster over to Eire against the former's will'. This was a prophetic claim, but de Valera was not prepared to accept that Britain was flexible, responding that Irish nationalists would not believe that a united Ireland could be obtained in this way. He asserted that the north would remain independent of Eire after the war in any case, because it had joined in the war from the beginning.

At this first meeting between the two politicians, MacDonald was under the illusion that he and de Valera agreed on the 'facts as they were', yet this was not the case. Despite MacDonald's appreciation of de Valera's difficulties and his evident goodwill, the defence of Britain took second place to what de Valera considered to be Ireland's interests. If Irish and British interests coincided then de Valera would negotiate for an outcome acceptable to him, but in his view this was rarely the case. Indeed there was a basic incompatibility in the aims of the negotiators. Britain wanted de Valera to end neutrality and he would not, apparently under any circumstances; de Valera wanted the British to impose a united Ireland on the north and agree to all-Ireland neutral status, which they would also not do under existing circumstances. Moreover, de Valera was unwilling to consider any compromise. Not only did he reject British troops in Ireland, neither was he prepared to accept French, Polish or dominion forces. He was also not prepared to intern German or Italian nationals who had not acted against Irish interests, as that would be 'an un-neutral act'. While agreeing to have them watched more closely, he was not willing to go further. MacDonald now challenged Irish behaviour in this respect, citing the arrest of Stephen Held the previous month in circumstances which questioned Irish security arrangements. Furthermore, he urged de Valera to take account of evidence that German nationals in Ireland would work with the German military when they invaded. De Valera was not persuaded by any of this, pointing out that Held was a 'naturalised Irishman', not a German national, while also questioning the significance of the evidence found at Held's home, although when pressed further, de Valera admitted that the Held case had in fact 'shaken him considerably'.

While both men agreed that Hitler had to defeat Britain within the next two months or so or the task would become far more difficult, de Valera also demonstrated that he had little interest in Europe or Hitler's domination of the continent. He asked why the British would not negotiate a peace settlement with Hitler, keeping the empire while Hitler controlled Europe. MacDonald's response illustrated the shift in opinion among those who had previously been members of Chamberlain's government – appeasers, as Churchill saw them. There was no basis for such a settlement, he responded. Britain would not tolerate Hitler's domination of Europe, nor would a negotiated settlement bring security to either Britain or Ireland. Such a settlement, he contended, would be taken as a sign of weakness by Hitler and in time he would use the resources available to him in continental Europe to prepare another attack (which is exactly what Hitler did in the case of the Soviet Union in 1941). De Valera spent the remainder of the meeting probing MacDonald on Britain's ability to hold off the Germans and the extent to which it could continue to maintain naval and air superiority. MacDonald gave a very upbeat assessment of Britain's drive to enhance its military defence production, as well as expressing confidence that in time his country would prevail. While believing that de Valera was impressed by this assessment, he also admitted that the taoiseach 'nevertheless remained sceptical'.

Towards the end of the meeting de Valera summarized what he wanted from Britain, including the recognition that Ireland would remain neutral unless attacked. He wanted Britain to provide Ireland with the necessary military equipment to resist attack, but also to provide immediate assistance if the Germans invaded. He emphasized that the help he most desired was from the RAF, perhaps because aircraft could be removed from the country more easily than troops. While willing to bring Ireland's defence needs to the attention of London, MacDonald reminded de Valera that Britain's needs were now far more pressing, while reiterating that Britain had little confidence in Ireland's ability to defend itself. The meeting ended on this note, with de Valera simply repeating that he and his countrymen would fight if invaded.[33]

These discussions would have been extraordinary under any circumstances and their nature and direction reveal both British desperation and their determination to do whatever was necessary to achieve victory. It is perhaps a truism that going to war is the most dramatic action a government can take, but it is also the case that in wartime what was impossible just a few weeks before can become a real possibility. Who in 1938 would have believed that within two years Churchill would be prime minister and that some of his closest associates would be members of the Labour party? Ernest Bevin was one of the key figures in the rapidly developing sequence of events that occurred between Monday and Friday of that June week. Chamberlain must have been discouraged by MacDonald's discussions in Dublin, yet the response in London was to explore virtually any alternative to invasion or occupation. On Tuesday the 18th Chamberlain wrote to Churchill recommending that the British government pursue an active policy in Ireland, one that would secure the defence of the island as a single unit. Bevin believed that there was a good chance that political unity could be achieved as well, underscoring his opinion with evidence that the Irish members of his trade union had been offered the opportunity to set up a specifically Irish union but had refused. Churchill accepted the need for a generous gesture but stopped short of forcing the northern Unionists into a united Ireland. On the same day, Leo Amery, secretary of state for India and Burma, wrote suggesting that stationing Canadian or Australian troops in Eire might prove more acceptable to de Valera and nationalist sentiment. Not all correspondence with the prime minister during the week was in favour of compromise with de Valera: Lord Londonderry wrote emphasizing the danger to Britain and dismissing Maffey's recommendations as based on ignorance of the facts of Ireland. However, although Churchill was receiving conflicting advice, those who favoured a moderate policy in respect of Ireland were dominant. Bevin and Amery, representing very different factions within government, both favoured the conciliatory approach, as did Chamberlain and Eden. What is also clear is that despite his misgivings so did Churchill. This did not prevent him from criticizing de Valera or from protecting Unionists, but it did provide the prospect of a very different type of negotiation with de Valera when MacDonald returned to Dublin.[34]

Arriving back in Dublin on Friday 21 June, MacDonald met de Valera then and on the following day. He told the taoiseach that the British were prepared to provide his government with some armaments, but that it was impossible to give them anti-aircraft guns, Bren guns or rifles as these were required for the defence of Britain. MacDonald impressed on de Valera the harsh reality that 'we thought the danger of a quick success for a comparatively small invading force was so real that we could not, in the present circumstances, contemplate letting him have valuable equipment'. This could change if Ireland could assure the British that 'resistance to the enemy would be effective'. One way of demonstrating this was for de Valera to accept the presence of RAF and British army personnel on Irish soil prior to a German attack. De Valera rejected this, forcibly adding that the best way to defend Britain was to provide him with adequate arms. He charged MacDonald with short-sightedness:

> Eire was exposed to attack; it was a back door through which the Germans might try to enter Britain, whilst they were at the same time trying to get through other doors on the shores of Britain itself. We ought not to keep all our guns to defend the British doors, but to send some to the back door in Eire.

MacDonald questioned whether Irish troops, brave though they might be, could in fact deter a German attack, as they were untrained and inexperienced in combat. The best way to meet an attack, he urged, was for the British navy to intercept the Germans before they even landed. De Valera was unwilling to risk national unity by accepting the Royal Navy into Irish ports. He asked if MacDonald feared that he would join with the Germans and fight the British, wondering if this was the reason for refusing to provide arms. MacDonald assured de Valera that he had no reservations in this respect, but that the British military and he himself had little confidence that Eire could repel an attack.

De Valera insisted that most Irish people wanted good relations with Britain. This would be the case, he added, whether Britain won or lost the war, as Ireland was 'largely dependent on Great Britain':

> The destiny of Ireland must be closely linked with that of Britain. It was unthinkable that, so long as Britain did not interfere with Irish freedom, Ireland should give the slightest assistance to Britain's enemies.

The 1938 agreements, which of course MacDonald had helped to broker, had established a new environment for relations between the two states and de Valera agreed that the British had lived up to their commitments 'in the letter and the spirit' of the agreements. He then said that if the British had brought an end to partition in 1938, 'there might have been an alliance between the two countries by now'. This was the opportunity that MacDonald had been waiting for. He now shifted the discussion to the question of Irish unity and held out the prospect of the British being willing to negotiate a solution to this outstanding problem. MacDonald suggested that the best opportunity for Ireland to become a united country was for north and south to fight on the same side: 'It seemed to me that the co-operation and unity which would be established in war could not be broken when peace returned.' MacDonald wanted to impress on de Valera that these views were not limited to him and could not have made his point in stronger terms:

> I could now tell him that this view was shared strongly by the War Cabinet in London. The Prime Minister himself, as well as Mr Chamberlain and others, had said that we should do nothing to discourage and everything that we could to encourage the unity of Ireland, so long as there was no coercion. The establishment of unity in war would almost certainly lead to the continuance of unity in peace.

MacDonald then pressed de Valera again to change policy and take a pro-Allied stance that would bring Ireland into the war. But if earlier de Valera had argued that the threat to Ireland justified the British

diverting large amounts of armaments to Ireland, he now grew sceptical concerning the possibility of a German attack, offering various
reasons why this might not occur. MacDonald agreed that it would be
a mistake to take a dogmatic view on the prospect of an invasion but
nevertheless insisted that 'the odds were in its favour' at that time,
given the circumstances in which both islands were placed. Further
discussion followed until the substance of the issue was refined down
to three possible alternatives. MacDonald's preferred position was
that Eire would remain neutral, that Northern Ireland would remain
in the war, that a defence council be set up on an all-Ireland basis
and that British forces be stationed in Eire to protect the island. De
Valera rejected this on the grounds that it would be a provocation to
Germany and that Irish neutrality would in effect be compromised,
notwithstanding MacDonald's claim. He was also concerned that if
British troops entered Irish territory the IRA would attack them. When
asked if this view was a personal one or was shared by his government,
de Valera replied that it was one shared by the government. De
Valera's preference was for a united neutral Ireland with its neutrality
guaranteed by both Britain and the United States. He immediately
added that American involvement was his own personal preference.
Some of his colleagues might oppose this, as the stance of the United
States was so favourable to Britain. However, few nationalists would
oppose such an agreement, and a neutral Ireland with United States
protection would deny the entire island to the Germans. If the Germans did attack Ireland then the United States would also be drawn
into the war and this could only work to the British advantage. De
Valera then offered another sweetener to MacDonald: 'he thought that
the neutrality of a United Ireland might well be short-lived; after a
while Ireland might enter the war on our side'. As usual in these
circumstances the important word was 'might'. De Valera did not
commit himself to anything substantive as a united Ireland could in
fact remain neutral.

MacDonald rejected this proposal, pointing out that there would
be strong opposition to it among Ulster Unionists and this would
deprive the new state of any stability. Ulster was in the war and
most of its people would not wish to desert Britain at this stage. If
all Ireland did become neutral this would deprive Britain of much-
needed productive capacity, in particular shipbuilding, which would

1. De Valera may have appeared aloof and austere to many, but to his supporters he was charismatic and engaging, as this photograph from a political meeting in Cork in 1934 shows.

2. A decisive moment for de Valera, when he arrives in Cork harbour to officially accept the handover of the ports by Britain in July 1938.

3. An anxious gathering outside the offices of the *Cork Examiner*, shortly after the British declaration of war was announced.

4. Many Irish citizens living in Britain quickly returned to Ireland after war was declared, as can be seen from a packed *Innisfallen* arriving in Cork in September 1939.

5. Winston Churchill: Britain's wartime leader and de Valera's nemesis.

6. After the fall of France, it was feared that Ireland would be the next target for Hitler's campaign against Britain. Although there was often a shortage of uniforms and weapons, there was considerable enthusiasm and volunteer forces were quickly mobilised.

7. De Valera associated himself closely with recruitment for the defence forces. Here he visits Tralee in County Kerry in June 1940.

8. The belief that Ireland would be invaded as a back door into Britain led to the abortive talks between de Valera and Malcolm Macdonald in June 1940. This cartoon suggests that Northern Ireland might not have been able to veto a deal between Britain and Eire, despite de Valera's misgivings.

9. By the end of 1940, as British shipping losses mounted, Churchill had lost patience with de Valera. This cartoon was published shortly after widespread criticism of de Valera's refusal to agree a deal on the ports in Eire.

10. De Valera here takes the salute at the march-past outside the GPO in Dublin at the twenty-fifth anniversary of the 1916 Rising in 1941. De Valera frequently linked the fight for independence with the need to defend Irish neutrality against all comers.

11. 'The night the Fianna Fáil backbencher contradicted Dev'. De Valera's control over his party was legendary, especially during the Emergency. This November 1941 cartoon suggests that dissent was virtually non-existent within Fianna Fáil.

The Night the Fianna Fail Backbencher contradicted Dev.

(Mr. de Valera said that, when he was young, he wanted to be a ploughman.)

THE PLOUGHMAN: "Thank goodness, I have them pulling together, and on a straight line, at last!"

12. 'The Ploughman'. There was widespread agreement among the political parties to defend neutrality. Fine Gael found it impossible to openly disagree with de Valera, despite private misgivings.

13. When the United States entered the war in December 1941 the Irish were shocked by American hostility to neutrality. The president had little sympathy for Irish concerns and relations between the two states quickly deteriorated.

14. In August and September 1942, the Irish army organized an ambitious exercise, which involved most of the military force under its command. One division marched from Dublin to Cork, engaging in military exercises before marching back to Dublin. De Valera takes the salute in Cork city.

15. Army personnel assembled in Cork city as part of the army manoeuvres, September 1942.

16. 'Strict neutrality'. Signposts were removed in Eire for the duration of the war in the hope that an invasion force would not know where it was going. This was considered naive by British opinion.

17. Religious enthusiasm was widespread during the Emergency. During this period the alliance between Church and state was cemented. This is a Corpus Christi procession in Cork in 1942 with Irish army participation.

be of primary importance if air raids destroyed capacity in Britain itself. There were also strategic considerations. MacDonald also doubted that the United States would be prepared to defend Irish neutrality in these circumstances. De Valera sought to meet these objections, but MacDonald reiterated the positive aspects of the status quo, adding forcibly, 'If our forces had to withdraw from Ulster, the net military result would be to expand the area of weakness on our western flank, and increase the size of the territory which Germany might successfully invade.' De Valera did suggest that the British army might remain in the north until Irish troops were capable of defending the area but MacDonald again refused to contemplate Ulster as part of a neutral Ireland.

The two proposals were mutually exclusive. MacDonald now attempted to square the circle by placing a slightly different emphasis on unity, but demanding a real shift from de Valera:

> That there should be a declaration of a United Ireland in principle, the practical details of the union to be worked out in due course; this united Ireland to become at once a belligerent on the side of the Allies.

There is a subtle contrast between this and the original MacDonald proposal. It indicated that the British position was quite flexible – or their situation desperate enough for them to contemplate this change in policy. De Valera seemed to recognize this, though he was still reluctant to change Ireland's status:

> If there were not only a declaration of a United Ireland in principle, but also agreement upon its constitution, then the Government of Eire might agree to enter the war at once. He could not be certain about this. Perhaps the existing Government would not agree to it, and would be replaced by another government which did. But the Constitution of a United Ireland would have to be fixed first.

There was a hint of uncertainty here that MacDonald recorded and it would be surprising if this were not the case. After all, de Valera wanted Irish unity more than virtually everything else and the 1937 constitution had been designed with this in mind. De Valera suggested that this constitution provide the institutional basis for any new political arrangement. MacDonald demurred at what might have been a temporary flight of fancy on de Valera's part, pointing out that the constitution could not simply be forced upon the people of Ulster without serious negotiation or it would leave a legacy of ill will. During the discussion that followed, de Valera seemed tempted by the possibility that the proposal offered, yet ultimately adopted a cautious attitude. Most illuminating, however, was de Valera's elaboration on his earlier comment that Eire might enter the war if Irish unity was in place. He now emphasized that the use of 'might' had a 'very big question mark' after it. This prompted MacDonald to retort that a 'might' would not be sufficient for his colleagues to change policy in such a radical fashion; London would require something far more substantial if it was to deliver a united Ireland and a new constitution for the country. At this stage de Valera clearly drew back from contemplating any radical departure on his part:

> A mere declaration of union in principle would not be enough. His people would recognise the difficulties which would lie in the way of working out an agreed constitution, and they would suspect that there never would be an agreement, and that the declaration of principle would never be implemented. And even if we got an agreement on a constitution he still could not go further than a 'might'.

This dismayed MacDonald, but he pursued the issue a little further. He asked if de Valera's view reflected the opinion of his government. The taoiseach at first answered in the affirmative, but MacDonald sensed some unease in the reply. De Valera then admitted that some of his colleagues might vote differently from him, though he did not think this would be the case, but that he at least would maintain the position he had just outlined. De Valera also emphasized that the threat of invasion would be a powerful influence on his government's position. He revealed that 'some of his colleagues and advisers were almost in a state of panic' and that when the defence situation was discussed immediately after MacDonald's previous visit, 'there was some talk which was thoroughly defeatist'. De Valera may have been disingenuous here. If his reference was to the Defence Conference which took place on 19 June then there is no reference in the minutes to defeatism or indeed to anything untoward in the discussions. While various routine aspects of local defence and matters of security were indeed discussed, the minutes reflect a cooperative spirit between government and opposition members and no sense of panic or concern. MacDonald sought to reassure de Valera that adequate protection would be provided by British forces in the event of Ireland joining the war, but did admit that there would be real problems. This did not mollify de Valera, though he did agree to report the conversation to his colleagues on his return from a visit he was making to Galway.[35]

Rather enigmatically, de Valera told MacDonald that the purpose of his visit to Galway was to address what he described as a 'pro-German element' there, though he did not elaborate. Maffey told MacDonald the following Monday that, prior to leaving Dublin for Galway, de Valera called in Gray to ask if the United States was going to abandon neutrality. While Gray was not prepared to give a definite answer to this question, he impressed on de Valera that 'in every possible way except physical participation in war, America was already no longer neutral'. De Valera then asked if the United States would guarantee the security of a united Ireland, but Gray replied that no such guarantee could be given. Maffey commented, 'it is a strange mind which thinks it possible for Northern Ireland to withdraw from the war and also thinks that America would pledge her armed forces on behalf of an island on the fringe of Europe', not appreciating that this is precisely what the United Kingdom was asking of the American president at that time.[36]

While de Valera travelled to the west of Ireland, MacDonald reported to the cabinet in London. Surprisingly, perhaps, he remained cautiously optimistic despite de Valera's considerable reservations. He believed that de Valera's willingness to discuss options provided the basis for further initiatives and he placed considerable emphasis on the possibility of a more favourable response once the proposals had been discussed in the Irish cabinet. Yet what MacDonald had missed in his discussions with de Valera was the taoiseach's admission that there was defeatist sentiment among his colleagues and advisers. MacDonald did not know that the secretary of the Department of External Affairs, Joseph Walshe, one of de Valera's closest advisers, had concluded that Britain would be defeated in the very near future. Walshe was a conservative who considered Portugal under Salazar the 'best ruled country in Europe' as it was 'under an admirable Catholic government'. This sentiment was widespread in certain Catholic circles in Ireland, as was the view – also expressed by Walshe – that the fall of France was a consequence of the influence of Freemasons and the left. Catholic opinion was often sympathetic to the Vichy regime and to its leader Marshal Pétain. While this attitude should not be equated with pro-Nazi views, those who held it were often anti-British and not slow to predict the fall of the British empire in June and July of 1940.

*

While MacDonald was back in London exploring possible responses to de Valera, Walshe was providing de Valera with an extensive review of the political situation. On the Monday after the latest round of talks Walshe informed de Valera of the 'hourly increasing gravity of the war situation' and sought to assess what impact this would have on Ireland. This 'most secret' memo for de Valera recorded the changes in Britain's fortunes, emphasizing both German strength and the loss of France. In contrast to Churchill, who denounced the peace settlement imposed on France by the Germans, Walshe concluded that the surrender terms were not as severe as they might have been. There was now, he continued, an open breach between France and Britain. The British offer of union between the two states had been rejected, he added, because the French government had decided that 'a British defeat was inevitable'. Walshe extended his analysis by reviewing developments around the world, concluding that continental Europe was under Hitler's control, the United States, especially the Republican party, was becoming isolationist and that President Roosevelt 'seems to have over reached himself' in his pro-British policy. Accordingly, 'It does not seem that there is a single organised State left in Europe or Asia which is not ready to profit by what they regard to be the impending downfall of Britain.' Walshe feared that a British attack on Ireland could not be ruled out, because British shipping would now be routed to the west and more open to U-boat attack. Walshe also reported that Dulanty, the Irish high commissioner in London, had described Lord Caldecote, secretary of state for the dominions, as deeply distressed, unshaven and highly critical of French behaviour. Dulanty had had lunch with Chamberlain's private secretary, who said to him, 'you are going to have a terrible time, you will all be murdered'. Walshe then drew attention to the Catholic composition of the Pétain government, predicting moves towards totalitarianism accompanied by a campaign against Jews and Freemasons. His conclusion was profoundly anti-British and unsympathetic to its cause:

> The probability [of totalitarianism] has been increased by the foolish policy of Britain in ignoring the movement towards the Right in France and Spain and in supporting elements who did not represent the fundamental traditions of the people. Britain's final folly was committed during the weekend, when Churchill, by his accusations and his support for de Gaulle, threw France into the totalitarian bloc and made England's defeat inevitable.[37]

In a subsequent memorandum, again produced for de Valera, *Britain's Inevitable Defeat*, Walshe described a world where Britain was alone and on the defensive:

> The entire coastline of Europe from the Arctic to the Pyrenees is in the hands of the strongest power in the world which can call upon the industry and resources of all Europe and Asia in an unbroken geographical continuity as far as the Pacific Ocean.

If the British response to this was defiance, Walshe nevertheless asserted, 'Neither time nor gold can beat Germany.' He then predicted that an isolated Britain could not hold out, nor could she expect much support from the United States, which would look after its own interests. All over the world, he maintained, Britain's allies were deserting her and her enemies preparing for her defeat at the hands of Germany. Walshe predicted civil war in South Africa and revolts in the colonies, concluding, 'It is a fair deduction from the course of events that some members at least of the British cabinet must be turning their thoughts to peace.'[38]

Neither Walshe nor de Valera fully appreciated the seismic shift in British politics that had taken place over the previous month, nor could they understand the determination of even the previously appeasing members of the government to fully support the war effort. By the end of June 1940 there was widespread popular enthusiasm for Churchill and increasing support in the House of Commons. When 'Rab' Butler gave the impression of defeatism in a conversation with a Swedish diplomat, he immediately offered his resignation from the government to allay any suspicion that this might be prevalent.[39] Walshe's analyses for de Valera weakened any possible Irish support for Britain in the war. Walshe was close to de Valera and his influence was reinforced by Frank Aiken, who also believed that Britain would lose the war and may actually have hoped that this would happen.[40] The Catholic bishops provided unanimous support for de Valera's position, circulating a statement on the war couched in anti-partitionist and anti-British terms. It also completely ignored the wishes of Ulster Unionists, who continued to support the British war effort:

> Fortunately for us, our country, or at least that part of it which is subject to the national government, has not been involved in the devastation of war and we must hope and pray that the neutrality which our rulers have so scrupulously observed may continue to be respected by all the belligerent powers.

The statement included the hope that Ireland would be united in the near future.[41]

Despite the lack of progress with de Valera, opinion within British governing circles was moving towards taking an important initiative on Ireland. Independently of MacDonald's negotiations, John Betjeman, who was working with the Ministry of Information, had been in Dublin assessing Irish opinion and seeking to determine the best strategy to pursue in respect of Ireland. On his return to London he circulated a memorandum that demonstrated a keen appreciation of Irish concerns and British interests. While Betjeman recognized that these did not coincide, nevertheless he advised that certain initiatives could have an impact. Betjeman had spoken with Seán MacEntee, minister for industry and commerce, whom he described as having 'pro-British leanings'. In contrast, Walshe at the Department of External Affairs he saw as 'if not actually pro-German . . . certainly somewhat of an isolationist'. Despite their differences, both Walshe and MacEntee agreed that 'the Government will come into the open on the Defence question and will co-operate with British forces in Ireland to resist enemy invasion once some unification of the Six counties and Eire is achieved'. Significantly, they also insisted that military cooperation would not be sufficient if it occurred without 'some sort of symbolic union of Ireland' being established in advance.[42] Betjeman recommended that 'everything should be done towards voicing in the press an outcry for the abolition of partition'. This had quite an impact in the Ministry of Information and a letter was then sent to the Dominions Office incorporating Betjeman's recommendations. The Ministry of Information accepted that its function was to influence Irish opinion and not to dictate policy, but it suggested that it was now important to improve British perceptions of de Valera and to influence Irish attitudes towards Britain. There was a strong emphasis on taking positive action on the partition issue. It concluded:

> The idea is that the present critical situation in regard to defence gives an opportunity to appeal to the British or Irish patriotism of all parties to reach a settlement which would not be possible under less urgent conditions.

While the Dominions Office did not share the Ministry of Information's enthusiasm, considering some of Betjeman's thinking confused, it recognized that action over partition could be beneficial to Britain. Interestingly, the Dominions Office was equally critical of both de Valera and Craigavon, whose attitude is described as 'stay put'. It was agreed that a policy that promoted an end to partition would be agreeable to the Dominions Office.[43]

Chamberlain again persuaded the cabinet to respond positively to de Valera and Irish opinion. In what was his last major political initiative, he introduced a memorandum on Tuesday 25 June summarizing MacDonald's report. Chamberlain acknowledged that de Valera's views on the war seemed clear, but this did not seem to be the case with all members of the Irish cabinet. He also recognized that the very reason the British were now promoting a new initiative was also the reason the Irish cabinet was less likely to agree to it. The enhanced power of Germany and the perceived weakness of Britain, as outlined by Walshe for de Valera, made the Irish extremely cautious. However, Chamberlain recommended that the British test the possibility that some members of de Valera's government might consider an end to neutrality if a British offer was sufficiently generous. He remained concerned that the Irish government underestimated the threat of invasion and now proposed a six-point plan which MacDonald would put to de Valera as the considered offer of the war cabinet. This plan incorporated much of what MacDonald had been discussing with de Valera and was Chamberlain's attempt to break the logjam:

1. A declaration to be issued by the United Kingdom Government forthwith accepting the principle of a United Ireland.
2. A joint body including representatives of the Government of Eire and the Government of Northern Ireland to be set up at once to work out the constitutional and other practical details of the Union of Ireland. The United Kingdom government to give such assistance towards the work of this body as might be desired.
3. Joint Defence Council representative of Eire and Northern Ireland to be set up immediately.
4. Eire to enter the war on the side of the United Kingdom and her allies forthwith, and, for the purposes of the Defence of Eire, the Government of Eire to invite British naval vessels to have the use of ports in Eire and British troops and aeroplanes to co-operate with the Eire forces and to be stationed in such positions in Eire as may be agreed between the two Governments.
5. The Government of Eire to intern all German and Italian aliens in the country and to take any further steps necessary to suppress Fifth Column activities.
6. The United Kingdom to provide military equipment at once to the Government of Eire.

Clause 6 referred to an extensive appendix listing the armaments that would be made available for the defence of Eire if de Valera's government agreed to change policy. These included the anti-aircraft batteries that de Valera badly needed, but also anti-tank weapons as well as aircraft for the Irish air force. Quite tellingly, Chamberlain told the cabinet that:

> If that reply [from de Valera] be favourable I do not believe that the Ulster Government would refuse to play a part in bringing about so favourable a development.

Chamberlain knew that the real hurdle was de Valera. He thought that the most likely response would be negative, advising his colleagues that if this was the case he had no further suggestions to make in respect of Ireland.[44]

When MacDonald returned to Dublin on Wednesday 26 June he had a clear set of proposals and the authority of the British cabinet to negotiate with de Valera. However, though the discussions went on for two and a half hours, the prospects for success were not good, as he quickly learned. It is clear from de Valera's general discussion with MacDonald that the briefs that Walshe had prepared for him over the weekend had had their effect. At one stage his words were almost identical to those used by Walshe. The taoiseach now insisted that 'there was no limit to their [German] capacity to produce', insisting that Britain 'could not destroy this colossal machine'. While this specific exchange came at the end of the meeting, the attitude permeated the entire conversation. De Valera's attitude was less forthcoming and more pessimistic than it had been on the previous Friday, a consequence of Walshe's memorandums but also due to the conversations de Valera had had with his colleagues.

In the circumstances MacDonald had a difficult if not impossible task, but he returned again and again to the loss of Ireland's freedom if Germany invaded and if Britain lost the war. When MacDonald introduced Chamberlain's six-point plan, he argued that it was an attempt to meet de Valera's objections and persuade nationalist opinion of Britain's good intentions. He insisted that entering the war on these conditions meant that the Irish would be fighting for the freedom of Ireland. This would provide a strong moral appeal to de Valera's supporters and would probably neutralize the possibility of invasion in any case as German success could not longer be guaranteed. If de Valera was not prepared to accept this offer, MacDonald warned that the 'opportunity might never present itself again'. Furthermore, 'After the war we in Great Britain would not be in the least interested in encouraging the establishment of a united Ireland, if during our time of difficulty Eire had stood aside whilst Ulster had fought with us.' As anticipated by Chamberlain, de Valera rejected the proposals on the ostensible grounds that a united Ireland would not be guaranteed by the British.

MacDonald went to considerable lengths to convince de Valera that Britain was seriously committed to ending partition if the plan was accepted, but to no avail. De Valera called the offer of a united Ireland a 'deferred payment' that fell well short of what 'his people' could accept. MacDonald highlighted the interim steps that would be taken to give effect to the plan, emphasizing the positive role that Britain would play in delivering Irish unity. But de Valera would only accept 'the setting up of a united Ireland at once' and entirely on his terms. He then suggested that 'some far more impressive demonstration of the impending change was desirable', sketching out a plan where the two Irish parliaments would be merged into one with sovereign powers to legislate on 'matters of common concern for the whole of Ireland'. It is difficult to know if de Valera was simply probing here or if it was a genuine attempt to see how far MacDonald would go. MacDonald indicated that he thought such a proposal could be included in the negotiations and certainly would not be ruled out in advance. As if alarmed by this response, de Valera quickly turned away from this line of thought and stated emphatically that the best outcome would be for Northern Ireland to become part of a neutral united Ireland under the existing constitution. De Valera then focused on other objections to the scheme, including his entirely realistic fear that Germany would 'punish' the Irish for ending their neutrality. MacDonald countered these and other objections, but agreement could not be reached. The parties agreed to meet again the following day after de Valera had circulated the proposals to the cabinet. MacDonald attributed de Valera's reluctance to reach an agreement to the Irish leader's belief that Britain would lose the war.[45] MacDonald then telegraphed London to enquire if it was possible to compromise on the demand that Eire should declare war, if a method be found short of this to allow the British into the ports and airfields. MacDonald was sanguine as to the outcome:

Fact that de Valera is making counter-suggestions is a measure of his temptation. I do not think situation is hopeless though odds are still heavily against affirmative reply to our plan. Prospects of success are being deeply influenced by de Valera's inclination to think that we are definitely losing war and if you send me any morsels of encouragement about the fate of the French fleet this will have beneficial effect.

The following morning Chamberlain replied that Britain was prepared to compromise on the issue of declaring war if that helped the negotiations, adding that MacDonald 'can certainly assure Mr de Valera that if his Government is prepared to accept the plan, our acceptance of the principle of a United Ireland is regarded by us as a pledge which we are bound honourably to fulfil'. While the assent of the Northern Ireland government would be required, 'we should do our best to obtain this and do not doubt our success'. At the same time Eden was mobilizing American support, reporting to the war cabinet that the American ambassador Joseph Kennedy was going to ask Roosevelt to bring pressure on de Valera to agree to the proposals. Likewise, Kennedy was going to contact the president to mobilize Gray in Dublin to support the initiative.[46]

MacDonald had hoped that he could discuss the proposals with de Valera's cabinet colleagues before the measure was placed before the Irish government. However, de Valera pre-empted this by holding a cabinet meeting and rejecting the offer prior to meeting MacDonald for lunch on Thursday 27 June. Frank Aiken and Seán Lemass accompanied the taoiseach to the meeting with MacDonald. De Valera chose Aiken and Lemass because they represented different viewpoints within the cabinet. In the conversation that followed, MacDonald's fears were realized. He concluded that de Valera had not put the proposal to the cabinet with the force that MacDonald had shown the previous evening. An alternative but not incompatible interpretation is that de Valera simply imposed his will on the cabinet, having made up his mind in advance. Later in life, Lemass described what it was like to be in the cabinet room with de Valera:

> He relied upon the force of physical exhaustion to get agreement. In other words he'd never let a cabinet debate on any subject end with a vote of ministers. He always wanted to get unanimity and he sought this unanimity by the simple process of keeping the debate going – often till the small hours of the morning, until those who were in the minority, out of sheer exhaustion, conceded the case made by the majority. This technique was quite effective in his case.[47]

Despite this setback, MacDonald attempted to persuade Lemass that there was more to the proposals than de Valera might have led the cabinet to believe. He recognized that Aiken was the more doctrinaire nationalist and that Lemass might be more appreciative of both the British position and the implications of the offer. Although he reiterated the British commitment to a united Ireland once the plan was accepted, MacDonald could not sway Lemass, who accepted British assurances but said that their own supporters could not be convinced that a united Ireland would actually result. MacDonald asked his Irish counterparts to acknowledge that practical difficulties would prevent an immediate united Ireland, but that the plan set the process in motion. He urged them to consider this as an opportunity, adding that the British government would, if the Irish wished, put forward an amendment to bring into effect de Valera's suggestion that the two parliaments be merged. MacDonald emphatically stated that 'the establishment of a united Ireland was an integral part of our plan, from which there would be no turning back'. These comments seemed to impress even Aiken, who now engaged actively with MacDonald. But if Aiken ever intended to change his mind on this issue, the temptation did not last long and he quickly returned to de Valera's position that the only acceptable solution was a neutral united Ireland. As on previous occasions, MacDonald rejected this view as unrealistic. Lemass then asked if it was absolutely necessary for Ireland to enter the war to meet British requirements. MacDonald had been authorized to compromise on this, and replied that this would not be necessary if facilities were made available to Britain to defend Ireland. In this scenario Ireland would not declare war, but British troops would be stationed in Ireland at the invitation of the Irish government. This may have been unrealistic as well, but Lemass seemed intent on pursuing the issue. However, de Valera intervened to stop the line of discussion by claiming that in effect Ireland would be at war if British troops entered the country. De Valera also asked what guarantees the British could provide that Northern Ireland would accept a united Ireland, if they would not coerce them:

I said that we certainly would not coerce Northern Ireland. We would not and could not march troops into the six counties to force a policy upon their government. But if the Eire Government accepted the plan, we hoped to be able to persuade the Northern Ireland Government also to accept it, and we felt that present circumstances offered a very good chance of such an agreement being reached.

Neither Aiken nor de Valera was prepared to accept these assurances, though it is not clear what Lemass's position was. Aiken then responded by recommending that the British tell the government of

Northern Ireland that it was in the best interests of Britain's security that they join with the south in a united neutral state. MacDonald, who expressed his views with some heat at this stage, emphatically rejected this view. Aiken then implied that the British were lucky that they had handed over the ports in 1938, remarking that if that had not been the case Ireland would have been in the war but against Britain in order to secure them. He suggested the most that Britain could expect was 'friendly neutrality' on the part of the Irish. Finally, in a last effort to save the talks, MacDonald asked the Irish delegation not to reject the offer, offering to amend the existing proposals in the light of the discussion.[48]

*

Chamberlain had said earlier in the week that the six-point plan was the last initiative he was prepared to make and he now confided to his diary, 'the de Valera people are afraid we are going to lose, and don't want to be involved with us'. Despite this pessimistic assessment of the outcome of the negotiations, he drafted a further letter for de Valera that attempted to meet Irish objections raised at the meetings. The letter went further than before, stretching to the limit what the British were prepared to concede. Following a further cabinet meeting on 28 June it was agreed to amend the original offer and this was incorporated into Chamberlain's letter to de Valera. Chamberlain tried to allay de Valera's doubts in respect of Northern Ireland: 'I cannot, of course, give a guarantee that Northern Ireland will assent, but if the plan is acceptable to Eire we should do our best to persuade Northern Ireland to accept it also in the interests of the security of the whole island.' Furthermore, a number of the clauses in the original proposal were amended:

1. A declaration to be made by the United Kingdom Government forthwith accepting the principle of a United Ireland. This declaration would take the form of a solemn undertaking that the Union is to become at an early date an accomplished fact from which there shall be no turning back.
2. A joint body, including representatives of the Government of Eire and the Government of Northern Ireland, to be set up at once to work out the constitutional and other practical details

of the Union of Ireland. The United Kingdom government to
give such assistance towards the work of this body as might be
desired, the purpose of the work being to establish at as early a
date as possible the whole machinery of the Union.

Chamberlain also tried to anticipate any objection that these changes
would not be enough to secure nationalist support for the proposals
and assured de Valera that his suggestion to merge the two parliaments at an early stage would be given 'immediate consideration with
every desire to reach an arrangement satisfactory to all the parties
concerned'. Perhaps most importantly the British government was
also prepared to forego Irish participation in the war and amended
clause 4 accordingly:

4. The Government of Eire to invite British naval vessels to have
   the use of ports in Eire, and British troops and aeroplanes to
   co-operate with the Eire forces and to be stationed in such
   positions in Eire as may be agreed between the two
   Governments, for the purpose of increasing the security of
   Eire against the fate which has overcome neutral Norway,
   Denmark, Holland, Belgium and Luxembourg.

Despite these changes de Valera's reply on 4 July effectively ended
the British government's search for a solution to the Irish problem in
the context of the war. De Valera's letter reprised previous objections
to the British plan, emphasizing in particular the view that Unionists
could at any time undermine the process towards unification. Moreover, de Valera offered no alternatives to the Chamberlain proposals,
while he went on to insist that 'our present Constitution represents
the limit to which we believe our people are prepared to go to meet
the sentiments of the Northern Unionists'. He also reiterated his view
that a neutral Ireland (north and south) was the only solution. Chamberlain informed the cabinet that the negotiations were now over and
wrote to his sister:

The real basic fact is that it is not partition which stands in the way
at this moment but the fear of Dev [*sic*] and his friends that we
shall be beaten. They don't want to be on the losing side and if

that is unheroic one can only say that it is very much the attitude of the world from the USA to Roumania and from Japan to Ireland.

*

Thus ended the last serious attempt to unify Ireland in the twentieth century. It may not have been a feasible solution but it did represent an opportunity for substantial change. It also marked the effective end of Chamberlain's career, and he died later in the year. However it is a testament to the individual that he was prepared to expend such time and energy in an attempt to achieve a solution that might have addressed both British and Irish needs at a time of crisis for British society.[49]

*

In 1937 Walshe had told a British counterpart that de Valera 'would do almost anything to realise the ideal of a united Ireland' but, as we have seen, when MacDonald brought such an offer to Dublin in June 1940 de Valera rejected it after days of discussion. But could the result have been different if de Valera had continued to negotiate with Britain into July? We know that the British proposal was rejected and the tendency is to conclude that this was probably the only outcome possible in the circumstances. Was this a missed opportunity for a united Ireland or a rational response from de Valera and his government? There is evidence to support both points of view. A major concern for Walshe and de Valera was that they believed Britain would be defeated, as did even pro-British elements in Ireland. Supporting the British at this stage was certainly a risk, but then the prize was a significant one and it was not to be expected that it could be obtained without some sacrifice on Ireland's part. There was also the question of whether the British could actually have delivered Irish unity even if there had been an agreement between the two states.

The balance of probability is that the British government sincerely wanted an agreement with de Valera in 1940, and indeed later. It is also likely that they would have gone to considerable lengths to achieve this. Churchill was willing to negotiate a union of Britain and France in 1940 to keep the French in the war, a radical and desperate proposal born out of crisis. In these circumstances, the offer to de Valera was clearly genuine and British willingness to negotiate on the matter and respond to Irish fears and suggestions provides further evidence for this. The amended British offer may have been disingenuous in stating that Eire would not have to enter the war but was a clear indication that Britain was flexible. It is difficult to judge how far Britain would have gone if the negotiations had continued into July 1940, but it is important to recall that they remained conciliatory with the Irish until towards the end of 1940. It is possible that a more positive and nuanced negotiating strategy on Eire's part in July and August 1940 would have achieved considerably more, though this suggestion is speculative. Long after the end of the discussions British officials were insistent that the cabinet was committed to an agreement that would secure unity. Ernest Bevin insisted during a meeting with Dulanty in 1942 that he had been instrumental in including an 'absolute guarantee for a United Ireland' as part of the proposed agreement. Bevin also said that Churchill strongly favoured a united Ireland and had told him that he would do anything short of 'using physical force to compel these people [Unionists] to take a course against their will'. Churchill himself had told Dulanty in 1941 that he was in favour of Irish unity and had always been so. He also said, 'What chance was there now when their friends in the North of Ireland were fighting with them and we were standing aside. He was afraid we were perpetuating partition.'[50]

A more serious challenge to the notion that 1940 represents a missed opportunity was the attitude of Ulster Unionists. Craigavon would have resisted any attempt to change the status quo and would undoubtedly have had considerable support for such a position. However, he was dying in 1940 and Unionism was in some disarray. Brian Barton has suggested that some Unionists would have accepted a negotiated settlement with de Valera if that had brought Irish participation in the war. It would have been difficult for Craigavon to oppose an agreement between Britain and Ireland in wartime if this had been promoted as part of a defensive strategy against Germany. At the very least it would have split Unionism as some in Northern Ireland would have placed loyalty to Britain above their attachment to the six counties in such a crisis. However, even figures more sympathetic to the British position in Dublin such as Lemass were concerned that Britain could not guarantee unity and this was of course true. But this is to assume that all factors remain constant. An agreement between Britain and Ireland would have changed everything and placed immeasurable pressure on Northern Ireland. Though Churchill was not prepared to send troops in to force the Unionists to comply, this did not exhaust the British government's options. Opinion in Britain would have been unsympathetic to Unionism and its many failures could have been highlighted. Unionists would have been faced with a divided community at home and pressure from the British and Irish governments plus President Roosevelt to accept a negotiated settlement. Moreover Craigavon did not control a state, but was the leader of a devolved government within the United Kingdom with a questionable civil rights record. De Valera on the other hand was the head of an established state within the commonwealth and could draw on considerable political and diplomatic resources to promote his position.

But even if Unionist objections had been overcome, would public opinion in Eire have abandoned neutrality in exchange for the possibility of achieving unity? De Valera put forward two arguments against changing Irish policy. The first was that it would lead to serious instability in Eire, the second that Germany would attack the country as a result. Richard Mulcahy estimated in July 1940 that if de Valera and Cosgrave opted to end neutrality about one third of the population would be opposed. He thought that Fianna Fáil would divide on the issue, with Aiken, Traynor and some backbenchers refusing to accept de Valera's change of policy.[51] But as with Northern Ireland this argument assumes that all factors remain constant. Policy change during a crisis brings opportunities as well as instability and threats. A split in Fianna Fáil cannot be discounted but might well have been contained if an agreement had been shown to be generous and the outcome portrayed in a positive light. De Valera could have used his considerable influence to persuade his followers that this was the right path to take. The Irish government controlled the media and this would have enabled them to place a very positive gloss on any agreement. The IRA was on the defensive at the time and it is unlikely that the Irish army or the Garda would have revolted on the issue. If an agreement had had Roosevelt's endorsement, which in all likelihood it would, this would have been particularly influential. This is not to say there would not have been dissent, but it is to suggest that the options available to the Irish government in the summer of 1940 were considerably greater than is sometimes thought. De Valera had certainly missed an opportunity to forge a new relationship with Britain and Northern Ireland, one that need not necessarily have entailed Eire entering the war.

5. NEUTRALITY IN PERILOUS TIMES: MAY 1940 TO JUNE 1941

As the strategic position deteriorated for Britain in the spring of 1940, Eire's importance was enhanced. The attention was not welcome to de Valera's government, as comment frequently focused on the negative impact of neutrality on Britain's war effort. The *Daily Mirror* was seized and banned in April when it published a cartoon suggesting that the German legation in Dublin could be used as a listening post. George Orwell noted in his diary a little later that the use of Ireland as a back door into Britain had not been appreciated prior to this, but should have been obvious.[1] The arrest of Stephen Held in May had exposed the links between German intelligence and the IRA, and Irish intelligence also expressed concern that former Blueshirt leader Eoin O'Duffy and successful businessman and former government minister J. J. Walsh would form a pro-German collaborationist alliance with the IRA. This was taken seriously because Walsh and O'Duffy had contacts which would allow them 'to influence a number of people even in State service'. Germany's military successes in May and June lessened any possibility that de Valera would reach a political agreement with Britain, but also provided a stimulus for anti-British sentiment in Eire. Nor was all the attention concentrated on potential German collaborators; concern was expressed about pro-British figures such as James Dillon TD and Senator Frank McDermott, though there is no suggestion that they were involved in sedition.[2]

De Valera appreciated the seriousness of the situation. Frank Gallagher recounts a visit to de Valera during which he received news that a parachutist had landed in County Clare. De Valera responded immediately, 'Tell Maffey at once,' and put down the phone. Gallagher remonstrated with de Valera: 'You're a nice Republican: a parachutist lands and the first person you tell is the British Minister.' De Valera went very serious, asking his information director who was endangered by such a landing. The rationale offered by de Valera was persuasive: 'We must play an absolutely straight game or we will never come through this war alive. I have promised I will not allow this territory to be used as the base for an attack on Britain and I will fulfil my word fully. That parachutist did not come to harm us but the British.'[3]

While the main threat to Irish neutrality came from Germany in the summer of 1940, the Irish authorities had to act cautiously towards Britain. In July Churchill received a report that German nationals were purchasing property in Eire to prepare landing sites for an invasion. Churchill wanted the matter discussed at cabinet, but the potential crisis was defused when Maffey reported that the claims were ill-founded. Incidents such as this explain de Valera's fears, but also underline the continuing importance of Maffey in Dublin.[4] Reports from Maffey and other reliable sources had a greater impact on official British thinking than sensational stories. Thus it quickly emerged that the German and Italian communities in Eire were small and indeed not all fascists. Exaggerated reports of U-boats refuelling in the west of Ireland were challenged, while Irish efforts to protect the country and decommission airfields had a decisive impact on British official attitudes. This is not to say that reports became totally reliable – some were clearly highly exaggerated or products of fantasy – but in the main Churchill received reliable information from the best of these reports.[5] Irish behaviour persuaded the British that their neutrality was real and would be protected. Maffey put it succinctly: 'public opinion here became firmly wedded to the policy of neutrality and whatever individual politicians may have thought here and there no government, and no party, could get the country to abandon neutrality against the present background'.[6] Military intelligence and the police closely monitored members of the German legation, though this could lead to unfortunate results. One young woman and her husband were placed under surveillance when she telephoned a friend who was visiting the flat of one of the German legation's staff.[7]

De Valera complained to Maffey that relations between the two states had deteriorated as Britain's difficulties increased. He alleged that there was an orchestrated campaign in the British and American press to obtain air and naval facilities in Eire. The censors were hard at work dealing with these reports, some of which were malicious but others simply critical of Irish neutrality.[8] Walshe also pressed Maffey on the changing atmosphere, attributing much of it to Churchill. He told Maffey that there was a widespread view that Churchill hated independent Ireland and wanted to 'set the clock back with a strong hand'. The atmosphere was worsened by the arrest of a number of British agents in Eire between May and July. Walshe complained that the Irish government had been 'open and frank' with Maffey, but that these incidents jeopardized the existing cooperation. The Irish government was now concerned that these intrusions were a prelude to military intervention, one result of which was that staff talks between the British and Irish military were now 'hedged about with mental reservations' on the part of the Irish authorities.[9] Whether the intrusions were part of a concerted plan or a consequence of overenthusiasm on the part of the military in Northern Ireland, it is still difficult to say. However, an element of probing the south was to be expected, if nevertheless unwelcome to the Irish authorities. In response to Irish protests, such activities were stopped – according to its official history, MI5 did not employ 'trained agents' in Eire during the war. Britain and Ireland cooperated closely on security matters after this, which controlled 'rogue' elements, satisfied the Irish and provided Britain with detailed information on most but not all occasions. In addition, British intelligence agreed to share its information with the military to obviate the need for it to collect its own in Eire.[10]

The Irish also had continuing difficulties with the Germans. The German navy landed three agents on the west coast of Ireland. They had £900 in English banknotes, detonators and various explosives. Unfortunately for the agents they were fairly conspicuous on the isolated roads of West Cork; it did not help that one of them was an Indian and the other two South African. They boarded a bus for Cork city, but were soon arrested, quickly tried and sentenced.[11] Other agents were more successful, causing considerable difficulties for the Irish security forces and some strains in Anglo-Irish relations.

While German success had altered Irish opinion and narrowed the political possibilities for Britain there, Maffey concluded that a German attack was unlikely due to undertakings given by de Valera to Hempel in respect of neutrality. What was not clear to Maffey in July was what Britain wanted from de Valera. He asked if the ports were still required, because if this was not the case then 'we need not worry about Mr de Valera and his neutrality provided we could secure a neutrality of a reasonably benevolent character'. Maffey was also critical of some aspects of the MacDonald negotiations, maintaining that Britain had been prepared to change policy radically for relatively little in return from Eire. The implication was that the British would have given away far more than was required for what they would gain in the event of a German invasion, especially as they would get it anyhow if this occurred. Despite this reservation, Maffey continued to believe that Northern Ireland was the key to future relations, but now thought that the unity offer had come too late to have any political impact. He speculated that opinion might move against de Valera if what had been on offer became widely known. This was unlikely as Aiken, who was the main opponent of any concessions, controlled censorship and chaired the Defence Conference, and was not going to permit any publication on this or related matters. Aiken was so effective that Cosgrave did not wish to hear the terms of the offer from Maffey, despite being in favour of a change of policy. Cosgrave's deputy Mulcahy complained at the limitations imposed by Aiken on the Defence Conference, alleging that the government was using it as a means to persuade the country that the main political parties were united behind its policies. Mulcahy further complained that the proceedings were so narrowly framed by Aiken that discussion on the most serious issues was effectively ruled out.[12]

Sir Eric Machtig wrote to Maffey immediately after the failure of the MacDonald initiative emphasizing the importance of Eire in British considerations:

The danger of an invasion of Eire is regarded as so serious, not merely from the Eire point of view but also from our own, that the government here were prepared to go to the lengths which they have in order to try and create a situation in which they could be reasonably confident of resisting or overcoming any such attempt. In other words while we have always agreed with you in thinking that a Union of the North and South with the consent of both parties was an ideal to be aimed at, it was not until the last phase of the war that we were prepared to face the risk of exercising sufficient pressure to afford a chance of this being achieved.

Despite these concerns, Britain was now reluctant to arm Eire, as there was a fear that in the event of an invasion the Irish army would collapse and Germany would obtain a significant supply of British armaments to use in the invasion of the neighbouring island. Machtig acknowledged the importance of Irish neutrality for de Valera's government, but wanted it to be flexible enough to allow British armed forces into the country before an invasion.[13] This was unrealistic, as the MacDonald talks had shown. Maffey complained, 'it is the old story, to offer nothing until we are in the soup and when we are in the soup what we have to offer is not attractive'.[14] Just two weeks later, Maffey reported a 'subtle and progressive change in the general and political atmosphere here'. He was concerned at the shift in Irish opinion, which was now more sceptical of Britain's chances of winning the war and increasingly pro-German. Maffey admitted that 'during the last three weeks opinion here has swung steadily over to the view that we are now the probable aggressors', a view shared, he conceded, by many of Britain's friends in Ireland. The fall of France was the catalyst for this change of opinion, consolidating the Irish commitment to neutrality as well as mobilizing support for the Fianna Fáil government. Maffey now also concluded that in the face of German victory no party or individual would openly oppose neutrality or advocate that Ireland abandon it.[15]

Fine Gael remained the party most sympathetic to the British in Eire, but its leadership was reluctant to oppose de Valera, believing that its own members had embraced neutrality as the best policy. On 9 July Cosgrave wrote to de Valera. It was said that Cosgrave and de Valera disliked one another; they never met socially or formally, even though they were the leaders of the two largest political parties in the state.[16] Cosgrave was uneasy about Eire's position, warning that if an invasion took place within the following month the country was defenceless. In contrast to the position adopted by the government, the primary issue for Cosgrave was not neutrality or belligerence but how to secure national security. Cosgrave painted a horrendous picture of the impact of an invasion on Ireland. He urged de Valera to consider the possibility of inviting in outside support 'before immense damage to person, life, property and morale has been done'. It is clear Cosgrave believed the only invasion that might occur would be a German one: 'we share the Government's view that a hostile invasion by Britain is not contemplated'. Cosgrave's fear was that if a German force did land and the Irish army was not capable of repelling it without British assistance, then Ireland would become a battlefield between the two belligerents with the most severe consequences for the country. This issue was a military one, but he urged de Valera to reconsider how to achieve the best balance in terms of policy. There was a political decision to be made, a difficult one, Cosgrave admitted, 'between adhering to neutrality for too long a period or on the other hand abandoning neutrality too soon'. Cosgrave accepted that any change to Ireland's neutral status could only occur in a context where national unity was maintained and the new policy was supported by the mass of the people. These conditions, he conceded, were not present when Britain made the offer on unity. Cosgrave wanted the all-party Defence Conference to discuss policy matters, not simply day-to-day detail, which had been the case up to then. The government continued to decide all policy issues, while the opposition effectively had a role only in implementation. This was not only unsatisfactory for the opposition but, Cosgrave complained, it also did not address the urgency of the present situation. It is clear from Cosgrave's letter that he believed the opposition was being excluded from policymaking in the most important areas: 'if proposals have been made from any other Government on defence matters, absence of knowledge of these proposals makes the discussion of defence measures unreal'. Cosgrave was echoing his colleagues' frustration at the operation of the Defence Conference, where Fine Gael members had his full confidence. He added that his party had already given assurances to members of the government on 2 July that Fine Gael would give full support to any change of policy in respect of neutrality. This, he suggested, demonstrated the goodwill of his party and himself.[17]

There is a note of irritation in Cosgrave's letter. He clearly felt that the opposition did not have the ability to make informed decisions on the important strategic and defensive issues facing the country. He further told de Valera that the future of political parties and indeed of politics itself was of little importance when the leaders of the parties were asking young men to risk their lives to defend the country. A new approach was required. De Valera did not reply to Cosgrave until 13 July, having discussed his suggestions with his cabinet colleagues.

More importantly, Walshe provided de Valera with a detailed memorandum on the 11th, making a trenchant argument as to why Ireland
should not give up neutrality. Walshe admitted that there was a
possibility that Germany would invade, but insisted that this was not
an adequate reason for abandoning neutrality. He realistically pointed
out that an invasion would be a fairly hazardous undertaking for the
Germans. In any event, he confidently predicted, in contrast to Cosgrave, that the Irish defence forces 'at least with the help of the British
Army' would quickly neutralize such an attack. Walshe also identified
but probably exaggerated the impact of a German invasion on American opinion. He concluded that Hitler would be sensitive to this and
would seek to avoid American intervention in Ireland. These were
reasonable counters to Cosgrave's concerns – he would probably have
accepted them – representing as they also did the views of the Irish
military at this time. However, Walshe also challenged Cosgrave's view
of neutrality and Ireland's relationship with the world:

> Neutrality was not entered upon for the purpose of being used as
> a bargaining factor. It represented and does represent, the funda-
> mental attitude of the entire people. It is just as much a part of the
> national position as the desire to remain Irish, and we can no more
> abandon it than we can renounce everything that constitutes our
> national distinctiveness. If either party invades us, we are then
> going to fight to defend our integral national life against an enemy
> who wishes to destroy its essential character in time of war. In
> defending our neutrality against an invader by force of arms, we
> are not giving it up – quite the contrary.

Neutrality is seen as a core attribute of Irish national identity, a central
value associated with nationalism.

But there was also a practical application for this ideology. Walshe
insisted that remaining neutral confers certain rights on a state, even
if it is later invaded and overrun, as was the case with Belgium or the
Netherlands. In a revelatory assessment, Walshe dismissed the British
view that Germany wanted to dominate Europe: 'The fact that
Germany regarded these territories as essential to her for waging war
against England and France does not necessarily mean that they are
to be incorporated ultimately into the German State.' Walshe argued
that these neutral countries, though occupied, would retain a status

and sympathy in world politics not available to a state that had given up neutrality prior to invasion. Ireland would lose goodwill and sympathy – especially in America, he believed – if it now entered into an alliance with Britain against Germany. There was also a cynical aspect to this. If Britain won the war, relations would inevitably return to normal; but if Germany won, forgoing neutrality now would lead to complete loss of independence later. Walshe also concluded that Britain was facing defeat and that some sections of its elite must be seeking terms with Germany. At the heart of Walshe's memorandum was the belief that Churchill wanted to keep Ireland weak, because a strong Ireland would endanger Britain. The obverse of this, which Walshe seemed to endorse, was that a strong Ireland would strengthen Europe (or Germany?) against Britain. In this context, Walshe argued it would be politically and strategically mistaken to abandon neutrality: 'England is already conquered. That is also an elementary fact for everyone who has not allowed himself to be overcome by Britain's belief in her permanent invincibility.' Walshe asserted that defeat on the continent had undermined Britain's strength, a situation that American aid and support could not alter, he maintained. Walshe predicted that America would soon withhold its support from Britain and that Italy's involvement and Spain's virtual participation would effectively destroy the British capacity to resist Germany or retain its military power. Accordingly, Europe 'will bow to fate when they see Britain abandoned by all her former adherents, and Germany will have willing populations to aid her in her schemes for a new Europe'. Walshe was also dismissive of 'some priests who have no world Church outlook and, overcome by hatred for the passing phenomenon of Nazism, say we are bound to join the fight against Germany'. Walshe rejected their argument by pointing out that the pope did not seem to share these views. For the Irish government, especially Walshe, the role of the Vatican and its neutrality remained a model to be emulated.[18]

De Valera's reply to Cosgrave, though without the material on Britain's defeat, owed a lot to Walshe. The taoiseach accepted that there was little difference between himself and Cosgrave on the grave threat to Ireland. Where they did differ was that the government rejected the view that military assistance should be agreed prior to an attack. This would be the same as taking sides, and Walshe had warned de Valera of the consequences of this. The government continued to believe that the best way to preserve neutrality was to take whatever steps were necessary to avoid either side intervening in Ireland. However, de Valera went further than this and rejected Cosgrave's claim that the threat was only from Germany: 'the assumption that hostile invasion need be feared from one side only is one which cannot in all circumstances be relied upon'. De Valera endorsed Walshe's view that remaining neutral was the best policy for avoiding attack, whereas inviting assistance from Britain would lead to immediate involvement in the war. De Valera also shared Walshe's view that remaining neutral placed Ireland in a better negotiating position once the war was over. In a more conciliatory vein, de Valera showed willingness to be more forthcoming with the opposition in the Defence Conference. He was also now prepared to arrange discussions in addition to the conference for representatives of Fine Gael and Labour. However, he made it clear that policy matters would remain within the remit of the government. This must have been disappointing for Cosgrave, who in his reply did not engage further in argument about neutrality. He reiterated the view that if the government decided to change policy, then Fine Gael was prepared to support such a change. Cosgrave also agreed to make arrangements for further discussions between the government and the opposition on defence.[19]

Nothing came of de Valera's promises. The Defence Conference continued to do useful work on detail, but Aiken refused to extend its remit beyond this. By November, Cosgrave was frustrated with the government's refusal to share information with the opposition or to include him in defence policy deliberations. He complained, 'we have felt it our duty to refrain from all criticism of the government's foreign policy and to give assistance as was in our power to improve our defence measures' on the grounds that public divisions on these crucial issues would invite outsiders to engage in adventures in the country. Cosgrave continued to agree that national policy should be aimed at avoiding reconquest by Britain or, if Britain lost the war, occupation by Germany. Despite this active support for the government, Cosgrave maintained that it was not clear what policy the opposition was supporting. He questioned whether the government itself had a clear conception of the danger or was adequately prepared for it, and was left in the dark by the government on whether either

Britain or Germany now posed a real threat, especially in November after Churchill's bitter speech criticizing Eire for refusing to provide port facilities to Britain. As he put it, somewhat in despair, 'Neither my colleagues in the front bench nor I have any information regarding the problems likely to arise or what measures have been taken or are under consideration for dealing with them.'

Fine Gael had publicly stated that it was prepared to accept responsibility for government policy if it were communicated to them, yet de Valera's reply to Churchill in November on the ports had been sent to the press without any consultation with the opposition and prior to them receiving a copy of it. Cosgrave recognized that he could not publicly state that no consultation had taken place, as this would undermine national unity and morale and show up divisions within the country. Yet, 'it is clearly impossible for us to accept the position in which we must say ditto to a statement which we have never seen or about the background of which we know nothing'.[20] De Valera and Fianna Fáil had effectively boxed in Cosgrave and Fine Gael by this stage. The government was not prepared to concede any influence over policy to the opposition, in part because it believed it had the monopoly on policymaking, but also because Fianna Fáil did not trust Fine Gael, who they continued to identify with pro-British sentiment in Ireland. The opposition had only two alternatives: 'say ditto' or openly challenge the government on policy and take the consequences. Fine Gael took the first option, though in doing so it provoked James Dillon to take his stand against neutrality the following year. Mulcahy told Maffey that the government was unwilling to conduct an open dialogue with the opposition and attributed the widespread support for neutrality, even among ex-Unionists, to the feared consequences if Ireland entered the war.[21]

None of these disagreements appeared in public. What did appear, much to the annoyance of the Irish government, was a report that a military pact had been agreed with Britain. Walshe believed that the Ministry of Information, which he claimed had a strong anti-Irish bias within it, was placing this and other press reports in the media.[22] By mid-July 1940 many in Fine Gael, including Cosgrave, feared that the British were creating the political conditions in Britain for an invasion of Ireland. On the 17th Maffey had a difficult meeting with de Valera, who complained that public discussion of the rumoured military pact was causing great harm. According to Maffey, de Valera 'begged that our military and staff liaison should be kept as secret as possible. This was in our best interests.'[23] De Valera also told Maffey that Ireland's defence strategy had previously assumed a British attack, but in September 1939 that policy had been changed and the focus for defence concentrated on a possible German invasion. However, de Valera had recently held a meeting with his military staff at which he had cautioned them to include the possibility of a British attack as well as a German one. The assumption among many Irish nationalists was that if Britain wanted something badly enough, it would take it, especially in the context of the threat from Germany in July 1940. Churchill's reactionary cousin Lord Londonderry certainly advocated taking the ports in defiance of Irish opinion, though this was an increasingly unrepresentative view, even among the Irish aristocracy.[24] The dominions secretary, Lord Caldecote, replied to Londonderry, emphasizing the various initiatives taken by the British government to persuade Ireland to become involved in the war. The best that could be expected, he cautioned, would be close cooperation if the Germans invaded Ireland. Caldecote rejected the call to invade Ireland, advising Londonderry that the vast majority in Eire not only supported neutrality but would oppose the British, and continuing:

> Obviously we could not likely undertake the conduct of another war in Ireland at the present time. It may be that circumstances will arise in which no other course is open to us, and that we may have to choose what, at the time, appears to be the lesser of two evils. But anyone who remembers the extraordinary difficulties experienced in military operations in 1920 and 1921 and who considers the extremely bad effect on relations with the United States which such a step would have, must necessarily hesitate before recommending that such an extreme step should be taken.

Nor did Churchill accept his cousin's implied criticism of government policy. The prime minister noted that Ireland was being closely watched and the government would respond as necessary.[25] In response to a memorandum circulated from the prime minister's office, the War Office replied in late July, 'I think there is little doubt that the policy will be not to jump in until we are asked to do so.'[26] While this does not provide definite proof that the British were not going to invade, it indicates that both the Dominions Office and the War Office recognized the difficulties if they did so. It is also important not to neglect other influences on Churchill. Shane Leslie, also a relative of Churchill, visited the prime minister at various times during the war. Leslie was sensitive to Irish neutrality but not uncritical of Ireland's stance and in his conversations with Churchill would have given him a more balanced account of opinion in Ireland.[27]

In Dublin Maffey was anxious to maintain good relations with de Valera and his cabinet; indeed he argued forcefully that the Ministry of Information in London and the Dominions Office should 'soft pedal' on Ireland. He highlighted the alarmist articles in newspapers and the rumours that circulated in London and elsewhere concerning Ireland and hinted that many of these were mere prejudice and did not help his job in Dublin. He complained bitterly that the situation could 'get out of focus, due to these rumours' and that military attachés recently appointed to his office were responsible for both alarmist and inaccurate reporting. One such report merited a disciplinary charge, according to Maffey. He understood Irish anxieties, advising the Dominions Office that German propaganda and anti-British sentiment could be addressed adequately without playing 'the German Game':

There is an immense volume of pro-British feeling in this country. If we do not mishandle the situation that feeling will grow. It has waxed with our misfortunes. It waxed with our determined action against the French fleet, but it will wilt at once if we tread on the sensibilities of Eire.[28]

Walshe now prepared a detailed brief for de Valera on American and British criticisms of Irish neutrality. Maffey had previously assured Walshe that he 'was the master of the situation on the British side as far as the channel of communication between the two countries was concerned', but Walshe told him that he seemed unable to control the situation in the media or the various agents at large in Ireland. Walshe warned that his government was now suspicious of British motives and concerned that they were contemplating destabilizing or at least interfering with the internal affairs of Ireland. Walshe added ominously that the very presence of British agents jeopardized the genuine cooperation that Maffey had received since he arrived in Ireland.

Walshe threatened to call for Maffey's recall if the incidents continued. According to Walshe, Maffey was distressed by the presence of these agents and appealed to him to use the Irish high commissioner in London to pressurize the British government to stop all such agents being sent to Ireland.[29] After his dressing-down by Walshe, Maffey telegraphed London with a toned-down but still fairly accurate description of the conversation. Although not stated explicitly, Maffey's dispatch left London in little doubt that the Irish were seriously concerned and that there was a danger that relations between the two countries would deteriorate if action were not taken. In particular, Maffey warned that staff talks would be difficult if the Irish were not conciliated.[30]

Though Walshe continued to criticize what he considered anti-Irish articles in British newspapers during July, the situation quickly improved. Maffey returned to London for discussions and Walshe confided to de Valera a little later that the British and American press were now dealing with Ireland in a more positive fashion. By the end of the month Walshe was able to report that the British had agreed to supply Ireland with military equipment that had previously been refused, adding this 'is a further conclusive proof that, for the time being at any rate, the British government have changed their policy towards us'.[31] The British authorities also transmitted warnings to Ireland on a number of occasions when a German attack was possible. There was some concern the Irish might think this was scare-mongering so to show good faith British intelligence authorized Maffey to provide de Valera with secret information based on British intelligence summaries. At the end of June 1940 Walshe could write to David Gray, the American minister, confiding that 'it does happen to be the case almost by a miracle of history, that our neutrality, though for very different reasons, suits both sides in the present conflict'.[32]

*

De Valera's wish that all contacts between the British and Irish on defence matters be kept secret did not prevent discussions taking place or plans being developed. The British War Office was concerned that if an invasion took place Eire could be cut off from Northern Ireland and British military headquarters would not have reliable information upon which to act. This presented an obvious difficulty for the Irish authorities, as they were adamant that they should control the timing of any British military entry into the south. One suggestion discussed was the possibility of sending one Irish officer by air and another by car to pass on the information. In early August General Harrison, former governor of the Channel Islands, arrived in Dublin to meet de Valera and other senior officials to discuss how best to coordinate military liaison between the north and south. Harrison confided to de Valera that an attack on Northern Ireland was the most likely option for the Germans, though Donegal was an obvious target as well. He was also realistic enough to admit that no attack could take place until the British navy was 'put out of action'. Harrison wanted discussions with senior Irish army staff so that liaison would be effective if Ireland had to call for assistance. Though Harrison thought it important to get to know Irish staff officers, de Valera demurred at anything more than him developing a personal acquaintance with one or two members of Irish General Headquarters staff, and even here he only promised to examine the possibility of him doing do. De Valera insisted that formal staff talks were impossible as Ireland was neutral and used the opportunity to ask again for armaments, a request that Harrison supported. The Irish were somewhat sceptical about Harrison's abilities, noting that his view of warfare had more in common with 'the easygoing wars of the Indian frontier'.[33]

Writing in 1944, the Irish chief of staff, General McKenna, maintained that 'there can be no doubt that in the present war our neutrality must have created a problem for Great Britain which fortunately for us, she was not strong enough at the appropriate time to regulate by force'.[34] McKenna based this opinion on evidence received in the spring of 1941 that the British army in Northern Ireland had developed plans for an invasion of the south which would involve the use of ten divisions. Interestingly, McKenna's reference focuses on 1941, with the evidence for a German invasion pointing to the autumn of 1941. The period between June and December 1940 is not discussed, yet this is the time when other sources suggest heightened tension, even a real possibility of invasion.

As noted above, the Irish authorities were engaged at various levels with British military and intelligence organizations during 1940. In a memorandum to his minister in June 1940 McKenna advised that Ireland could anticipate an attack from either Britain or Germany. His assumption at this stage was that Britain would occupy various ports and also maybe Dublin. The Irish army would defend the ports and destroy their guns if they were likely to be overrun. In the case of Dublin, a decision had to be made either to defend it or declare it an open city. If the latter, then plans to evacuate the civilian population would have to be quickly formulated. The Defence Conference discussed the possibility that Dubliners should be encouraged to leave the city voluntarily in July 1940. It was noted that the army authorities were strongly in favour of families who could leave Dublin doing so immediately.[35] A German invasion was likely to involve sea and air attacks between Waterford and the Shannon in the south of the country, though secondary attacks on Dublin were also to be expected.[36]

Although McKenna warned his staff that an external attack might come from either side, most of the planning after May 1940 was concerned with either internal subversion or with an attack from Germany. At the very time that de Valera and Walshe were telling Maffey and other British representatives that they had everything under control, the Irish military were concerned that the IRA was planning a major operation. A rising in the country could not be ruled out, while a foreign power might send in parachutists, land troops by aircraft or support the uprising in other ways. Even if this did not occur, extensive gun-running was possible, as were bank raids and attacks to seek weapons within Ireland – the Magazine Fort debacle cannot have been far from the minds of the Irish military at this time.[37] Military concern was echoed by a circular issued by the Crime Branch section of the Garda to divisional officers warning them of the threat from the IRA:

> In view of the startling developments in the European war and in view of the recent instructions to the IRA it is apparent that the utmost vigilance is necessary. The IRA apparently expects external assistance which may take the form of a landing of arms.

The chief superintendents were warned that if a landing did occur, diversions would be staged to draw attention away from the area. Quite dramatically the warning continued:

Such diversions must not be allowed to divert the Gardai from its primary task, the cutting off of the landing area by a cordon, backed when possible by military. If a situation occurs in which the use of arms is necessary, and the use is considered desirable by the Chief Superintendent, the nearest military station will furnish a supply of arms.

By the end of May, the military had moved into the docks, oil terminals and areas around airports to protect them from attack.[38]

On 24 May Operational Order No. 1 was issued. It considered that an attack was likely to take place in the south-west of the country as the British were laying an extensive minefield off the east coast. This presumed a German attack. By June the British minefield had been extended to the south-west, off the Waterford coast to the Tusker Rock, and to the coast of Cornwall. The mines were located just outside Irish territorial waters and were designed to push a German invasion fleet out into the Atlantic, where the Royal Navy could intercept it. By late June de Valera, Aiken and Traynor were engaged in detailed discussions with General McKenna on various aspects of the threat to Ireland. De Valera took a detailed interest in all aspects of the army's preparedness and plans, questioning the chief of staff closely. McKenna confirmed that the army now had a force of 8,000 men who could engage with invading troops 'without unnecessary delay', though it was recognized that this was not sufficient to stop a major invasion. Of the 24,000 men available to the military at this stage, some 18,000 were considered trained. Following these discussions, Operational Order No. 2 was issued on 10 July and contained more detail. While an invasion could still be expected from either belligerent:

From information at the disposal of the General Staff it does not appear that the British Forces have any offensive intentions at the moment . . . generally speaking it is felt that the Germanic group is more likely to take the initiative against us.

However, the possibility that changing circumstances would alter this threat could not be ruled out, it was maintained. The primary task of the Irish defence forces therefore would be to resist the Germans, while the secondary mission would be to take account of a possible

British attack. Remarkably, there is little evidence that the Irish army had detailed plans for cooperation with Britain in the event of an attack. Indeed, the assumption was that Ireland would hold the line against an enemy for some time. As Order No. 2 explained it:

> If, despite such initial efforts, hostile forces succeed in establishing themselves, prompt action will be taken and no effort will be spared to dislodge them by use of available resources. Pending arrival of such reserves, troops in contact will impede enemy action to the utmost.

Apparent in Operational Orders 1 and 2 is the need of the political and military leadership to demonstrate that independent Ireland had the capacity to defend itself. This may have been a suicidal strategy, but it was an understandable, if old-fashioned, one. It rested on the belief that a robust defence of sovereignty by the Irish army would secure a more favourable position for the country, even if it were defeated in the initial engagement.[39]

*

The Irish authorities were extremely sensitive to British conditions for cooperation between the two states. Walshe called in the British representative at the end of June to complain that conditions attached to a delivery of anti-aircraft guns were unacceptable. The British wanted their own military personnel to man these weapons in Ireland, but Walshe insisted that the Irish army had more than enough trained personnel to handle the new equipment. This meeting was clearly a tense one; though Maffey himself claimed to understand the Irish position he was not sure the War Office would. However, Maffey's representations proved successful and the following day it was agreed that the weapons would be delivered unconditionally.[40]

The Irish military were also reluctant to allow the British to dominate either the strategic planning involved or the day-to-day side of cooperation. While inter-staff talks were considered essential, Irish officials were suspicious that the British and Irish did not agree on what the best strategy should be:

> We for our part, are quite satisfied that our own strategy is undoubtedly – if not the best possible – the best for us in our

present circumstances. Indeed we can claim to possess an exceptionally unified doctrine in this matter.

To achieve Irish supremacy in strategic staff talks with the British, it was deemed necessary to persuade the British that the Irish plans were well advanced, took account of all circumstances and were strategically sound. If the British could be persuaded of this, then the Irish plans would be more easily accepted. The Irish military recognized the challenge facing them: to persuade the British that they wanted to cooperate, but at the same time achieve a position where Irish planning strategy would become the agreed method of action. To do this, it was necessary to exclude the politicans from the discussions as they were considered lacking in understanding of the strategic, technical and military contexts. Furthermore, it was assumed that the British military were out of date, still attempting to apply the lessons of the First World War to a situation that did not warrant it, although it was admitted that many Irish officers thought the same way. However, the priority was to clarify the situation between the two staffs and this needed to be completed as quickly as possible.

The Irish were not prepared to accept a relationship with the British similar to that of those Poles, Czechs or Belgians who had accepted British military control. These exiles' countries had been conquered by Germany and they had no alternative but to accept British authority. Ireland was still in the field both politically and militarily and this made a fundamental difference to the relationship between the two states and military staffs. The Irish military also had considerable confidence in its own ability:

> We ourselves are probably the only people in Ireland quite devoid of any technical 'inferiority complex' vis-à-vis the British. We are quite equal to holding our own with them in any technical discussion – and that too without in any way offending their sensibilities. It is highly probable that, far from being overawed in the course of military talks, we could assume a technical ascendancy over them.

The Irish military clearly knew the assumed theatre of war better than the British and this provided them with a clear advantage in terms of leadership and strategy. However, British troops had been blooded in Norway and France, and though defeated they had acquired considerable battle experience, something the Irish did not acquire at any stage during the war.[41]

Two plans were developed by the army to defend Ireland in case of attack. GDP1 was designed to meet a German invasion, while GDP 2 was focused on Britain. In July 1940 the taoiseach decided to give priority to defence plans presuming a German invasion over plans to counter a British attack, although the Irish still had serious reservations about Britain. The chief of staff issued an order to all staff commands on 14 September 1940:

> Should an invasion of our country be intended by Germany, it is believed that the next month or so is of special importance, and should be regarded as a period of special vigilance. While no scare should be created, arrangements should be calmly made in each command to have each unit held in such a state of readiness that the greater part of it can move to action at short notice at any hour during this period.[42]

There remained a general fear in Fianna Fáil that Britain would seek to reconquer Ireland. While this threat was normally seen in terms of a British invasion, there was also concern about the consequences of a military alliance with Britain; the decision to keep Harrison at arm's length in August reflected unease about the intentions and reliability of the British. General McKenna noted in September 1940 that if a German invasion did take place, the Irish army was not prepared to fight under British leadership. The political difficulties would be immense, but in McKenna's view the competence of the British officer corps was also seriously in doubt:

> In the present war the British have already given a glaring example of gross incompetence when a minor ally gave them a free hand on its territory. The command in Norway was British, and it should be quite sufficient to convince the most pro-British that nothing of a profitable nature could be looked for in similar circumstances.

McKenna knew that it would come as a shock to the politicians 'that our own staff are definitely more efficient than the British'. Moreover, he added that for operations in Ireland itself the Irish officer corps was superior to the British. There was a degree of national pride in this, with the chief of staff of a small army emphasizing the military prowess of his men compared with the forces of a major power. In McKenna's mind, and this would surely have been a shock to the British, an Irish officer should also be in command. This view only extended to the army; he conceded that the leadership of the Royal Navy and the Royal Air Force was of a superior calibre and there could be no objection there. It is clearly relevant in this context that Ireland did not have an air force or navy of any consequence so did not have the personnel to direct a sea or air campaign. McKenna's position may have been more politically driven than he admits, as the army was the only section of the Irish military with the experience to lead if the need arose. Similar reservations applied in the event of cooperation with the Germans, but with a different rationale: 'We would have to reject German command; not because it would be incompetent, but because it would subserve our national interest to theirs in every possible direction. This has invariably been the case in all instances in which the Germans have commanded an allied force.'[43]

*

In May 1940 the Czech consul in Dublin, D. K. Kostal, wrote in a report to the Czech government in exile in London that most Irish newspapers were neutral towards Britain, that there was widespread approval of Lord Haw Haw's radio broadcasts and that support for Hitler was evident in the general population. He concluded that the Irish regard the 'war as an English enterprise, something which generally speaking has nothing to do with Ireland'. While Kostal noted pro-German sentiment, overall his reports suggest an Irish distance from the moral issues of the war. In September he analysed de Valera's interview with the *Christian Science Monitor* and the Irish justification for neutrality. In effect, de Valera had rejected the suggestion made by Churchill early in the summer that an American fleet might be stationed in Ireland to preserve its neutrality. Kostal noted that this interview was a response to the hostile press that Ireland was receiving in the United States, but also an attempt to mobilize Irish–American opinion in favour of some sort of guarantee of Ireland's neutrality. Kostal may not have realized it but his reports were being read by Irish intelligence, which noted that the 'first officer of the Ministry of Commerce' had been in discussion with Kostal. In a strange conversation with Maffey, Walshe pointed out that the Irish government had to keep an eye on foreigners in Ireland who did not have an official position. He referred directly to Kostal, adding, 'it might even happen that Czechoslovakian citizens send reports to their government in London'.[44]

Far more serious from the Irish viewpoint was Kostal's report that the Germans had delivered a note to the Irish government in August which threatened the country if it continued to trade with Britain.[45] Kostal had also pointed out that the Germans had attacked a number of Irish ships, actions which he viewed as a warning to the Irish government. He was well informed on this occasion as his information came from a senior civil servant. De Valera had been deeply concerned about this note and instructed Walshe to convene a meeting of the secretaries of the Departments of Supplies, Industry and Commerce and Agriculture to discuss a response. There were two aspects to the German note. The first concerned the institution of a blockade of trade with Britain, while the second included an offer to the Irish government to exclude shipping entering Ireland with essential supplies from attack. The meeting took the blockade issue seriously. The Germans wanted the Irish government to prohibit all travel and trade between Britain and Ireland. The possibility of agreeing to the German demand was discussed but it was quickly conceded that the British would probably retaliate. However, it was also necessary to avoid conflict with Germany, and here the meeting did not have a clear sense of direction. There was some discussion of the legality of the German blockade, but the consensus was that it was not illegal. In the event of a blockade Ireland would not arm its ships or provide naval protection, as the Germans would consider this an act of war. Notwithstanding the legal position, there were strong reasons for not taking a robust position in respect of Germany:

> Politically an official attitude of defiance and resistance to the German blockade measures would be liable to maximise the political repercussions of such incidents as did occur and to lead to a severe strain on our relations with Germany.

The meeting agreed that there was no easy answer to the blockade issue and the threat to Irish citizens and shipping. It was agreed that a formal protest would be ineffective, though it was hoped that private representations to Hempel would lead to the Germans exercising a degree of discretion in respect of Ireland. Nevertheless, it was apparent that a blockade could only be successful if universal and therefore such an appeal would probably not be entertained by the Germans.

If the blockade caused serious political difficulties for Ireland, the German offer to exempt Ireland from it under certain conditions caused consternation. The German conditions effectively placed all Irish shipping under German control – they would decide the terms of exit and entry. The Germans wanted a formal agreement, as they wished to trumpet what would be a major political coup: a commonwealth dominion entering into a formal agreement with the Reich. It was noted anxiously by the Irish that 'the spirit in which the proposal is put forward by the Germans is not such that we can afford simply to ignore it'. Meanwhile the British were engaged in trade talks with Ireland, one aspect of which was a request for Irish ports to be used for transhipment facilities between the United States and Britain. It was agreed that there was little room for manoeuvre on the German offer. Accepting it would provoke Britain, while there was a fear that if the blockade were successful, opinion in Ireland would question the reasoning behind rejecting the German offer. As a consequence, though there were good reasons for rejection, there were 'almost equally strong reasons for trying to keep open the possibility of making an arrangement on the lines suggested at a later stage'. The meeting decided to place the emphasis on a defence of Irish neutrality. It was settled that no formal agreement could be made, but that Hempel might be persuaded to make the Irish case to Germany. It was intended to prepare a note for the Germans, pointing out that no re-export or transhipment facilities had been available in Ireland since the beginning of the war and it was not anticipated to provide them. Furthermore, 'the general idea would be not to reject the German offer out of hand and to keep it open for the present'. Hempel would be informed verbally that the Irish government was 'looking into the possibility of making, in an emergency, practical arrangements of a kind which would enable us to put forward suggestions' at a later stage. In addition, Hempel would be informed that attacks on ships coming into Ireland from countries not at war with Germany would be against international law. The Irish would claim compensation in these circumstances. Walshe transmitted these conclusions to de Valera and they agreed that Walshe should meet Hempel to try to secure an easing of the situation. Walshe warned de Valera that the real danger was that Britain would use this as an opportunity to draw Ireland into the war.[46]

However, it was the Germans who now took the initiative. Just a week later two aircraft attacked targets in County Wexford. The first attacked Ambrosetown and the second Campile. Intelligence reports stated that the planes were Heinkels and an unexploded bomb was undoubtedly of German manufacture. Most worrying for the Irish government was the information that visibility was 'exceptional'; indeed the Welsh coast could be seen from County Wexford according to Irish air force personnel who flew over the area later the same day. Moreover, on the basis of an analysis of the bombs and detonation methods, military intelligence concluded 'that the destruction of buildings was intended'.

Dillon raised the bombing at the Defence Conference, claiming that there was evidence that the Germans had publicly threatened certain companies, including one at Campile, if they continued to trade with Britain. Aiken was reluctant to issue a statement in respect of the attacks, and though the issue was raised on a number of occasions at the Defence Conference, little seems to have been done. Whether the attack on County Wexford was deliberate retaliation or a warning is difficult to say, but it is possible that the Germans wanted to send a strong message to Ireland to maintain its neutrality at a level acceptable to the Reich.[47]

*

When the German note arrived in mid-August, the Irish government was negotiating a trade agreement with Britain. If the Irish assumed in 1939 that its farmers would benefit from agricultural exports to Britain, as in the First World War, they were mistaken. Britain now exercised much closer control over its economy than had been the case in the First World War. Keynes had been brought into the Treasury and had designed a control model for the wartime economy which provided the government with sophisticated mechanisms to guide and manage a capitalist economy in wartime.[48] The aim of the Irish government early in 1940 was to obtain prices for its exports equal to those paid to British producers. Lord Woolton, the British minister for food, was reluctant to engage in full ministerial discussions with Ireland or to accept the principle that Irish producers should receive the same prices as their British counterparts, although Churchill agreed with Eden that an agreement would be 'most desirable' on political grounds. British objectives included maintaining the 1938 trade agreement, specific deals in respect of imports and exports and a pricing mechanism for agricultural products acceptable to both sides. The British thinking was:

> In general it must be borne in mind that Eire's economy is complementary to and not competitive with that of the United Kingdom and consequently that, so far as possible, undertakings should be avoided which would further force Eire in the direction of economic self-sufficiency.[49]

The Irish ministerial team arrived in London at the end of April and it quickly emerged that the main sticking point between the two sides was the prices on offer from Britain. Despite objections from Northern Ireland, negotiations proceeded and considerable progress was made. By 4 May, there were still substantial differences over the prices for cattle, butter and bacon, but the Irish ministers agreed with Eden that an agreement was now possible. Irish Minister for Agriculture James Ryan accepted that 'there was no fundamental difference of principle, on the issues, but there were a number of outstanding problems to be resolved'. According to Sir William Brown of the Board of Trade, agreement with the Eire representatives had been reached on all matters except for the prices to be paid for butter, bacon and cheese. One might have thought that these would be serious exceptions, yet officials worked hard to resolve the difficulties over the next few days. When Walshe met Stephenson in the Dominions Office on 8 May he admitted that the British offer was a very generous one, but that agreement had not been reached within the Irish cabinet.[50] Irish ministers were also anxious about transhipment facilities the British might demand as part of the trade deal.

Walshe wrote to de Valera outlining the evolution of the discussions and highlighting the friendly atmosphere in which they were taking place. Some days before Walshe had told Eden that Ireland's benevolent neutrality 'placed Britain in Ireland's debt'. Although Walshe was mainly concerned with the political aspects of neutrality, he also pressed Eden on trade, arguing that an agreement would have a positive impact on Irish opinion. Likewise, Maffey, who had accompanied Walshe to London, was using his influence to persuade Britain to make concessions.[51] Despite the goodwill generated in London, political considerations prevailed in Dublin and the proposals were not accepted. The unease in Dublin reflected circumstances in Europe and a concern not to be locked into Britain. However, alternative proposals were now developed by Ireland, and John Leydon transmitted these to the UK on 17 May. While his proposals focused almost exclusively on the issue of pricing, his brief mention of political circumstances was designed to pressurize the British to make a better offer. This had a salutary impact and by the end of May draft heads of agreement had been drawn up. Britain had accepted most of the Irish proposals and Dulanty informed the United Kingdom on 6 June that Dublin was prepared to accept the agreement.[52]

Despite this, the agreement was not actually concluded and by the end of July one British official was complaining that Dulanty was 'skirmishing around Departments enquiring about his comprehensive agreement on prices'.[53] This activity had been prompted by concerns in Dublin that despite the extensive discussions exporters in Ireland still had no clarity in respect of markets and prices. This was causing some dissatisfaction among producers. The impasse seemed to have been broken on 21 August, when Lord Caldecote met Dulanty – who the Irish high commissioner found 'stiff-necked, on this occasion'. Caldecote informed Dulanty that the cabinet had decided to accept the Irish demands, but only if these were part of a comprehensive agreement. Dulanty remonstrated with Caldecote, but the British cabinet wanted an agreement that included transhipment facilities. Caldecote attempted to mollify Dulanty by saying that it would only be an extension of existing arrangements and would not endanger Ireland's neutrality. Dulanty also met a number of British officials who informed him privately that there had been serious disagreement within the cabinet over making concessions on prices; Caldecote could only achieve agreement by accepting transhipment as a quid pro quo. Maffey then met Walshe on the demand for transhipment facilities. He must have startled Walshe by telling him that Britain had little interest in Irish cattle as everything was now rationed. He said that in the light of Ireland's 'special difficulties' they were prepared to accept an agreement if transhipment facilities were available in Irish ports. Walshe minuted de Valera that 'it is, of course, quite impossible for us to accept the condition, which – as they well know – would lead us straight into the war'.

In another development Beaverbrook approached Dulanty to enquire if the Irish government would offer facilities to train civilian pilots in the country. Dulanty was concerned that this was one of the reasons the British had delayed an agreement on trade. He phoned Lord Caldecote, who denied there was any connection between this request and trade, but implied that Britain would ask for transhipment facilities. Dulanty then phoned Walshe to discuss how best to meet these developments. Walshe told Dulanty to reject both suggestions, while Dulanty revealed that at the Anglo-Irish May ministerial meetings, Lemass and Ryan had given the decided impression that something might be done about granting transhipment facilities. Walshe responded tartly that any impression given in May no longer applied. He urged Dulanty to take a vigorous line with the British, as he believed that neutrality was now more seriously threatened than it had been in May.[54]

The British proposals arrived at the beginning of September and duly included storage and transhipment conditions as well as repair facilities for merchant ships. They were circulated to the various government departments in Dublin, who quickly responded. The Department of Finance identified both positive and negative aspects to the proposals, while recognizing that Britain placed considerable importance on the shipping aspects of the agreement. The Department of External Affairs questioned whether a neutral could provide transhipment facilities, though conceded that there was no objection in international law to doing so. However, Irish circumstances, the nature of the war and the German blockade of the United Kingdom precluded them from adopting this policy.

As noted already, the Germans were pressing Ireland to enter into a formal agreement while Irish diplomats were endeavouring to persuade the Germans to accept that Irish trade with Britain was a vital national interest. It was acknowledged that the Germans had accepted the Irish position on trade with Britain but the quid pro quo was not to agree transhipment facilities. Indeed, William Warnock, the Irish chargé d'affaires in Berlin, was authorized to inform the Germans that

Ireland had not and would not provide facilities for Britain to tranship goods through the country. The Department for External Affairs was not prepared to make a case for transhipment, insisting that it was up to those departments or ministers who believed a change in policy was essential to make the necessary case. However, the DEA painted a very negative picture of the consequences of a change in policy, predicting that this would lead the country into war on the British side. It was further emphasized that Germany had not been attacking Irish ships taking cattle to Britain, and that more generally the Irish shipping situation had been 'relatively satisfactory' since the beginning of the war. Consequently, it was strongly affirmed that the status quo was the best position to maintain.

From a separate memorandum by Walshe himself it is clear that the real obstacle to transhipment was fear of the Germans. Walshe admitted that providing such facilities and storage to the British did not break international law, but that doing so would have a negative impact on Ireland's relationship with Germany. Added to this was the fear that German action against Irish ports would lead in turn to Britain stationing naval vessels at the ports to defend their own vessels. Public opinion was also a factor, as Irish citizens would take different views on the arrangements and this could lead to 'considerable political alarm and criticism of the government'. But the primary reason for rejecting transhipment was the need to conciliate Germany:

> We are at present making an effort to secure that Irish ships and Irish trade with Britain will enjoy some measure of immunity from German blockade measures. Any hope there may be of achieving this object, now or in the future, would probably disappear if we were at this stage to allow our ports and waters to be used for the transhipment of British cargoes.

On 19 September a detailed memorandum was sent to the government, which largely reiterated these and other arguments. The memorandum nevertheless presented a stark picture of the consequences of not accepting the British agreement: 'on purely economic grounds there is, therefore, an unanswerable case for making every effort possible to accept such terms of any draft agreement as are reasonable and do not endanger the country's neutrality'. But neutrality was the key point. It is clear that some departments were in favour of accepting the agreement as the negative features of it were balanced by advantages in terms of employment and economic benefits.[55] However, the government decided at its meeting on 24 September to reject the British draft as unacceptable. Notwithstanding this, discussions continued into October through various channels. By late October the Irish had produced fresh proposals, which excluded storage and transhipment facilities. This was not acceptable to Britain. Machtig wrote to Maffey on behalf of Lord Cranborne, the secretary of state for the dominions, reminding him that transhipment had been included in the first series of discussions in May and was not an afterthought as the Irish claimed. He insisted, 'it is about the only, if not the only, item in the proposed agreement which can definitely be regarded as a "quid pro quo" from our point of view', though he did add that it was not clear that Britain would actually use the facilities. If this was intended to disarm the Irish, there was no disguising the hardening of the British tone and strategy towards Ireland. The secretary of state was less diplomatic than Machtig, criticizing Ireland's position on the grounds that Britain was doing far more for Ireland than it was getting in return. This toughening stance was confirmed at a cabinet meeting in late November, when the Irish counterproposals were rejected as they did not include transhipment.[56]

*

The failure of trade negotiations was just one aspect of deteriorating relations between Britain and Ireland at this time. The British were deeply concerned at the way Irish public opinion generally and elite opinion in particular waxed and waned. After June 1940 it became evident that Britain would have to act in a positive and proactive fashion if it were to maintain the residual goodwill that all agreed existed. By September the Ministry of Information had realized that the manipulation of news for Irish consumption was self-defeating, in part because censorship in Dublin was so effective, but also because the Irish authorities could see through what was being done and could protest – as they inevitably did. Although alarmist in the circumstances, one ministry official warned, 'it is practically impossible to counteract the unfortunate influence that certainly seems to be exerted in Dublin by our ill-wishers'.

One inspired decision at this time was to appoint John Betjeman press attaché in Maffey's office, to match the appointment in the German legation.[57] Some of the information received by the British Ministry of Information was poor, even when from staff with good Irish family connections, though it was not necessarily prejudiced. However, it must have been bracing to receive a report from one member of staff, who identified herself as Anglo-Irish, noting that even among her close friends in Ireland – most of whom had been educated in Britain and retained close links there – there were some who seriously questioned Britain's moral right in the war and others who if not pro-German were certainly anti-British. This Miss Maxwell expressed surprise at the attitudes held by many of her Anglo-Irish friends, as she had assumed they would be the same as hers, but what she had ignored was how changed Ireland was as a result of independence, and how much Britain had changed as a result of the war.[58]

A more objective and reliable account of Irish opinion was provided by Elizabeth Cameron – better known as the novelist Elizabeth Bowen – who visited Ireland in July 1940. Bowen was originally refused permission to travel by the Dominions Office as her trip involved spending some time working on a novel; the Dominions Office was only prepared to sanction trips to Eire at this time if it could be shown that the visit was of importance for the national interest. However, the Ministry of Information insisted that Bowen could do some good while in Ireland. Betjeman supported her trip, pointing out that Dulanty and the writer Stephen Gwynn, 'two people to whose voices we should certainly listen', supported her visit to Eire to collect information as an 'entirely unofficial and unpaid correspondent'. Dulanty believed that Bowen would provide independent and objective reports on the state of opinion in Eire, presumably ones that would allow for a more nuanced approach by the British. Whether Dulanty was acting on his own initiative is difficult to judge, but de Valera was minister for external affairs and Joseph Walshe maintained close contact with Dulanty throughout the war.

There was some embarrassment at the United Kingdom representative's office in Dublin when Bowen arrived. She was confused with another writer, Marjorie Bowen, but 'fortunately this was discovered before anyone talked about the wrong books'. She noted with surprise that aside from normal customs formalities no checks were made on

her when she arrived at Rosslare by boat. She was not asked for any
travel documents, nor were her papers examined. This may be attributable to the Irish accepting any individual's bona fides once they had
been given permission by the British to travel. She noticed that at one
level life went on as if the war was not taking place, emphasizing the
social round and people planning summer holidays. At another level
there was great fear that Britain would invade and that this was more
likely than a German invasion. These sentiments, she concluded,
reinforced the common view that neutrality would not be respected
and contributed to pro-German feeling within Ireland. She noted that
support for neutrality was widespread among every sector of society;
indeed she noted the increasing identification of independence with
neutrality. Bowen also reported that men with a Unionist or Protestant
background who volunteered for the Irish military frequently asked if
they would have to fight Britain if it invaded Ireland and were told in
categorical terms that they would. Many had had second thoughts as
a consequence, while those who nevertheless joined or remained in
the services hoped that Britain would not make the mistake of doing
so. Bowen's reports in July and August noted that the fear of a British
invasion had diminished, but the shift in opinion may just reflect less
concern on the part of the elite and officials in Ireland – who successfully communicated this to the general public. Bowen's views echoed
those of de Valera, Walshe and the army chief of staff at this time.[59]

Bowen returned to Ireland in October and her notes in November
made sombre reading for British policymakers. She claimed that
Churchill's speech on 5 November had undone most of the goodwill
towards Britain that had existed in late July and strengthened over the
following months. While Bowen criticized what she calls the childish-
ness and obtuseness of the Irish, she also wanted her readers in
Britain to appreciate how Irish sensitivities were hurt by British
criticism of neutrality and the pressure to reoccupy the ports. Bowen's
insights here are quite acute:

It may be felt in England that Eire is making a fetish of her
neutrality. But this assertion of her neutrality is Eire's first free
self-assertion: as such alone it would mean a great deal to her.
Eire (and I think rightly) sees her neutrality as positive not merely
negative.[60]

When Betjeman visited Dublin in June 1940 he provided a similar insight into Irish opinion in terms of neutrality, the ports and the commitment to resisting attack by Britain or Germany. Betjeman viewed de Valera's position positively, recognizing that neutrality had itself neutralized many IRA supporters. Betjeman believed that the partition question would have to be resolved to de Valera's satisfaction if Britain and Ireland were to effectively cooperate in the event of a German invasion. On de Valera, Betjeman promoted his view that he was not pro-British, as some ministers were, but that he and the majority of his colleagues believed that Ireland's interests were best served by a British victory. Betjeman concluded, 'Mr de Valera is Britain's best friend in Ireland.'[61]

Bowen's notes from November were circulated to a number of leading politicians and civil servants in London. Churchill eventually received a copy, despite the rather critical assessment of the impact of his speech, and wrote to Lord Cranborne asking him to thank Bowen. Whether Churchill appreciated the comments in Bowen's notes we have no record; what we do know is that he became increasingly irritated with Eire's neutrality as the autumn progressed.[62]

*

By September the RAF had won the Battle of Britain, and the likelihood of an invasion receded as winter approached. This provided a breathing space only and Churchill watched anxiously as shipping losses mounted; the figures for October 1940 were the highest so far. Churchill's exasperation with de Valera was clearly conveyed in his House of Commons speech of 5 November when he complained:

> The fact that we cannot use the South and West coasts of Ireland to refuel our flotillas and aircraft and thus protect the trade by which Ireland as well as Great Britain lives, is a most heavy and grievous burden and one which should never have been placed on our shoulders, broad though they may be.

De Valera reacted furiously. He interrupted a Dáil debate on the 7th to defend Irish neutrality and to insist on the good faith of the Irish government. He threatened both belligerents with 'bloodshed' should they try to bring pressure on Ireland to change its policy. De

Valera's remarks were accompanied by an orchestrated campaign in the *Irish Press* against the Churchill speech and in favour of Irish neutrality, while the censors directed the debate into channels congenial to the government. This was posturing on the part of de Valera. When Dillon asked Aiken at the Defence Conference held on 6 November if the British government had made any approach to the government or to the high commissioner in London in respect of the ports after Churchill's speech, the meeting was adjourned. When Aiken returned he reported that the taoiseach had asked him to tell the meeting that no approach had been made by Britain.[63]

General McKenna convened a conference of army planners in direct response to Churchill's speech on the ports. This followed correspondence between the assistant chief of staff, Aodh O'Neill, and McKenna in which they decided to give priority to plan GDP2 focusing on possible British aggression, while putting GDP1 on the 'back boiler'. O'Neill believed that an attack from Germany was not likely before the spring of 1941 and the most likely threat now came from Britain. The changing nature of British popular opinion was noted as evidence that an invasion might be in the offing. O'Neill offered the view to his chief that:

> If the British decided upon military action they could act at once, they are not dependent upon weather conditions to the same extent as the Germans. They might desire to have the Irish situation cleared up and naval and air bases consolidated in Ireland prior to the opening of the spring campaign.

This was not an unrealistic conclusion to draw if indeed Britain intended to invade. However, a little later in the month, McKenna told his staff that personally he did not anticipate any aggression until diplomatic efforts had been exhausted, 'but that did not absolve us of the responsibility for preparing for surprise actions'.[64]

The national executive of Fianna Fáil was also much exercised by Churchill's speech, discussing how prepared the country was for war as well as congratulating de Valera on 'reaffirming the national position in regards to the ports'.[65] Maffey reported to London that de Valera was in an agitated and bitter mood when he met him. The Irish were now seriously questioning the motives of the British in respect of Ireland.

Maffey returned to London for discussions after de Valera's reply to Churchill on 7 November. He arrived back in Dublin on Saturday the 9th, but, to Walshe's concern, did not contact his department for five days after this. Maffey then informed Walshe that the Dominions Office was concerned at Churchill's statement: it was 'typically Churchillian' and the Dominions Office had not been consulted in advance. Maffey insisted that there was no threat in the speech to take the ports; it was simply a statement of regret. According to Walshe, there was now an orchestrated campaign against Ireland in the House of Commons and in the British media, making the situation in Ireland worse than it had been.

In a subsequent meeting Maffey confided to Walshe that everything was being done in London to control press attacks on Ireland, but the Irish government had to recognize that the media was giving voice to real concerns about shipping losses. Irish censorship was more severe than in Britain, even though Ireland was not at war. Maffey wanted to assure Walshe that no one in Britain was considering occupying the ports. There was then according to Walshe a very indiscreet conversation initiated by Maffey, who said that Churchill was temperamental and might not remain in office. He was prime minister because of the severity of the situation and the belief that he was the best war leader, 'but when the war becomes less critical, changes were likely'. Walshe then asked Maffey if it were possible that Ernest Bevin would replace Churchill, to which Maffey replied that he hoped so as a leader from Labour would be more favourably disposed to Ireland and would 'avoid any action which might be permanently detrimental to the good relations between the two peoples'. This is a somewhat bizarre exchange which, if reflective of Maffey's and Dominions Office opinion, displays considerable unease with if not opposition to Churchill. However, there is a danger that Walshe heard what he wanted to hear, as there is no supporting evidence for this conversation in the Dominions Office files.[66]

*

To what extent was there a threat to Irish neutrality from Britain in November and December 1940? The answer depends on the evidence used and how it is interpreted. The Dominions Office and Maffey were certainly opposed to any direct action against Ireland to take the ports, and the Irish chief of staff considered in early November that no action would be taken until diplomatic options had been exhausted. It is also likely that de Valera misunderstood Churchill's speech, as he focused exclusively on one sentence out of a speech running to seven pages of text. It is true that Churchill's remarks on the ports came immediately after a discussion of air raids and shipping losses and clearly he considered the issue important. Yet the context was one of success on the part of Britain against the worst that Hitler could do. For Churchill, 'the course of events at home has not been unexpected nor, on the whole, unsatisfactory'. The speech was often upbeat, reflecting a degree of confidence that Britain would win out in the end. Immediately after referring to the Irish ports, Churchill continued, 'however, this period of stringency is perhaps passing', referring then to the acquisition of fifty American destroyers. Churchill was also confident that 'the invasion danger has for the time being diminished', a view supported by the intelligence services in late October, who concluded that 'it appears that the invasion of United Kingdom and/or Eire is not imminent'.[67]

Providing context does not clinch the matter, as many other variables were at work including the importance attached to the ports by Churchill and whether Eire was a major strand in British strategic planning and operations during these months. In fact, the focus at that time was on Italy, Greece and the eastern Mediterranean, not on Ireland. This was also the prime concern of MPs, according to Harold Nicolson. Nor was there discussion of Eire at Defence Committee meetings around this time. On 8 November there was a discussion on the Irish ports and shipping losses, but no evidence of an invasion being considered. What there was, was a personal message from Churchill to President Roosevelt urging him to help Britain get the ports. It is telling that on this occasion, as on others, Churchill's initial action was to contact Roosevelt on Ireland. America loomed large in Churchill's considerations in November and December 1940, and actions in respect of Ireland have to be placed in this context. If the British had been considering an invasion, the United States would always have acted as a brake on the more adventurous impulses of the prime minister.

On 12 November Churchill nevertheless wrote to Eden in ominous fashion. The prime minister wanted a significant increase in the garrison in Northern Ireland 'with a view to a decisive move on a broad front, should this at any time become necessary'. However, Churchill made it clear that this was a planning exercise not a change in policy on the part of his government. The advantage for Churchill was that the arrival of six divisions in the north would become known and 'might have a salutary effect'.[68] The war cabinet discussed Eire on 21 November. The prime minister opened the discussion by referring to Maffey's view that attitudes to Britain had been improving but that reopening the ports issue had badly affected this sentiment. Churchill then went on:

> One line of reply would be to say that this country had a very real appreciation of the fact that, if Eire was now at war with Germany, she would be exposed to the same perils as ourselves, but that at the moment she had no adequate defence. The last thing we wish to do was to lay Eire open to such attacks before adequate defence was available, and we were prepared to go to the limit of suffering. If, however, a time arrived when the use of Eire ports became a matter of life and death to this country, we might have to take another view. Clearly, however, no reply or statement should be made without further discussion in the war cabinet.

The general opinion of the cabinet was that it would be better not to make any statement which might provoke controversy, but there was also a recognition that postponement might not be possible given likely agitation over the ports and shipping losses in Britain itself. Most importantly, Churchill concluded the discussion on Ireland by stating, 'Every expedient must, of course, continue to be tried, both in the political field, in order to bring influences to work on Mr de Valera, and in the field of naval measures which might enable us to overcome the threat to our shipping without the use of the Eire ports.'

Maffey was now exasperated with de Valera, saying at one point that he was a 'complete dictator', and recommending that no new offer be made to him:

> It is quite wrong to suppose that de Valera will ever respond to a generous gesture. He is completely ruthless and has achieved great success by never allowing his gaze to be diverted to right or left. He is a most astute politician and understands exactly what his people will do and what they will not do.

Maffey concluded that de Valera, Walshe and many members of the Irish government expected a German victory, and some were preparing for this outcome.[69]

By 23 November Churchill was discussing with Woolton the impact on Britain and Ireland if Irish food supplies were cut off. Woolton thought that economic sanctions would bring Ireland to the negotiating table within three months. This prompted Churchill in early December to consider various sanctions in retaliation for Eire's refusal to concede the ports. British shipping losses were still mounting and the use of the ports was considered even more vital than previously. On 3 December Churchill proposed withdrawing all subsidies from Irish cattle, noting also, 'we must now consider the military option'. More dangerous for Ireland, Churchill was now fulminating against 'the de Valera-aided German blockade'. In his letter to Roosevelt of 7 December Churchill appealed for increased aid and asked the president to consider using the American navy to protect convoys crossing the Atlantic. He also asked Roosevelt to 'obtain bases in Ireland for the duration of the war' and, if this were not possible, for his assistance and influence in procuring 'for Great Britain the necessary facilities upon the southern and western shores of Eire for our flotillas, and still more important, for our aircraft working westward into the Atlantic'. Although Churchill reiterated his unwillingness to coerce the Unionists in Northern Ireland he also indicated to the president that the British government would certainly support the establishment of a defence council for the island of Ireland and that this could form the basis of unity at a future date.[70] By the middle of December 1940 then, Churchill's cabinet was considering action against Ireland, but not of a military kind. The war cabinet was more concerned with events in the Mediterranean, believing that Spain might go to war to take Gibraltar and occupy the North African coast. Early the following year George Orwell dismissed a call to invade Ireland from a German anti-Nazi living in Britain. His own position was that if the British invaded Ireland to occupy the ports it would have a disastrous impact on public opinion in Britain – not just in the United States. Orwell touched on an important aspect of the changing nature of politics in Britain: despite Churchill's imperialist leanings and prejudices much of the public did not share these views and believed in a democratic outcome to the war. The invasion of a neutral democratic country for strategic reasons would have to be justified in the most serious terms or could not take place.[71]

Although Irish officials were not aware of all these developments, they were deeply concerned at Britain's toughening attitude. De Valera would not accept that Irish neutrality harmed Britain, refusing any responsibility for shipping losses. In this he was certainly correct as the Germans had broken British codes and could locate convoys with lethal effect. However, there was also a more general belief in Britain that bases in Ireland would allow the British fleet and its aircraft to roam considerably wider than was currently the case. This was recognized by Irish military intelligence, which concluded that the British were no longer seriously concerned with the southern ports, but desperately wanted facilities in Lough Swilly in the north of Eire and in the Shannon estuary up to Limerick city. These would, it was suggested by Colonel Archer, 'be most valuable, particularly the Shannon with its air base at Rynanna, which could be used to intercept German bombers which are now active off our west coast and causing the British grave concern'. General McKenna authorized an improved intelligence network in Northern Ireland, as the existing one was not providing satisfactory results.[72] Irish staff officers prepared further plans not only to defend the country against a British assault but also to cooperate with the Germans militarily. These plans assumed that Germany would intervene if Britain attacked, and drew on lessons from Greece and Crete as well as Norway. They presumed that the Germans would be anxious to avail themselves of any opportunity to arrive in Ireland as allies. Among actions to be taken by the Irish army to aid the Germans were the provision of naval facilities in Donegal, the organization of collaboration with the IRA in Northern Ireland and the identification of areas for German parachutists to land. The Irish suggested that the Germans might bomb Ulster urban centres such as Portadown and Coleraine, which were predominantly Unionist, but parachutists should be landed in South Armagh, South Derry and in the Glens of Antrim, where nationalists were strongly represented.[73]

By the middle of December de Valera was worried enough to call a meeting of senior staff officers and government ministers in his office. The situation had deteriorated to such an extent that Christmas leave was cancelled for the armed forces. De Valera told the meeting 'that there was a danger that the British might attempt a rapid and surprise occupation of the country'. The taoiseach warned those attending that the British should not be provoked, for 'we must not be put in the position of making an aggressive move first'. Notwithstanding this caution, he also emphasized that if conditions changed, 'we should assume the offensive particularly in the six-county areas where the population was friendly'. De Valera seemed keen to stress that:

> The British have done nothing hostile but that there has been a definite change and the situation has worsened. He was anxious that nothing provocative should be done and that in implementing the decisions now taken they should be constantly borne in mind.

The chief of staff then announced a neutral zone extending ten miles from the border to avoid any clashes between British and Irish forces, but all units were placed on alert and extra resources sent to Donegal. Information was received that members of the British forces in Northern Ireland with Irish backgrounds were being moved elsewhere. Also, whereas the British army in Northern Ireland had previously provided the Irish with its order of battle, by the end of the year as troop reinforcements were moved in this information was withdrawn.[74]

Within a year Ireland had become a potential battlefield, and even if no invasion was threatened in December 1940, de Valera was right to see the situation as extremely serious for him and his government. He had met with ruthlessness the IRA threat, had countered the incursions of German agents, only now to be faced with the possibility that Britain might reoccupy the south. Nor did matters get better. On 3 December 1940 Hitler said, 'The occupation of Ireland might lead to the end of the war.' While Ireland was not the only focus for German plans at this time, it was now clearly a factor in Hitler's calculations.

De Valera was due to enter a nursing home just before Christmas for treatment on his deteriorating eyesight, but on 19 December Dr Hempel called on Walshe. Hempel said that he had just received an urgent message from Berlin that three new staff members were being appointed to Dublin. They would arrive two days later by aeroplane. Walshe immediately rejected Hempel's request that the Germans be granted entry, making it clear that this would embarrass the Irish government. He then went to see de Valera. After this meeting, William Warnock, the Irish chargé d'affaires in Berlin, was instructed to inform the Germans that the appointments could not be accepted. The Irish also ignored Hempel's plea that the German aircraft be cleared for landing in order to save time.

Hempel returned on 20 December to insist on the appointments. He threatened Walshe with a possible break in diplomatic relations if his request was not granted, arguing that Germany was within its rights to increase its legation staff. Walshe conceded this was technically so but urged Hempel to accept that political conditions were not suitable. Although Hempel agreed to contact Berlin, he again demanded that landing clearance and call signals for Shannon be given to him. Walshe, who immediately contacted both the minister for defence and Frank Aiken to alert them to the threat, rejected this demand. De Valera, when informed, issued instructions that the Germans be immediately arrested if they landed, and Robert Fisk reports that a German aircraft flew low over Rynanna around this time, but left without trying to land.

Hempel was extremely agitated during these meetings with Walshe – not surprisingly as the additional staff were most likely intelligence officers. Ribbentrop also expressed considerable annoyance that Ireland was refusing his request, a refusal that Hempel told Walshe would have 'serious consequences'. Hempel and Walshe met on numerous occasions over the Christmas period, and the minister met de Valera when he came out of his nursing home on 28 December. De Valera reiterated Walshe's original position, telling Hempel in very direct fashion that the request would be refused. On the 29th Hempel told Boland that 'he was worried as to what the reaction would be'.[75]

It is probably no coincidence that German planes attacked Ireland two days later, bombing Dublin among other places. Shane Leslie arrived in Dublin on 1 January 1941, finding it 'white with snow but bright with lights'. Given the absence of a blackout, the Germans clearly knew what their target was. In the course of the bombing a number of people were killed and Leslie reports that the archbishop of Dublin was blown out of his bed. This attack was followed by further bombings on the nights of 2 and 3 January. Aiken admitted to the Defence Conference that the planes were German, telling his fellow members that a protest had been lodged in Berlin. He 'believed personally' that the attacks were mistakes, made due to bad weather conditions. The government was certainly of this view as they decided not to bring the air-raid warning system into operation.[76]

The early months of 1941 were the most uncertain of the war for de Valera and his government. Army Chief of Staff Dan McKenna believed that both the British and the Germans had designs on Ireland. By the time the Germans bombed Dublin in January, it was evident that Britain was also taking a tougher line with neutral Ireland. Churchill's patience with de Valera was exhausted and he minuted Sir Kingsley Wood the chancellor of the exchequer to consider economic sanctions against Eire. The objectives were first to bring home Ireland's dependence on Britain for shipping, supplies and other necessities and second to ensure Ireland suffered the same wartime deprivations that Britain was experiencing. The issue of the ports was never far from Churchill's mind, but he told Lord Cranborne the dominions secretary on 17 January 1941, 'I do not consider that it is at present true to say that possession of these bases is vital to our survival. The lack of them is a grievous injury and impediment to us. More than that it would not at present be true to say.' In March Churchill rejected Cranborne's appeal for a more moderate approach, while the same month the deployment of additional British forces in Northern Ireland caused considerable concern in Dublin. A fresh crisis over conscription in May did not improve the situation.[77]

Despite these continuing points of tension, relations between Britain and Eire were managed on a day-to-day basis to the advantage of both states even though Irish officials feared a British invasion. Officials in the British Foreign Office and Dominions Office only reluctantly supported Churchill's aggressive stance, advising caution in respect of Ireland. Though an invasion could not be entirely ruled out, the membership of the British cabinet, Maffey's position in Dublin, military considerations and the possible impact on public opinion in Britain and the United States reduced that possibility to manageable levels. The threat to Ireland receded further when the Soviet Union was invaded in June 1941. By this time Eire had something to offer. Britain was seriously short of labour by early 1941 whereas unemployment in Eire had created a manpower surplus there.

Bevin persuaded the cabinet and Churchill that the benefits of regulated Irish immigration into Britain far outweighed any disadvantages. Various conditions were imposed on Irish labour coming to

Britain but MI5 concluded in June 1941 that the intelligence services could deal with the migration without serious security problems. In July Churchill complained about the presence of German diplomats in Dublin but reluctantly recognized that Irish labour would be useful to Britain's war effort. Once the two governments agreed on the conditions governing the movement of labour into Britain, large numbers of Irish citizens crossed the Irish Sea to work in Britain's war industries. It is likely that as many as 200,000 Irish men and women were working in the war industries by 1945. Not only did these workers make an indispensable contribution to industrial production, but the agreement between the two states also reduced the possibility of a British attack on Ireland.[78]

Nevertheless the sense of threat felt by the Irish elite was also present in the general public. A national recruiting campaign had begun in June 1940 and in just five weeks nearly 25,000 men volunteered for service. There was considerable enthusiasm among those who volunteered, reflecting genuine concern that Ireland might be attacked. While recruiting subsequently levelled off, the government and especially Frank Aiken made considerable efforts to persuade people to join the auxiliary forces as well as the regular army. Aiken would later claim that over 200,000 Irish citizens joined up during the Emergency, describing this as 'one of the most remarkable popular movements that has appeared in the history of the nation'. Despite this influx Irish army chiefs remained worried that the army was not in a position to effectively meet an attack on the country.[79]

If relations between Britain and Ireland in early 1941 were tense but manageable, the Irish relationship with Germany was far more uncertain. Given Hitler's willingness to take considerable risks, an attack on Ireland as a way into Britain could not be discounted. In August 1940 IRA leader Seán Russell and Frank Ryan were sent to Ireland from Germany in a U-boat but Russell died on the way and Ryan returned to Germany. In addition a number of German agents were successfully landed in Ireland during 1940 and 1941. While most of them were quickly apprehended, some evaded arrest for some time. The most successful of these agents was Herman Görtz, who arrived in Ireland in May 1940 and was not apprehended until November 1941. Görtz was protected by the IRA and also by a group of republicans he described as 'independent patriots'. He was also in contact with senior members of the Irish army, in particular Major-General Hugo McNeill, who may have been assigned this task by the chief of staff. Irish intelligence chief Dan Bryan subsequently noted that Seán MacBride, former IRA leader and later minister for external affairs, was 'closely involved in German activities'; but 'has never been questioned about the matter'. Görtz also met members of the Dáil and possibly even members of the Fianna Fáil cabinet during this crucial period.

Mark Hull has provided the most comprehensive study of German espionage in Ireland, demonstrating that Hempel was deeply involved in espionage throughout this period. While German activities in Ireland were not notably successful, one of the major puzzles of the period is how Görtz was able to evade capture for so long. It may be that during the second half of 1940 and in early 1941 the Irish authorities wanted him free to maintain an unofficial conduit to the Germans. He certainly seems to have had some sort of government protection and it is remarkable that General McNeill could have met and had discussions with him at a time when the security forces were looking for him.

The Germans certainly brought the war home to Ireland when its air force attacked Dublin in May 1941, dropping bombs close to the president's residence in Phoenix Park and that of the United States representative close by. However the most devastating attack was on the North Strand area of Dublin when thirty-four people were killed and hundreds of homes destroyed. It is likely that this and other attacks by the Germans were intended to terrorize the Irish population and to emphasize the costs of giving up neutrality. If so they were clearly successful.[80]

6. THE (LOST) AMERICAN CARD:
FDR, GRAY AND THE NEUTRALS 1938–41

David Gray warned de Valera in May 1940 that neutrality would not save his country if Germany won the war. It was a stark warning and, coming as it did from President Roosevelt's personal representative in Eire, must have shocked the Irish leader, who only a year earlier had been planning a visit to the United States, his place of birth. Not only was Gray a relative by marriage of Roosevelt, he and his wife Maude were close to Eleanor, the president's formidable wife. Gray was also a Democrat who supported the New Deal and had an abiding admiration for Roosevelt, well attested to in the voluminous correspondence in Gray's own papers and in White House files. Gray may have been appointed to Ireland because of his connections – he had the sort of access to FDR that few others had – but his appointment was not simply nepotistic. He belonged to the progressive wing of the Democratic party (in which Eleanor was also a significant figure) and, as he informed the president on various occasions, his only objective in Ireland was to promote Roosevelt's policies. In addition to his formal diplomatic correspondence with the State Department, Gray also corresponded privately with the president. Gray's letters to the president supplemented those of Churchill and others and provided a framework for the president on Irish policy.

Gray urged the taoiseach to reconsider his position in respect of neutrality and to assess how he could assist 'in the defeat of Germany'. This exhortation was unwelcome to de Valera, who retorted that he 'was waiting further on events'. Gray reported to Roosevelt that the Irish government was now 'waking up to its danger', but did not hold out much hope of decisive action. What de Valera wanted from Roosevelt was a declaration that the United States would protect

Ireland against invasion. If the United States responded favourably to this request, de Valera told Gray, he would consult the Dáil and make a formal approach. Gray concluded that de Valera was frightened by the changing military situation, 'but not prepared to cope with it'.[1] Gray and Roosevelt wanted de Valera to negotiate a deal with the British on the Irish ports, Gray suggesting that the ports be leased to Britain for the duration of hostilities, but de Valera was seeking to maintain the status quo of early 1940 and if possible extend neutrality to the rest of the island. While the United States might have been sympathetic to Irish neutrality, it was sceptical about extending it to the whole island. This was particularly true after the German military successes of May and June 1940, when Britain was isolated. Roosevelt replied to de Valera early in June, refusing to make any commitments of the type de Valera wanted. 'Such a declaration,' the president claimed, 'would imply that we were departing from our traditional policy in regard to foreign affairs and would undoubtedly lead to misunderstanding.'[2]

While this was formally true, Roosevelt was doing everything he could to advance the British cause. In his first letter to Churchill after he became prime minister, Roosevelt was understandably cautious about the specific nature of the aid that might be forthcoming from the United States. Nevertheless, the president's inclination was to provide what aid he could within the restrictions imposed by neutrality legislation. Roosevelt was prepared to give 'the most favourable consideration' to requests for anti-aircraft equipment, while 'we are doing everything in our power' to create the conditions for Britain to buy aircraft. Churchill had suggested that an American naval squadron should visit Irish ports, a visit 'which might well be prolonged', but certainly not a suggestion that would meet with de Valera's approval. Roosevelt identified closely with Churchill and Britain, but though he was not prepared to give the prime minister any guarantees, he offered what help he could.

This period marks a clear shift in the global balance of power. The most obvious expression of this was Hitler's victories, but the most significant was the recognition by both Britain and Germany of the rise of the United States to world-power status. American power was acknowledged by de Valera's appeal to Roosevelt to protect Irish independence, but also by Churchill's belief that American involve-

ment could secure the ports for Britain. Globally, American dominance was acknowledged by the desperate attempts of Britain and
France to obtain arms and supplies, as well as political support, from
the Roosevelt administration.

In providing assistance Roosevelt was restricted by neutrality legislation, but he also insisted on exacting a price for US help. In their
crucial exchanges of July and August 1940, Roosevelt told Churchill
that support for Britain must also promote the 'national defence and
security of the United States', insisting that Britain provide bases for
the USA in the West Indies. Furthermore, in the event of Britain being
unable to control the seas around its island home, the British fleet
was to be moved to other parts of the empire to avoid the Germans
gaining control of it. Roosevelt was playing very clever domestic
politics, disarming critics of his foreign policy, but he was also using
his strength to expand American power and influence. Churchill may
have disliked this, but there was little he could do if he wanted to
contain Hitler in 1940 and 1941.[3]

Gray shared Roosevelt's liberal outlook on foreign policy and like
him was anti-Nazi. In the summer of 1940 de Valera asked the United
States to provide arms for Irish defence. His extensive shopping list
was sent to Robert Brennan, Ireland's minister in Washington and a
close personal friend, who forwarded it to the State Department. It
was an exhaustive list, and the State Department seemed anxious
to work with Brennan to provide introductions to officials in the
United States who could help him in his task. Gray warmly supported the Irish approach, warning the State Department that fears of
an invasion were not exaggerated. He also reported that, as matters
stood, the Irish were not in a position to defend their country. Gray
was extremely sympathetic to Ireland's position in the summer of
1940, making various suggestions about how American support might
be provided.[4] What the Irish did not seem to realize was that the
United States administration was sympathetic to the Irish request
only if granting it aided Britain. Secretary of State Hull contacted
the American embassy in London to ascertain what the British
attitude would be 'in regard to possible efforts on the part of this
Government to facilitate and expedite the purchase and delivery of
these arms'. The response was surprisingly positive, and the British
ambassador in Washington Lord Lothian was instructed to 'assist

the Irish Government as far as possible in obtaining the material desired'. However there was an important caveat: 'provided it does not impede or postpone delivery of any similar items ordered by the British Government'.

While there was considerable goodwill in Britain and the United States towards Ireland, there were clear limits. Brennan had been irritating State Department officials by calling every day at the department to gain an answer to the Irish request; he would have been mortified to learn that whatever he would achieve was entirely dependent on British goodwill. State Department officials agreed in June that information received from London provided them with enough to 'let the Irish Minister know what quantities of the desired arms could be purchased in this country and when they could be delivered'. Shortly after, Hull assured Gray, 'it is understood that the Irish Government's needs can be met at least in part'.[5] Gray asked Hull to appreciate the delicacy of the political situation in Ireland and the impact on the morale of the new volunteer force if the United States provided the arms. 'If humanly possible make it yes,' he urged.

Two days later Brennan was informed that the materials requested were not available from army surplus stock, but that there would be no objection to the Irish government purchasing the material from private companies. This was a blow to Irish hopes, as the cost of obtaining armaments from companies would be much higher than from the military authorities. On 26 June Brennan learnt that the delivery of any armaments to Ireland would be impossible 'within any reasonable length of time'. He then asked if surplus rifles could be purchased and was directed to the War Department. Hull again assisted Brennan, but little progress was achieved. Gray asked Hull if the negotiations with Ireland were stalemated, pleading, 'Is there yet hope for delivery. Need for these arms unquestionably pressing.' Gray was to be disappointed. In August virtually all the surplus rifles were sold to Canada. Most significantly, when Roosevelt made the decision to permit this sale both the Irish and the Canadian requests were on his desk. The president noted on the document, 'O.K. for Canada', but ignored the Irish request. American officials suggested that if Ireland wanted any rifles, then these would have to come out of the Canadian delivery. This was however no longer an American concern; the Irish would need to approach the Canadians and the British to see if some of their allocation could be diverted to Ireland.[6]

The Irish government also approached the United States for a warship to defend its coastline. Gray was dismissive of this request:

> As a matter of fact, the Irish government has no more use for one destroyer than I have for a white elephant. To defend this coast with a navy would require, in the opinion of experts a fleet of submarines and fast torpedo craft, entirely beyond the means of the nation.

While Gray was probably accurate in his assessment, the Irish government had been remiss in failing to develop a navy adequate to defend its coasts. Gray may have been closer to the truth when he indicated what might have been the real reason for the Irish request:

> The acquisition of one or more destroyers flying the Irish flag can only be regarded as a tribute to national pride and a very heavy burden on the national purse.

Gray however admitted that the purchase of 20,000 rifles was both necessary and within Ireland's means. He remained worried that these guns would not be made available:

> These rifles are very badly needed, and if it is the policy of the Department that the Irish government should be assisted in obtaining them I recommend that an effort should be made, unless the sale is prohibited by law, to hurry up delivery. Very serious results might possibly ensue from the failure of these rifles to reach this destination in time to be of service.[7]

Little had been achieved by the end of 1940, though Gray continued to impress upon the State Department and the president the danger that Ireland was exposed to. Relations between Ireland and Britain had deteriorated and Roosevelt increased his support for Britain rather than Ireland. Just before the November presidential election, Gray warned Roosevelt to be on his guard when dealing with the 'Limies', whom he claimed would 'take your pants, if you go to sleep with them on'. Immediately after the election itself Gray wrote that he had received congratulations from many people in Ireland, both public and private, as well as from most of the diplomatic corps.

He thought it 'queer' that not a single member of Fianna Fáil offered congratulations on the election outcome, while noting that the papal nuncio had predicted that Roosevelt would lose. All of this puzzled Gray and he speculated, 'there has been some dirty work at the crossroads'.[8]

The immediate reason for the cooling of relations between America and Ireland was Roosevelt's public support for Britain against Germany, but it was also believed in Ireland that Britain's success in the United States was at the cost of Irish influence with the administration. In these circumstances it is likely that most Fianna Fáil members would have welcomed a Roosevelt defeat in 1940, as they feared that he would lead the United States into the war if re-elected. Gray would have been disturbed to learn that de Valera had authorized Brennan to mobilize Irish-American sentiment against the Roosevelt administration and to cooperate with German and Italian representatives in the United States to create a strong isolationist lobby against the president's pro-British foreign policy. It is perhaps no accident that immediately after the November election de Valera sent a message to the American Association for the Recognition of the Irish Republic, a pressure group closely associated with isolationist tendencies in the United States. De Valera warned delegates of a 'new menace' to Ireland and called on them to mobilize American opinion in support of Irish neutrality and his government's anti-partitionist policies. Insisting that Ireland had the same right to stay out of the war as the United States, he told the AARIR delegates to 'beware false parallels'. Ireland, he continued, 'belongs to the Irish people and our territory cannot be lent or leased to any belligerent for war purposes without involving us in the war'.[9]

As a direct consequence of this and other contacts, Irish-American organizations met in New York later in November and established the American Friends of Irish Neutrality to promote Irish interests and defend the country's right to neutrality. The relationship between AFIN and the Irish government was such that the Irish legation wrote to the organization to warn that it should not 'give the impression that the organization is being used by the Legation . . . as the official channel for the dissemination of governmental decisions and news reports'. The Irish legation complained that AFIN had issued statements which suggested a very close relationship between themselves and the Irish government, Robert Brennan in particular. The real danger for the Irish government was that the closeness of this relationship would force AFIN to register as an agent of a foreign power under American law, 'which you could not do unless the Irish Government authorised it'. The Irish also wanted AFIN to be careful not to identify itself directly with the Irish government as it might say something embarrassing which would have to be then repudiated. The value of AFIN and other Irish-American organizations to Ireland was that influence could be exercised independently of the Irish legation, especially within the Democratic party. This advantage would be lost if the government had to repudiate AFIN or if it had to register as a foreign agent.[10]

De Valera's Christmas message to the United States in 1940 was addressed to the anti-British and isolationists. He complained that there was a campaign in the United States in support of Britain seizing the ports. De Valera assured his listeners that his government would not agree to this. 'We are a small nation and we have no illusion about our strength. But should any attempt be made to put such a suggestion into execution we shall defend ourselves to the utmost of our power.'[11] The view in the Roosevelt administration however was that de Valera should reach an accommodation with Churchill on the ports, and many officials became increasingly unsympathetic towards Ireland for its failure to do so. Gray wrote to Roosevelt early in February 1941 pointing out how difficult it was 'to make any of these people realize what was going on in the U.S.A. or that the American people had very little understanding or sympathy with Mr de Valera's academic contentions'. Gray was obviously feeling some pressure from the Irish government and Fianna Fáil supporters as he asked Roosevelt how far he could go with the Irish: 'I have no one to consult about the line I ought to take and if I am getting out on a limb send me a telegram saying "careful".' Gray was anxious to assure Roosevelt that he was doing what the president and the State Department wanted him to in Ireland, though this did involve him interpreting what this policy might be and 'its implications to this government'. Gray was dismissive of the quality of the Irish government, in particular because de Valera did not consult the opposition over the Emergency. Roosevelt responded very positively to Gray, advising him that he need not 'be careful'.[12]

Gray was certainly right to feel uneasy about some official Irish attitudes towards him. The secretary at the Department of External Affairs was especially hostile to the Roosevelt administration and sensitive to criticisms of Ireland. American newspapers frequently slated the Irish stance on the ports and supported the British in what was increasingly portrayed in the United States as a war between democracy and totalitarianism. Nor was Roosevelt's advice to Gray not to be careful a personal attitude on his part. While still constrained by domestic political pressures, Roosevelt increased his support for the British in 1941. One expression of this was his decision to appoint Wendell Willkie, his opponent in the 1940 election, his special emissary. Willkie visited Britain, Russia and China in this capacity. In Britain, he had lunch with Churchill on 27 January 1941, and passed on a letter to Churchill from Roosevelt that showed the intimacy that had developed between the two leaders as a result of their cooperation. Roosevelt included lines from Longfellow's poem 'Building the Ship'.

> Sail on, O ship of State!
> Sail on, O Union, Strong and great!
> Humanity with all its fears,
> With all the hopes of future years,
> Is hanging breathless on thy fate.

If sentimental, these lines attest to the respect that Roosevelt had for Churchill and it was shared by his closest advisers, including Gray, Willkie and Harry Hopkins. More alarming from the Irish point of view, Secretary of War Henry L. Stimpson recommended a more robust role for the American navy in the North Atlantic, including armed action to 'secure a British victory'. Although Roosevelt did not accept this recommendation for political reasons, it was a view commanding increasing support in the administration. Harry Hopkins was already in Britain and had also developed an intimate relationship with Churchill, one that the prime minister was careful to cultivate. In December Secretary of State Hull and Assistant Secretary Welles had tried to persuade de Valera to offer the ports to Britain, but had been dismissed in bad-tempered fashion by Brennan. It was this exchange that led to de Valera's critical Christmas message to the United States in 1940.[13]

De Valera was clearly in a difficult position, yet his own narrow vision of the war and the weakness of his diplomatic representation in Washington meant that the implications noted by Gray were not, nor would they be, appreciated in Dublin. In a bizarre change of tactics Dublin tried to engage the sympathies of Willkie while he was in Britain. Irish officials wanted Willkie to come to Ireland during his visit to Britain and used their American supporters to put pressure on him. Paul O'Dwyer, chairman of AFIN, telegraphed Willkie in London (probably prompted by Brennan) to complain that he would not 'cross a few miles of channel to give the people of Ireland encouragement in their forthright stand'. The telegram expressed concern at attempts to force Ireland into the war and called on Willkie to support Irish requests for arms and munitions. It is difficult to know what AFIN or the Irish government hoped to achieve by bringing Willkie to Dublin for a meeting with de Valera. If he did not go, Irish sensibilities would be offended by what would be seen in Fianna Fáil circles as a snub. Yet it must have been well known that Willkie strongly supported Britain, a view that was reinforced by his visit as he openly admired the stoic nature of the British resistance to Hitler. His policy platform at the 1940 election had been essentially bipartisan on foreign policy, and this was the reason Roosevelt had asked him to visit Britain.[14] Willkie decided to go to Dublin on his own initiative, though Gray was opposed to him doing so. Gray had previously approached Hull and advised that if Willkie came he should do so under the auspices of the State Department or the legation.

Willkie made his own arrangements and Gray only learnt of his visit the evening before he arrived, driving in the dark to the airport the following morning to receive him. Gray met Frank Aiken at the airport, and on learning that Willkie's plane had been delayed in Manchester due to a puncture they had to wait for over three hours. The delay and Aiken's presence dismayed Gray, as it prevented him having a private conversation with the visitor. If the Irish had expected Willkie to be sympathetic to their position, they were disappointed, despite providing twenty-year-old whiskey for their American visitors. The whiskey was provided when they met de Valera in Government Buildings, where Willkie had a private discussion with the taoiseach at which he 'handed him a couple of jolts', as he recounted later to Gray. At the lunch that followed de Valera looked 'sour', and on being questioned about the discussion by Gray replied, 'Of course one has no time in an hour to explain our position.' This was de Valera's frequent response when he met someone who did not agree with him on partition or his other policies, a response based on his belief that his position was the only one possible. When Gray suggested that the invitation to Willkie was a courageous one, as it could outrage the Germans and Italians, de Valera shrugged his shoulders and replied, 'Oh well.' Gray commented that de Valera had been caught off balance by the visit, which he discovered had in fact been suggested by the Dominions Office in the belief that de Valera should learn what an American supporter of Britain was thinking about Ireland and the war.

Whatever he thought of de Valera, Willkie was certainly unimpressed by his visit. When he returned to London he attended a dinner in his honour at the Dorchester. He talked frankly about the conversation with de Valera, recounting how the taoiseach had produced a map of Ireland and pointed out the threat to his state from Britain as a consequence of its presence in Northern Ireland. Willkie was dismissive of de Valera's views, asserting that none of them mattered given the seriousness of the current crisis. Willkie had put it to de Valera that his refusal to hand over the ports to Britain was a 'disadvantage to the cause of freedom' and most importantly de Valera would not have American opinion on his side if there were a clash with Britain. According to Willkie's account, this startled de Valera, who accused the British government of stupidity to 'dodge and edge away' from Willkie's charge. Willkie finally asked de Valera if he wanted the British to win the war. When de Valera replied that he did, Willkie accused him of making such a victory more difficult. When de Valera then countered that Dublin would be bombed if the ports were leased to the British, Willkie was contemptuous, as he had recently visited some of the bombed cities in Britain and seen the courage of the inhabitants. Gray wrote to de Valera shortly after the visit to thank him for inviting him to lunch with Willkie, and emphasized that Willkie was a private citizen who 'made his own plans and time table'. However, Gray was being somewhat disingenuous as he then went on to note the possible impact of the visit on the American press.[15]

At this point, the relationship between Gray and de Valera remained fairly cordial. Gray regularly forwarded memoranda of his conversations with de Valera to the taoiseach's office as well as to the

State Department, though de Valera did not always accept the version that Gray had written. In early February 1941, for instance, Gray sent a memorandum he had prepared for Hull. The conversation had taken place on 22 January and in his note Gray displayed considerable admiration for de Valera and the Irish government. He had sent this particular memorandum so that de Valera could appreciate Gray's position in respect of the war and Ireland, even when the views of the United States and Ireland diverged. He recognized that de Valera might not consider the opinions either accurate or fair, but as he respected and admired de Valera Gray believed it was better to be open with him. 'I prefer,' Gray claimed, 'to have open differences of viewpoint.' Gray may have been well intentioned, yet it was a gesture that the Irish authorities never returned.[16]

*

The Irish government decided in February that another direct approach to the American government to obtain arms and supplies would be appropriate. Why this was so is not entirely clear. At a top-level meeting in December 1940 attended by de Valera, Aiken and General McKenna it was acknowledged that 'the prospect was very remote' that any arms could be obtained from America. Gray met de Valera during the afternoon of Saturday 22 February to discuss the decision to send a special representative to pursue the Irish case. Gray was strongly in favour of this initiative and endorsed de Valera's decision to send Frank Aiken on the grounds that he had de Valera's complete confidence and 'was in unconditional sympathy with his policy regarding the existing crisis'. When De Valera dismissed Gray's opinion that Aiken represented 'leftist' opinion within the cabinet, insisting that the minister was a 'centrist', Gray reiterated that what was important was that Aiken would not be 'influenced either by blandishment or pressure' while in the United States. Gray welcomed de Valera's frankness and openness at the meeting, though the two men disagreed on a number of matters. When Gray wrote to the State Department he emphasized de Valera's 'good faith and sincerity'.[17] He warned de Valera that the United States would require an understanding that any weapons that Aiken received would not be used against the British. De Valera responded that any weapons would only be used against the British if they invaded Ireland, as this would place them on 'the same plane as the Germans'. The taoiseach also confirmed that a defensive front had been established by the Irish military against the British forces in Northern Ireland as a consequence of Churchill's statement on the ports in November 1940.

De Valera feared that an orchestrated campaign was under way to prepare British opinion for an attack on Ireland, while Gray tried to persuade him that Britain and Ireland were in a vicious circle, with neither side prepared to give the guarantee that the other required. Gray continued to believe that it was a situation 'which men of good will should try to escape by mutual compromise'. Gray admitted that he did not change de Valera's mind on this issue.[18] Two days later Brennan was authorized to tell the State Department or others who might enquire that the Irish government wanted to send a senior minister to investigate possibilities on the spot. By 3 March Gray had informed de Valera that Hull was 'endeavouring to comply with this request', but more ominously Gray had been authorized to tell de Valera that American military production was already assigned to specific orders and delivery could take a year or more. Gray also reported Hull's view that American requirements would take priority but after that precedence would be given to 'Governments who are resisting aggression' – this did not include Ireland. The only way out of the difficulty that Hull could suggest was that the Irish government cooperate with the British Purchasing Commission in Washington. If they did so Aiken's task in the United States could be greatly eased and 'It might be possible for them to advance to your Government munitions shortly to be delivered in return for others which Mr Aiken might order.'[19]

While Brennan was organizing the American side of the trip, Gray wrote to Aiken providing him with an introduction to Eleanor Roosevelt from both himself and his wife Maude. Much has been made of Gray's closeness to the president, but the most intimate relationship was with Eleanor, with whom Maude Gray had grown up. In his letter to Aiken Gray wrote that he would find Eleanor 'interesting and sympathetic', and encouraged him to send the letter of introduction to the White House once he arrived in the United States. Gray assured Aiken, 'We are sure that as soon as possible she will arrange to meet you.' Gray then offered some advice to Aiken, which was fairly frank. He recollected that when he was appointed minister to Ireland he was warned not to ignore Fianna Fáil or he would learn little of the real politics of Ireland. He now hoped that Aiken would not be offended if he offered similar advice:

> If you associate yourself with the Irish nationalist circles, which you would naturally find sympathetic, you will return knowing no more of the sources of majority opinion, upon which the President's Government rests, than you know now.

This probably did not go down well, though Gray emphasized that Eleanor Roosevelt would introduce him to individuals in American politics with whom Brennan might not have close contact. In the letter provided by Gray for Eleanor Roosevelt, he was even more direct but not unsympathetic to Aiken. It is not difficult to guess how Aiken would have responded to Gray's views on his background:

> He is a very interesting example of what Irish ideals do to people of non-Gaelic origin, for his family, as I have been told, were Cromwellian settlers in Ulster.

According to Gray, the Aiken family had only recently become Catholic and nationalist. Gray recommended Aiken to Eleanor as 'He has very interesting ideas as to education and social reconstruction in Ireland as well as other matters in which you are interested.' Gray also told her that Aiken would provide her with an idea of the Fianna Fáil government's position on the current crisis more honestly than anyone else.

Gray was very positive about Aiken, noting that he and Maude 'have had pleasant social relations with him and his wife'. He described Aiken's wife Maud as 'a most intelligent, charming and distinguished woman'. Gray asked Eleanor on his and Maude's behalf to extend any courtesy she could to Aiken when she met him in Washington, including introducing him to interested parties. In a telling section of the letter he wrote:

> These are very difficult times for everyone here, but the courtesy, kindness, and fine manners of all the members of the Government make it possible for the American representative to have a happy time here, even though he is obliged to differ fundamentally with the Irish government on many questions.

If we take these letters at face value – and there is no reason why we should not as they are available in the files of the Irish Department of External Affairs – Gray had a favourable though not uncritical view of the proposed visit by Aiken. Gray and his wife were prepared to use their personal relationship with FDR's wife to assist Aiken in his search for support in the United States. Likewise Gray's correspondence with the State Department and with the president does not include any hostile comment on the purpose of the trip. In his discussions with de Valera Gray did warn that public opinion in the United States had changed over the previous few months, emphasizing that the mobilization of Irish-American opinion against FDR, the British and the lend-lease programme which provided Britain with vital military assistance on preferential terms was not winning favour or aiding Ireland's cause with the administration. Gray maintained close relations with various leading Fianna Fáil members and appears to have been on particularly good terms with some of them. He exchanged letters and jokes with Frank Gallagher, at least one of which he passed on to Roosevelt. Gallagher wrote a very friendly letter to Gray in February 1941, before Aiken went to America, in which he wrote, 'It would be impossible not to be at one's best wherever Mrs Gray and yourself are.'[20]

While de Valera and other Irish officials might not have wished to hear Gray's message, it was one that he made very clear, and it was the position also taken by the State Department. In early February 1941 Gray warned de Valera that he was not prepared to support an Irish request for arms if these were demanded 'on your terms', as it would not be successful. The best he could promise was to point out the state of American opinion and that Hitler's success posed a 'threat to the American way of life and a menace to American society'. In what must have been an uncomfortable exchange for de Valera, Gray baldly stated, 'those nations that are fighting the Axis powers are fighting for American security'. The unstated but clear implication was that Ireland was not and would not therefore be receiving American armaments and supplies. Gray was quick to add, 'This is no criticism of your policy of neutrality and implies no lack of friendliness on the part of my Government. It is simply the state of things made inevitable by our respective national states of mind.' This was clever, as De Valera had made much to the Americans and British of his inability to act in support of Britain because of public opinion in Ireland. Gray was now invoking American opinion. Nor was Gray demanding that de Valera hand over the ports or go to war at this time, but he was saying that if Ireland sided with America then he would strongly support Irish requests for arms.[21]

Hull's reply to Gray essentially reinforced these views and certainly could not have brought comfort to de Valera. However, Hull did hold out the possibility that the British and the Irish would cooperate in obtaining arms from the United States: 'it must not expect if it acts alone without the assistance of the British Purchasing Commission to be able to place considerable orders for munitions for immediate delivery'. This clearly established the low priority given to Ireland by the American administration but also ignored the Irish belief that relations between Ireland and Britain 'had steadily deteriorated' since November 1940.[22] Gray delivered Hull's message to de Valera on 3 March, after which there was a noticeable shift in emphasis in his reports to Washington. He now withdrew his support for selling weapons to Ireland:

> Last Summer I endeavoured to enlist your good offices to procure arms for Irish Government direct from America. I wish formally to recede from this position in view of changed conditions and fuller knowledge. This is not to be taken as an alarmist warning but as common prudence in view of unfortunate possibilities. If, as I suspect, you believe the decision to arm Ireland to be primarily a British responsibility I agree entirely.

Gray's view of Aiken also soured. He now worried that Aiken had 'the dogmatic obstinacy of the child mind', which might embarrass de Valera if he subsequently changed his political position on Britain or neutrality, although he did raise the possibility that Aiken would get 'straight talk' in America. Although Gray wrote the letters of introduction already cited, when he gave these to de Valera he asked if Aiken was pro-German. De Valera insisted that Aiken was not pro-German but pro-Irish, and asked Gray to believe him.[23]

*

Aiken left Ireland in early March. He went first to London, after which he travelled to Lisbon from where he flew on to the United States.

When he arrived in London a message was waiting for him from Colonel Bill Donovan, the personal emissary to Europe of President Roosevelt and Secretary of War Knox. Donovan was Irish-American, a Republican but also a close confidant of FDR. He is best known as the head of the OSS, the forerunner of the CIA. He had just visited Ireland as part of a European fact-finding mission during which he had made no secret of FDR's commitment to preventing the defeat of Britain. Such an attitude was not welcome in Ireland, nor was the fact that he was an Irish-American Republican who supported the British in the war, a matter of considerable sensitivity for the Irish government and for the legation in Washington. His visit to Ireland led officials there to complain that he had not stayed long enough to fully appreciate the Irish position, a similar observation to that made when Willkie proved unsympathetic. Yet Donovan had met Cardinal MacRory, then eighty years of age, whom he described as a 'determined eloquent, nationalist and vigorous man'. MacRory gave Donovan a memorandum on the oppression suffered by Catholics in Northern Ireland. This made a considerable impression on Donovan, as he included some of the complaints in his own report to Knox. He also discussed the complaints with Churchill when he met him in London, observing that the Catholics of Northern Ireland had a disproportionate influence on the Irish government because of the oppression suffered.

The main purpose of Donovan's visit was to see de Valera, who was at pains to assure him that the Irish government was friendly to Britain and not pro-German. However, he also argued that the best way for Ireland to aid the cause was for the country to be adequately armed. De Valera claimed that 'he could resist invasion successfully and save England a diversion of troops' if only his army had the weapons they had asked for, a point with added urgency now that Aiken was about to visit the United States. De Valera refused to consider any change of policy in respect of the ports, returning to this issue on a number of occasions, and insisted that Irish opinion did not trust Britain. He also made it clear that his government was going to remain neutral 'even over America's request'.

Donovan was persuaded that the Irish situation was a real problem:

I do believe that there are dangerous elements which may have consequences of a very serious nature to British defence if not dealt with. It is my opinion that they can be dealt with if we and the British act rapidly.

On Donovan's return to London, Churchill invited him to Chequers, where he also met the Australian prime minister, Robert Menzies. In conversation with the two leaders, Donovan warned that de Valera's policies, especially censorship, ensured that his own citizens were unaware of what was happening in the outside world. He also believed de Valera's assurances that his government was broadly sympathetic to the British but that he was not 'free' to act accordingly. Donovan told Churchill and Menzies that statesmanship was required, not military action. He predicted that if Britain occupied the ports against Irish wishes this would aid the Germans, as it would take considerable resources to defend them. Not only would this create a dangerous situation in Ireland, it would also alienate opinion in the United States.

Tellingly, Menzies interrupted to strongly agree with the American, noting that about a quarter of his people were of Irish origin and that the use of force would 'affect the opinion of the Australians'. Donovan argued forcibly that contact was an absolute priority and that the 'curtain of asbestos hanging between England and Ireland' needed to be removed. Liaison between Churchill and de Valera was required, he strongly suggested, if there was to be any prospect of Irish opinion endorsing action in support of Britain. Donovan passed on de Valera's complaint that such liaison was absent, and he urged Churchill to investigate Catholic complaints in Northern Ireland and deal with them if possible. Donovan was also anxious to bring Ireland 'into our sphere', as he put it, and he toyed with the idea, 'not an inconceivable one', of inviting de Valera to the United States. Donovan went on to think out loud: 'It is necessary for us to get rid of the veil of unreality under which Ireland is living if we really intend to influence her.'

While Donovan might not get de Valera to the United States, he recognized the importance of Aiken's impending visit. He speculated whether Aiken was going to America for reasons other than simply to discuss armaments, but nevertheless considered it important to impress him with the defensive measures that the United States had taken. In his report he recommended that Knox and other senior members of the administration take the opportunity to meet and talk to the visiting minister. Donovan had cautioned de Valera and repeated in his report to the president and the secretary of the navy that Ireland should not have any doubts that the United States would only provide arms to those states allied with Britain.

At Chequers Churchill promised to investigate the situation for Catholics in Northern Ireland, adding that 'although he was for a united Ireland he would not compel it'. He did promise however that if Ireland joined the war he would do everything he could to achieve a united Ireland. While this was not likely to satisfy de Valera or Aiken, it is significant that Churchill was prepared to support an initiative similar to that proposed by MacDonald the previous year and to do so in the presence of Donovan and Menzies. Donovan's own view was that the strategic value of the ports was significant and the issue serious enough for action. 'I am sure that our help in securing the Irish bases is greatly hoped for,' he concluded his report to Knox. Churchill, Donovan and Menzies agreed that the Australian prime minister would visit Ireland, north and south, to explore further some of the issues raised by Donovan.[24]

In London Donovan had a long discussion with Aiken at Claridge's hotel. They talked for over two hours and Aiken was not especially impressed with Donovan. Donovan 'interrogated', as Aiken put it, the Irish minister on neutrality, the ports and the charge that Aiken was pro-German. The American made it clear that while he was not asking Ireland to join the war, he personally believed that the British cause was morally superior and had a strong spiritual dimension to it. Aiken may have been irritated by Donovan's interrogative approach to the issues; he seemed to expect a yes or no answer to each question. There was however an interesting exchange between Aiken and Donovan when Dulanty, who was present, intervened to challenge Donovan's view that Britain had moral superiority in the conflict. Dulanty claimed the war was simply between two imperialist powers. Aiken then asked Donovan what difference it would make to America if Germany won the war. Donovan replied that he did not believe that Germany would directly attack the United States, but added that its dominance of Europe, the Middle East and the seaways would have catastrophic consequences and would undermine the 'American way of life'.

Aiken's position was that Ireland would not join a war on the side of a state that he condemned as an aggressor in Ireland – Britain. Ireland would only enter the war if it were attacked. He reiterated de Valera's policy that force would not be used to end partition and that Ireland would not be used as a base for attacks on Britain. However, he went on to question the extent to which Ireland would cooperate with Britain even if there were a German attack:

> We would not ask the British forces into our territory even though we were assured that the Germans were going to attack us within ten days, as the morale of our people required it to be clearly proved who was the aggressor.

The two men then discussed the possibility of a pre-emptive British strike in Ireland to occupy the ports, a most unlikely possibility according to Donovan. Aiken demanded that Britain arm Ireland, and asked for support from the American administration to stop anti-Irish propaganda in the United States. He did not welcome two points made by Donovan. The first was that the Americans had effectively been at war with Germany for two years, but that Hitler was ignoring this until he was in a position to attack them. The second was that Donovan wanted to see Ireland 'within the American orbit and taking the same line as America on all questions', perhaps an early warning of how United States policymakers viewed Ireland and the other neutrals. However, Donovan also admitted that he viewed every issue from an American perspective, despite his interest in Ireland and all matters Irish. Donovan and Gray continually emphasized that their primary interest was in securing the United States from German aggression and that Irish interests were at the most secondary.[25]

Aiken believed that Germany would defeat Britain, and had been even more convinced since the evacuation from Dunkirk, while back in Dublin Walshe at External Affairs remained perplexed at United States support for Britain. Walshe had written to Brennan in Washington in November 1940, 'Is the view you attribute to Americans about identification of interests with Britain universal? As there is a real possibility of a British defeat there must be some Americans who see that and who do not accept such a complete identity of interests.'[26]

After meeting Donovan, Aiken travelled to Lisbon, where he met the Portuguese dictator Salazar. This seems to have been a more congenial meeting than that in London. Salazar told Aiken that it 'was

the neutrals who were paying for the war', an opinion with which
Aiken clearly agreed. Aiken pointed out that Ireland had no trade with
Germany, unlike Portugal, and was therefore totally dependent on
Britain for shipping, but that British policy towards Ireland 'was a
form of economic pressure by squeezing', adding that 'we are in effect
blockaded by both sides'. Salazar interrupted to say that he thought
no country had suffered more than Portugal from the British blockade,
but Aiken then upped the stakes by telling Salazar that the Irish
famine of 1845–51 had been 'an artificial one' and that its impact on
the population had been worse than that of a war. This was the
politics of grievance in a big way, with the two men attempting to
outdo one another. It was also revealing of Aiken's views on politics
prior to his arrival in the United States. Salazar told Aiken that he had
read the Irish constitution in a French translation, offering his opinion
that some of its basic principles were the same as those that guided
his actions in Portugal.[27] British sources in Lisbon reported further
revealing remarks made by Aiken at a lunch with Irish members of
the Dominican order in the city. These included that Britain would be
defeated and a German victory was to be hoped for and that there
was no reason from an Irish perspective not to welcome German
success. John Winant, the new American ambassador in London,
forwarded this report to Washington. He added that in view of this
and other evidence, 'the principal object of Aiken's visit would seem
to be to influence feeling in favour of Eire's neutrality' and not
primarily to obtain arms.[28]

Gray reported James Dillon's view that de Valera was sending
Aiken to the United States to educate him. Dillon also believed
that Aiken was in a position to prevent de Valera from taking an
anti-German position, though how never became clear. Others in the
Irish government now shared Aiken's view that Britain would lose
the war, including some who had previously been considered sympathetic to the British cause. The Canadian high commissioner in
Dublin, John Kearney, told Gray that Lemass had said to him that it
made little difference to Ireland whether it was under British or
German control. Gray thought that Lemass's views were prompted by
his belief that Ireland was in 'economic serfdom' to Britain. Similar
views from other Fianna Fáil members were reported to the State
Department by Gray, including that of Tom Burke, who was both a

TD and lord mayor of Limerick. He asserted not only that Britain was beaten but that some benefit could come to Ireland from a German victory. Gray also noted admiration for German skills and organizational methods among some sections of the population. This led Gray to paint for Sumner Welles, who was preparing to meet Aiken, a dismal picture of the political leadership in Ireland. He considered de Valera in particular myopic in respect of the international situation and the threat to Ireland in particular:

> I think it is fair to say that, in all the circumstances, the policy of neutrality has been the only one that could have been maintained for the past eight months, but I think history will condemn him for having been unwilling to lead public opinion to a realization of the spiritual issues of the world conflict. It will condemn too for using the anti-British issue to keep in power against the ultimate best interest of the country.

Gray told Welles that the political environment had changed for the worse. He had asked de Valera if in return for arms he would provide assurances that in the event of a German attack he would invite the British in and provide them with facilities. De Valera was not prepared to do so. Gray then told de Valera that while the United States did not wish to criticize the Irish government it

> sorrowfully regrets that we do not see eye to eye and stand shoulder to shoulder in this struggle for the survival of Christian civilization and the rights of small nations.

Gray charged that Ireland was not prepared to acknowledge that its safety and supplies were dependent on the British navy and was unable to agree a formula that would 'contribute to the security of the ocean lanes'.[29]

This cannot have helped Aiken when he arrived in the United States, but his own predisposition against the British and the briefing material provided to him by the Department of External Affairs only compounded the situation and placed him on a collision course with the Roosevelt administration. External Affairs had become increasingly hostile to the American administration, asserting that 'no government with which we have direct diplomatic relations has been so grudging to admit our separate statehood as the American government'. Walshe

had been particularly irritated back in 1939 when the veteran republican Joseph McGarrity wrote to the State Department to enquire as to
the exact status of the Irish minister in the United States. The department's reply, though legally accurate, could only embarrass the Irish
government, as de Valera pointed out to Dominions Undersecretary
Devonshire earlier in 1939: 'The Irish Minister to the United States
bears letters of credence from King George, which are countersigned
by the Prime Minister of Ireland.' Walshe complained that the United
States continued to believe in the diplomatic unity of the British
empire, which in effect meant that the British ambassador would act
as a conduit for the Irish government.[30] What Walshe ignored was that
Eire was still a member of the commonwealth, but he still condemned
the State Department for showing 'a disregard for our separate status
entirely opposed to the normal relationship existing between states'.[31]

If this was not enough to prejudice Aiken against the United States
government, Walshe also described the State Department as having
become 'more arrogant' by condemning Ireland for not supporting
the British war effort. This then led to the claim:

> They are throwing off the mask of even superficial courtesy towards
> us, and we are almost told that we cannot expect any support or
> friendliness from the United States in a situation in which the
> British would consider it necessary to seize the ports.

This was a fairly crude characterization of United States policy towards
Ireland, and the recommendation to Aiken did not redeem the
situation:

> The time has come to let the more serious and discreet of the
> influential of the Irish-American groups into the secret, and to tell
> them, with the details which our Minister in Washington can
> supply, that the American policy towards Ireland is to force us into
> a war which they must know can bring nothing but destruction
> and suffering to this small nation.

This was precisely the tactic that Gray had warned Aiken not to
pursue, but clearly one the DEA thought appropriate to the situation.
It should be recalled that while Walshe wrote this and other notes for
Aiken, de Valera was minister for external affairs and exercised very
close control over its actions. The advice to Aiken would have been

read to de Valera by Walshe and agreed with him. It included a denial that possession of the ports had any strategic advantage for Britain and the allegation that the main reason the British wanted Ireland in the war was to 'remove the moral deficit' that Ireland's neutrality was causing. This was a strange argument to advance when Walshe and de Valera must have been aware that Gray, Roosevelt and Donovan all shared the view that the British cause was a morally superior one. There was also some arrogance in suggesting that Ireland's involvement would make the war more moral, but this was due to Walshe viewing the situation from a exclusively Irish standpoint. At the very least it expressed an isolationism of attitude and knowledge surprising in a foreign affairs department.[32]

Walshe had also been aggrieved by an appeal signed by prominent American Catholics in support of Britain and instructed Brennan to interview various Catholic bishops and prominent Irish-Americans to put the Irish position. Walshe also wanted it circulated that Colonel Bill Donovan, one of the appeal's supporters, was anti-Catholic.[33] Aiken was also provided with an extensive memorandum, *British claims to the Irish Ports*, which rehearsed various arguments against handing them over, and received a four-page memorandum on how to counter 'anti-Irish' propaganda while in America.

At the heart of the Irish position as Aiken landed in the United States was their view:

> Neutrality is of the very essence of Irish independence. It is based on the fundamental and universal will of our people so much so that no Government could depart from it without at once being overthrown.

Consequently there could be no negotiation on neutrality or the ports. Americans were to be urged to recognize that Ireland's 700 years of 'resistance to the aggression of a great power had contributed more to liberty and justice than any other country in the world'. The Irish government was also opposed to the lend-lease programme, which had been recently agreed by Congress, but given the generally pro-British sentiments of the Roosevelt administration and an increasing majority of the American public it was considered necessary to demonstrate that Irish policy was not based on 'historic hatred of England'. Walshe also claimed that there was no certainty of Germany occupying Ireland if it won the war. Indeed Walshe and other Irish officials believed – or at least hoped – that neutrality would give them some negotiating space with a victorious Germany. Even if occupied, a neutral people would have 'a right to the restoration of their freedom', but if neutrality was abandoned and Germany won, then a state could have no expectation of such a benign outcome. Irish policy therefore had to be based on the principle of 'securing the ultimate survival of the nation' and this could be best achieved by remaining outside the war. The alternatives were stated in stark form for Aiken:

> The government is, therefore, obliged to consider rather the immediate certain consequences for Ireland of entry into the war than *the possible or probable effect of that entry in determining the victory of the democratic states.* We should be exchanging the present certainty of immunity in neutrality for the certainty of destruction in war. (emphasis added)

The tone of the memorandum was also neutral as to outcome. The widespread view in America that Britain was fighting a selfless war was dismissed as 'child-like' and Americans were considered ill-informed and gullible. No moral difference was made between Britain and Germany; indeed to an Irish nationalist or an American isolationist the emphasis would have seemed anti-British.[34]

*

Prior to Aiken arriving in the United States, Winant in London forwarded information to Washington on the nature of his mission. Maffey had informed London that while Aiken was anti-British he was not pro-German, adding that the British authorities should assist in arranging transportation to the United States as this 'would help dispel the feeling in Ireland that British economic measures were punitive'. Maffey was rather naive here, for when Senator MacDermot tried to highlight British goodwill in arranging travel facilities his views were censored. Winant also reported that Foreign Office Undersecretary Sir Alexander Cadogan considered, as did Maffey, that the visit could be useful in educating Aiken in the realities of political life outside Ireland. But Cadogan also told Winant that Aiken's visit had nothing to do with British national policy, though they were prepared to work with Aiken in the United States to achieve his aim of purchasing arms, as long as Ireland's requirements could be met without reducing supplies to Britain.[35] In a press conference Roosevelt confirmed that an Irish minister was about to arrive, but emphasized that American weapons were only available to those resisting aggression or prepared to do so. When asked about which country such arms might be used against, the president laughed and said that was a delicate matter. He also said that no specific aid programme was being contemplated for Ireland and did not know if it would qualify for lend-lease. This press conference caused consternation and embarrassment in Dublin as Roosevelt was asked a question about Aiken and replied that he had no *official* knowledge of the visit. Walshe immediately called in Gray and demanded an explanation. Gray insisted that while there may have been confusion, no discourtesy was intended. This did not allay Irish fears and suspicions however.[36]

Immediately after this, de Valera broadcast his annual St Patrick's Day message to the United States. Gray wrote to Roosevelt, 'It will do him no good over there. He cannot get out of his self-centered dream world and realize that the Irish will be goose-stepping if Britain goes down.' In his broadcast de Valera reiterated what was now a common charge by members of the Irish government and its supporters: that both sides were blockading Ireland, with de Valera complaining that this was the case even though Britain and Ireland had worked out mutually accommodating arrangements for the first eighteen months of the war. He commended Aiken's visit to the United States and called for Ireland's neutral status to be recognized internationally so that it could avoid 'the hazards of imperial adventure', echoing Dulanty's remark to Donovan earlier in the month.

Gray was close to despair after the broadcast and angry about de Valera's hypocrisy. He wrote to Roosevelt that Ireland was completely dependent on British sailors risking their lives to bring supplies to the country. Despite this, the Irish government was not prepared to distinguish between the two sides in the conflict. The reality, according to Gray, was that Ireland could not defend itself against 'any third rate power unless it was British policy' to help it. This harsh appraisal was written for the president's eyes only, but it reiterated what Gray had been saying to the State Department and de Valera himself. Gray commended Cosgrave's policies on Northern Ireland and the commonwealth, but complained that de Valera had used these issues to promote his political success: 'this running a government on hatred for another country is a very dangerous thing and is bound to land him on the scrap heap eventually'. This extreme attitude to Britain and Northern Ireland prevented de Valera from securing an end to partition, he believed. Indeed Gray suggested that no solution was possible while de Valera was in power. Less than a year after arriving in Ireland, Gray recognized that he was not as welcome as he had been among government supporters; he clearly sensed a difficult time ahead.

The State Department noted early in March that Britain attached 'supreme importance' to Aiken's visit, adding significantly, 'It is not at all certain however that they attach importance to the success of his mission in terms of securing arms and supplies.' The department believed that at various times since 1939 Britain had favoured a policy of strengthening Irish defences and this goodwill was in evidence when 20,000 rifles out of a consignment previously purchased from the United States were passed on. More recent developments puzzled the State Department however; in particular the tension that had emerged between de Valera and Churchill over the ports. The stand-off between the two states was a cause of concern for American policymakers, as it was not clear what Britain wanted. On weapons Britain was seen as the decisive player, as 'it is believed we might ask Britain for a clarification of its attitude on the question of providing arms for Ireland'. Departmental officials prepared a memorandum for Sumner Welles incorporating the views of Gray, Donovan and Winant. It was a fairly critical brief and included the charge that Aiken was on the 'extreme left' and might be in the United States for reasons other than arms purchase. America's policy of selling arms only to those states committed to aiding the democracies fighting Hitler was again emphasized.[37]

Welles met Aiken on 21 March but was not impressed by his Irish visitor. Aiken complained that Ireland was still waiting for the transfer of ownership of two ships and wanted to know how soon this would be completed. Welles was emphatic that 'assistance to Great Britain came first and foremost' and that requests from other governments would only be considered in the context of that policy. This could not have pleased Aiken, but his own negotiating tactics clearly did not impress the State Department. Immediately after this meeting a note was incorporated into the department's file on the trip baldly stating, 'Aiken has the narrowest point of view – no cooperation with England while the Ulster question remains unsettled.'[38] Welles was extremely critical of Aiken, who had engaged in 'a rather extraordinary diatribe' against Britain. Welles wanted Aiken to realize that lend-lease was intended to give maximum support to Britain. The president's decision to sign the legislation indicated that America was committed to a British victory. He contended that 'British victory was indispensable' not only for Britain but also for the 'world at large'. While this could not have been welcome to either Aiken or Brennan, Welles also expressed his personal view that 'no patriotic Irishman could possibly believe that Irish independence would be secured if a German victory took place'. Welles provided a very upbeat interpretation of Anglo-Irish relations since 1922, confidently predicting that if Britain won the war the remaining differences between the two states could be resolved. He nevertheless expressed concern that Irish public opinion did not believe that a British victory was in Ireland's interest. A German victory would end Irish independence, he believed. Welles was clearly frustrated by Aiken, who instead of responding to these issues, focused on partition. Aiken criticized the British on a number of counts, both contemporary and historical, but this had no impact on Welles, who replied,

> At a time when the British were moving heaven and earth to get all the arms and ammunition from this side of the Atlantic, it was hardly reasonable to believe that they would transfer part of their own stocks held in Britain to Ireland when the Irish government refused to lift a finger to assist the British in their attempts at self defence nor to cooperate with the British in this common endeavour.[39]

The Irish summary of this conversation was somewhat more optimistic, though recognizing that the United States was committed to supporting Britain as a priority. Brennan's report to Dublin did not depart in substance from that of Welles, though the emphasis was quite different. Welles seemed willing to discuss Irish needs and asked for a list of requirements, after which he promised to arrange for Aiken and Brennan to meet officials to process the request.[40] Aiken was

critical of the British, remarking in one exchange that they were fools
for not realizing that Ireland would not change its policy. Aiken
confirmed Welles's contention that Ireland was not 'as keen on a
British victory as the Americans were'. Those who held those views,
Aiken retorted, 'were right', but the British had only themselves to
blame. According to Aiken, 'They had partitioned the country and that
was the worst sort of aggression.' At a later point in the discussion he
made it clear that Ireland could see little justice in Britain's position,
'as long as the country was suffering aggression'. When Welles
remarked that this made Americans uneasy with Ireland, Aiken sharply
replied, 'There was no use talking to the Irish people about a potential
aggressor when they were facing an active aggressor.' Aiken went on
to condemn the press campaign in Britain and America over the ports
and to insist that the British could derive no benefit whatsoever from
their use of them. At one stage Aiken seemed to imply that Ireland was
irrelevant to the war and should simply be left out of the calculations.[41]

*

Gray was becoming anxious about Aiken in America. He wrote to Hull
on 27 March asking about the positions Aiken was taking in the
United States. Gray feared that Aiken would alienate United States
officials at a time when the economic situation was deteriorating
rapidly in Ireland. When Gray met Tánaiste Seán T. O'Kelly, he warned
that de Valera's St Patrick's Day broadcast had not helped the Irish
case with the US administration. Gray noted that there was some
unease in Ireland concerning this speech, where James Douglas had
raised the issue in the Seanad, rejecting the charge that Britain was
blockading Ireland.[42] Gray concluded that de Valera was not prepared
to concede on the ports under any circumstances, but hoped that
economic and other pressures would 'rouse the government from
its dream of academic neutrality'. He worried that there might be
an increase in anti-Americanism when the Irish realized that American supplies were being directed to 'our friends' and that Ireland
no longer fell into that category. Less realistically he speculated that
this hostility might be directed at the Irish government rather than
the United States. Given the successful application of censorship for
the previous eighteen months this was most unlikely to happen.[43]

    Although Gray did not immediately know this, Aiken would confirm his worst fears in Washington. He met Dean Acheson on 2 April and repeated that Ireland would not give up neutrality. It was, he argued, 'a fixed factor in the situation'. Aiken also described neutrality as 'the crown and symbol of Irish independence', reiterating that if the Irish army were well armed it could hold off a German attack until the British arrived. He repeated that Britain was the aggressor in Northern Ireland and that his government could not be asked to fight against a potential aggressor 'on behalf of an actual one'. He launched a vicious attack on partition and on British policy, displaying a profound lack of political understanding not only of the Americans but also of the Unionist population in Northern Ireland. Acheson and Aiken went on to discuss the possibility of a German invasion of Ireland, with Aiken offering his view that an attack would come from the air and be followed by surface craft – as the British also believed.

Just a week later, Aiken and Brennan met Secretary of State Hull, after which Aiken was dismissive and contemptuous, saying to Brennan, 'The poor old man, why have they left him so long in that post?' Brennan complained in his memoirs that he and Aiken were lectured by Hull on the evils of Nazism and that Hull ignored Aiken's attempts to criticize the British massing of troops on the Irish border. Hull thought the conference had been 'cordial', but considered that Aiken's views on Britain 'related very little to the realities of the present situation'. Hull admitted that he spent a considerable portion of the meeting discussing the threat from Hitler, noting that Aiken had very little to say about the danger that Nazism posed to all countries. Hull wanted Aiken to recognize that Germany and Japan were involved in a campaign to conquer the world and that Germany was a real 'danger to humanity'. During the following few days Aiken met a number of other senior officials in the administration, including Vice President Henry Wallace and Secretary of the Navy Knox, as well as members of Congress, journalists and academics.[44]

Although Aiken met many influential figures while in Washington, he never saw Eleanor Roosevelt or the other senior Democrats recommended by Gray. Though Brennan emphasized that Aiken met representatives from across the political spectrum, his primary focus was on those sympathetic to Ireland and isolationists. This was a conscious decision by Aiken, as he left Gray's correspondence in Dublin. When Gray discovered this he forwarded copies to America, but Aiken disregarded these as well.[45] When Roosevelt postponed meeting Aiken until 7 April Brennan believed the president did not wish to see him. According to Brennan, he terrified White House officials by threatening to send Aiken back to Ireland if they did not set up the meeting. This is more naive self-importance on Brennan's part than reality. This was a difficult period for Roosevelt and the administration and Aiken's visit had a very low priority. Throughout this time Roosevelt was continuing his correspondence with Churchill, his attention concentrated on the Balkan crisis that erupted in March and April while expressing considerable concern at British setbacks in the Middle East. Furthermore, on 27 March the British and American military staffs completed what was probably the most important joint report on military cooperation to date and Congress appropriated some seven billion dollars for lend-lease.[46]

When Roosevelt met Aiken they had a vigorous, but from the Irish perspective unsuccessful, meeting. During the discussion Roosevelt claimed that Aiken had said that Ireland had 'nothing to fear from German victory', but Aiken denied this. Roosevelt's main concern was that American military equipment might be used against the British. Aiken's stock answer to this was to refer to de Valera's statement that Ireland would not be used as a staging ground to attack Britain. Roosevelt wanted Ireland to convince the British that it would not allow itself to be used to attack Britain. If they were able to do so and the British confirmed this was the case then he would see that armaments became available. Aiken responded that British policy was stupid and he hoped that 'the President should try and save them from their own folly'. Aiken boasted that if given armaments he could put 200,000 trained personnel in the field overnight, a claim the president did not accept. Roosevelt made various suggestions to try to draw Ireland into a more active role in respect of convoys and submarines, and when Aiken dismissed all of these, retorted that 'the Irish did not seem to realise what a German victory would mean'. Aiken confirmed the president's opinion by telling him that Ireland 'also feared an outright British victory', not a view that Roosevelt could have been expected to entertain.

The interview went well over time and various officials came into the room to try to end the conversation. Aiken ignored them and ploughed on with the perfidy of the British. It was coming to Roosevelt's lunchtime and some staff came in to set the table. Aiken asked Roosevelt if he could say that the president 'sympathises with Ireland's stand against aggression'. Roosevelt responded that he supported Ireland against German aggression, to which Aiken added 'or British aggression'. Roosevelt was angry by this stage and dismissed Aiken's suggestion as 'nonsense', adding, 'You don't fear an attack from England. England is not going to attack you. It's a preposterous suggestion.' Aiken clearly was not prepared to accept this and wanted to know why Britain would not give Ireland a guarantee on this, but again Roosevelt retorted, 'It is absurd nonsense, ridiculous nonsense. Why, Churchill would never do anything of that kind. I wouldn't mind saying it to him myself.' After further exchanges Roosevelt agreed to ask Churchill for a commitment along these lines.[47]

In his memoirs Brennan described a dramatic end to the confrontation in which the president became so incensed with Aiken that he pulled at the tablecloth being placed on his lunch table with such ferocity that the silverware 'was hurled across the floor'. This is a good story but the problem is that it does not seem to have happened. Brennan wrote his memoirs for popular consumption in 1958 and admitted that he had no access to departmental files. Not a single participant has left a contemporary record indicating that this incident occurred. Aiken's own account of the trip records the table being set but nothing untoward. He does recount the exchange with Roosevelt in detail, providing an important insight into his view of what happened, but his version is almost benign in tone. When Aiken met Charles Lindbergh after the visit to Roosevelt he discussed various aspects of the exchange but never mentioned such an incident. Brennan described the meeting as 'cordial' immediately afterwards and Roosevelt wrote to de Valera a little later noting that he had met Aiken and they had had an interesting talk. It is unlikely that at least one of the participants would not have mentioned this incident if it had occurred. Aiken was notoriously indiscreet and would have recounted it with relish, yet appears never to have done so. Whether Roosevelt recalled much at all from this meeting is a moot point; it does not appear to have made much of an impact on him and there is nothing in the presidential or State Department files to indicate that he lost his temper. He does not discuss Ireland at this stage in his correspondence with Churchill, nor have other members of the

administration left detailed memoirs or correspondence about Aiken
or Ireland for this period. In the circumstances the Brennan account
has to be treated with caution if not dismissed as entirely unreliable.[48]

Towards the end of April Brennan met Welles and immediately
noticed that the administration was more hostile to Ireland than
previously. Brennan seemed unaware of the changing war situation
between 18 March, when Aiken arrived, and his meeting with Welles
at the end of the following month. There was a grave danger that
Britain would finally be defeated in the spring of 1941, as the German
military machine seemed unstoppable in the Balkans and the Middle
East. Welles told Brennan that the negotiations on providing ships
and food were progressing, but that Aiken's visit 'had created a bad
effect'. Aiken was charged by Welles with displaying 'blind hostility to
England', as a result of which no arms would be available until the
Irish government showed a 'better spirit of co-operation with those
fighting against aggression'. The United States was prepared to sell or
charter two ships to Ireland but nothing beyond this. Brennan angrily
rejected the account of Aiken's position, asking if 'co-operation means
bases'. Welles replied that this was not what was wanted; what was
required was Ireland's willingness to discuss joint defence with Britain. Brennan answered that he did not think this would be acceptable
to his government, but asked Dublin for instruction on how to
proceed. He also asked if Aiken should break off his trip and return.
The atmosphere deteriorated further after this, with some Irish supporters distancing themselves from Aiken and the Irish legation.
Brennan believed that the administration was advising its supporters
not to see Aiken. Dublin was not worried by these reports, deciding
not to cancel Aiken's tour, but cautioned Brennan to inform them of
the change in the political climate.[49]

Aiken remained in the United States for a further seven weeks, not
returning to Dublin until 27 June. In the meantime he had little
contact with the administration and spent much of his time travelling
across the United States addressing meetings on Ireland. At these
meetings he repeated much the same message: Ireland was neutral;
it would remain so; and it was impertinent for American journalists
to demand that ports be transferred to Britain. At the heart of his
message, repeated by Brennan and AFIN, was that Ireland was under
threat and required arms for its defence.[50] If Aiken had returned to

Dublin at the beginning of May that might have relieved the situation diplomatically for Ireland, but the decision to remain and to engage in what was certainly seen by Roosevelt as an anti-administration tour could only harm the Irish case in the United States. Aiken may not have appreciated this but it was a view that became widespread among Roosevelt's supporters.[51] Nor do Irish diplomatic staff appear to have seen the damage being caused or taken steps to avert it.

Aiken was now associating closely with isolationist opinion. He met Charles Lindbergh at a private dinner in New York City on 24 April and told his fellow guests that Ireland feared an invasion from either Britain or Germany – he was not sure which would attack first. He admitted that he had not been successful in securing arms for Irish defence. In a private conversation Aiken told Lindbergh that he agreed with his isolationist views. In contrast to what he had told administration officials, he informed Lindbergh that shipping losses were much greater than publicized by the British and that German aircraft were responsible for a considerable percentage of these. German bombers were able to take off from France, fly unmolested along the west coast of Ireland, attack British convoys and then go on to Norway to refuel. Aiken was invited to visit Lindbergh at his home four weeks later, where he complained that the administration would not provide weapons for Ireland unless there was closer cooperation with Britain on the war. By the time he met Lindbergh for the second time, the administration had agreed to sell the Irish two ships and provide $500,000 for refugees in Ireland, and Aiken said, 'I'd hate like hell to think our nuisance value was only a half-million dollars.' Later in the conversation the two men discussed the war itself and the possible threat to Ireland, with Aiken now fearing the British threat more than Germany. Around this time AFIN Chairman Paul O'Dwyer attacked Eleanor Roosevelt for an article she had written on Ireland, claiming that Ireland was now the victim of a 'triple blockade'.[52]

Gray had warned both de Valera and Aiken that public opinion in the United States was changing and even Irish-America could not be relied on. Opinion polls tended to support this view. A Gallup poll in early January 1941 reported that 63 per cent of Americans agreed that Ireland should give up neutrality and provide Britain with the use of ports for war bases. Among Irish-Americans 40 per cent agreed with this proposition, while 52 per cent disagreed. Furthermore, the majority of Irish-Americans in Congress supported Roosevelt on the lend-lease legislation, demonstrating at least some sympathy for the British cause. Yet there were religious differences in the support for Britain and action that might be taken by the administration. Although Catholics were less likely to support Britain than Protestants, approximately 40 per cent were prepared to do so even if there was a risk that the United States would have to go to war. Religion and ethnicity are the main factors explaining levels of support, with Catholic Irish-Americans the most reluctant to favour Britain.[53]

This relationship between religion, nationality and isolationism was demonstrated on Sunday 11 May 1941, when Ireland's 'secret weapon' was unleashed across the United States. A significant proportion of Catholic priests led their congregations in saying the rosary 'to invoke the Divine aid to preserve Ireland from invasion'. Paul O'Dwyer announced that it was the 'greatest prayer movement in the history of the United States', calculating that some twenty-two million rosaries were said. Later in the year members of AFIN were involved in the Catholic Laymen's Committee for Peace, which polled 35,000 Roman Catholic clergy on two questions. The first asked if the priests were in favour of the United States becoming involved in a 'shooting war' outside the western hemisphere, while the second asked if they favoured the administration providing aid for 'Communist Russia'. Just over 12,000 priests endorsed the first and rejected the second proposition on a 37 per cent turnout. Both these events organized by isolationist opinion in the United States provided evidence that Aiken could expect considerable support from the Catholic as well as the Irish-American population if he chose to mobilize it. Indeed, when a little later he started a nationwide lecture tour it was with the active support of AFIN and isolationist groups.[54]

By this time Roosevelt's patience was running out. When longtime Irish supporter Representative James F. O'Connor of Montana wrote to the president complaining about the administration's treatment of Ireland, Roosevelt exploded:

When will you Irishmen ever get over hating England? Remember that if England does down, Ireland goes down too. Ireland has a better chance for complete independence if democracy survives in the world than if Hitlerism supersedes it.

As Roosevelt intensified his informal alliance with Churchill against Hitler, his irritation with Ireland increased. After his historic meeting with Churchill in August 1941 he would write to Gray expressing his hope that the meeting would do some good and that 'it may make a few more people in Ireland see the light'. Roosevelt was equally dismissive of pro-Irish isolationists in the Democratic party, but saved his harshest comments for Ireland itself:

> It is a rather dreadful thing to say but I must admit that if factories close in Ireland and there is a great deal more suffering there, there will be less general sympathy in the United States than if it had happened six months ago. People are, frankly, getting pretty fed up with my old friend Dev.

The Irish position, whether expressed by Aiken, Brennan or their supporters inside the USA, was to continually condemn the British and insist that nothing should be done to help Britain's defence unless partition was ended. In this Aiken was echoing de Valera's long-standing strategy of giving nothing away and waiting for the other side to concede, but this had little impact on Roosevelt, who was drawing ever closer to Britain. What Aiken and Brennan missed was that the Irish were supplicants and ill prepared to negotiate with a government openly supporting Britain. If Aiken had genuinely wanted to achieve something while in the United States it would have been relatively simple to nuance his comments and to provide the Americans with various assurances about Irish good faith. Instead his belligerent behaviour, his openly anti-British attitudes and his association with isolationists alienated not only the administration but also some of Ireland's supporters.[55]

It certainly alienated Gray, and from April 1941 it is possible to watch him distancing himself from de Valera and the Fianna Fáil government. At one meeting he told O'Kelly, who was one of Gray's main interlocutors in Fianna Fáil at this stage, that 'his chief had no idea what was going on in America and that the speech [St Patrick's Day] was as well calculated to prevent Ireland getting what she wanted as was possible'. Aiken then compounded the effect of de Valera's broadcast by his actions. Gray wrote to Roosevelt describing the position he was now taking with Fianna Fáil supporters as upbeat and cheerful but that he was telling them, 'Our things are available only for those doing their bit for democracy – don't be surprised. You can't have it both ways.'[56] Gray suggested to Roosevelt that economic pressure might work, but more realistically thought that as the Irish 'are gluttons for punishment' they would welcome the opportunity to play the martyr. Gray's reports to the State Department also became more critical. He accused the Irish government of using the Aiken visit to demonstrate American approval of its policies while continuing to engage in anti-British campaigns. He now believed that de Valera was playing 'both ends against the middle' and he wanted authority to take a strong line with the Irish government. Gray received authority to ask why Ireland was repeating its claim that it was being blockaded by Britain but instructions to take no further action. Hull clearly thought that Gray wanted to go further and warned,

> Beyond keeping in general touch with the Prime Minister and current public opinion in Ireland it would be inadvisable (repeat inadvisable) for the American Government representative to intervene at this time with the Irish Government either as to its future course of policy or its relations with other nations.

If this was a rebuke to Gray, there was also a sting in the tail for de Valera. Gray was to inform his Irish contacts of the extent to which the United States government was opposed to 'the forces of aggression' and that the president was backed by public opinion in the certain belief that democracy would win out.[57]

Though Hull was prepared to rein in Gray's more belligerent initiatives, there was nothing here to bring comfort to the Irish. Indeed in the weeks that followed Hull might have regretted cautioning Gray, as Aiken demonstrated to the satisfaction of the US administration his hostility to Britain. Gray met de Valera at the end of April for what proved to be an acrimonious exchange between the two men. Gray was authorized to discuss de Valera's claim that Britain was blockading Ireland and to deliver memoranda on the United States's positions on ships, arms and food. Gray informed the taoiseach that the United States was sympathetic to Ireland's difficulties and prepared to negotiate, but that Britain would take priority. Gray made it clear that the offer of the ships was being made directly to de Valera from Gray and that the administration would not deal with

Aiken, 'whose point of view appeared to be one of blind hostility to the British Government and the British people'. The Americans believed that Aiken's views were such that he failed to understand the dangers that faced Ireland, especially that 'The future security and safety of Ireland inevitably depends upon the success of the British cause.' Gray then spelt out the American position of support for Britain in fairly brutal terms, emphasizing that 'Any policy followed by Ireland opposed to this objective of the United States would naturally not offer any ground for fruitful and helpful cooperation between the two countries.' Although the United States was prepared to negotiate on food and shipping, it was not prepared to do so in respect of armaments. It wanted Ireland to take a more cooperative attitude to the democratic states at war and only then would the possibility of armaments arise. Gray finished in confrontational mode, 'The United States does not question the determination or the right of Ireland to preserve its neutrality, but it holds that there is a clear distinction between such a policy and one which, at least politically, affords encouragement to the government of Germany.'

Gray also left a note with de Valera complaining about the blockading reference in his United States broadcast, and pointing out that this had been repeated by other senior members of the government. He then presented considerable evidence to show that Britain was not blockading Ireland, but in fact was facilitating the import of necessary supplies. Gray wryly pointed out that whereas the Dublin government had announced that Irish shipping had been attacked and sunk by German forces, no such attack had been attributed to the British. Gray was clearly incensed with what he saw as de Valera's use of the war for his own political ends and his refusal to acknowledge that Britain was doing what it could to protect Ireland. 'It is obvious,' the memorandum ended, 'that in the present emergency, policies antagonistic to the British war effort are antagonistic to American interests.'[58]

In Washington Brennan, who understood the bad feeling against Aiken, was called in to see Welles, who delivered the same memoranda to him. Welles assured Brennan that Irish–American cooperation did not entail giving up the ports. Aiken confirmed this in his own account of the trip written a little later. He cited approvingly a public statement by Hull that the United States government was not asking Ireland to hand over ports to Britain nor had the United States government entered into negotiations with him to achieve that objective.

De Valera noted his own disagreement with American policy, asserting to Gray during their April meeting that he no longer considered the United States to be neutral. He defended Aiken and rejected the view that he was anti-British and obsessed with partition:

> I said that that was a completely mistaken view; that he [Aiken] naturally resented the partitioning of his country and the cutting off of the people of the territory in which he was born from the main territories of the Irish nation.

He went on to reject Gray's request for an explanation for his statement that Ireland was being blockaded by Britain. According to Gray's account, de Valera got red in the face, shouting out, 'This is an impertinence to question the statement of the head of a state.' Gray seems to have gained some satisfaction from de Valera's irritation with him on this occasion, though he confided to Roosevelt that he was of the view that de Valera never told his cabinet of the incident.[59]

De Valera's bad temper is an indication of his increasing hostility to Gray. It seems de Valera disliked being contradicted, and his use of censorship to protect himself is but one indication of this. But it also prevented him from seeing what was going on around him. He had a fixed view of the world and the war and would not stray from this. More worrying from the American and British points of view was that censorship was also being used to control perceptions of Aiken's visit to the United States. Aiken had authorized Knightly to prohibit any report that might jeopardize the mission, which meant that Irish readers had little knowledge of Roosevelt's attitude to Ireland or of the problems associated with the visit. Censorship was applied systematically to create the impression that the Aiken mission was a success; all criticism was prohibited, even when voiced by senior opposition politicians such as Mulcahy. Coyne confirmed in a letter to the minister for defence that 'Mr Aiken gave us this instruction and even if he had not done so we would have taken appropriate steps on our own initiative to see that there was no sabotage or stabbing in the back while he was away.' Moreover, censorship was not limited to the trip itself but continued when Aiken returned. This placed the mission on the same level as the defence of the country. As with other political matters, the government and the censors decided what was appropriate for public consumption, and in this case as in most others decided that the less known the better.[60]

The Aiken visit was nothing less than disastrous for Irish–United States relations. He alienated the American administration by his personal behaviour and by courting isolationist forces, while his views on the United States were influential within the Irish government and affected its foreign policy. As a result Gray distanced himself from the Irish government and viewed de Valera with increasing suspicion. This coolness reflected the very different postures of the two neutrals. The United States provided maximum support for Britain in defence of democracy, whereas Ireland's neutrality was based on isolationism and indifference. If tension was high during the second half of 1941, relations would inevitably deteriorate further when the United States entered the war that December.

7. NEUTRALITY, POLITICS AND PARTY IN THE EMERGENCY

Wars bring uncertainty on many fronts: on the battlefield but also in domestic politics. When a country is neutral, it will be some distance from these uncertainties but nevertheless affected by them. At times, de Valera sought to impress on his fellow countrymen a sense that Ireland was in the war if not actually at war. On one occasion he warned, 'in a sense, we are fighting for our lives at present', almost as if Ireland was a belligerent. Indeed, he asserted, 'We are, in fact, threatened with the same danger of destruction as if we were in physical conflict because a small state, no matter how strong we feel our rights are, is not in a position to make good these rights.' In this context Fianna Fáil often blurred the boundaries between party, nation and state. Aiken and de Valera frequently invoked the national interest when it was the interest of the government or the party that was actually involved. De Valera also asserted that criticism of him as taoiseach could be against the national interest and should be censored:

> We are faithfully carrying out the policy of the State in so far as it is humanly possible for us to do it. It is not in the interests of the community that the head of the Government, in circumstances like these, should be represented by any body, or that an attempt should be made to build up a case to represent him as being biased, as being animated by hatred or any such motive against one belligerent. It is untrue, to start with, and it is not in the interests of the State. As long as this Government is here, it is not in the interests of the State that that should be done.

What this meant in practice was that de Valera could make an assertion, believing it to be in the national interest, and refuse to permit the opposition to question his reasons for making it or provide a rationale for it. This approach was echoed in Aiken's January 1940 memorandum, 'Neutrality, censorship and democracy', which provided a detailed justification for limiting democracy and free speech in the context of neutrality.[1]

While Aiken and de Valera were anxious to claim that censorship only applied to foreign policy, neutrality and the belligerents, as time went on its application came to include most policy areas. In the Seanad in December 1940 Aiken provided a rationale that essentially justified the government censoring any matter that it considered necessary for the preservation of order during the Emergency. Thus, publicity circulated by the Kimmage and Crumlin Tenants' Association campaigning for lower rents and a statement by the Dublin Trade Union Council on refugees could be and were censored on these grounds. More seriously, one of the leaders of the tenants' association, Neil Goold-Verschoyle, a leading Irish communist, was interned for his activities, none of which could be described as threatening the state or neutrality – though possibly Fianna Fáil. Aiken admitted, 'I could imagine more freedom being given, or less censorship, even in a belligerent country, provided that it was located less dangerously than we are.'[2] But compared with Sweden or Switzerland the threat to Eire was considerably less. An extraordinary aspect of de Valera and Fianna Fáil's behaviour in the Emergency was the sense of insecurity that they promoted. Occasionally, they were justified, but anxiety was a permanent feature of Irish public life from May 1940 to August 1945. Indeed, the safer Ireland became, the more emphasis the government placed on its insecurity. It may be that de Valera and his government were genuinely paranoid, though this is unlikely. A more plausible explanation is that this was a deliberate attempt to orchestrate support for the government and to undermine challenges from opposition parties.

When Elizabeth Bowen arrived back in Ireland early in 1942 she thought the country more isolated than ever. This was not just distance from the war; she noticed a more profound sense of displacement. Her overall impression was that 'the country was morally and nervously in a state of deterioration. Intimidation was having malign effects. In general, people seemed to have lost face – with themselves, with each other.' Rumour fuelled rumour, when there was no real news or when – more likely – the censors manipulated the news to give expression to the government point of view. American entry into the war caused much excitement and considerable resentment, as if Irish public opinion had been betrayed by the United States. Irish nationalists found it difficult to accept that American opinion cared little for Irish neutrality and was critical of the country's stance.[3] The fears and confusions evident in Ireland in 1942, in particular the widespread view that the United States would invade, were a consequence of previous news management. The general public were not permitted to see, never mind discuss, alternative views on neutrality. According to Aiken, censorship was operated 'to keep the temperature down internally and to prevent it from rising between ourselves and other countries'. One of the consequences of keeping the temperature down internally was to create the moral isolationism that Bowen noticed in February 1942, an attitude that led to the intimidation of opinion that did not agree with the government. De Valera admitted that free expression would have to be controlled, arguing that no democracy could successfully fight a war unless this freedom was curtailed. Yet Eire was not at war, although de Valera and Fianna Fáil created an atmosphere that made it seem as though it was. According to de Valera, 'When a decision was taken as a state decision that decision should be implemented and all the citizens should obey it. In other words, it was made law.'[4] Aiken was willing to intimidate and vilify journalists in public and private, but then use censorship to deny the individual the right to reply. In one case, where a journalist revealed that salmon stocks had been killed by chemical discharges, Aiken insisted that the report would damage the tourist industry in the area and therefore should be censored. He believed the journalist 'should be taken by the back of the neck and given a couple of years in jail', a fate that was only avoided because of the intervention of the censors, he boasted.[5] Aiken also became short-tempered with interventions in the Dáil, on one occasion in 1942 replying to a point by saying, 'There are a lot of Deputies who in this house and elsewhere should censor their own tongues.'[6]

Aiken defended the right of the censors to delete sections of a book review that referred to the Civil War and the Blueshirt movement (it may be no accident that the reference was unfavourable to de Valera and positive about the Blueshirts). It was necessary to avoid controversy on matters that might affect national unity, Aiken asserted, but clearly the censors were employing political criteria in areas likely to affect Fianna Fáil. While on this occasion the censors were prepared to permit publication of the reviewed book in order that the allegations in it could be refuted, the policy was that 'it would be contrary to the public interest to allow a fresh controversy to break out in the press regarding either the Civil War or the Blueshirt movement'. Aiken admitted that this consideration could be used to justify the suppression of 'all political controversy', though circumstances would affect each decision, he assured the Dáil.[7] The increasing blurring of normal political issues and emergency issues placed intense pressure on the political system itself. On 29 January 1942 the Agricultural Committee of Fine Gael met members of the government to discuss cereal prices, which were set by the government and imposed on the farming community. Fine Gael issued a statement after the meeting criticizing the government's position, but this was immediately censored. Aiken defended this decision on the grounds that critical publicity might discourage farmers from growing cereals at the fixed prices. Dillon accused the censors of prohibiting a statement by an opposition party that disagreed with the government position, asking Aiken if he approved of this. Dillon added that the issue was important because the government had subsequently adopted the Fine Gael position. On this occasion the government changed its position after discussion with the opposition, but would not permit Fine Gael's criticism or its own policy shift to be publicized. There then followed a remarkable exchange between members of Fine Gael and Aiken. The minister insisted that while TDs could say what they wanted within the Dáil, this right would not be extended to speeches or statements made outside the house. In consequence matters of controversy were routinely censored. Thus, Fianna Fáil decided in early 1941 that Ireland was blockaded, but Fine Gael, independent members of the Seanad, the United States and the British all denied this. However, the only view that appeared in the press was the government version. When Senator James Douglas addressed the Seanad on the matter, his remark that Britain was providing Eire with a share of its supplies was censored. The reasoning behind this was that while the statement might indeed be true, it could provoke an attack by drawing attention to these supplies.[8]

More serious from a political point of view was Aiken's insistence that the government maintain the right to determine what was prejudicial to public safety and required to preserve the state. Censorship would be applied to pre-election speeches, if he considered this necessary. This Dáil exchange in 1943 led Dillon to question whether it was possible to have a free election in Eire. Aiken concentrated his remarks on neutrality, yet under questioning agreed that it was even acceptable to censor statements and correspondence dealing with allowances paid to soldiers' wives.[9] In support of this position, Walshe argued that any speech at election time or otherwise should not be published if it seemed 'likely to weaken or compromise Ireland's position as a neutral state'. This was the question asked by Dillon: whether he could go before his electors and oppose neutrality. The answer seemed to be no, or at least he could do so but his views would not be published. What this meant was that there could be no debate on neutrality during an election. Walshe even extended this prohibition to those who 'pretend to accept the neutrality policy', an indirect reference to Fine Gael. Walshe recognized that there might be theoretical reasons for allowing greater flexibility in interpreting how neutrality might be protected in this way, even conceding that in Spain 'un-neutral' speeches had been made by cabinet ministers without the country experiencing retaliation. The most that Walshe would permit was that a 'pro-war' candidate, as he described them, could make a speech advocating entry to the war if it did not offend one of the belligerents. The electorate could then identify such candidates and vote accordingly, said Walshe. Walshe considered that 'any relaxation of the stricter censorship rules now might in itself seem to the belligerents like a break with the strict correctitude which this country has imposed on itself in their regard.' Thus, the very severity of censorship was considered as important as neutrality itself, and like neutrality could not be given up. This, of course, was a circular argument. The main proponents of neutrality may not have been in favour of limiting free speech in the abstract, yet if they shared Aiken's view that 'words can be a lot more dangerous than any bomb ever thrown by Hitler or the British' then the close control exercised could be justified, even when this limited political debate or strayed into areas of policy only indirectly related to neutrality.[10]

The Irish media was successfully managed by the censors in order to promote Fianna Fáil's view of neutrality; the Government Information Bureau and the government itself were complicit in this. A secondary and only marginally less important aim of censorship was to use the media to promote a sense of danger threatening Ireland – not on every occasion, but at crucial moments. When the United States entered the war de Valera broadcast to the country demanding national unity and hard work in the face of possible adversity. He invoked a vision of 'calm courage' in the face of death, assuring his listeners that there was indeed life after death. How reassuring such speeches were is difficult to judge, but they cultivated crisis while implying that only Fianna Fáil could preserve the conditions to prevent disorder. De Valera often seems anxious during these years, not only in public but when dealing with his own party. He intervened during an acrimonious debate of the parliamentary party in March 1941, when members protested at the decision to withdraw employment assistance from married men in rural areas. The party had profited politically in the past from the extension of these benefits to rural areas and rural TDs complained that their withdrawal would cause hardship (and perhaps also affect their own chances of re-election). The reason for the change in policy was to coerce labour in rural areas to work on the land to achieve maximum output, and the decision was reinforced by an order prohibiting farm workers from leaving their area. De Valera's contribution on this occasion was one of the most extended recorded in Fianna Fáil party minutes and one of the most bizarre. He warned the party that 'this was a most important time', continuing ominously:

> If we do not work, someone else will. If we are to get out of the present position, we must have organisation. If this country were not neutral, we would not in all probability have these problems. We would have war work, and we would have a better chance of securing supplies. There are people amongst us who will do everything to bring about defeat. They will complain about supplies: they will accuse the government of failure to take this step or that; they will arouse discontent.

De Valera appealed for increased production of food for town and country. Bread was according to him 'the foundation food'; cereal production should fulfil all requirements and after this potatoes were the priority. De Valera insisted that where shortages did occur 'rigid economy' must be imposed. He also appealed to employers not to dismiss workers even when production was affected by shortages and cutbacks.

While he admitted that mistakes had been made, de Valera urged the party not to restrict those who were attempting to do useful work. The taoiseach also played the anti-British card: 'We are a blockaded country. We are prevented from getting the things we require by circumstances.' However, the best way forward, according to de Valera, was to promote 'a campaign for the production of food and for the production of fuel', but most importantly 'for a better public spirit'. He wanted his TDs to work with him to eliminate 'that feeling that it is a smart thing to fool the state'. Yet he finished on a pessimistic note, saying that unemployment was 'almost certain' to get worse and work would not be available to all those who wanted it.[11]

At a Fianna Fáil national executive committee meeting a few days later, allegations were made that financial support was being provided for unemployed workers to leave Ireland to, as the minutes judiciously put it, 'get employment elsewhere'. Backbencher Donnchadh O'Briain expressed the view, shared by many of his colleagues, that he had 'no sympathy' for the single male worker in terms of benefits or unemployment, but that married men required support. Later in 1941 O'Briain complained at a party meeting about increased migration to Britain. While the Department of Industry and Commerce claimed that levels of emigration had dropped the previous month, O'Briain pointed out that on each occasion he had travelled in recent weeks the train had been full of young men moving to Britain to work. Yet O'Briain's lack of concern for the employment prospects of young men in wartime was one of the main factors forcing these people out of the country.[12]

*

De Valera's remarks reflected the unease and uncertainty at the heart of government about the impact of neutrality on Irish life. For the most part Eire was unaffected by the war until the end of 1940. In January 1941 on three successive days German aeroplanes bombed various parts of the country, while in May there was a devastating raid on Dublin itself. This brought home to the average citizen the exposed position of the country. Perhaps more seriously, by the end of 1940 the supply position, which had been satisfactory up to then, became much more precarious. This was in part due to Britain reducing supplies to Eire, but was also a consequence of complacency on the part of the Irish authorities. Reserves were low and by early 1941 some commodities had disappeared. By 1942 imports were down two-thirds on pre-war levels, while exports were down by about one-third. The cost of living was also increasing well ahead of incomes, which were now effectively controlled by the Wage Standstill Orders (1941). It was claimed in the Dáil in 1942 that the price of working men's boots had increased by 66 per cent, while the cost of a shirt had gone up by 80 per cent. The minister for finance did not challenge these figures, which suggest very considerable increases indeed.[13] The Department of Supplies imposed a rationing system backed up by draconian powers of enforcement. Appeals to the public to tighten their belts on patriotic grounds were not always well received and the increasingly limited supply of tea provided symbolic ammunition for critics of the government.

There were attempts to deflect criticism by blaming shortages on the 'blockade' by Britain, but this defence did not always work. Part of the problem for the government was that in effect the Department of Supplies had become the central purchasing agency for all goods imported into the state during the Emergency. Once imported, goods were distributed in a closely regulated fashion to shops and stores throughout the country, or to factories and businesses for use in production. While this was the most efficient method of allocating limited supplies, it also entailed that when there was a shortage of tea, tobacco or any other commodity, shop owners were liable to tell customers that the problem rested with the government and not with them. By the end of 1940 the Department of Supplies estimated that there was only four weeks' supply of tea, eight and a half weeks of petrol, and eleven of coal. By late 1941 the situation had deteriorated further. Virtually all petrol-driven vehicles had disappeared and coal for railway engines was in short supply. Electric trams in Dublin replaced buses, while the rail system ran on briquettes manufactured from turf. Even then there was only one scheduled train between Cork and Dublin per week. Horse and cart, pony and trap and bicycle became the main forms of transport, and bicycle theft the most common crime in urban areas. Imports fell dramatically and much of Irish industry, dependent on imported raw materials, collapsed. Between 1939 and 1944 the cost of living increased by approximately 40 per cent. The Wage Standstill Orders were an attempt to regulate wages and salaries, but those in paid employment felt disadvantaged by their application.

It was estimated that a selection of goods costing one pound in August 1939 cost thirty-four shillings in August 1944, a 70 per cent increase, but agricultural labourers, despite four regulated wage increases, were only earning an extra thirteen shillings. This real decline in income was not restricted to farm workers.[14] The impact of low income and shortages was particularly felt by women, especially in poorer urban areas. The Irish Women's Workers Union drew attention to the effect that shortages of fuel, sugar, fats and cereals had on the health of children and women on low incomes. Unemployed women were receiving benefit of twelve shillings per week at a time when price inflation was seriously limiting their ability to purchase even essential supplies for the family. The union condemned the 'middlemen' – a group often blamed for the problem. What was required was strict control of pricing and distribution; in particular fixed prices should be introduced for basic foodstuffs, the union urged. The government was cautioned that 'If the poorer sections of the urban community are to survive the fuel and food emergency now existing without disastrous results to health, the provision of centrally cooked meals should be widely extended.'[15] A number of allowances were introduced during this period, including a subsidy on fuel for poorer sections of the community, but in early 1944 it was estimated that at least 3,000 children were not attending school in the inner city areas of Dublin because they did not have adequate footwear. In March, in the face of objections from Finance, the cabinet agreed to provide footwear for those in need.[16] Nor were hardships confined to the poorer sections of the city. Seán Lemass lived on Palmerston Road, a fashionable area of Dublin, but three of his daughters became ill with TB and one of them was confined to hospital for two years. His wife Kathleen nursed the other two at home, a difficult task given the absence of drugs to counteract the disease.[17]

Irish sources also suggest that the average working-class family in

Ireland had less disposable income than its British counterpart as it spent a much higher proportion of its income on food and clothing. This was due to lower income per head in Ireland, larger families and more children in Irish households as well as a higher dependency ratio. In one study it was assumed that a normal middle-class family of five had an income of approximately five pounds per week. This remained fairly stable during the Emergency due to the controls on income, but in 1939 overall expenditure was calculated at £4 16s. 9d., whereas by 1944 it had risen to £6 7s. 9. despite the imposition of price controls. A further estimate suggested that over this period a family needed an increase of 60 per cent in income to meet its needs in full. Children's allowances were introduced in 1943, but even with this bonus most middle-class families either went into debt or cut back on expenditure.

The table overleaf provides some insight into purchasing patterns in wartime. Expenditure on turf (for fuel) increased from zero to twelve shillings per week, while that on coal declined to zero. Shortages of fruit and bacon (rashers) are notable, while increases in the cost of vegetables and potatoes are particularly noticeable. Some items declined as a proportion of expenditure, but this was due to shortages. More telling is what is left out: no alcohol, no tobacco, no account taken of holiday. Nor is expenditure on insurance or medical costs taken into account, an important item for middle-class families. However, the situation may not have been as sombre as this suggests; many urban families had relations in the countryside and would have had access to additional food resources. Nevertheless the evidence suggests that in urban areas and among the poor in rural areas there was considerable deprivation for many and severe austerity for some. It is likely that the exodus of large numbers of males from urban areas between 1942 and 1945 was largely due to deprivation and opportunities in Britain for enhancing income.[18]

A conservative official assessment concluded that there was a considerable difference between the cost of living in urban and rural areas, with Dublin being the most expensive place in the state. An additional concern for the government was the very high dependence on the state for employment. Statistics produced just before the war showed that approximately 26 per cent of the labour force was employed in protected industries or was heavily subsidized by the

FAMILY BUDGET (WEEKLY COSTS 1939 AND 1944)

Item	1939	1944
Fish and meat	12s	18s
Butter	4s 1d	5s 1d
Sugar	1s 3d	9d
Tea	1s	5d
Oatmeal	10d	1s 9d
Bread	4s 8d	6s 9d
Milk	4s 4d	7s
Eggs	5s 10d	7s 6d
Rashers	1s 2d	—
Vegetables	1s 9d	2s 6d
Potatoes	1s 4d	1s 10d
Cheese	4d	6d
Fruit	2s 6d	—
Clothes	5s	7s
Polish, soap, etc.	6d	1s
Turf	—	12s
Coal	5s	—
Gas	5s	7s
Electricity	1s 11d	2s 4d
Rent	£1 10s	£1 10s
Income tax	—	—
Schooling	3s	5s
Transport	3s 6d	6s
Boot, shoe repair	1d	2d
Newspapers	7d	1s 2d
Union subscription	1s	1s
Total	*£4 16s 8d*	*£6 4s 9d*

Dublin *Standard* 28 July 1944

state.[19] One mitigating feature of the situation however was the increasing flow of remittances from workers in Britain home to families in Ireland. During December 1941 over £45,000 in British money and postal orders was cashed in County Mayo in the west of Ireland, for example. By early 1942 Irish officials estimated that some £300,000 per month was being sent from Britain. Further estimates suggest that in 1942 remittances and money brought home by individual workers amounted to about £4.1 million, more than double the figure for 1941. Throughout 1941 and 1942 the number of Irish moving to Britain for war work increased dramatically, and later in the war a figure of £12 million per annum was cited.[20]

The playwright Denis Johnstone provided another insight into Irish life in a BBC broadcast to the United States in September 1941. He reminded his listeners of what Dublin had been like before the war, assuring them that in many respects little had changed. Restaurants were full and considerable choice still existed, while Indian and Austrian restaurants had also opened. Nevertheless subtle changes were observable on menus including the stark notice, 'It is illegal to serve wheaten foods with more than one course', a reflection of bread shortages. A key issue for most of the Emergency period was the quality of bread and adulteration was a common complaint. Despite a significant increase in arable acreage, the quality of Irish wheat was frequently below that required for bread production. As early as 1940 the author Maura Laverty was producing recipes utilizing potatoes and oatmeal as substitutes for wheat flour, while the diet of lower-income families was already poor, as items such as fresh fruit were considered luxuries.[21]

Community kitchens were opened in urban areas to provide meals for the poor and unemployed, and the government introduced a food voucher scheme to ensure at least a subsistence diet in times of shortage. Remarkably perhaps, while there was considerable loss of employment in urban areas by 1942, the rate of unemployment in 1942 was lower than it was in 1939, a figure directly attributable to mass emigration to Britain to work.[22]

*

By mid-1942 conditions had worsened. There was a severe cigarette shortage, chocolate was fast disappearing and there were few sweets due to controls over sugar. There were complaints by Fianna Fáil TDs of shortages of beer, stout and whiskey just before the local elections in 1942. Elizabeth Bowen found that the better-quality restaurants in Dublin were cheaper than in London and provided better food and a wider choice. She was especially impressed by the plentiful supply of wine, still at pre-war prices. If the well-off could continue to enjoy their pleasures, the same could not be said of lower-income families. Food prices continued to rise during that year, and cheaper restaurants pushed their prices up in response. When a member of the Cadbury family visited Dublin in connection with its chocolate business there, he noticed oranges and lemons on sale – unavailable in Britain – and fairly unrestricted menus in the restaurants. However he thought that Dublin had become a backwater during the war, though a very pleasant one.

Perhaps this was an impression fostered by the difficulty of travelling between the two countries, as it now took eight hours longer to travel from London to Dublin than had been the case before the war.[23] When David Gray travelled to the south and south-west of the country in the spring of 1942, he noticed few motor vehicles on the roads besides his own. There was an occasional truck, mandated by the Department of Supplies; otherwise horse-drawn transport was widespread. He recorded some discontent due to economic pressures on families, but little dissatisfaction with the government or its policy of neutrality. Most of the discontent was in the towns, where shortages of bread, sugar and flour had led to serious difficulties. Gray commented that farmers were fairly self-sufficient in basic foodstuffs, including potatoes, poultry and eggs.[24]

De Valera's response to the supply challenge was to insist that Ireland 'had [not] suffered tremendously during the past three years'. He attributed this to self-sufficiency, a policy that should be maintained after the war.[25] This was not a view shared by the population generally. When Bowen returned to Ireland for her second visit in 1942, she found Dublin politically apathetic, despite the forthcoming local elections scheduled for August. However, in rural Ireland, the situation was quite different. Bowen noted considerable interest in the war, though individuals were not prepared to come down on either side. She reported that whenever her husband or herself met people in their neighbourhood, talk invariably returned to the war.

The main reason for this was the absence of news. The *Cork Examiner*, which was widely distributed in Munster, only arrived in the village in the late afternoon and of course was heavily censored. In addition, paper was rationed which reduced coverage; after the local government elections the *Examiner* was reduced to just four pages. Radio news was now unavailable to most people in the countryside. Electricity was limited to cities and towns or to big houses with independent power plants. Most of those living in rural Ireland were dependent on battery-powered radios and by mid-1942 batteries were no longer readily available. Up to that time it had been common for those – especially men and boys – who did not have a wireless to walk to a neighbouring house to listen to the war news. Radios themselves were unevenly distributed across the country. While there was one licensed radio per nine persons in Dublin, the figure was one for thirty-two in Kerry and one for thirty in Galway. This may have been simply due to licence evasion but is more likely to do with poverty.[26] Bowen insists that country people were intensely interested in the war; they sought information from every source available and discussed it in considerable detail. This keenness Bowen associated with men rather than women, noting that when the newspapers did arrive they were read with close attention. There is a striking image in one of Bowen's reports of country people meeting at bridges and crossroads in the evening to discuss the latest news.

While intrigued by the war, the rural Irish were also distant from it. Bowen thought that their interest was a type of escapism from the routine aspects of country life. She noted a lack of interest in politics more generally:

> With regard to Eire domestic affairs the country people are at once bored and depressed. A sense of immediate dullness, fretted by deprivations, seems to cloud life here. The 'war' stands for drama, events in a big way, excitement. All this appeals to the Irish temperament.

In an editorial shortly before the local elections the *Cork Examiner* criticized the 'uninformed citizen' for paying too much attention to the war and not enough to local politics. The editor warned that there could be a low poll due to indifference and encouraged his readers to pay attention to Irish affairs and to go out and vote. The fear among government critics, including the *Cork Examiner* and the *Irish Independent*, was that the government was fostering apathy by emphasizing the non-partisan nature of the contest, and at the same time holding the election in the middle of the harvest period to reduce turnout.[27]

By 1942 neutral Ireland had settled into a state that essentially was to persist until the end of the war. Large numbers of men and some women were going to Britain to work in the war industries or join the armed forces. At home, a certain dullness fell upon the country now that the threat of invasion or internal subversion had receded. Rationing and its concomitant the black market were all-pervasive, as well as being the focus of conversation for women in particular. Censorship limited access to news and while British radio could be received, the newspapers only contained what the Irish authorities permitted. Censorship was extended to film and other media in a draconian and successful neutralization of opinion in favour of neutrality itself. Irish sovereignty seemed secure; the threat from Germany was now more distant, and while the United States – now a belligerent on the side of Britain – might be irritating, its influence was not hostile. Political life was seriously circumscribed. A number of Dáil seats were vacant due to the death of the incumbents, yet no by-elections had been held as the government was reluctant to engage in open political conflict during the Emergency, a decision that affected the nature of politics itself.

In the summer of 1942, however, the general torpor was punctured by the decision to hold local elections in August and by the packed mail trains returning from England with Irish workers with cash to spend. Those on paid holiday from war work were coming home to enjoy themselves and share their good fortune with friends and relatives. At the same time trains from Belfast were packed with northern holidaymakers. Many of these were seeking to avoid the Unionist 12 July celebrations but for others it was an escape from wartime austerity to the relatively better-off south. According to Bowen, who was in Dublin when the influx of northerners occurred, 'they frequented the cheaper hotels, crowded the shopping streets and crowded the cafes and restaurants. Dublin is undoubtedly flattered to find herself in the role of a pleasure city. They are said to be down here chiefly to eat.' While all clothing was rationed by this stage, coupons for clothing were readily available on the black market. Inflation had affected the price of these coupons. In early July 1942 a book of clothes coupons was available for fifteen shillings, but once the northerners arrived the price went up to around two pounds. A *Dublin Opinion* cartoon has a street seller outside the railway station where the northerners arrived, offering Charles Dickens at 3d., Walter Scott at 2d. a copy, but a ration book for twenty-five shillings. There was also a steady market within Dublin for clothing coupons. If an individual did not have adequate coupons for a particular item, some form of exchange would be negotiated with friends or neighbours to allow the purchase. Bowen noticed that the wealthy rural Irish were spending their time and money in Dublin rather than in London or Paris, as they would have done before the war. Upmarket clothing stores in Dublin seem to have benefited in particular. Bowen commented, 'random and often extravagant shopping has been one of the few amusements left' for this section of society. The wives of British officers and wealthy northerners also travelled to Dublin to shop. The coupons had been introduced to control this trade and that of Irish workers who bought clothing before returning to Britain and selling it on at inflated prices. The government did its best to control abuses of the coupon system. Between 1941 and 1943 there were 5,000 prosecutions for black marketering. The conviction rate seems to have been fairly high. Seán Lemass as minister for supplies (sometimes called minister for shortages) was at the heart of this campaign, but also hoped to lead by example. Despite being a cabinet minister, Lemass travelled around Dublin on a bicycle rather than use motor transport.[28]

*

In his report for the year ending March 1942 General McKenna, the army chief of staff, acknowledged that the threat from both Germany and the Allies had diminished considerably and recognized that a degree of stability had entered the military situation in respect of Ireland. However, he also noted that recruitment to the armed forces had fallen off appreciably, probably reflecting the public view that the threat to Eire was no longer serious, despite the government continuing to emphasize threats to neutrality at every opportunity.[29] Local elections had been due in 1940 but had been postponed with all-party support. Within Fianna Fáil there had been grave misgivings over the appropriateness of holding any elections during the Emergency.[30] By the summer the government had operated under the Emergency for just under three years, but despite various crises and controversies no election had taken place. The government could perhaps be forgiven for wanting to maintain the broad agreement reached in September 1939 on the need to protect neutrality, and in July 1940 Cosgrave had conceded that 'national security is the supreme issue', although emphasizing the need to maintain party politics in other respects. By the end of that year Cosgrave was nevertheless complaining that Fianna Fáil was taking Fine Gael's support for granted by refusing to include it in discussions on matters of importance to Irish national security.[31] Both Fianna Fáil and Fine Gael wanted to avoid political controversy during those years, especially from the summer of 1940 when the state appeared to be genuinely threatened for the first time. Subsequent threats and challenges reinforced this desire, as did the realization that shortages would be a fact of life for Irish citizens and in some cases there would be considerable deprivation. By early 1941 the full impact of Britain's decision to cut back on supplies for Ireland and the increasing hostility of the United States administration to Ireland was being felt by the government if not yet by the general population.

In these circumstances a pact to postpone elections until after the Emergency might have proved attractive to Fianna Fáil and Fine Gael, if not to the other parties in the Dáil or to the country itself. In the United Kingdom Labour and the Conservatives had suspended hostilities and there was a coalition government, though this did not prevent maverick candidates appearing at by-elections. It seemed at first that Eire would have a pact of some sort, but the constitution imposed restrictions: an election had to take place within five years of the previous one, which meant a general election by June 1943 at the latest. However, the situation in respect of local elections was less clear. In theory these should have taken place every three years, yet successive governments had postponed them. Fianna Fáil had done well at the 1934 elections, but then postponed them when due in 1937 and again in 1940, though this time with Fine Gael and Labour support. Irish governments generally have been dismissive of elected local representatives, and the central state had eroded most of the authority vested in local officials by the time of the Emergency. The 1940 County Management Act came into operation in August 1942 and deprived local government of most of its existing functions, instituting a managerial system often hostile to local interests and answerable to the state rather than to the locality. This reflected the centralizing nature of the Irish state under Fianna Fáil but also unease by state institutions at local power. If the new managerial system was a reflection of pre-Emergency state concerns which had been strengthened by the Emergency, the reluctance to hold elections nevertheless disturbed the opposition. Norton asked MacEntee in April 1942 if local elections would be held. MacEntee replied that while the government would like to hold them, the Emergency had imposed serious restrictions. He cited transport difficulties and a shortage of paper and other materials required for electioneering as obstacles and advised that it was probably unrealistic to expect elections in 1942.

This seemed to be confirmed in June, when MacEntee introduced a bill in the Dáil to provide him with the authority to postpone the elections until the end of September 1943.[32] Fine Gael decided to oppose the government, arguing that it was vital to hold elections despite the practical difficulties that might be encountered. MacEntee's remarks were alarmist, warning the Dáil that danger pressed on the state at every turn:

> We in this House and the country must remember that at any moment the peace and security which we now enjoy may prove to be short-lived, specious and deceptive. So long as there is war all around us, we in this island are not masters of our fate and all our plans must take account of that fact. If therefore today it might seem practicable to hold the elections, overnight circumstances may so change that tomorrow that course might, with equal conviction, be held to be impracticable and unwise. Even if we were still at peace, the position, say in regard to such a matter as supplies, might have so changed in the interval that it would be improvident to hold the elections and it might be better to abandon our original intention.

He admitted that supplies and transport were not his main concern but fear of disorder. Consideration had to be given also to the consensus achieved among the political parties during the Emergency. Mulcahy retorted that MacEntee was denying the rights of those defending the state by depriving them of the opportunity to vote. He asked if they were not to be regarded as citizens.

MacEntee said he did not want confrontation in the Dáil or at election rallies, openly questioning whether the spirit of inter-party cooperation would survive an election. In an extraordinary intervention the minister then asked the Dáil whether they should contemplate the alternative to elections, and here he may have been addressing his own colleagues as much as the opposition:

> But if we are to have authoritarianism in local affairs, why not in national affairs also? Why not an authoritarian government, and why not an authoritarian state? That is the dilemma with which we may be confronted if the local elections are much longer postponed, and if we permit the principle of elective representation on the local authorities to become fossilised and to be set aside.[33]

Immediately after this remarkable comment MacEntee conceded that elections should be held as soon as possible, but warned that it was a choice between two evils. The best that could be hoped for, he continued, was a non-party approach to the elections, one that would elect 'honest, upright, earnest and intelligent' citizens to local government. In his response to MacEntee, Mulcahy went to considerable lengths to meet the minister's concerns. He agreed with much of what had been said, including the need to play down the party aspect of the elections. De Valera then intervened to support holding the elections. While no decision could be taken on the general election due in 1943, de Valera did suggest that it could be postponed if a majority in the Dáil decided that this was the best course of action. This discussion seems to have been decisive for Fianna Fáil; with de Valera leading, MacEntee returned to the Dáil a week later, confirming that it was now intended to hold local elections on either 12 or 13 August.[34]

This was uncharted territory for the government, which was nervous that the electorate might punish it for the shortages affecting most parts of the country.[35] Consequently it was in the interests of Fianna Fáil to depoliticize the elections; surprisingly Fine Gael shared this view. Mulcahy seems to have made a principled intervention in the Dáil in respect of holding elections, but accepted the Fianna Fáil view on the non-competitive tone of the elections themselves. Liam Burke, the secretary of Fine Gael, told the *Irish Times* that the party did not in general contest county council seats in elections and left it to the local party organization to decide whether each election should be fought or not. The party position was to encourage support for independents or candidates from parties other than Fianna Fáil. In certain counties, Louth and Carlow in particular, no candidates were put forward, while in other places Fine Gael candidates only came forward when it seemed unlikely that an electoral panel would be filled.[36]

In the event the elections were fairly low key, but nevertheless gave a clear warning to Fianna Fáil and indeed to Fine Gael. Turnout was high in some parts of the country but low in others. The *Irish Times* thought the electorate had been apathetic, but this may have been because the newspaper was unduly focused on Dublin. There the turnout was around 40 per cent; in Cork city it was 49 per cent, while in Limerick it rose to nearly 80 per cent. In some rural areas where harvesting was under way, turnout was as low as 25 per cent, whereas in nearby townships returns of 50–70 per cent were recorded. In an editorial comment the *Cork Examiner* noted 'a definite break away from political alignments'. It identified the success of independents as one of the key features of the elections, though, as Ó Driscoll has pointed out, many 'independents' were members of Fianna Fáil or Fine Gael downplaying their party affiliations in implicit support of MacEntee's non-party hopes for the election.[37]

Nevertheless, the two major parties suffered. The *Cork Examiner* commented that 'the government party is clearly on the descendant', speculating that this might have serious consequences at a future general election. Overall, Labour did well, independents very well and Fianna Fáil quite poorly. That Fine Gael did not make an impact was a result of its lack of distinctiveness and the demobilization of the party itself. Its organization was weak in 1942 and this problem was to plague the party for the next two decades. The *Irish Times* election analysis sought to diminish Labour's success. It pointed out that low levels of turnout in the cities, along with holidays and harvesting, had affected both Fianna Fáil and Fine Gael. The paper suggested that Labour's success rested on its ability to get its vote out, calculating that it had mobilized 100 per cent of its supporters in Dublin. This seems unlikely when one considers the large number of workers who had travelled to Britain in the course of 1942. The trend to Labour was not confined to Dublin, though its impact was greatest in the capital. Fianna Fáil lost about half its strength and Fine Gael two-thirds. Labour doubled its vote, while others (including independents) increased theirs by about 50 per cent. Farmers' candidates won control of Roscommon and Kerry County Councils in a rural revolt against the major parties. In other western areas farmers' candidates polled well, including in the Fianna Fáil heartland of Galway. The direct outcome of this success was the formation of a new farmers' party, Clann na Talmhan, which was to challenge both major parties at the 1943 general election.

Fianna Fáil's review of the elections identified five factors that contributed to its poor showing: bad party organization, dissatisfaction among farmers and rural Ireland generally with the government, hostility on the part of public employees in urban areas to government wage policy, similar hostility in the private sector, and what was described as 'mischievous propaganda' by the Labour party and Fine Gael over the Trade Union Act of 1941.[38]

An *Irish Times* editorial immediately after the elections discussed the prospects for change in Irish politics. It argued that the major divisions between Fianna Fáil and Fine Gael had all but disappeared and there was now little to distinguish them, especially as both parties supported neutrality. It also endorsed the proposal of independent TD Alfred Byrne that the two parties establish a coalition government for the duration of the Emergency and postpone elections until after the war. Yet readers were reminded that while de Valera and Cosgrave agreed on the need for unity and increasingly shared the same political viewpoints on many issues, neither man would make the move to end the division between the two parties. This was 'a public danger', according to the *Irish Times*, as it undermined appeals for national unity.[39]

This editorial demonstrates the extent to which the *Irish Times* had reconciled itself to the new order in Ireland and to Fianna Fáil in particular. In effect, the Emergency provided a basis for national unity, one that the *Irish Times* was prepared to endorse. This in turn created the conditions for a formal end to the divisions between the two main parties. Yet this did not happen. Whatever misgivings Fianna Fáil might have had concerning elections, it was unlikely to enter into a coalition with Fine Gael. There may have been individual Fianna Fáil members prepared to consider such a proposal, but there is little evidence that such ideas were being generally developed in the party. De Valera had hinted that he would postpone the general election if he gained all-party support in the Dáil for such a move, but this was not forthcoming. De Valera's suggestion was not concerned with forming a national government, but maintaining the Dáil without an election. When all-party agreement was not forthcoming, de Valera called a general election for 22 June 1943. Even then there was considerable unease in the government and it was decided to adjourn rather than dissolve the Dáil in order to ensure continuity of government in case a crisis occurred while the election was taking place, though this was more a reflection of the government's paranoia than anything else.[40] De Valera wanted all the other parties to maintain the consensus with Fianna Fáil, but would not even consider providing time for a discussion on a national government in the Dáil. The tanaiste, Seán T. O'Kelly, declared that the electorate should decide on the issue in the election.[41] Surprisingly, James Dillon also recommended that a national government be formed under de Valera. He considered an election in 1943 reckless.[42] Dillon accused de Valera of not being prepared to share power even in the face of a crisis, condemning him for wanting a cabinet of yes-men. Elizabeth Bowen described a visit to the Dáil the previous year, after which she expressed her concern and disappointment at the content and level of the debate and speeches. She described de Valera with his head in his hands and his fingers laced over his forehead and ascribed his attitude to 'intellectual weariness', but also said that he had the 'very barest degree of tolerance' for most of the speakers.[43]

In the months prior to the general election Fine Gael confirmed the view of the *Irish Times* at the time of the local elections that there was little difference between the two parties. Interestingly, while Fine Gael continued to support the commonwealth, it now did so on economic grounds rather than for political or constitutional reasons. Its main criticisms of the government were focused on public expenditure and taxation, a major concern for Fine Gael's core constituency among exporting farmers. While party candidates were

urged to be positive and stress the future, most of the focus at the
election was on past success, with little new to challenge Fianna
Fáil.[44] Fine Gael favoured a national government, though given
Fianna Fáil's reluctance to share information with the opposition,
never mind power, this seemed a forlorn hope and perhaps also a
reflection of Fine Gael's inadequacy. To make matters worse for the
party, James Dillon had broken with neutrality some time before in a
surprise speech at the Fine Gael Ard Fheis in February 1942. This was
in response to American entry into the war and according to Bowen,
who was present, had the impact of a bomb exploding among the
delegates. Dillon wanted Ireland to end its neutrality and openly
support Britain and the United States against Germany. Despite
some support for Dillon at the Ard Fheis he became effectively isolated as a result and resigned from the party. Bowen described Fine
Gael at this time as a party with limited ambition and little positive
to offer the country.[45]

Fianna Fáil opposed a national government, arguing that what was
required was a single-party administration to protect Ireland from
instability. Fianna Fáil used censorship to circumscribe the opposition, and despite the changes in Irish politics since 1938, was still
extremely confrontational; every threat to its majority was claimed as
a threat to the nation, neutrality and on occasion religion itself. Fine
Gael was criticized for wanting a coalition – these had always failed,
according to Fianna Fáil. The Labour party was communist, while
Clann na Talmhan was either fascist or communist, depending on the
speaker. Fianna Fáil had reason to worry. Its performance in 1942 had
been poor, and the Labour party and Clann na Talmhan were now
challenging in core urban and rural constituencies. Erskine Childers
had warned the party after the local elections that Fianna Fáil should
fight the coming election with a positive ideal. His reasoning was that
Fianna Fáil success in the past had rested on having a clear policy
that mobilized its voters and maintained party unity. He urged that
'some general plan for future social progress, given purely on condition that circumstances permit, should be included as a distinctive
and separate item in the election and that the emergency policy of the
party should be realistic, frank, outspoken and quite separate'. Of
greater concern to party officials were criticisms from the constituencies. The chief whip asked party TDs to let him have examples of

criticisms so that party headquarters could use them to plan the election campaign.[46]

The campaign itself was unusual in a number of respects. Clann na Talmhan challenged both Fianna Fáil and Fine Gael. Led by Michael Donnellan, a former Fianna Fáil member and Galway footballer, its candidates emphasized the corruption of Irish politics and the isolation of the established parties from the people. For Clann na Talmhan the 'real' people lived in rural Ireland, not the towns or cities. One party poster condemned poverty, emigration, politicians and job hunters, urging the electorate to 'Smash the racketeers and politicians. Give the country back to the people. Vote for the Farmers Candidates'. On another occasion, Donnellan told a political rally:

> You could take all the TDs, all the senators, all the ministers and members of the judiciary and all the other nice fellows and dump them off Claire Island into the broad Atlantic. Still, Ireland would succeed. But without the workers and producers the country would starve in twenty-four hours.

Clann na Talmhan drew on the sentiment widespread in the Irish countryside that the state was both intrusive and ineffective in terms of rural problems. The new party was an alliance of eastern, western, large and small farmers, and its appearance in 1943 provided colour in the wartime gloom and a focus for dissatisfaction among the rural population.[47]

The other notable aspect of the election was the emergence of the Labour party as a force in urban Ireland. Labour had received significant support in 1942 in part because of dissatisfaction with wartime austerity among the urban poor, but also due to the failure of the two main parties to deal with these difficulties. Organizationally, the party had expanded rapidly. In 1941 it had 174 branches, but by 1943 this had grown to 750. A number of factors stimulated this expansion, including reactions against the Trade Union Act of 1941, the Wage Standstill Orders, censorship and the depoliticization of the election process by the two main parties. For Fianna Fáil, MacEntee ran an extremely aggressive campaign, dismissing Fine Gael as Blueshirts – suggesting they were fascists – while also defending the Trade Union Act on nationalistic grounds.[48] As the campaign progressed, MacEntee focused most of his attention on the threat from the Labour party.

This was seen as being on a number of levels: Labour was a challenge to Fianna Fáil's power base in the urban working class; it was a challenge to political order; it had links with communism. MacEntee stressed all of these, and placed them at the centre of his defence of the state and nationalist rhetoric of unity. On one occasion he explicitly claimed that the state was in danger and only a Fianna Fáil victory could protect the nation from domestic as well as external threats. MacEntee linked the domestic to the foreign by invoking a communist threat to Ireland through the Labour party. This might appear far-fetched, as the Communist Party of Ireland had effectively dissolved itself rather than oppose Irish neutrality, which it would have had to do after the German attack on the Soviet Union, but the majority of Irish communists had joined the Labour party and attempted to push it to the left. Coinciding with this, leading left-wing activists Jim Larkin and his two sons were nominated as candidates for the Labour party in 1943, increasing the tension already existing between them and the moderate leader of the ITGWU William O'Brien. One of MacEntee's attacks was to accuse the Larkins of being communists and then to ask of another Labour party member, John de Courcy Ireland, what his real name was and 'when was he last in Russia'. Jim Larkin had split from the ITGWU in 1924 and founded the WUI amid great bitterness. The Larkins and the WUI provided a focus for radical alternatives to the Labour party and O'Brien's leadership. In contrast to Britain, where communism, Stalin and the British party experienced some popularity as a result of the war against Hitler, anti-communism in Ireland remained well entrenched and the the war did not change this.[49]

MacEntee rejected the claim made by critics, especially Labour, that the average citizen had suffered a fall in living standards since the beginning of the war. He countered this with the assertion that the policies introduced by Fianna Fáil prior to the Emergency had assured that despite four years of war 'we stand unique among the states of Europe, whether neutral or belligerent, in the fact that the standard of living of our people has been left little affected by the widespread calamity'. To underline this claim MacEntee drew attention to the 'truly liberal constitution' that regulated government and secured individual rights.[50] There was no real social message from

MacEntee, despite what Childers had urged a little earlier; instead, he grasped at a speech by Mulcahy, who in his campaign had highlighted the absence of real differences between the two major parties. Mac-Entee agreed with this view, condemning what he called the deterioration of Irish politics that personal resentments had caused, and emphasized that 'the day on which they are ended will be a good day indeed for the Irish people', but spoilt the effect by demanding that Fine Gael acknowledge 'the great services which the Taoiseach had rendered to the Irish people'. This was asking too much of the Fine Gael leadership, but then it is likely that MacEntee wanted to emphasize de Valera as a focus for loyal Fianna Fáil supporters.[51] During the campaign de Valera was irritated by a radio broadcast on the election given by Francis Stuart, who recommended his listeners in Ireland to vote for republican candidates, excluding Fianna Fáil from his list. De Valera immediately ordered the Irish chargé d'affaires in Berlin to protest against what he described as interference with Irish internal politics.[52]

MacEntee's attacks were deeply resented by Labour, but there was also discontent in Fianna Fáil. Lemass wrote to MacEntee in the middle of the campaign, asking him to moderate his tone. Leading Fianna Fáil ministers including Ryan and Traynor conveyed the opinion of party activists that MacEntee's attacks were actually helping the Labour party. Lemass warned that there was a danger that Fianna Fáil would lose working-class support.[53] There is no evidence that Mac-Entee moderated his attacks on Labour, but there is considerable evidence that support for the party was enhanced in the final week of the campaign. Labour increased its total vote by 80,000, receiving over 200,000 first-preference votes. This was its best performance since the state was established, giving the party nearly 16 per cent of the vote and seventeen seats in the new Dáil, an increase of nine, four of which were in Dublin. Overall, the party increased its vote by slightly less than 6 per cent over 1938, but in Dublin it went up by just under 10 per cent. The most controversial results were the election of Jim Larkin and his son, Jim Junior, to the Dáil on the Labour ticket. These were to have serious consequences for the party in the future. The other major success in 1943 was Clann na Talmhan, which received 130,000 votes and won eleven seats, most of them in the west of

Ireland. Over 300,000 votes had been cast for two parties deemed radical or anti-system by the government. Eleven independent candidates were also elected.

Fianna Fáil and Fine Gael lost substantially. In six out of eleven losses for Fianna Fáil, Labour won the seat. The remainder of the seats lost by the governing party and most of those lost by Fine Gael were in constituencies where Clann na Talmhan polled well. Fianna Fáil suffered because it was in government, Fine Gael because it had become indistinguishable from Fianna Fáil. Of the independents, Oliver J. Flanagan supported the IRA and was strongly anti-Semitic, while James Dillon ran in County Monaghan, doing well enough to retain his seat despite his criticism of neutrality. A report by an MI5 agent claimed that the election had been particularly quiet and that economic issues were at the forefront. While noting significant Fine Gael losses, including that of Richard Mulcahy, it claimed that women voters had strongly supported Fianna Fáil because the government had kept Ireland out of the war. This suggestion is an intriguing one, if not one that can be easily demonstrated from available sources. The report also suggested that Lemass and MacEntee were unpopular candidates but were elected because of their response to the German bombing of North Strand in Dublin in May 1941.[54] However, in other accounts of this period there is no support for the suggestion that Lemass or MacEntee were in political difficulty and both were elected on the first count, as they had been in 1938. The turnout in the two constituencies was not significantly lower than in 1938; indeed while Fianna Fáil's overall vote dropped in Lemass's Dublin South constituency, his personal vote actually increased. However, MacEntee faced considerable criticism from within Fianna Fáil after the election.

Because the party had done so badly, many members went looking for a scapegoat and found MacEntee. On Friday 25 June Fianna Fáil ministers met to discuss the election results. The main conclusion was that MacEntee's campaign strategy had had a negative impact on the Fianna Fáil vote in areas where the Labour presence was strong. This view had already been promoted by Lemass, Ryan and Traynor, but now de Valera joined other leading members of the party in accusing MacEntee of being 'selfish and self-seeking' in his campaign. This MacEntee deeply resented. He responded that this was not the first time he had had to defend himself against criticism from within the party, but now de Valera had sided with the critics and this was unjustified. In the past MacEntee had attributed de Valera's criticism to him being ill informed; 'On this occasion, however, you choose to attack me before those with whom, hitherto, I have been sitting as an equal in the Cabinet, and it is not possible for me to allow it to pass in the same way.' MacEntee's bitterness can be appreciated from his accusation, 'nor are you now dependent upon others for what may be read', a reference to de Valera's sight, a particularly sensitive issue among Fianna Fáil members.

In the face of this criticism MacEntee prepared a powerful defence of his tactics, but offered his resignation from government to de Valera. MacEntee's trump card was his own success in being re-elected, but he was equally scathing over accusations that his attacks on Labour could have affected the Fianna Fáil vote in rural constituencies such as Roscommon. MacEntee argued that Fianna Fáil was still suffering from the effects of poor organization, rural dissatisfaction and working-class alienation due to its wages and trade union policies. These weaknesses had not been attended to since the local elections and it was here, rather than in his statements, that the party's difficulties could be found. The shortage of potatoes in cities and towns contributed to public discontent, while MacEntee also criticized the public record of some of his colleagues, implying that they deserved to lose their seats, and provided a vigorous defence of his own campaign in the Dublin Townships. He attributed his success to effective organization and a stout defence of the government's policy on trade unions and wages. While Labour increased its vote in his constituency, he claimed Fianna Fáil was also able to attract working class votes as a consequence of his strategy. MacEntee also drew attention to the decision by Fianna Fáil voters to use their lower preferences to help elect James Larkin Senior and defeat General Mulcahy.[55]

*

The 1943 general election was a serious setback but not a disaster for Fianna Fáil; despite being in a minority in the Dáil it still commanded considerable political resources and could point out that while it had received over 40 per cent of the vote, Fine Gael had polled only 23 per cent. There was little likelihood of an alternative government, as Labour's new confidence and radicalism excluded a coalition between it and Fine Gael. In any event Fine Gael and Labour together could only command 39 per cent of the vote, less than Fianna Fáil on its own. Nor would the Clann enter a coalition at this time, given its general anti-system stance. In these circumstances, de Valera was easily elected taoiseach by 67 to 37 votes on 1 July. Neither the Labour party nor Clann na Talmhan voted against his nomination, but perhaps significantly Donnellan visited de Valera prior to the vote. While there was a degree of uncertainty in the months after the election, government continued despite de Valera's fears of chaos. Publicly, Fianna Fáil ministers complained that a minority government could not give undivided attention to protecting the state in its hour of peril nor attend to economic and social development. On previous occasions when he did not have an overall majority, de Valera had waited for an opportunity to call a snap election. This tactic had advantages: the government could present itself as constrained by its lack of a majority. Past experience showed that a snap election normally worked to the advantage of Fianna Fáil. For example, de Valera had caused consternation within the party in 1933 when he decided to call an election, but was proved right when the party received an overall majority.[56] The smaller parties and independents were ill prepared for another election so soon after 1943 and money was a serious problem for Labour, Clann na Talmhan and the independents. Also Fianna Fáil was usually better organized than the other parties. All of these considerations and more operated when de Valera used the occasion of a minor defeat in the Dáil on 9 May 1944 to call another general election. By that time the political situation had been transformed to the advantage of Fianna Fáil.

W. T. Cosgrave, Fine Gael's long-time leader, retired in January 1944, leaving the party without a clear successor as Richard Mulcahy had lost his seat in 1943. Indeed by 1944 Fine Gael was in serious political difficulty. It was poorly organized and financed and its coherence as a national political force was seriously in question. The Irish electoral system operated on a proportional basis with a single transferable vote in multi-seat constituencies. Candidates were usually dependent on lower-order transfers to be elected. This required candidates from the same party to secure preferences from one another but also from other parties. Fine Gael's internal party transfers were

18. 'Keeping an eye on Russia?'. Irish military planners were more frequently concerned with the possibility of the Allies or Axis invading the country.

19. An anti-aircraft battery in Dublin. Despite this, Irish defence against air attack was woefully inadequate.

20. The German bombing of North Strand in Dublin in May 1941 brought home the destructive nature of modern warfare.

21. The remains of a child's car taken from the rubble in North Strand.

22. Many allied and Axis planes crash landed in Ireland. This one is a Heinkel HE 111H that came down in Bonmahon County Waterford in April 1941.

23. Would resistance have been futile for the Irish defence forces? This gun emplacement in Cork harbour offered limited defence for the state but would have been destroyed rather than handed over to invading forces.

GARDA SIOCHANA

£500 REWARD

The above sum will be paid to any person giving information resulting in the arrest of HANS MARSCHNER, German internee who escaped from custody at Mountjoy Prison on the night of 15th February, 1942

30 yrs. of age, 5ft. 9ins., complexion pale, hair dark brown, eyes brown, scar between eyes and on left cheek. Speaks English well.

Information may be given to any Garda Station.

Proportionate rewards will be paid for information concerning this man which will assist the Garda in locating him.

24. A number of German agents were arrested in Ireland during the war. This is a 'wanted' notice for Hans Marschner (an alias for Günther Schütz) who escaped from Mountjoy prison and was protected by the IRA before recapture.

25. The Belfast–Dublin train was used by visitors from the North to travel to Dublin in search of goods not easily obtained in wartime Belfast, while many Irish citizens used it to travel to Northern Ireland to join the British forces.

" Come, come, Mrs. McEntaggert, I tremble to think of what would happen if this should ever come to the notice of the Minister for Supplies."

26. Ration books became a valuable currency for those who arrived in Ireland to avail of its food, clothing and other goods. The bookseller in this cartoon is selling ration books outside the railway station in Dublin where the Belfast train arrived.

27. During the Emergency virtually every type of good was in short supply, which according to this cartoon gave the shop worker new power.

" Oh, very good, Miss Murphy ! . . . The customer will not be right till after the emergency."

"——and *our* candidate knows so much of what it is not in the public interest to hear that we have had to gag him."

28. Eire had two general elections during the war. The impact of censorship on the quality and diversity of debate is lampooned in this cartoon.

"No opposition! No opposition! . . . If I'm not careful, I'll begin to mellow."

29. Fianna Fáil's decisive victory in the 1944 general election and the opposition's disarray prompted a wry reflection in *Dublin Opinion*.

JUST A FRIENDLY SNAP FOR DER FÜHRER'S ALBUM

30. 'Just a friendly snap . . . '. The American note in February 1944 was greeted
with outrage by the Irish government. Yet, the Allies were deeply concerned that
a German diplomatic legation remained in Dublin while they prepared
to invade continental Europe.

31. 'Victory Festival'. De Valera refused to give up neutrality, even when it was safe for
Eire to do so. His refusal to identify with the victorious Allies (as an increasing number of
states did) and his visit to the German Minister to offer condolences on Hitler's death
bewildered American and British opinion.

32. The front page of the *Irish Times*, 8 May 1945, entitled 'Peace To-Day in Europe'.

33. A return to normality? Oranges arrive in Cork after the end of the war.

weaker in 1944 than on any previous occasion, confirming a trend towards individual campaigns and personality politics that was to characterize the party for over two decades. In 1944 Fine Gael no longer had the appearance of a potential governing party; its candidates sounded tired, repeating old slogans without any passion. Seán Milroy experienced a considerable degree of apathy among Fine Gael supporters from 1941 onwards; on one occasion he had to cancel a meeting because so few people turned up. In Leitrim the party organization proved to be weak and largely ineffective.[57]

Fianna Fáil captured just over 49 per cent of the vote in 1944 and 76 seats, providing it with a comfortable overall majority. One striking feature in 1944 was the party's campaign: in contrast to the previous year, it emphasized the defence of the state and neutrality but also social progress under Fianna Fáil. MacEntee's campaign most effectively illustrates this point. While De Valera had not accepted his resignation, there continued to be unease within the party about both his conservatism and his brutal realism. In this election MacEntee emphasized the economic and social benefits of Fianna Fáil government and the promise of more to come. He identified the introduction of children's allowances, which he had opposed in cabinet, improved old-age pensions and widows' allowances as well as benefits for TB patients as typical welfare improvements introduced by the party. He also drew attention to the Transport Bill, the new Conditions of Employment Act and legislation to improve drainage as important contributions to the improvement of the country.[58]

This emphasis on welfare and social progress was only one aspect of the election campaign; others were perhaps more important. De Valera used the opportunity provided by an American note in February requesting that German and Japanese diplomatic representatives be withdrawn to create a major crisis between Dublin and the Allies. The Allied decision in March 1944 effectively to cut off Ireland from continental Europe and to impose severe restrictions on travel between Eire and the United Kingdom also contributed to an atmosphere of crisis. Not only did de Valera reject the American request, but he ordered a general call-up and called the cabinet into emergency session. Despite assurances from the American government that the note was not an ultimatum, de Valera decided to give it the worst possible interpretation. He emphasized the threat to Ireland, insisting that it was greater on this occasion than ever before: 'Since the war began I have pointed out to the people and given cogent reason to show that, until the last shot has been fired in this war, we shall be in danger and at times in great peril.' Significantly he added, 'The danger becomes greater as the theatre of war moves more in our direction and the efforts of the belligerents against each other reach their climax.'[59] The note was leaked to the press, but in circumstances carefully orchestrated by the censors. De Valera's attempt to create a crisis did not prevent Maffey and Oscar Traynor, the minister for defence, sitting together at a football match, to the puzzlement of spectators. Nor was the Irish army deeply concerned. The chief of staff, writing in April 1944, described the note as 'not unexpected' and concluded that public opinion remained apathetic. Nor did the major review of the defence forces completed in 1944 focus on the note as a threat, though it did refer to other occasions when invasion might have been possible. Early 1944 was not about a threat of invasion, but the creation of a crisis to benefit Fianna Fáil's electoral chances.[60]

The 1942 local elections and the 1943 general election had demonstrated a demand for change that had benefited Labour in particular. With wages effectively controlled by the state, the trade unions were effectively redundant and discontent could best be expressed at elections. Surprisingly perhaps, MacEntee's anti-communist campaign at the 1943 election bore fruit twelve months later when Fianna Fáil was the beneficiary of the political controversy that erupted in the Labour Party over the communist issue.

The origins of the controversy go far back into the early years of the Irish state, when James Larkin returned from the United States to find O'Brien in control of the ITGWU. Larkin established a rival union, the Workers Union of Ireland. O'Brien subsequently attempted to force the trade union movement to reorganize to give his union dominance over general workers, but this failed at the 1939 Irish Trade Union Congress meeting. The Fianna Fáil government then compounded this tension. The party had been broadly sympathetic to the trade union movement and this was reflected in legislation and the generally supportive attitude of the Labour Party to the government. Trade unions had benefited from Fianna Fáil legislation and membership had increased in the favourable conditions. However, a number of issues remained unresolved by the time the war broke out. The first of these was the disorganized and at times chaotic nature of the trade unions. In many firms different workers were represented by different unions and demarcation disputes led not only to conflict but a reluctance by union members to cross picket lines set by other unions. These problems were compounded by the emergence of local trade unions in competition for members with existing unions with headquarters in Belfast or in Britain. These Irish trade unions were nationalistic in ideology and resentful of the British-based organizations, which they considered should not be allowed to operate in an independent Ireland. All these issues prompted the Irish government to intervene in trade union matters.

Pressure was building up within Fianna Fáil during the 1930s for the state to exercise control over the trade union movement, or at least to establish parameters within which the unions should operate. In late 1938 the parliamentary party discussed a proposal to introduce compulsory arbitration in industrial disputes, while Childers, a representative of the employers, urged the party in 1940 to establish an industrial court.[61] By early 1940 the Department of Industry and Commerce had trade unions under serious review, due in part to a strike wave in the early months of the war but also to concerns about neutrality, public order and national cohesiveness. One delegate to the ITUC in 1939 complained about the disorganization of the union movement, but the unions themselves failed to address this problem or appreciate that the government was likely to intervene. The war intensified the search for an institutional solution to the problem. The government had used the state decisively between 1932 and 1939 to redirect the Irish economy and to exercise control over many aspects of society. Fianna Fáil's exercise of control however brought a cost, as it demanded that organisations within the state accept the national interest as defined by the party.

The conflict that erupted in the Labour party after the 1943 election brought into the open smouldering resentments between the two most mercurial personalities in the trade union movement. O'Brien had been a founder member of the ITGWU and closely involved in the Irish labour and trade union movement since 1904. He was the key figure in the expansion of the union between 1916 and 1920 when membership increased tenfold. O'Brien had also been chairman of the administrative council of the Labour party from 1939 to 1941 and had served briefly as a TD. Larkin was best known for his involvement in the violent 1913 Dublin lockout, when his fiery speeches and journalism had provided solid support and motivation for the workers against the employers. He had spent nine years in the United States, where he was jailed for his political activities. He visited the Soviet Union in 1924 and was Irish delegate for a time to the Communist International.

The divisions in the trade union movement continued up to 1939, with Larkin representing the more radical wing of labour politics during this time. His son Jim Junior was elected to Dublin Corporation as a communist in 1930 and won a seat in the Dáil in 1927, standing as an Irish Workers League, or communist, candidate. Jim Larkin Junior became chairman of the new Communist Party of Ireland established in 1933. In contrast, O'Brien was a social democrat, a nationalist and a reformer. He had considerable skills as an organizer and was committed to working within the system whereas Larkin was at his best when involved in a strike or political agitation.

The differences between the two can best be seen when Fianna Fáil decided to institute the Wage Standstill Orders to protect the state from inflation and a trade union bill to regulate the labour movement. Larkin was at the centre of opposition, mobilizing support from working-class and left-wing activists in Dublin especially. O'Brien was much more cautious; he was sympathetic to Fianna Fáil and supported Irish neutrality. He believed that the trade union movement could achieve more by negotiating and cooperating with the government than by openly confronting it. In contrast to Larkin, O'Brien had a clear understanding of power in wartime Ireland, recognizing that the state was powerful enough and had the political will and support to achieve its objectives. O'Brien's address as president of the ITUC conference in Drogheda in 1941 captures his position quite well. He invoked his long association with the congress; this was his fourth time as president. But he also struck a nationalistic note by reminding delegates of his address to a special trade union conference in April 1918 which had called for a general strike against the British government. O'Brien was critical of the government decision to introduce wage controls and a trade union bill, but he complained that the trade union movement had only itself to blame as it had failed to act decisively. In fact, O'Brien had cooperated with MacEntee and officials at Industry and Commerce on the draft bill, though this was not known to the delegates at this conference. His views however were clear:

> We all, of course, can understand that no matter what the proposals in the measure were, there would be an outcry from the superfluous unions which we all want to be eliminated – or to use an expression in fashion in some quarters, 'liquidated'.

O'Brien did not push this idea further, but his own union effectively moderated its opposition to both the 1941 Trade Union Act and wage controls. Early the following year the minister for industry and commerce was to report to the cabinet that about 60 per cent of unions were now prepared to accept the authority of the 1941 Act. Finally O'Brien reminded his listeners that the trade union movement had changed beyond recognition, implicitly warning them that forms of organization appropriate in 1914 were no longer so:

> We are not now as we were twenty-five years ago a movement of social outlaws denied the ordinary rights of human beings. We are an organised body whose right to speak on behalf of a large number of the wealth producers of the nation is not denied. It means that we are in a position to take our place in the public life of the country on level terms with other sections and that our increased responsibility and status carries with it duties as well as rights. No rights without duties, no duties without rights.[62]

This was not a view shared by the Larkins or by the recently dissolved Communist party. Larkin fused the energy of the outlaw with communist ideology. For him, the working classes were the wretched of the earth and only full confrontation with state and society could achieve equality and liberation. Larkin's political base was the Dublin Trades Council, around which much of left-wing Dublin opinion organized during the war. It is perhaps no coincidence that Larkin and his sons joined the Labour party in December 1941, not long after the communists decided on a policy of working through that body. This was certainly what O'Brien thought, and his views were shared by other moderate social democrats. O'Brien was also concerned that the British-based unions would threaten Irish neutrality by promoting a pro-Allied position within the Irish trade union movement. At the 1942 ITUC conference O'Brien opposed an anti-fascist motion, essentially on the grounds of neutrality. These divisions were further exacerbated when Jim Larkin and his son were nominated as Labour candidates at the 1943 general election. When O'Brien failed to have the Larkins expelled, he led his union out of the Labour party. As a result five Labour TDs sponsored by the ITGQU also left and established the National Labour Party (NLP). The NLP reflected nationalist, Catholic and anti-communist tendencies within the Irish labour movement and tended to be more sympathetic to Fianna Fáil than the Labour party. This was followed by a split in the trade union movement when it opposed a proposal to send delegates to the World Federation of Trade Unions. This was characterized by O'Brien and his union as anti-neutrality and when the ITUC agreed to send a delegation, the ITGWU and a number of other unions left the ITUC to set up a new organization, the Congress of Irish Unions.

The political impact of the split in the Labour party was felt in the 1944 general election. Not only did Fianna Fáil win an overall majority, but the combined Labour party and National Labour party vote slumped to just over 11 per cent. Labour lost nine seats; the NLP won four, a net loss of five over 1943. Labour lost two seats in Dublin to Fianna Fáil. In Leinster it lost four seats, three to the NLP and one to Fianna Fáil. The total vote for Labour dropped to 139,000, a loss of over 60,000 between the two elections. This was an impressive victory for Fianna Fáil and conservatism. The theme of the election had been the security of the state and the maintenance of the progress already achieved by the government. Fine Gael continued its decline, while the Labour party was rent by defections and accusations that it was pro-communist. Lemass, director of elections for Fianna Fáil, could be pleased with his strategy, though one feature of the election caused some concern. It was noted that transfers from other parties to Fianna Fáil were weak, though some were received from the NLP. The transfers from Labour 'reveal definite hostility to Fianna Fáil'. It appeared that Fianna Fáil could not expect to attract lower-order preferences from other parties; the party would have to bring out its vote and ensure that its supporters voted for all Fianna Fáil candidates on the ballot. The 1944 election ushered in a new style of politics with important implications for the future. A chasm had opened between Fianna Fáil and all the other parties – the rest. The big question after 1944 was whether the rest could ever gain enough votes and enough seats to form a government.[63]

8. TO WAR: IRISH VOLUNTEERS
IN THE BRITISH ARMED FORCES

In late April 1995, almost fifty years after the end of the Second World War, Taoiseach John Bruton made an emotional speech at the Irish National Memorial Park at Islandbridge in Dublin in which he paid tribute to the 150,000 Irish people who had 'volunteered to fight against Nazi tyranny in Europe, at least 10,000 of whom were killed while serving in British uniforms'. This ceremony was the most public acknowledgement of the contribution that Irish volunteers had made to the Allied victory. Bruton's speech was all the more remarkable as it was made in the presence of representatives of Sinn Fein and the Ulster Unionist party, as well as the parties represented in the Dáil. It is highly unlikely that such a ceremony would have taken place a decade earlier and it reflected a growing acknowledgement of the need to recognize different traditions on the island of Ireland as well as the links with Britain. Bruton's brave contribution also drew attention to a little-known aspect of Irish involvement in the Second World War. It remains a controversial one, though it is now possible to provide a more measured assessment than in the past; for much of the post-war period the Irish state and popular nationalist opinion ignored the contribution of the volunteers or even questioned the motives of those who left Ireland to fight.

As Bruton implied, all those from the island of Ireland who joined the British armed forces during the war were volunteers. Everyone from Eire was of course a volunteer as the country was neutral and each individual had to take a conscious decision to leave his or her home and join up. The situation in Northern Ireland was complex. Unlike in Britain, conscription was not introduced in Northern Ireland, due to political opposition from de Valera and Irish nationalists.

However, there was considerable sympathy and empathy for the British among the majority Unionist population and surprisingly also among some sections of the Catholic (if not republican) community. Nevertheless, in all cases those who joined the armed forces between 1939 and 1945 were volunteers.

In his speech Bruton took it for granted that the figures for those who volunteered and those who died were accurate, but there is some doubt about this. One reason is that for the duration of the war and for a long time after highly inflated figures were circulated for propaganda reasons by the Irish government and its supporters in many parts of the world. It was in the interests of the Irish government to enhance the numbers who had volunteered from Eire and deflate those who had come from Northern Ireland. Implied though never overtly stated was the suggestion that despite Irish neutrality Eire had made a major contribution to the Allied war effort and therefore should not be disadvantaged because of its neutrality. The counter-argument, usually developed by Ulster Unionists, was either that the figures for Eire were inflated or that joining the British forces was due to poverty and starvation in Eire. The British government was also reluctant to engage in a public debate on the issue for diplomatic and other reasons.

*

When Australian Prime Minister Robert Menzies arrived in Belfast in April 1941 he was surprised to hear that recruitment in Northern Ireland was slow and that numbers were only being kept up by the flow of recruits from Eire. Menzies was given figures that suggested approximately 650 men a month were joining from the south, which if true would be about 8,000 in a year. On the basis of incomplete information, G2 Irish intelligence concluded in late 1943 and early 1944 that some 200 Irish citizens were being recruited into just the RAF every week. If this rate was stable, then a yearly figure of 10,000 is not out of the question. G2 estimated after the war had ended that recruitment into the RAF was continuing apace and by November 1945 a figure of 1,000 per week travelling to Belfast was considered realistic. More alarming from the point of view of the Eire authorities was evidence of large-scale desertion from the Irish army during the Emergency. It was estimated that some 4,800 members of the Irish armed forces deserted, most of whom then joined the British.[1] What this all suggests is that a large number of Irish citizens for one reason or another took it upon themselves to travel to the border, allowed themselves to be harassed by the RUC and then went on to Belfast to join one or other arm of the British armed forces.[2] In a 1946 letter to *The Times* General Sir Hubert Gough insisted that he had reliable information that by the middle of 1944 the official British next of kin list included 165,000 addresses in Eire. This is a figure often cited, and just as frequently dismissed, though it should not be immediately discarded as Gough though a friend of Ireland was a lifelong Unionist.[3]

British officials around the same time were dismissive of what were thought to be inflated claims regarding the numbers of Irish volunteers, though the Dominions Office may have come close to the truth when it commented that it had got to the stage when 'all Irishmen, whatever their views as to Eire's neutrality, find it impossible to believe that Eire's contribution to the Armed Forces was not on a scale which the slightest reflection would show to be incredible'.[4] Perceptions that the numbers were enormous were widespread and seem to have emerged quite early in the war. Someone as level-headed as Seán Lemass told one British visitor in 1943 that there were 100,000 Irish men in the British armed forces and a further 150,000 in civilian work. Lemass's concern was with possible social and economic disruption at the end of the war when large numbers of Irish nationals returned to look for work. In the meantime the Irish government was keen to benefit politically from their volunteers to offset Allied criticism of Irish neutrality.

The Irish high commissioner in London, John Dulanty, wrote to the *Spectator* in March 1944, immediately after the American note controversy, defending his government's stand on neutrality. This was a period of tension between the Allies and Eire, and Churchill had just announced that the country would be cut off from the rest of the world in the interests of security prior to the invasion of Europe. Dulanty claimed that though Eire had been neutral since the beginning of the war, its policies had not disadvantaged the Allies nor was it hostile to their aims and objectives. As evidence for this, Dulanty highlighted the 170,000 Irish working in British war industries and in other sectors of the economy. The implication was that Irish nationals were contributing by their work to the war effort, though this was something the Irish government refused to acknowledge publicly. The high commissioner also drew attention to the large number of Irish citizens serving with the British forces, continuing:

> No difficulty or hindrance was placed in Eire in the way of those who wished to join the British Army. The large proportion of Irish who thus volunteered represents a considerable proportion of Eire's population – especially in the military age group – and a good many of these volunteers have, as you know, outstanding achievements to their credit.

Dulanty did not reveal to readers the exact number of Irish men and women in the British forces, but the implication of the letter was that it was quite large.[5] The actual figures have been a source of considerable controversy ever since. The Dominions Office reported in 1946 that Irish sympathizers around the world were claiming that as many as a quarter of a million Irish nationals were in the British armed forces by this time. Indeed such claims got as far as President Roosevelt's office: a telegram arrived to tell him among other matters that 300,000 Irish were fighting for the Allies and this gave Eire the right to participate in the peace conference.[6]

The issue was also both sensitive and controversial for the commonwealth, because the higher the number of Eire citizens who had volunteered to fight, the less valuable the contribution from other dominions appeared. Churchill always acknowledged the role of the Irish in the British forces, though he was inclined to be sentimental about it. Around the time that Dulanty was writing to the *Spectator*, the prime minister was announcing the restrictions to be imposed on Eire, adding:

> I need scarcely say how painful it is to us to take measures in view of the large numbers of Irishmen who are fighting so bravely in our armed forces and the many deeds of personal heroism by which they have kept alive the martial honour of the Irish race.

Churchill was careful to distinguish between the 'good' Irish, who identified with Britain, and the 'bad' ones, such as de Valera, who at the very least were indifferent to the struggle against Hitler. Yet there was a serious issue for Britain as well as de Valera. Here was a state that was officially neutral yet if the figures could be believed its human contribution to the war was out of all proportion to the size of its population when compared with Canada, Australia or South Africa. More politically sensitive was the claim that the number of volunteers from Eire was proportionally higher than from 'loyalist' Northern Ireland, questioning the loyalty of the region. The Unionist government in Northern Ireland was especially sensitive to this charge. In May 1943 Prime Minister Sir Basil Brooke informed Stormont that on the basis of the incomplete information available to him the best estimate for the number of Northern Irish volunteers was 27,600 men and 5,000 women. Just a year later the *Belfast Newsletter* reported that some 66,000 individuals had joined the British forces in Northern Ireland. The breakdown of these figures is quite interesting: 37,000 northerners and 29,000 from the south. The figure of 37,000 for Northern Ireland is not far off Brooke's total estimate of the previous year (33,600) plus additional recruitment for the year. If these figures were accurate, there was serious doubt as to the extent to which Northern Ireland identified with the struggle. One of the reasons Churchill returned to the issue of conscription in 1943 was his concern that American troops in Northern Ireland preparing for the invasion of Europe would see the limited extent of involvement by British citizens in the war effort.[7]

The estimates escalated as the war came to an end. In Dublin Maffey came to the conclusion that Frank Gallagher, head of the Government Information Service and de Valera's confidant, was orchestrating a campaign to present Irish neutrality in the best possible light, especially in the United States. On 2 August 1945 Maffey had a bad-tempered exchange with him, during which Gallagher argued that the Allies were wrong to assert that Irish neutrality had affected the outcome of the war. Gallagher promoted the view that Irish neutrality had not disadvantaged the British or the United States in any way, indeed that its impact had either been even-handed or positive for the Allies. British officials believed that this Irish campaign during 1945 had been effective. Not long after the war ended one British diplomat reported that a clergyman preaching at St Patrick's cathedral in Dublin at an armistice commemoration had used the figure of 160,000 volunteers. Even more remarkable from the Irish standpoint was a series of articles written by Randolph Churchill (Winston's son) which appeared in the *Irish Times* in November 1945.

These articles had been commissioned by an American press syndicate to review the position of various countries at the end of the war. When Churchill came to Dublin to research his article, Irish officials went to considerable lengths to convince him that the Irish position in respect of neutrality had been the correct one. This had been so successful that there was some concern that Churchill's enthusiasm for the Irish cause might have been overdone. Frederick Boland, assistant secretary at the Department of External Affairs, told one British official he was worried 'that the articles might almost give the impression that Eire's attitude had been tantamount to non-belligerency in our favour and so have an adverse effect on the internal political situation'.[8] British officials predicted that the articles would be used by Irish diplomats to 'rehabilitate' Eire in the United States and provide the basis for anti-British campaigns on partition there.

Such attempts had begun as early as 1942. At the end of July that year the United States chargé d'affaires in Dublin reported that Boland had admitted to him that while the government did not have accurate figures for the number of Irish nationals who had volunteered for the British forces, at least 150,000 individuals had joined up and many of these were women. Boland added that at least 100,000 additional Irish citizens had crossed over to Britain to work in the war industries since 1939. Boland was concerned that at the end of the war as many as 340,000 Irish nationals in Britain would return to Ireland. This, he believed, would cause real problems, but he suggested that the Irish government was considering a deal with the British: 'as Eire had been helpful to England in their time of difficulty, it was hoped that so England would try to help Eire to reach a solution of her post-war unemployment problem'.[9]

By 1943 the propaganda value of the Irish volunteers had increased considerably. An Irish intelligence report later that year confirms the Irish authorities were convinced that a large number of Irish citizens were in the British forces. This report referred to an article on Ireland that had appeared in the *Atlantic Monthly* written by Hugh O'Neill Hencken, who is described as having 'a more informed mind on Irish affairs than the average foreign writer on Irish subjects' and mentioned specifically his figure of 150,000 as the number of Irish volunteers in the British forces.[10] In 1944 the secretary of the Department of Industry and Commerce in Dublin Robert Ferguson, who is described as 'pro-British and pro-Ally', cited a figure of 300,000 as the total number of persons of Irish origin in the United Kingdom. He estimated that 150,000 of these were in the British forces and the others in civilian occupations. When an American diplomat challenged Ferguson's figures, he responded that he had the statistics for civilian employment in his office and that figure was probably accurate. However he also defended his figure for volunteers, though he did not appear to have actual statistics on this. Ferguson readily accepted that the normal calculation for mobilization in wartime would be approximately 10 per cent of the relevant population (presumably men 21–45). He attributed the higher level of recruitment among Irish nationals to the more warlike nature of the Irish, a characteristic they shared with the Scots. Therefore he calculated that a figure of 15 per cent of the population rather than 10 would be more accurate in the case of Scotland and Ireland. He also added to demonstrate the strength of his position that some twelve million pounds in remittances was now being sent back to Ireland by those working in Britain every year. By 1945 the figures seem to have inflated even further. An article in the *Boston Pilot* in 1945 written by the Reverend James M. Gillis reported that he had it on the authority of the Irish consul general in New York that between 250,000 and 300,000 Irish nationals had volunteered for the British forces.[11]

Maffey argued that this was all part of an Irish government plan to prepare the ground for an anti-partition campaign in the United States, although most British officials concerned with the issue believed that Irish neutrality during the war had weakened de Valera's appeal in the United States. Accordingly, 'Irish stock has never before stood so low' in America or among Irish-Americans. Reports indicated that even Irish-Americans disapproved of Irish neutrality and 'the representatives of the Eire government have found it advisable to lie low and wait until the atmosphere improves'. On this basis and for the foreseeable future, 'We have nothing to fear from Irish attempts to stir up trouble between us and the Americans.'[12] British officials were dismissive of Irish government attempts to use the volunteers to redeem their position with the Allies: 'We have nothing to gain from a controversy with the Irish over a delusion as harmless as George IV's belief that he took part in the battle of Waterloo.' Whatever the British thought, the Irish certainly believed they had much to gain by promoting the importance of the volunteers and in 1945 and 1946 made considerable efforts to persuade the Allies of the benign nature of its role in the war and the positive contribution made by Ireland to the war effort even though neutral. However, there was also a very un-benign feature to this offensive within the closed world of Irish nationalism.

As the war came to a close, the worst fears of Maffey and of Ulster Unionists seemed to be realized. An editorial in the *Irish Press* entitled 'Crusaders?' openly challenged Northern Ireland's contribution to the war effort and more elliptically the status of the war itself. The editorial was written in response to Unionist criticisms that Eire had stood aside 'in the greatest crusade for freedom known to history while Ulster fought in partnership with Great Britain against devilish men and evil things'. The *Irish Press* instinctively reacted to any slight on Irish neutrality or to any suggestion that de Valera or Fianna Fáil might be wrong. Its rather pompous reply began, 'We, like the Poles, can leave to one side the definition "the greatest crusade for freedom known to history",' and went on to challenge whether Northern Ireland had made any reasonable contribution to the war. It claimed that the register of electors in Northern Ireland included a column showing those who had enlisted in the armed forces and gleefully emphasized the total as 24,914, also claiming that the majority of these were Catholics. It condemned Unionist politicians for hypocrisy in demanding conscription when most of their own people did not volunteer for the war. The editorial contrasted this with mobilization in the south, stating that 200,000 men had joined the Irish defence forces when called upon to do so by the state when the country was in danger. Nationalists in Northern Ireland used these figures and the figures for Irish volunteers in the British forces to embarrass the Unionist government, which responded defensively. Of considerable importance however was the evidence that northern Catholics were prepared to volunteer out of proportion to their numbers in the population and in an environment that was especially unsympathetic to them. Lord Craigavon had promised at the outbreak of the war that there would be 'no slacking in loyalty. There is no falling off in our determination to place the whole of our resources at the command of the government.'[13] But at the end of the war nationalists could point out that Unionists were not so loyal when their lives were at risk. One aim of Irish nationalist propaganda was to deflect criticism of the south by suggesting that despite being neutral it had contributed more to the cause than Northern Ireland – an integral part of the United Kingdom, as Unionists never failed to remind them. Unionists were acutely aware during the war of growing criticism of devolved government in Northern Ireland. Moderate Unionist opinion was also alert to this and both within and outside Stormont there was unease at the style of government under Craigavon and his successor and at the failure to prosecute the war with vigour. The issue of numbers volunteering in Northern Ireland and in the south thus took on much more significance than might at first appear.[14]

The Dominions Office sought to counter Irish nationalist assertions but found reliable figures hard to come by. One official commented that 'he could not believe the [Irish] figures bore any resemblance to the truth'.[15] The War Office assembled data in June 1942 for those born in Ireland: for the north the figure was 28,287, for the south 23,549. This was for the end of January 1942, and did not include those serving in the navy or air force. The need for reliable data increased as Frank Gallagher and the Irish diplomatic service circulated what were considered inflated figures to suit their interests. A decision was taken to revisit this issue and determine the exact numbers involved. The Home Office calculated that approximately 100,000 Irish nationals were working in British war industries, confirming Boland's 1942 claim. At the end of 1944 the Dominions Office concluded that a 'very approximate' figure might be 40,000–70,000 in the armed services. Concern was expressed that British and Dominion public opinion would take offence at the claim that proportionally neutral Ireland had contributed more to the war effort than not only Northern Ireland but the dominions as well.[16] Reliable information for the period between 1941 and the end of 1943 confirmed that some 130,000 Irish nationals had crossed to Britain to work in the war industries, while it was considered likely that 40,000 could be added to this figure for the period between 1939 and 1940 and for 1944. The total of these figures conforms to Dulanty's estimate of those in war work, but leaves out of consideration how many actually joined the armed forces. There continued to be difficulty obtaining accurate figures for the numbers of those who actually joined up from Ireland.

The 1942 War Office figures were based on place of birth as given by individuals, though this was considered by the Dominions Office a 'very unreliable basis for various reasons'. Machtig now announced that it was time to bring the figures up to date and to gather them from all three services. The secretary of state for the dominions, Lord Cranborne, agreed that the figures should be obtained if possible, but added rather cautiously, 'I should be strongly against publishing them or giving them in the House of Commons, if it can be avoided. There is no value in making public necessarily incomplete or inaccurate statistics.'[17]

The discussion continued to be hampered by incomplete statistics. The new War Office figures did not deviate significantly from those of 1942, and as on previous occasions were based on individuals providing place of birth. The numbers for Eire in 1944 were 27,840 men and 3,761 women, giving a total of 31,601 in the British army. The comparable figures for Northern Ireland were 26,579 and 2,152 respectively, a total of 28,731. When the figures for 1942 are compared what stands out is that the number born in the south had increased by over 4,000 whereas there had been a decline of some 1,700 in the total for Northern Ireland. This decline was attributed to casualties not being replaced by new recruits from Northern Ireland. However, the percentage of casualties from the south would have been just as high yet their numbers actually increased. This points to the continuing willingness of individuals from Eire to join the British army, despite the increasingly hostile attitude of the Irish authorities to them. The composition of those serving also highlights another contrast between north and south. At the end of 1944 there were 3,493 serving officers from the south, whereas the north provided 2,414. In the women's services the south contributed 837 officers and 2,924 other ranks, while the north provided 372 officers and 1,780 other ranks. One reason for this was that there was a considerable amount of work for women in Northern Ireland, whereas in the south not only was work in short supply but there were considerable institutional obstacles to women working. Even though incomplete and inadequate in many respects, the data remains a remarkable testament to the sustained movement of Irish citizens into the British armed forces, leading one official to note, 'it will be born [sic] in mind that the population of

Eire is three millions against one and a quarter million for Northern Ireland', but in a handwritten addition, 'on the other hand Eire is neutral and Northern Ireland is not'.[18]

The figures for the other services proved less encouraging for the Irish case. The Admiralty provided figures based on where an individual lived when he or she joined the service, and concluded that 715 had volunteered for the Royal Navy from the south; the figure for the north was 5,539. The Admiralty admitted that these figures were limited but argued that more detailed information could only be obtained if advanced statistical machines were used and these were required for the war effort. The Air Ministry was more forthcoming, providing RAF figures of 12,200 for Northern Ireland and 11,050 for Eire.[19] The totals for all men and women in the army and air force thus come to 41,950 for Eire and 40,660 for Northern Ireland. These figures are based on the same criteria: place of birth as provided when joining up. As the Admiralty figures did not follow this method, its data can be considered unsatisfactory. The Dominions Office concluded that the total for the navy for all of Ireland was no more than 6,000, but in contrast to the figures provided by the Admiralty thought that this should be divided equally between the two parts of the island. The Dominions Office remained unsure how to proceed with the matter, though it was decided to work through the Ministry of Information to deflate the Irish numbers being circulated. Concern was expressed that in the absence of reliable figures for the navy, 'it would not be right to use them as the basis of an official statement'. It was also decided that Britain could gain little from publication, but that informal circulation might temper the Irish case. This was thought an appropriate task for the Ministry of Information, which was authorized to confirm that volunteers from Eire numbered no more than 50,000 and that this was a generous estimate. The intention was to counter Irish exaggeration.[20]

Maffey, however, opposed any off-the-record release of data on the ground that the numbers were unreliable and in the absence of any direct benefit to Britain in doing so. Machtig wrote to Cranborne after the discussion with Maffey, admitting that the figures were not 'firm' and publicity could generate a serious challenge to their reliability. There was a real danger, he added, that more harm than good would be done in the circumstances. Maffey also feared that those unsympathetic to Eire in the United Kingdom would highlight the large numbers of deserters from the Irish forces now in the British military and that this would have an unfortunate effect in Ireland. In addition Maffey believed that the Irish government would not 'directly or indirectly, claim credit for the number of volunteers serving with the forces'. Cranborne accepted the strength of this argument, fearing that Irish sympathizers such as Sir Hubert Gough would challenge any official figures, even though they might be 'approximately correct'. Cranborne would have liked to 'prick the bubble of Irish propaganda', but recognized that this might rebound on them and not achieve the political objective desired.[21]

*

British officials were to be mistaken if they hoped to keep the issue from the public eye. Both sympathizers and critics of Ireland were quick to use the volunteer issue to promote specific views on the situation. One Soviet expert on the British empire cited the figures approvingly to demonstrate that the Irish were indeed anti-fascist despite the official position of the government. In contrast, the author St John Ervine challenged Sir Hubert Gough's figures on the numbers volunteering during the war, a challenge actually endorsed by David Gray. In Northern Ireland Unionists and nationalists argued over the merits of Irish neutrality and the numbers of volunteers for their own ideological ends.[22] When the future president of the United States, John F. Kennedy, visited Dublin in July 1945 he found the higher figures widely cited by those he met. He was told that approximately 250,000 Irish nationals had travelled to Britain during the war. 'How many of these went direct into the armed forces has not been disclosed, but the fact that residents of southern Ireland received seven Victoria Cross while people in the North received none has caused some satisfaction among the people in the South.'[23] The volunteer issue went to the highest level of British politics when unofficially the new prime minister, Clement Attlee, confirmed an estimate of 40,000 for Eire and 37,000 for Northern Ireland, though in public the government sill insisted that complete data was not available. Northern Ireland Prime Minister Basil Brooke wrote to the British home secretary expressing his displeasure and irritation: 'I am sure you will appreciate that I am put in a position of some embarrassment by not being able to refute the claims that are being made that our contribution to the Armed Forces was very much smaller than Eire's.' Sir Eric Machtig wrote to the Home Office asserting that the 'figures are incomplete and not water tight'. However, the Dominions Office was prepared to reconsider its position not to publicize the statistics it did have in consideration of Brooke's plea to them.[24]

In a major policy review in March 1946 the Dominions Office revealed that one of the reasons it wished not to publicize the numbers was that the British government wanted 'to promote the restoration of friendly relations between the two islands' and that therefore it was 'desirable to avoid raising controversial issues'. The Dominions Office also argued that 'there is some advantage from our point of view in not discouraging Eire from claiming credit for the participation of southern Irishmen in the war'. On further consideration, however, this was not a view that actually commended itself to the British state. It was recognized that whatever the short-term gain for Britain in Eire the loss in Northern Ireland would be considerable. It was accepted that Northern Ireland had nothing to gain from the circulation of Eire's exaggerated figures; indeed the loss to its prestige would be great. The British government had to defend the honour of Northern Ireland against what were conceded to be fabrications by nationalist propagandists in pursuit of a dubious objective. Brooke would vigorously defend Ulster's good name and the government had to recognize that any advantage gained by allowing Eire's propaganda to continue was trivial when 'compared with the injury which it would inflict upon Northern Ireland'. If the Irish were angry at any refutation of their figures, it would be ironic for them 'to be forced into the position of maintaining, in effect, that whatever we may say, the youth of Eire rushed as one man to join the colours and to fight for the British Empire'. It was important to act as it was reported from Dublin that de Valera himself now believed that 180,000 Irish nationals had fought for Britain during the war. It was now necessary, 'In fairness to Mr de Valera himself as well as Sir Basil Brooke . . . to dissipate this delusion as soon as possible'. This was not going to be easy, as the myth of Eire's contribution to the war effort was now deeply embedded in public consciousness.[25]

The issue was further complicated when the Air Ministry announced that it would not stand by the figures circulated in January

1945. Given the clear evidence from Irish sources that as many as 200 men per week were volunteering to join the RAF in Belfast, this was strange. The ministry also let it be known that it did not hold separate figures for those who joined from Eire or Northern Ireland prior to January 1943. In January 1945 two separate figures had been circulated: estimates of 11,050 volunteers from the south and over 12,000 from the north. By March 1946 these figures had been withdrawn and a new estimate provided which significantly reduced overall numbers. It was now calculated that only 3,110 men and women had joined in Northern Ireland and it was further maintained that the earlier statistics 'could no longer be verified and that they were unable at such a distance of time to say precisely where they came from or how they were obtained'. The Home Office then circulated a note to Brooke which provided him with a figure of 37,282 for those of Northern Ireland origin who had volunteered during the war for all the services. In this case place of birth was used to determine the figure, considered the least satisfactory method of calculation.

In April Henry Harrison and other Irish supporters in Britain issued a circular entitled 'How Many? Irish Volunteers Served in His Majesty's Armed Forced in the War 1939 to 1946' in which the figures were again disputed. Harrison argued in some detail that official definitions were not adequate when assessing the Irish contribution and showed considerable gaps in the methods used to assess numbers from Eire. He pointed out that figures for the RAF did not take account of first-hand evidence that large numbers of Eire citizens travelled to Belfast to join up. Harrison also challenged the lack of information, claiming that data on place of birth for RAF personnel was centralized and available. He then enumerated eight categories of volunteer which needed to be included to reach a more accurate figure:

1. Eire citizens serving at the outbreak of war.
2. Those recruited in the United Kingdom when under no legal compulsion to serve.
3. Citizens of Eire recruited to the Royal Navy and marines, including men 1 January 1945 to 31 August 1945 and women 3 September 1939 to 14 December 1943.
4. Irish citizens who joined the army between 1 January 1945 and 31 August 1945.

5. Eire citizens among army dead 3 September 1939 to
   31 December 1944.
6. Eire citizens discharged from the army 3 September 1939 to
   31 December 1944.
7. Eire recruits to the RAF 3 September 1939 to 31 December 1942
   (who appear to have been attributed to Northern Ireland).
8. Eire volunteers not identifiable by address on enlistment but
   identifiable by next of kin as opposed to place of birth.

Harrison also argued that the number of awards to Irish nationals
during the war lent support to the view that far more people of Irish
provenance were in the armed forces than the official figures would
suggest. Thus, Canada with a population of between ten and eleven
million received ten Victoria Crosses, while those with connections to
Eire received eight VCs and one George Cross.[26]

Harrison's wider criteria are important because many of those in
the British forces in 1939 or resident in the UK at the time continued
to consider themselves Irish. Eric Dunlop was one such individual
who made a conscious choice to join the war effort, though he could
have left his employment and returned to Eire. Indeed, for Dunlop
the question was even more difficult as he was in Belfast, where there
was no conscription. At first the war had very little impact on him,
as was generally the case with people living in Northern Ireland. However, by May 1940 with the collapse of France he recognized that the
world had changed appreciably and that he had to take a decision:

The German menace was no longer a remote, impersonal thing
cushioned from us by a huge effective French army. . . . I quickly
realised that the old world of 1939 had vanished and I should now
have to listen to my conscience and try and decide what, if
anything, I should do.

His decision was to join the RAF, on the fatalistic grounds that 'It was
better to be in a service where you either survived intact or were
written off.'[27]

Decisions were individual and often complex. Basil Baker who
was from Fermoy in County Cork recalled that there were military
personnel on both sides of his family. His grandfather had been a
general and Baker used to visit his house and play with uniforms and

swords. At least three of his classmates at school also joined the forces. James Hickey volunteered in September 1940. This was clearly expected by his family as he recalled that he would have 'been given the white feather' if he had not done so. Aidan McCarthy, a doctor from Cork, recalls that when he joined the RAF in 1939, 'he was actually looking forward to the war'. Desmond Fay was already a committed anti-fascist when the war broke out, providing him with an opportunity to fight Hitler. Fay was living in Britain but his view of his identity is interesting. He considered himself Irish not British: 'the fact that you were brought up in a foreign country doesn't seem to me to alter your nationality'. Dennis Murnane had visited Germany before the war and been deeply affected by what he had seen there. He recognized that there would be a war and believed that even a neutral Ireland would not be immune from the consequences of a British defeat. Many in Murnane's family had fought in the First World War, but he believes this was not the main reason for him volunteering. Fay, Murnane and many others believed that they were fighting as much for Ireland as for Britain. Living in Ireland, one could choose to join up or not, a luxury not available to those who lived in Britain when conscription came in, so it is true to say that all Irish people who joined up did so voluntarily, though this should not disguise the often subtle pressures to do so. In some firms in Dublin men of military age were encouraged to volunteer and there was tacit acknowledgement that jobs would be held open for those who did so. What is not clear is whether sanctions were imposed on those who did not. Even where this was not the case, it is clear that in firms with many veterans of the First World War there was a social context that pressurized individuals to join. In Northern Ireland some of these pressures may have been stronger but it is difficult to judge this without further research.[28]

Many Irish people in Britain believed that the British government did not have the moral right to impose conscription in Northern Ireland, but some also extended this view to Britain itself. Alexander McCann wrote to the Department of External Affairs in Dublin just after war broke out urging the Irish government to take action in defence of Irish nationals living in Britain who would be eligible for conscription because they had been resident there for two years or more:

I must add that while many Irishmen here feel they have obligations towards Britain in return for domicile and livelihood yet most
of them would feel bound in conscience to resist conscription into
an army which continues an occupation of part of their country
and upholds there a regime as immoral as the one against which
Britain insists Irishmen take up arms.

It is difficult to judge how widespread this view was among the Irish
in Britain, but there was certainly a view that their Irish identity gave
them a special status.

When the war started the British government agreed to provide
exit visas for all those Irish people who might be liable for conscription
on condition they left for Ireland and did not return to the United
Kingdom for the duration of the war. Dulanty provided a letter in such
cases indicating that the individual had a home in Ireland to return
to. Sometimes he refused to do so. Dulanty refused James O'Rourke
such a letter while conceding that he was an Irish citizen as he had
been born in Britain of Irish parents and had lived there all his life.
The assumption was that he was using his Irish background to evade
his obligations under the Military Training Act. Likewise the Department of External Affairs in Dublin replied to Mrs J. Curran, who had
written on behalf of her son in Britain, pointing out:

> Your son being registered as an Irish citizen would not, however,
> exempt him from liability to conscription if he is liable to be
> conscripted under the British Military Training Act of 1939 (as a
> resident of Britain for two years or more). You will understand that
> the application of the British Military Training Act, 1939 is a matter
> outside the Minister's control.

The Irish Citizens' League, an Irish lobby group in Britain which had
earlier opposed the imposition of conscription on Irish nationals living
there, conceded that the British government was justified in suspect-
ing that some sections of the British public were using Irish citizenship
to evade their responsibilities. Indeed the League asserted that it 'is
aware of many such cases'.

In October 1941, much to the embarrassment of the Irish government, an Irish citizen was charged in Paisley in Scotland with refusing
to be conscripted. Faulkner actually had a travel document from the

high commissioner but had not applied for an exit visa as he believed he could fight conscription in the courts by using his Irish citizenship. This was clearly a test case for the Irish nationals living and working in Britain. He lost his case and was found guilty as charged, an outcome that dismayed officials in Dublin, who concluded that the British courts would not be sympathetic to Irishmen living and working in Britain who used their citizenship to avoid conscription and remain in well-paid employment while others had to go and fight. Boland was sure that Irish nationals would not receive justice in British courts: 'It is merely going to law with the devil in the court of Hell. Even if we had in our favour any law which the British courts would regard as binding on them, British magistrates and judges, even the most upright of them, are certain to take the same view as Sheriff Hamilton took in the court of Paisley – namely that Irish citizens are British subjects, and that that being the case, they are liable under the National Armed Forces Act to military service on the conditions laid down in that act.' He advised that any attempt to avoid conscription on legal grounds would be 'absolutely fruitless'.

Irish officials were also concerned that court cases would publicize the arrangements made between the British and Irish governments in respect of the movement of Irish labour and open them to criticism in both countries. In particular Boland argued that the current situation was favourable to Irish citizens and that publicity might force the British government to reopen discussion on these matters. His advice was to reach a formal agreement with Britain to ensure that no further prosecutions were undertaken and that Maffey, Dulanty and the Dominions Office work out an agreed method to deal with any such problem if it occurred in future. It seems that the Irish government was more concerned with the publicity than with the prosecution of its citizens.[29] Although Faulkner obtained an exit visa and returned to Ireland in 1942, the problem did not go away. In 1942 Michael Murray and four others appealed against the fines imposed on them for refusing to be medically examined under the terms of the National Armed Service Act 1941. Murray and his co-defendants based their case on their Irish citizenship but were found guilty on the grounds that they were in fact British subjects. On appeal, Lord Caldecote, the lord chief justice, delivered a verdict in favour of the lower court, concluding that under British law the individuals charged were indeed British subjects, notwithstanding the changes in the Irish legal and constitutional environment since 1932. De Valera responded robustly, denying that Murray was a British subject and insisting that Eire's citizenship laws be accepted by Britain.[30]

*

Notwithstanding arguments about jurisdiction and sovereignty, large numbers of Irish people from the north and the south clearly volunteered to fight in the Second World War. Most figures circulated in the past are either seriously inflated or too conservative to provide an accurate appreciation of the numbers involved. The problem with the higher figures is that little evidence has been provided to sustain them; the best case made for large numbers is that made by Harrison. However, we now have two sets of calculations that place the actual numbers in some perspective, though they still do not give us a complete picture. Richard Doherty has shown that when the war started there were approximately 20,000 individuals of Irish origin in the British armed services. Three quarters of these were in the army, and given the historical association between Ireland and the British army this was to be expected. The rest were in the RAF and Royal Navy. Doherty uses the accepted formula which holds that for every twenty-two members of the forces there was one death. On this basis the 4,468 Irish war dead give 98,296 for the army. He provides additional figures of 9,500 for the Royal Navy and 12,000 for the RAF. This gives an overall figure of 120,000 Irish military personnel serving during the war. If there were 20,000 Irish nationals already serving in 1939, then we have a residual figure of about 100,000 volunteers for the war period itself. Further calculations lead Doherty to conclude that 78,826 service personnel were from Eire and 52,174 were from Northern Ireland.[31]

A refinement of these figures has been undertaken by Yvonne McEwen who, with a first-class piece of statistical analysis, has contributed significantly to our knowledge of the composition of the Irish regiments and put a human face on those who were conscripted and those who volunteered for these units. McEwen has established the name, age, rank, date and place of death and country of birth for all but a handful of Irish men who died in the Second World War. When she initially searched the databases she discovered that some 967 were unaccounted for in this way, especially when it came to place of birth.

She cross-referenced the Army Roll of Honour with the data available from the Commonwealth War Graves Commission to reduce this number to forty-nine. For the purposes of her research, McEwen included Irish volunteers from both north and south but excluded men with Irish parents not domiciled in Ireland. Her calculations for war dead are 2,241 from Northern Ireland and 2,302 from Eire. This makes total volunteer war dead 4,543 and multiplied by twenty-two gives a figure of 99,946 volunteers from the whole island. Divided between north and south the figures come out as 49,302 for Northern Ireland and 50,644 for Eire. These numbers differ somewhat from Doherty's due to the different methods of calculation. I have accepted McEwen's figures as the more accurate, but should emphasize that they do not include those serving in the forces in September 1939, nor do they cover the Royal Navy or the RAF. If we include Doherty's figure for the air force and navy – approximately 22,000 – then McEwen's total increases to just over 120,000, making the two sets of figures roughly comparable. Irish intelligence reported that large numbers of Irishmen joined the RAF during the war so the figure might be somewhat higher. It is probably therefore safe to conclude that at least 60,000 Irish citizens actually served in the British forces during the Second World War, though if we adopt a higher figure for the RAF then it might be justifiable to push this up to 70,000. What this shows is that the figures circulated by the de Valera government were extravagant, but that nevertheless a significant number of Irish men and women from neutral Ireland did join the forces. What it also puts in perspective is the contribution made by Northern Ireland. Here again a figure of approximately 60,000 is not unreasonable and was a significant contribution from such a small population, challenging the charge that those who lived in the north were reluctant to volunteer for war service.[32]

The research also provides some fascinating details. Although men of Irish origin won eight VCs during the war, only one of these was a soldier in an Irish regiment. Of the total Irish dead of 4,543, those from Irish regiments accounted for 1,385, suggesting that the majority of Irish volunteers found themselves in non-Irish regiments. McEwen discovered that in the Royal Irish Fusiliers those of Irish origin constituted 31 per cent of the total, whereas those of English origin accounted for 61 per cent. In the London Irish Rifles the figure for those of English origin reached 72 per cent while the Irish contingent was 20 per cent. In some units Irish representation was much stronger, particularly in Ulster regiments; nevertheless the interesting conclusion is that for whatever reason traditionally Irish regiments had a majority of non-Irish. This was not due to a paucity of Irish volunteers, but to other reasons not yet entirely clear.

It is impossible to determine if servicemen in Irish regiments or indeed other units of the armed forces were of Irish origin but not birth, or Irish born but domiciled in Britain. Using popular Irish names, for example, allows one to detect a considerable number of individuals of English birth who could have had an Irish background. A number of those interviewed by the Cork Volunteers Project had been born in Britain or had lived there for a considerable time, yet considered themselves Irish because their parents had been born in Ireland or because of their own birth. In some other cases we have evidence that individuals born in England of Irish parentage considered themselves Irish. Desmond Fay stated that while born in England he thought of himself as Irish. In addition there had been an exodus of Protestants from Ireland after the Irish Free State was set up, and though some of these individuals would have identified more closely with Britain than Ireland, those with Irish antecedents could have been attracted to regiments with an Irish association. We can conjecture that English of Irish origin would have been more likely to apply for Irish regiments for sentimental or family reasons. Some regiments had specifically Irish customs attached to them, such as the distribution of shamrock on St Patrick's Day. In other cases the customs were more informal but nevertheless important to the character of the regiment. The Shamrock Club was opened in Hertford Street in London as an open house for Irish servicemen passing through the city; Leslie claims that some 40,000 service personnel had signed in by the end of the war. These points are suggestive, while Doherty's and McEwen's work has extended our knowledge of this topic substantially, but we still have no way of knowing how many individuals of Irish origin gave British addresses when they enlisted. Next of kin might appear to provide a satisfactory answer to this, but as yet we do not have enough information to confirm Gough's 1946 claim that 165,000 Irish citizens volunteered.[33]

*

The volunteers were the most tangible and public expression of the war for many Irish people, while the impact of the conflict was also very direct for the families of the two thousand or so Eire citizens who died. This is over twice the number who died in the Civil War, yet their sacrifice has barely been acknowledged by Irish society. The families and surviving comrades remember, but only recently has the wider community begun to appreciate the significance of what they did. One reason for this was the unwillingness of an isolationist society to confront the fact that large numbers of its citizens had left to fight for another country. Another was the effectiveness of censorship during the war in excluding the volunteers from public knowledge. The *Dublin Evening Mail* ran into trouble with the censors in September 1939 when it published a recruiting notice for the Irish Guards and an appeal from the British Legion. The following year the *Irish Independent* was ordered to submit all copy before publication when it published a photograph of an Irishman in British army uniform. In 1943 the editor of the *Drogheda Independent* remarked on the problems of policing material on the volunteers:

> So many people in my circulation area are either dying for foreign powers or marrying other people who are preparing to die for foreign powers or are having christened the children of people who are feared to have been lost in the service of foreign powers, I have to be continually on the lookout.

In effect, the censors wanted to exclude all matter that might suggest large numbers of Irish people were fighting in the British forces or that there was sympathy for the British cause.[34]

De Valera expressed his unease at the prospect of large numbers of Irish citizens returning to Eire in British army uniforms to Maffey at a meeting in October 1939. When Maffey responded that the military authorities in Britain would have difficulty providing their personnel with civilian clothing, de Valera suggested that an overcoat covering the uniform would prove adequate. He then recounted a story about a visit he had received from a friend then serving on the western front during the First World War. De Valera had given his own greatcoat to the individual, who was then smuggled out of the Irish leader's home.[35] While the British did attempt to deal with this problem by providing clothes depots for Irish military personnel, the system did not always work nor did some Irish servicemen want to accept the restriction on wearing uniforms in Ireland. Some of those interviewed by the Volunteers Project mentioned the uniform issue, and while all were aware of the clothes depots not all used them. Martin Lynch returned to Limerick on leave and wore his British uniform without incident there. Others were not as lucky; James Farnan recounted how while coming out of mass he was told not to wear his uniform by the local gardai. Though warned not to wear it again, he continued to do so; indeed he was married in his uniform shortly after this and continued to wear it while on honeymoon in Kilkenny. Brian Bolling-brooke recalled that when one of his friends was to be married in Ireland all those who returned for the wedding smuggled their uniforms in with them and wore them at the ceremony.[36] Clearly there were differences between the official position and day-to-day experience in various parts of Ireland. Nevertheless, the Irish government was extremely sensitive to public expressions of pro-British sentiment of which this was the most tangible.[37]

As in other areas of public life censorship was applied with draconian vigour to the volunteers. Restrictions were placed on death notices for Eire citizens killed fighting in the war, but these did not satisfy Aiken, who decided in 1941 that 'the time has come to stop all this business'. Aiken's decision effectively prohibited all information concerning Irish deaths in combat. At first it was permissible to publish information on cause of death, rank and regiment for individuals with addresses in Britain but not for those with homes in Eire. However, even this was prohibited when it was discovered that many families were publishing two death notices, one with a British address containing all the military details and the other with an Irish address duly sanitized. From May 1943 all newspapers were prohibited from publishing any information in a death notice that alerted readers to the individual's involvement in the war. Aiken personally made some exceptions for political reasons, but in effect those who volunteered and died had entered a shadowy world from which they never reappeared. The restrictions could have comic as well as tragic aspects to them. One item that irritated the censor read:

The many friends of Mr John A. Robinson, who was involved in a recent boating accident, will be pleased to hear that he is alive and well . . . He is a particularly good swimmer and it is possible that he owes his life to this accomplishment.

Robinson had been an *Irish Times* employee but joined the Royal Navy. In December 1941 his ship the *Prince of Wales* had been sunk, and his survival could only be reported in this indirect fashion. Even then, the censors were appalled and complained bitterly to the editor of the *Irish Times* about the impact of the item. For this and other misdeeds the newspaper was ordered to submit all copy prior to publication from the end of December 1942 until the war ended.[38]

The tragic consequences of this policy can be appreciated in the correspondence between Lady Gore-Booth and Independent Newspapers Ltd concerning an obituary for her son Hugh, killed in action in 1944. The censors would not permit the inclusion of the phrase 'killed in Leros' so his mother had to amend the text. The sanitized version appeared in the *Sligo Independent*, his local newspaper, and it defies belief that anyone reading it would not have been aware that Hugh had been killed on active duty. By prohibiting the place and cause of death the censor was in a way excising a part of Ireland that he and his minister were uneasy about. His mother described Hugh Gore-Booth in the obituary as follows:

> He was at heart Irish to the core, and not in any narrowly accepted sense or from any dogmatical or doctrinaire point of view, or based on set views. By birth baptised Church of Ireland, he was however persuaded by the plain and puritan form of Presbyterianism, which fact may have been the result of his sojourn and contact with the Scots. However he was a Gael too (it had grown into his blood) and an Irish Speaker. In no way could he be more happy than by spending his holidays in the Gaeltacht of his native Connaught and in the south west of Ireland. By his death we have lost the kind of man we can ill afford to lose and Ireland has lost one of her sons in whom the Irish spirit of thirst for adventure, romance and love of knowledge was traditionally exemplified.

It is probable that Aiken and Coyne were unable to appreciate the complexity of an identity such as this and therefore failed to nurture it as a more sophisticated society might have done.[39]

Aiken defended his policy on the grounds that publication of details which alerted readers to a deceased's involvement in the war would threaten Irish neutrality, though he also questioned the motives of those wanting to put in such information. The censors maintained that publication would lead to serious breaches of public order, though why this might be the case is never clearly explained. More telling is the view expressed by Coyne to one journalist: that those who volunteered had not done so for moral or idealistic reasons but were in fact mercenaries. This is a view difficult to sustain given that individuals could earn a lot more working in British war industries than risking their lives fighting in North Africa or Italy. However, it is a view consistent with Irish nationalism's belief that those who joined the British forces did so for reasons other than well-intentioned ones. The majority of those interviewed by the Volunteer Project confirmed that there were many and complex reasons for volunteering.[40] Those who deserted from the Irish armed forces to do so were vigorously pursued. The Irish government took the decision, apparently prompted by de Valera, to distinguish between those who had deserted and remained in Ireland and those who joined the British war effort. The latter were to be treated more harshly by the authorities; indeed their punishment was taken out of the hands of the military and brought under the Emergency Powers legislation. Towards the end of the war the government also introduced an amendment to the legislation to exclude those who had deserted to Britain from any publicly funded employment. This was a deliberate decision to punish those who had run away *to* battle not *from* battle, the normal reason for desertion, according to Dr T. F. O'Higgins in the Dáil. Though the government made its case that it had to punish those who had deserted, the fact that they isolated this one group and introduced special legislation to punish it suggests that vindictiveness was one of the motives behind this. In addition, the government wanted to avoid embarrassing court cases involving individuals who had fought all over Europe and even been in prisoner of war camps which would highlight the extent of both volunteering and desertion.[41]

This vindictiveness was extended beyond deserters to include those who had volunteered for the Allied cause. At the end of the war American troops visiting Dublin were permitted to wear their uniforms but Eire citizens returning home were not. In November 1945 the government banned the annual British Legion commemoration march to the Garden of Remembrance on public order grounds. This decision was fiercely criticized by James Dillon in the Dáil, who argued forcibly that the government had withdrawn the protection of the constitution from one section of the population. The grounds for the ban were weak and it is likely that the government simply did not want a show of pro-British sentiment on the streets of the capital so soon after the war. While the government and its supporters were prepared to use the volunteers in a self-interested and cynical fashion to repair the country's image with the United States during and after the war, they was less interested in recognizing the actions of their own citizens in fighting against Hitler and fascism. This confirms not only the indifference of the Irish government to the outcome of the war, but also its continuing unease about that significant minority in Eire which considered its responsibilities extended beyond the island's shores.[42] Larry O'Sullivan had gone to war to 'fight for civilisation against dark ages'. As a sailor he was sunk three times during the war, once off Norway, then at Dunkirk and finally in the Java Sea where he was captured by the Japanese and spent three years in a prisoner of war camp. Such was his treatment that he believes that the atomic bombs dropped on Japan saved his and his comrades' lives. For others who visited the death camps in Europe in 1945 the enormity of what had been at stake during the war became apparent for the first time. For many Irish men and women who joined the battle there was a sense of disappointment that the Irish neutrality which they often defended could be used to ignore what they had achieved.

9. DIPLOMACY AS IDEOLOGY:
NEUTRALITY JUNE 1941 TO AUGUST 1945

After the Nazis invaded the Soviet Union in June 1941, the war became more complex. The invasion provided Britain itself with a welcome breathing space, but there was little respite for its armies in North Africa and elsewhere. The ferocity of the German attack on Russia was such that even well-placed observers concluded that the Soviets would soon collapse. So convinced was Hitler of his success that he dismissed any thought of a negotiated end to the conflict on the eastern front. For Churchill, it was a godsend, as he famously told one of his confidants: 'if Hitler invaded Hell [I] would at least make a favourable reference to the Devil'.[1] He was no less enthusiastic in public: 'any man or state who marches with Hitler is our foe ... it follows therefore that we shall give whatever help we can to Russia and the Russian people'. Though a staunch anti-communist, Churchill saw his opportunity and quickly linked British fortunes with those of Stalin's Russia. A similar, if less enthusiastic, decision was made by Roosevelt in the United States, which was still neutral. Anti-communism was deeply embedded in the American consciousness yet Roosevelt decided to provide support for the Russians even when officials warned that this would deprive Britain of much-needed help. That the Soviet Union was communist, anti-democratic and militarily aggressive was not ignored in America and Roosevelt's decision gave ammunition to the isolationist lobby. Writing to Hull from Dublin, Gray reported that the alliance between Russia and Britain was also being used by anti-British elements in Ireland. Gray believed that the Irish censors were permitting articles stressing the anti-religious activities of the Soviet Union while articles condemning Germany for its religious policies did not appear in the press. The Irish minister in

Washington also identified with isolationist views on Russia, remarking in a letter to Walshe, 'recent events raise doubt that this war is a clear-cut issue of liberty and democracy. It is not a purely world conflict between tyranny [*sic*] and issue of Anglo-Russian alliance has dissipated that illusion'.[2]

Despite Russia's involvement, as the war progressed its democratic aims became the main focus for Roosevelt and Churchill. The unofficial alliance between the United States and Britain prior to Pearl Harbor was based on democratic assumptions. Though Churchill may have had sentimental attachments to empire and imperial grandeur, the changes in British politics after May 1940, the role of the dominions in the war and American influence established a political framework that was essentially non-imperial, if not yet post-imperial. The meeting between Roosevelt and Churchill at Placenta Bay, Newfoundland, in August 1941 marked an important step in the democratization of the war, as well as bringing the United States closer to active participation. Roosevelt was the dominant figure, with Churchill painfully aware of his dependence on American supplies and support for the continuation of the war. This was reflected in the Atlantic Charter, agreed between the two leaders, which in its eight paragraphs assumed a world without empires but with national self-determination and economic liberalism, as well as the introduction of basic freedoms for all. Even more significant, in September 1941 the American navy extended its protection to all Atlantic convoys between North America and Iceland.[3] The Roosevelt administration was still faced with considerable opposition to declaring war on Germany, but as a result of the meeting at Placenta Bay and the new role of the American navy, there was now an effective alliance between the United Kingdom and the United States. This worried Brennan, who wrote in October that 'the trend is definitely towards war', in Washington.[4] Roosevelt wrote to Gray after the conference with Churchill that he thought it 'had done good', adding that 'it may make a few more people in Ireland see the light'.

Roosevelt was dismissive of Irish-American isolationists. He complained that David Walsh, who was close to Brennan, hated England more than he loved the United States. Roosevelt was also increasingly dismissive of 'my old friend Dev' and sceptical of the Irish army's ability to defend the country without British help.[5] The president wanted an agreement between the Irish and British governments in advance of an invasion of Ireland to deal with any German threat. He was not prepared to provide Ireland with weapons he considered likely to fall into German hands unless some agreement could be reached. Roosevelt's scepticism concerning Ireland had increased because the Irish and British military staffs had not developed any plans together to meet such an attack. What de Valera never seemed to recognize was that there were no circumstances under which the United States would provide arms to Ireland unless he committed the country to an anti-German, pro-British position. In July 1941 Gray warned de Valera that his lack of action in respect of the German threat, his failure to cooperate with Britain on defence matters and his criticism of American technicians in Northern Ireland would not be viewed with sympathy by most Americans, and especially not by the administration. Gray told de Valera that the British were now likely to turn Northern Ireland into a fortress in order to defend Britain from any threat from the north Atlantic, and in doing so would effectively ignore Eire.[6]

Gray went to Derry in September 1941 to assess work being carried out under lend-lease. De Valera had threatened to openly denounce the involvement of American technicians if it appeared that the United States was going to take over any bases there. According to de Valera American actions in Northern Ireland infringed Irish sovereignty. Gray identified Walshe as one of those most hostile to Roosevelt and American policy, but also noted that some wives of Fianna Fail politicians frequently engaged in criticizing the United States.[7] Gray's view of de Valera and Fianna Fáil grew increasingly pessimistic as 1941 progressed. His reports now contained bitterness towards those he considered anti-American and anti-Roosevelt. He was particularly incensed by Aiken's views, caustically reporting that Aiken had boasted on his return from the United States that less than 10 per cent of the American public would support Roosevelt in a war. Gray concluded that de Valera did not want a German victory, but he did want a draw that would weaken Britain and the commonwealth. He also noted that the *Irish Press* reported news from the United States with an isolationist bias. He warned the Irish government not to expect sympathy from an American government under attack from Irish-American groups, many of which were supported by the Irish government and close to Brennan in Washington. Not surprisingly Gray became in his own words 'as popular as a skunk under the veranda' with Fianna Fáil. Despite this, he continued to provide the State Department with realistic assessments of Axis activities in Ireland. Gray considered such activities neither as widespread nor as important as the media claimed. De Valera, he thought, was neither anti-German nor pro-British in the strict sense, but is 'neutral and pro-Irish. All he asks of the world is that his country be left alone.' The IRA was no longer a serious threat in Ireland nor were they of much significance to the Germans, as the Irish government had largely emasculated them. Gray remained fairly positive about the Irish government, believing that censorship was fairly even-handed, but with a slight bias towards the Axis. He emphasized that there was widespread fear in Ireland that the country would pay dearly if it ended its neutrality. Gray took the view that the German bombing raids had served as a warning to the Irish of what would happen if the country did join in the war, claiming on one occasion that the Germans had reinforced this idea by bombing Ireland a short time after Roosevelt made a speech condemning German aggression.[8]

Despite Gray's balanced assessments American policy was becoming more critical of de Valera. After the Placenta Bay conference and the redeployment of the US Navy American support for Britain became more determined and active and Gray became more critical in his private correspondence with Roosevelt. He asked the president if Aiken had been linked with any sabotage trial in the United States and wanted the FBI to investigate. De Valera he now dismissed as 'grim and obstinate and blind'. Gray also complained that the Irish were ignoring his stated view that 'we do not like to be pressure grouped by any hyphenated minority. It is a good deal of a blow to him for they have come to take playing politics in our back yard as a right.'[9] In October 1941 Gray travelled to London, where he met the new American ambassador, John Winant. Winant and Gray were to develop a good working relationship over the coming years and cooperated closely on Irish policy. By this time Gray had concluded that the Irish ports could not be obtained unless the country was invaded. He recommended concentrating on Derry and building up defences there. The view to take with the Irish government was, according to Gray, 'that we were preparing to get along without their help, valuable though that would be, that we would probably respect their position as isolationists but that neither we nor the British would probably make sacrifices for them in the future'. Gray noted anxiety on de Valera's part, but also a continuing view among Irish government supporters and members that Germany would win the war. He cited Conor Maguire, president of the High Court and former attorney general in a Fianna Fáil government, and Cardinal MacRory as holding those views. MacRory wrote to Gray for example:

> My position is that whatever Hitler may be, you ought to try to make peace with him now, because you may have to do so later on. If he wins you shall be forced, I suppose, to accept his terms; and if the war be fought to stalemate, it will be necessary to make peace with him.

On another occasion the Cardinal was quoted by Walshe as saying 'a victory for America and England would be worse for Christianity than a victory for Germany. He said he believed that Catholicism in Germany was strong enough to eliminate in time the doctrine of Nazism, but he was very much afraid of the effects on the world of Anglo-American materialistic humanitarianism.'[10]

Gray sensed from these and other conversations that there was a part of Irish opinion, especially within Fianna Fáil, which believed that Britain and the United States should reach an accommodation with Germany before they were beaten.

In late October 1941 Gray demonstrated his own acute sense of danger for the United States, writing 'before you get this Japan may touch things off'. Gray also openly wondered what de Valera would do if Roosevelt directly asked him for the ports while also offering American protection. Quite realistically, Gray considered 'there is a great deal of loose talk here even in high civil service quarters, that he could not refuse. I think he both could and would refuse unless it suited his book to accept.' Walshe, probably at the behest of de Valera, was by October 1941 organizing opinion against Gray and the United States in Ireland. Gray was being blamed for the policy of not supplying arms without conditions to Ireland and he recognized that his position in Dublin might become untenable if the United States decided to do a deal with de Valera. If the occasion arose, he assured the president:

Of course you understand, if the position I have taken here ever embarrasses you in the least, tip me off and I'll get out: it may be that I have fulfilled my usefulness, that is insisting on American rights and policy instead of serving Irish policy as Dev expects an American Minister to do. There is no question that Dev is gunning for me and will probably try to work through political friends of his in America.[11]

Irish irritation at the close working relationship between Britain and the United States increased when the Irish legation in Washington sent an aide-memoire to the State Department requesting that the American administration advise the Irish government of its intentions in Northern Ireland. When no reply was received Brennan wrote again in a formal note, reiterating the Irish government's concerns in respect of Northern Ireland and its vital interest in the area. The State Department reply, annotated 'Very good' by Roosevelt, repeated a statement by the president confirming that Americans were in Northern Ireland working on a number of projects paid for by the British government. The most stinging part of the reply from an Irish perspective was the insistence that as Northern Ireland was part of the United Kingdom, issues arising from the Irish note should be taken up with the British government.[12]

*

The tension between the United States and Eire increased appreciably when American troops arrived in Northern Ireland early in 1942, after the United States had entered the war. In a letter to Roosevelt just after Pearl Harbor Gray confessed that his first reaction was one of relief: 'any number of wars are easier to fight than what you have been through for two years'. This may have been true but isolationist opinion did not disappear. One of the main criticisms of Roosevelt after Pearl Harbor was that he paid more attention to Europe than to Japan, which after all had attacked the United States. Confident of his own victory in Europe, Hitler had declared war on the USA; he had been of the view that the United States was effectively at war with Germany before Pearl Harbor, but had not previously acted to counter Roosevelt's pro-British policy. It is probable that Roosevelt would have declared war on Germany in any event, but this made it easier.

Roosevelt considered Hitler a greater danger than Japan, despite the specific Japanese attack. Since Munich at least he had believed Hitler a threat to world peace, to the existing international order and to liberal democracy, and his actions between then and December 1941 confirmed Roosevelt in this view.[13] Ireland's diplomats never appreciated this aspect of British or American policymaking. There is little doubt that Irish policy was focused primarily on self-interest and survival, and what de Valera and Walshe, among others, missed was Roosevelt's genuine desire to defend and promote democracy as an alternative to totalitarianism and authoritarianism.[14]

In March 1941 Maffey had a discussion with Walshe on the morality of the war. Walshe said that 'England was fighting for herself, for her life, and nothing else. America was thinking of nothing but her own interests. Ireland would fight for herself and nobody else.'[15] This narrow focus was also notable in de Valera's views on the war and the Allies after the United States entered the war. Gray nevertheless drew some very positive conclusions from the initial Irish reaction to American entry into the war. He recognized that Aiken and his supporters in Fianna Fáil would remain hostile to the United States but thought that de Valera might be more flexible. Gray suggested that it might be an appropriate moment to provide Ireland with weapons to defend itself, advising that the United States act judiciously in order to draw the country closer to the Allies. If Germany protested that this was a break with neutrality, Gray thought this would move Irish opinion closer to the United States. He advised Roosevelt in the circumstances to play up the evidence that some 150,000 Irish volunteers were already fighting for the Allies. Gray thought that de Valera's options had become quite limited, adding, 'Isn't it our cue to get the Irish people behind us with a few good deeds?'[16] Gray also issued a statement to Associated Press that he had been approached by a number of Irishmen wanting to volunteer to join the American forces now that the United States was at war. One reason given by the men and highlighted by Gray was that remittances from the United States had allowed them to remain in education and they wished to repay this kindness.[17]

De Valera made his first public statement on American entry into the war during a speech in Cork on 14 December. He emphasized that the extension of the war was a 'source of anxiety and sorrow for everyone in Ireland' and highlighted the links between the two countries. He went on to say that it would be unnatural if Irish people did not have a special sympathy for the United States but then referred to those 'strangers who do not understand our conditions' who asked why Ireland did not enter the war in support of the USA. This question, he said, had been answered in advance of the United States's entry to the war: 'the policy of the State remains unchanged. We can only be a friendly neutral.' He then cited partition, the absence of national freedom and the possibility that ending neutrality would lead to political conflict in the country as reasons for maintaining neutrality. This speech was not about the United States; it was about Ireland and the fear that it might be affected by the war. The course taken by Ireland was a just one: 'God has been pleased to save us during the years of war that have already passed.'

Despite the reference to the special relationship between the United States and Ireland, de Valera continued to place the belligerents on the same level and equally opposed to Ireland. On Christmas Day de Valera returned to some of these themes. He once again invoked the protection of God for Ireland in his radio broadcast to the United States. He recalled that on previous occasions he had been addressing a neutral nation, but now America was at war he could 'no longer speak as freely as before'. He wanted his American listeners to accept that 'Ireland's fate is bound up with the maintenance of the present policy of the Government' but that it would fight if attacked. When American troops arrived in Northern Ireland in January 1942 de Valera condemned the British and the American governments for not consulting with Eire, complaining that this reinforced partition, and adding, 'No matter what troops occupy the Six Counties, the Irish people's claim for the union of the whole national territory and for supreme jurisdiction over it will remain unabated.' He also sought to link partition with the defence of small states elsewhere, implying that German attacks on neutrality and small nations were comparable to the situation in Northern Ireland.[18]

Although Roosevelt had decided not to extend lend-lease to Ireland in November 1941 American participation in the war altered strategic thinking in Washington. Gray had recognized the possibilities when he had advised Roosevelt to consider providing armaments, but he quickly lost his enthusiasm for de Valera. He described de Valera's

Christmas message to the United States as 'fatuous', complaining that Roosevelt's note in reply to de Valera had been effectively censored and would not be read by the mass of the Irish people. As a result of censorship the average Irish person was unaware of how 'friendless' the country was. Gray's own suggestions were somewhat confusing at this stage. He warned against providing Ireland with anything that would deprive Britain or the United States of necessary materials, yet at the same time he did not wish to alienate the Irish people or the Irish army – as distinct from the government – which he considered friendly. He then speculated on the best course to follow in the future. One possibility was to take 'strong action' and attempt to split the country from the government; the other was to wait for a German attack while building defences in Northern Ireland. With the Irish military Gray was taking the line that he was prepared to recommend arms be supplied to them, but he also wanted the US administration to appreciate the positive impact of goodwill gestures. Gray now recognized that neutrality had widespread support among Fine Gael supporters; only Dillon now openly opposed neutrality. He also drew attention to the German airborne assault on Crete, suggesting that Ireland might receive similar treatment, and repeated a conversation he had had with de Valera's confidential secretary, Kathleen O'Connell, who had exclaimed, 'Who would have thought a year ago that America would be in the war!' Gray had responded he was surprised that no senior Irish official had believed that the United States would enter the war. When O'Connell did not reply he went on to say that de Valera, Walshe and others had laughed at him when he had repeatedly stressed that British and American interests were closely linked. Gray now believed the Fianna Fáil government and senior diplomats such as Walshe had a 'twisted and blinded' viewpoint on American policy. He was particularly shaken by the continuing Irish refusal to accept or publicly say that its economic and political survival was linked to that of Britain. Gray was also increasingly concerned at the security of his communications. He believed that there were German agents in the Irish postal service and that the German legation was operating a wireless link. All in all he thought, 'it is a bad situation'.[19]

*

Though Gray began 1942 by saying that 'here we are in it up to the neck', he seemed both positive and enthusiastic about the future. He was not the only one to feel that the situation deserved a new approach to Ireland. Churchill with his usual enthusiasm had telegraphed de Valera on 8 December through Maffey, who contacted de Valera at 2 o'clock in the morning saying that he had a message from the prime minister. It seems that de Valera panicked, believing it was an ultimatum or possibly that an attack was about to be made on the country; he contacted the military and political authorities putting them on standby. However, Maffey's early-morning telegram from Churchill was not concerned with the ports but contained the message:

> From Mr Churchill to Mr de Valera. Personal. Private and Secret. Begins. Now is your chance. Now or never. 'A nation once again.' Am very ready to meet you at any time. Ends.

De Valera's biographers describe this as an enigmatic message but it appears to suggest that Churchill thought that de Valera would take a different attitude to the war now that the United States was involved. However, Churchill did not appreciate that de Valera's primary commitment was now to neutrality and Irish sovereignty rather than to taking a risk on partition. De Valera's own views confirm this:

> On being handed the written text I concluded that it was Mr Churchill's way of intimating 'now is the chance for taking action which would ultimately lead to the unification of the country'. I indicated to Sir John Maffey that I did not see the thing in that light. I saw no opportunity at the moment of securing unity, that our people were determined on their attitude of neutrality

Nothing came of Churchill's initiative, though some behind-the-scenes correspondence and discussion did continue over the following week or so. Churchill's enthusiasm did not extend to the Dominions Office, where Lord Cranborne was anxious to maintain good relations with de Valera and the Irish government. At a meeting with de Valera later in December Cranborne was effectively dismissive of Churchill's telegram. No progress was made at this meeting or subsequently.[20]

When Maffey informed de Valera that American troops were to arrive in Northern Ireland early in 1942 he reported that the taoiseach looked depressed and deeply resentful. He reported that de Valera had said to him, 'if only Ireland were attacked by Germany it would simplify things'. Frank Gallagher recounts a conversation with de Valera in 1941 during which he had said to Gallagher with a smile, 'I wish there was some way of knowing who will win the war. It would make decisions much easier.'[21] Gray believed that Aiken had been wrong-footed by American entry into the war, having been told that Aiken had assured the government on his return from the United States that America would not become involved. Pearl Harbor nullified any such assumption and placed the Irish government in an invidious position. Gray now recommended that a full oil embargo be placed on those countries not receiving lend-lease and that unarmed neutral ships not be permitted to travel in American-protected convoys. In a memorandum in February to General Marshall, Roosevelt praised Gray, saying 'he had done exceptionally well there' and suggesting that the combined staffs consider his recommendations. The State Department was opposed to any action in respect of neutrals that might further alienate them, however.[22] This followed Roosevelt's reply to Brennan's note complaining about American troops in Northern Ireland:

> The decision to despatch troops to the British Isles was reached in close consultation with the British government as part of our strategic plan to defeat the Axis aggressors. There was not, and is not now, the slightest thought or intention of invading Irish territory or threatening Irish security. Far from constituting a threat to Ireland, the presence of these troops in neighbouring territory can only contribute to the security of Ireland and of the whole British Isles, as well as furthering our total war effort. [23]

However, de Valera was not prepared to accept this as a final statement of the position between the two countries. He replied to Roosevelt's note on 20 April accepting his assurances that no invasion was intended but completely ignoring his pointed remarks that the troops would be effectively protecting Ireland. He returned to the partition issue and asked again for armaments to defend the country. De Valera argued that it would be a mistake to leave Eire exposed even though neither Britain nor the United States was now going to attack. Ireland had a quarter of a million men ready to fight, but no adequate arms for them. De Valera ignored the fact that if Germany was now the only threat, then there was a case for closer cooperation with the Allies, but he wanted the weapons unconditionally. Roosevelt wrote to Hull that no reply was necessary, 'that means no reply at all', adding that he wished de Valera would 'come out of the clouds and quit talking about the quarter of a million Irishmen ready to fight'. He was equally dismissive of the fighting qualities of the Irish army, offering his personal view that there were probably no more than a thousand trained soldiers in the country and ending with the jibe, 'even they are probably efficient only in the use of rifles and shotguns'.[24]

Roosevelt's position was echoed by Churchill when he told the foreign secretary in 1942 that de Valera should not be provided with armaments unless he joined the war, though Britain should be prepared to supply some arms if Ireland provided services for the British. Churchill wanted the foreign secretary to request that the United States also not supply weapons. Winant wrote to Hull after discussions with Churchill and other British politicians that there was widespread opposition to providing arms for Ireland.[25] The State Department had meanwhile concluded that no progress could be made with Ireland that would be 'even remotely satisfactory' to the United States. Dean Acheson noted that extensive discussions with Aiken and other Irish officials had convinced him that another approach to Ireland would be mistaken, as they would take this as a signal to dictate terms to the United States and not as an opportunity to enter into negotiations over the war. Accordingly, the only acceptable position for the United States would be to take a sympathetic view of any Irish approach, but only to make concessions on issues of importance to the United States. The USA, he concluded, should not be 'offering something which they might accept upon terms satisfactory to them'. Acheson also reported that Roosevelt had been giving consideration to Ireland, deciding that an approach to Ireland on lend-lease 'would run counter to the general direction of his thinking'.[26]

The exasperation of the Americans at what they considered Ireland's shortsightedness was demonstrated on a number of occasions throughout 1942. Nor did Irish representations help. When General McKenna approached Gray in connection with obtaining arms in March 1942 he immediately introduced partition into the discussion.

It is very likely that McKenna was instructed to include the issue by de Valera, but Gray quickly dismissed any possibility of discussions on this matter. Gray pointed out to McKenna and Oscar Traynor, who accompanied him, that de Valera's complaint about American troops in Northern Ireland had lost sympathy for Ireland in the United States and 'the sooner that aspect of the situation was suppressed, the better for Irish security'. Gray had been deeply concerned at the inadequacy of the Irish military, sharing Roosevelt's opinion of their ability to defend the country. He had feared that a German invasion would quickly overrun the country and defeat the British in Northern Ireland, gaining control of the whole island. He had written alarmist reports on this, even before the United States entered the war, on one occasion recommending that the United States establish a network of agents – what he called a fifth column – in border areas to facilitate the entry of American or British troops into Eire in the event of a German invasion. Gray admitted later that he had pressed the British on these matters prior to December 1941, but that Maffey and others were reluctant to provide him with details of intelligence and security arrangements between Britain and Eire. When the United States did enter the war, Gray was quickly informed about these now well-established arrangements between British and Irish military staffs. Gray admitted that these contacts went well 'beyond what might reasonably have been believed possible'.[27]

Some of Gray's interventions were due to his enthusiasm to play a role in the war effort, leading him to suggest misguided or ill-thought-out schemes for obtaining facilities he considered beneficial to the Allies or to draw Ireland into a closer relationship with them. But his enthusiasm also led him to misread the political situation in Ireland, as diplomats frequently do. For example, he had believed that James Dillon could have split the country on the ports issue, possibly putting together a pro-Allied majority if the United States and Britain demanded the ports from de Valera. This overestimated Dillon's political influence and the extent and depth of pro-Allied sentiment in Ireland. Gray did recognize later that whatever validity there had been in this view disappeared once Dillon openly supported the United States in the war and resigned from Fine Gael. Gray now recommended forcibly occupying the ports if they were considered necessary for the Allied war effort. He sketched out a plan which included dropping leaflets explaining the action to the Irish people, occupying the ports, and if necessary bombing the main Irish military barracks in Dublin and on the Curragh. This, he asserted, 'would be the most merciful way of shutting off opposition'. A little later in 1942 Gray sent a fairly pessimistic report to Roosevelt, noting that Hempel, whom he calls 'this bastard', was flying the swastika on his car and had been surrounded by 'obsequious Irish' at the All-Ireland Hurling Final on Sunday 6 September. He was concerned that the Germans were planning something 'serious', warning Roosevelt of this on a number of occasions.[28] The president remained strongly supportive of Gray's work in Ireland and wrote to him about a visit from a friend of de Valera's, 'a typical professional Irish-American', who complained that the Irish people were starving. Roosevelt gleefully recounted how he gave him what he described as the 'absent treatment' and added, 'I looked at him in a much interested way and remarked quietly "Where is Ireland?"' Roosevelt thought the 'absent treatment' was the best way to deal with de Valera, and did disguise his annoyance with the taoiseach:

> I do wish people as a whole over there could realise that Dev is unnecessarily stirring up trouble because most people over here feel that Dublin, by maintaining German spies and by making all the little things difficult for the United Nations, is stirring up a thoroughly unsympathetic attitude toward Ireland as a whole when we win the war. That is a truly sad state of affairs.

Coming as this did from the president of the United States and to an official who was close to him, it boded ill for Ireland for the rest of the war.[29]

This changing atmosphere also created the conditions for misunderstanding, tension and possibly conflict, as the Irish were increasingly hostile to Gray. De Valera, Walshe and other Irish officials were inclined to dismiss Gray as a loose cannon rather than as a representative of the United States, appointed because of his connections with the president. De Valera told Fine Gael deputy leader Mulcahy that he would have demanded his recall if it had not been for his friendship with the president. This was to misconstrue the relationship between the two men and to misunderstand Gray's role in Ireland. Gray represented the United States and the president and expressed what he believed to be American views in Ireland. He did not represent Ireland in Washington, as Walshe wanted him to, except in so far as America's interests were involved. It is unlikely that Roosevelt would have maintained Gray in his post simply because of friendship, and as he made clear on several occasions he believed Gray to be doing the job in Ireland he was sent there to do. In the circumstances of 1942, when Allied victory was not certain, the possibility of conflict between Gray, now energized by American involvement in the war, and de Valera increased dramatically. The issue of the troops in Northern Ireland was but one flashpoint, but for Gray a crucial one. Walshe complained that the Americans in Northern Ireland 'wounded the feelings of all Irish who thought along nationalist lines'. One result of this expressed view was that Gray explicitly linked de Valera's condemnation of American troops in Northern Ireland with an IRA statement in August that attacked the Americans as invaders and threatened violence against them. Gray also condemned de Valera when he appealed for IRA men who had murdered a policeman in Northern Ireland to be reprieved. According to Gray, de Valera seemed more interested in this than in the war against Nazism or helping the Allies. If de Valera, Walshe or Aiken were now hostile to Gray, he in turn became increasingly bitter at the nationalist posturing of de Valera and his close associates. [30]

When Gray complained that de Valera's agitation over the IRA men was exacerbating an already volatile situation, de Valera emphasized their patriotism. He also told Gray that opposition to partition was part of his neutrality policy. Gray provides a telling insight into the mind of de Valera at this stage in the war:

Mr de Valera's inner conflict between his emotional urge to the Left and his reasoned long-range view of the situation, unquestionably was the factor that made him drift into the civil war that almost wrecked the new born Free State. His mind tells him that his only hope of ending partition is with our help and with the help of British liberal opinion, but his emotions apparently prevent his acting on this premise, similarly, his mind tells him that only by the defeat of Germany can Eire be preserved as an independent state, but again his nationalistic emotions blind him and he will exert no leadership in this sense. [31]

The leader of the opposition, William Cosgrave, told Gray in October 1942, 'Eire is afraid of America,' appreciating that the United States could use force if the Irish government refused facilities urgently required by the Allies. Gray clearly knew this, but suggested to Roosevelt that if a demand were to be made for the ports by the United States then it should be clearly linked to resolving the partition issue.[32] After Operation Torch, the Allied invasion of North Africa on 8 November, Gray complained to Roosevelt that de Valera had immediately made a speech in favour of neutrality and threatening to fight all-comers in response. Gray remarked cynically that in his speech de Valera had said his troops were now better armed, but never told his audience that the arms had been supplied by Britain. Gray added, 'It is that kind of rancid ingratitude which excites my contempt.' This feeling percolated through to Irish government sources. Seán T. O'Kelly complained that prominent Americans were no longer arriving in Eire for visits, being especially shocked that Eleanor Roosevelt did not come to Dublin when she visited Belfast. O'Kelly's wife told Maude Gray that the Irish government would offer a similar reception to Hitler or Mussolini as they would to Eleanor Roosevelt, which Gray noted was precisely the reason Eleanor Roosevelt did not come. Maude Gray was even more critical of Ireland than her husband. Writing to Roosevelt after meeting Eleanor in Belfast, she encouraged the president to watch Eire carefully and not to be fooled when the Allies won the war. Maude had noticed more openness to the Allies on the part of some sections of Irish opinion, especially after the invasion of North Africa, but thought 'our success is a surprise and they are not yet willing to admit that we have got them on the run'.[33]

*

There was a shift in Gray's emphasis towards the end of 1942 and the early part of 1943. He now concentrated on establishing long-term policy for the United States, Britain and the dominions in respect of de Valera's Ireland, warning that de Valera would seek at the end of the war to convince the Allies that Eire had done everything to aid the struggle. Whereas in May 1942 Gray had been proposing decisive action to acquire the ports if they were needed, by November of the same year he had formed the conclusion that the ports were not too strategically important. Visiting London to discuss Irish policy with

Winant and British officials, he was concerned that the ministers he met, including Attlee, Morrison and Cranborne, no longer considered Eire a primary concern, especially in the context of British–American relations at the end of the war. What he did detect was weariness, at times almost disgust, with de Valera and Eire even among those most likely to be sympathetic to Ireland. These impressions were to an extent confirmed when Gray attended lunch at 10 Downing Street with Churchill and General Charles de Gaulle. Gray found Churchill charismatic: 'he makes history with a light touch', he remarked a little later. Most conversation revolved around de Gaulle as the leader of the Free French bitterly complained that the Allies were undermining his position by their recent arrangements in North Africa with Vichy leader Admiral Darlan.[34] Although Gray did not make the comparison, the similarities between de Gaulle and de Valera were striking, each emphasizing his grievances, the importance of his nation and its concerns at the expense of all others. But Ireland was discussed and Gray was gratified to have the prime minister confirm that Britain had fought the war for three years without the Irish ports, had developed its own response to the threat at sea and, though the Irish ports would have been valuable, they could now win the war without support from Eire.[35]

This provided Gray with some breathing space in respect of Eire, but with the ferocity of the renewed U-boat campaign in early 1943 the issue of facilities in Ireland re-emerged. Gray was by this time coordinating Allied policy in Ireland with Maffey and with Kearney, the Canadian high commissioner. The three were agreed that with Allied successes in North Africa it might be more difficult for de Valera to refuse facilities to the Allies. Gray believed de Valera would not agree but thought it important to place his refusal to work with the Allies on record with an eye to possible post-war difficulties. Gray quoted an American newsman who had cited de Valera's opinion that Ireland would be safe after the war because Britain and the United States would fall out and compete with one another. Gray's views at this time echo those of the president, who wrote, 'Ireland has lived in a dream under the rule of a dreamer.' Gray took the position, and presented it forcibly to those Irish people he met, that while Ireland might have been prudent to avoid involvement when it looked like Germany would win, this was no longer the case:

Your neutrality is voluntary and gratuitous and if it means that you see no difference in the two causes, that you are as friendly to Germany as to us, American opinion is certain to resent it. Further-more you deny all moral obligation for our supply and security without which there would be hunger and freezing in Dublin and the breakdown of [the] Irish economy.[36]

One of Gray's tasks in Dublin was now to insist that de Valera's government and Irish opinion generally recognized and took account of the help given to Ireland and of the moral superiority of the Allied position. He believed Irish opinion was shifting when Walshe went to London in November 1942 with a request that Eire be represented at any post-war reconstruction conference that might take place, but if he thought that this would make it easier to convince Walshe or de Valera that Ireland should cooperate more closely with the Allies, he was to be quickly disabused. As the tide turned in the war, de Valera seemed as insistent on preserving neutrality as ever. Just three weeks after General Paulus and the German Sixth Army surrendered at Stalingrad, Maffey had a long conversation with de Valera, who continued to insist that Ireland needed arms to defend itself against Germany. Maffey assured him that Hitler was unlikely to attack Eire, but if he did the RAF was in a position to deal with the threat. De Valera challenged this in the strongest terms, though Maffey wondered if the taoiseach actually believed his own words. Maffey attributed de Valera's heated response to his unwillingness to accept that Eire was no longer of strategic interest to the Allies and that even if security threats emerged Britain had no need of Ireland's cooperation. It was in de Valera's interests to play up the German threat not only to secure advantages with the Allies, but also to create an atmosphere of uncertainty at home. Maffey and de Valera discussed various issues, some more controversial than others. At one point, to counter a proposal from Maffey de Valera insisted that 'neutrality had become the religion of the country', but he could only regret the situation when Maffey told him, 'England would not forget that while she was fighting for her life Dublin harboured Axis Legations and interned British airmen.'[37]

The question of the Axis legations in Dublin now took on greater importance for the Allies. While German, Japanese and Italian diplomats were resident in Dublin, there was always a danger that crucial information might be obtained and transmitted to Germany. As the Allies prepared for the invasion of mainland Europe, the issue concentrated attention. Maffey had raised the issue when Gray visited London in November 1942, suggesting that it might provide a stronger opening gambit to de Valera than the ports, which increasingly the Allies could do without. In March 1943 Maffey told Gray that the British military was no longer concerned with the Irish ports, as the facilities available in Northern Ireland, Iceland and elsewhere provided the necessary protection for convoys. However, popular opinion in the United States was not as easily assuaged. Brennan complained to Welles in May 1943 that American newspaper articles were pushing the United States to occupy the Azores and Cobh in County Cork to meet the U-boat threat and to protect convoys. Brennan wanted the administration to censor the newspapers, but Welles retorted that the US administration had no control over newspaper opinion – he might have added unlike the Irish government. Welles replied to some further remarks on the war from Brennan by remarking, 'It had seemed to us for a long time past that the Irish people felt that a victory which was of vital importance in assuring them their own security in the future would be won by the United Nations without their having to lift a finger themselves to bring that victory to pass.'[38] When in October the Portuguese government under intense pressure from the United States provided facilities in the Azores for US forces, the Irish were distinctly alarmed, but Gray did not think that de Valera would change his mind. Both Maffey and Gray reported that de Valera appeared disappointed by what he considered to be Salazar's weakness. In conversation with Maffey, de Valera expressed surprise at Salazar's decision, implying that changing policy was in some way disreputable. De Valera also insisted that the Portuguese position was inconsistent with neutrality, though Portugal and its stance had been viewed positively in Ireland up to that point. Maffey concluded that de Valera would continue to adhere obstinately to neutrality, even though Allied newspapers were now unfavourably contrasting the actions of the Portuguese dictatorship with those of democratic Eire.[39] Gray believed that this was the best time psychologically to demand concessions from de Valera, although this may not have been the case, as the Portuguese decision was one that de Valera disagreed with. It is clear that for de Valera the preservation of neutrality was more important than Allied victory over Germany, even though the risk to Ireland was now significantly lower than at any time since early 1940. This attitude infuriated Gray and he now threw himself into the task of placing the Irish leader on record, or, failing that, then forcing him to concede on either the ports or the legations.

*

Conscription also returned to the agenda. Churchill urged Roosevelt to support the introduction of conscription in Northern Ireland. He expressed his sensitivity to 'young Americans taken by compulsion from their homes to defend an area where young fellows of the locality loaf about with their hands in their pockets'. While he anticipated a 'loud caterwaul' from de Valera, he also thought that circumstances had changed. While Roosevelt was not prepared to oppose conscription on this occasion, neither was he prepared to give Churchill his active support. Roosevelt left the policy to Churchill's judgement, while neither he nor the State Department were overly concerned at its impact on American opinion or on relations between the north and south of Ireland.[40] Although conscription was not introduced in Northern Ireland, Roosevelt remained concerned with Ireland and interested in developments there. For example, he asked Cardinal Spellman, a close supporter, to travel to Europe on his behalf in 1943. One of Spellman's tasks was to obtain increased Irish cooperation with the Allies, something he failed to achieve. At a dinner at Gray's residence, attended by de Valera, O'Kelly, Maffey and Archbishop McQuaid, Spellman proposed a toast to 'the president of the United States and the cause he serves', a sentiment that must surely have been a bitter pill for the taoiseach to swallow.[41] In early May Churchill wrote to the dominions secretary encouraging action against Eire. Churchill believed it was possible to take 'stronger action' against Eire now that the United States was in the war and was particularly anxious to have the Axis diplomats expelled from Dublin, fearing that they would imperil plans to invade Europe. He also gave voice to his own irritation, which had built up over a long period:

Their conduct in the war will never be forgiven by the British nation unless it is amended before the end. This in itself would be a great disaster. It is our duty to try and save these people from their selves. Any proposals you make to terminate the enemy representation in Dublin will be immediately considered by me. We ought not to shirk the difficulties unduly for the sake of a quiet life.

Churchill was anxious to discuss this and the possibility of introducing conscription with Roosevelt and hoped to do so when he visited Washington in the near future.[42]

On 14 May, after consultation with Maffey and Kearney, Gray recommended to Roosevelt that the United States approach de Valera to obtain clarification from the Irish government regarding its position in respect of the Allies. The method to be employed was to ask for concessions advantageous to them. If the request was refused, 'Eire would be definitely on record as having refused a specific request made now for the first time.' It was agreed that a joint Anglo-American policy towards Ireland should be formulated and implemented. There was still some uncertainty as to whether the ports should be the focus for the approach, as from a strategic point of view both British and American military opinion considered that the Allies could continue to operate without them. Gray told his government that Irish policy towards the Allies was unlikely to change. Nor would de Valera be inclined to take 'a more realistic view of the situation or . . . pursue a policy actively helpful to the United Nations'. Gray in effect wanted the United States in cooperation with Britain to consider two things. The first was to test if the change in the war situation had made de Valera more forthcoming in terms of Axis diplomats in Dublin, the ports and airfields and other matters of importance to the United States. The second was whether the United States should take any steps to forestall Irish attempts to mobilize Irish-American opinion against the Allies while the war continued and divide the United States and Britain thereafter. Gray also argued that there was an anti-American tendency among nationalists in Eire, mostly prompted by an obsession with partition. He wanted decisive action against Eire while the war continued, as this provided a unique opportunity to forestall any post-war campaign of grievance by de Valera. Gray also made the important point that de Valera and the Irish nationalists were not serious about resolving partition 'on any basis of reason and compromise'. He had concluded that 'the grievance is politically of more importance than the solution' and believed, on the basis of discussions with British officials and politicians, that if Eire had participated in the war Britain would have made considerable efforts to end partition. He further noted, again realistically, that Northern Ireland's position had been enhanced and Eire's diminished by their respective involvements in the war. What had become clear, he affirmed, was that partition had been reinforced by the war and the possibility of Irish unity diminished. Gray recognized that any initiative by the Allies involving de Valera and Eire had difficulties attached to it, yet he argued that inaction would have more serious consequences not only for the war effort, but also for the future of the United Nations after the war. Now was the time to act, Gray asserted, and decisive action could achieve a considerable amount.[43]

Gray's memorandum was read with considerable interest by the president, who asked Hull what action could be taken on Ireland. Roosevelt mused that it might be possible to lease the Irish ports for the duration of the war and endorsed Gray's view that de Valera should be got on record, continuing, 'We shall undoubtedly be turned down. I think the strongest fact is that we are losing many American and British lives and many ships are carrying various supplies to Ireland without receiving anything in return and without so much as "Thank you."' Hull replied that Gray's wish to get de Valera on record was 'almost unanswerable'. He also agreed that air and naval facilities in Ireland would be useful to the war effort, a view that the military also informally endorsed to him. While Hull and the State Department did not wish to become involved in the partition issue, Hull did want a clear statement from the chiefs of staff that there was a 'sound military basis' for demanding the facilities. In fact, while the chiefs of staff agreed that the facilities would be useful, they suggested exploring the issue in general with Eire 'without committing the United States at this time to a definite programme for the establishing of air or naval bases in Southern Ireland'.[44] This fell well short of what Gray had in mind and over the following weeks his ambitious initiative was whittled down to a more limited intervention. Gray returned to the United States in August 1943 to consult with the State Department and to investigate the attitude of Irish-Americans to Irish neutrality, partition and the future relationship between the United States and Britain. After discussions with Sumner Welles at the State Department,

Gray went to Roosevelt's home in Hyde Park to sketch out a draft note on how best to deal with Ireland.

Gray's inside access was of immense influence on this occasion, as Roosevelt and Churchill arrived at Hyde Park after their conference in Quebec to find Gray already there. As a result, Gray was able to show the president and prime minister his rough draft and to discuss it with them. While Churchill approved the initiative in principle, he warned that any decision would be taken by his government, not solely by him. Gray quickly won over the president, but the British proved resistant to an Irish initiative. In the course of September and October, the State Department became more anxious that the British government was opposed to Gray's plan and wanted to put Ireland on the back boiler. Eden, now foreign secretary, revealed to Winant that while Churchill was in favour of the initiative, a number of senior ministers had serious reservations. The Labour party leader Clement Attlee was the most prominent cabinet figure to oppose action on Ireland. This debate within the cabinet attests to the sea change in the relationship between Britain and Ireland since September 1939, and especially since June 1940. Those opposed to action based their arguments on strategic concerns and not on concern for Ireland's sovereignty or neutrality. Indeed, it was now widely accepted in Britain that if de Valera had achieved a united Ireland before the war, the entire island would have been neutral in the present conflict. This would have further disadvantaged the already hard-pressed British and perhaps even justified intervention. The argument now went that Britain had survived for four years without Eire's ports or airfields, but had been able to use Northern Ireland for much-needed bases, industrial production and airfields. The decision not to support Gray's initiative in 1943 thus became a decision to maintain partition for the foreseeable future and was an unintended but not surprising consequence of Eire's neutrality. In October the American ambassador made another approach to the British, reminding them that 'the President is personally interested in this matter'. Nothing came of this and Hull dolefully wrote at the end of October, 'If therefore the British really wish to kill this proposal their long continued inaction is well calculated to accomplish this end.'[45]

Gray was critical of what he considered a half-hearted initiative on the grounds that de Valera would dismiss the issue as previously. He added that de Valera was likely not to respond unless there was a specific demand or request for the bases. Hull informed Gray that the president was of the view, as was he, that the approach should be based on military considerations only. He implied that the intention was not to alienate de Valera or the Irish government by highlighting previous disagreements, but to couch any approach in friendly terms. He admitted this might have some disadvantages, but he believed a moderate tone would be better. Hull reasoned that if de Valera agreed in principle to hand over the ports, it would provide a better basis for demanding the withdrawal of Axis legation staff at a future date. He did add however that if the Dublin government was not prepared to give a definite answer to the request, this would be taken as a refusal by the American government. Hull nevertheless agreed with Gray that the message should not come from the president, but should be a communication between the two governments. Finally, Hull also sought to assure Eden and the British government that the United States had 'not the slightest desire to be dragged into' the partition issue. This was a problem for Britain and Ireland, not for the United States.[46]

After further discussions with Maffey in Dublin, Gray reported back that anti-de Valera sentiment was strong in the British cabinet. This was based on the view that he should not be given any credit for changing his position at such a late stage in the war. By the end of 1943 there was also a change in emphasis from Gray, who now was pressing for action against the Axis legations in Dublin. Hull agreed that this would be a more attractive option than the ports, though again the Americans ran up against British pessimism. Eden told Winant that the Irish government was even more committed to its definition of neutrality than previously and that de Valera had been privately criticizing neutrals such as the Portuguese who were prepared to offer facilities to the United States and Britain because the tide of war had changed. Eden feared that any approach to de Valera would reopen the partition issue, which would not only be 'extremely embarrassing' to the British, but 'would be likely to give rise to acute difficulties'. Hull drew on Gray's correspondence to produce a draft note for the president at the end of December, but Roosevelt decided at that point to let the matter rest.[47]

*

The build-up to D-Day in early 1944 reinforced the Americans' determination to demand the withdrawal of Axis diplomats from Dublin.
In this they were quickly supported by Churchill, who in early February set out the choices facing the Allies:

> Much more dangerous even than the information betrayed about
> the movements of Anglo-American troop convoys, is what will
> certainly be passing in a stream about our preparations for OVER-
> LORD. If the German and Japanese ministers remain at their posts
> in Dublin, it may be necessary on military grounds to sever all
> contacts between Ireland and the Continent in the near future for
> a period of months. At present anyone can get in an Irish ship to
> Spain and give the latest news he has picked up in England about
> British and American preparations. Even if complete severance by
> sea was instituted, it would not prevent the German Ambassador
> from sending a wireless warning of zero, even though that was the
> last he was able to do.[48]

Churchill and the Americans were impressed by evidence that
German spies had been operating in Ireland, if not always successfully,
while of more direct concern at the beginning of 1944 was the
shipping link between Ireland, Portugal and Spain. MI5 knew that in
Lisbon German agents were attempting to recruit Irish crew members
as agents. In February 1943 one crewman, Christopher Eastwood,
had attempted to send a ciphered message to the German consulate
in Lisbon. Unfortunately for Eastwood, his Portuguese contact was a
British agent and the information went straight to British intelligence,
who then passed a version on to the Germans. As a result, British and
Irish intelligence were able to control this situation from a very early
stage, though the contact was closed down when the Germans discovered Eastwood's contact was an enemy agent. The shipping route
was a slow and cumbersome method, but it nevertheless provided a
means for information to be passed on if needed. In addition, the
Germans parachuted two agents with radio sets into Ireland. They
were to acquire information of use to the German defence of the
European mainland but were quickly apprehended. It is remarkable
that despite the restrictions imposed on travel between the two
countries in advance of D-Day, Irish citizens could still return to
Dublin. Lord Killanin, who was intimately involved in planning the

invasion, paid a visit home just two weeks before the invasion. He recalled, 'No one tried to stop me. If I'd been disloyal or alcoholic I could easily have spilled the beans. I knew absolutely everything except that there was going to be a postponement of D-Day by twenty-four hours because of the storm.' Despite the vigilance of Irish intelligence at least one American agent spent over six months unde-tected in Ireland in 1943. Martin Quigley's front was his position as the representative of the American film industry, but in reality he was an agent of the OSS. If Quigley went undetected, it is possible that other agents evaded capture or identification. The German legation in Dublin had a secret radio transmitter capable of connecting Ireland to Nazi Europe. The Dublin government persuaded Hempel to hand it over in December 1943, though this was not known to the Allies who continued to fear that the Germans had the capacity to send messages out of Eire. Consequently the presence of German, Italian and Japan-ese diplomats in Dublin remained a cause for concern in the run-up to the invasion of Europe. More generally, IRA supporters in Northern Ireland and Britain were in a position to acquire details of airfields, troop movements and other preparations and transmit this infor-mation to Dublin.[49]

It was these security considerations that led to the so-called Ameri-can note crisis that began at 3.30 p.m. on Monday 21 February 1944. Gray arrived at Government Buildings and presented de Valera with a note which in diplomatic language requested that Dublin seek the withdrawal of the German and Japanese legations from the country. The key point in the text reads:

> Axis agents enjoy almost unrestricted opportunity for bringing military information of vital importance from Great Britain and Northern Ireland into Ireland and from there transmitting it by various routes and methods to Germany. No opportunity corre-sponding to this is open to the United Nations, for the Axis has no military dispositions which may be observed from Ireland.

According to Gray's account, de Valera looked 'very sour and grim' but did not appear to be angry. He did ask Gray if the note was an ultimatum, and Gray responded that it was a request from a friendly state. De Valera emphatically rejected the note: 'Of course our answer will be no; as long as I am here it will be no.' On de Valera's personal copy of the note there are a number of handwritten comments. Next to the claim that Ireland's freedom is at stake no less than that of the United States, de Valera commented, 'We must judge that,' while he wrote 'NO' against the claim that Irish neutrality was working in favour of the Axis. De Valera also rejected the charge that intelligence could be compiled and forwarded to Germany from the legations, the principal fear of the Allies in the run-up to D-Day. At the heart of de Valera's response was his fear that if the American note were accepted, it would mean that any neutral would be at the mercy of 'any warring state'. After reading the note de Valera not only rejected it, but also praised the German minister, Hempel, who, he insisted, 'has behaved very correctly and decently and as a neutral we will not send him away'.[50] The following day Maffey went to see de Valera with a message from the British government supporting the American note on the withdrawal of the diplomats. This time de Valera was visibly angry, complaining that it was not a reasonable request. In response, Maffey insisted that there was a real problem for the Allies with the Axis diplomats on their doorstep. He challenged de Valera's view of Hempel, saying it would be a mistake to believe that he would betray his country by not engaging in or promoting espionage.

De Valera then called in the Canadian high commissioner, Kearney. He wanted the Canadians to persuade the Americans to withdraw the note, though it is not clear why de Valera thought the United States might do so after raising the issue. Nor were the Canadians very helpful. While Kearney passed on de Valera's request to the Canadian prime minister, Mackenzie King, he could not see how the United States or the United Kingdom could withdraw their requests. Moreover, while the Canadians were critical of the form and timing of the note, they remained in favour of removing the diplomats from Dublin. After all, Canada also had military forces poised to invade the European continent and was as anxious as the Americans or the British to protect them from espionage. In London, the Irish high commissioner, Dulanty, appealed to the Australians to intervene, but this was also rejected.[51] Immediately after receipt of the note, de Valera placed the Irish army on alert. Whether he believed that an invasion was imminent is difficult to determine, yet he certainly suggested it was possible to various individuals immediately after the note was delivered. In Washington Brennan went to the State Department in an agitated state and expressed himself deeply concerned that the Allies would invade Ireland. John Hickerson, a senior official at the State Department, was dismissive of Brennan's concerns or the fears of an invasion. In what appears an offhand remark, though probably a sentiment widely held at the time, Hickerson told Brennan, 'The principal sanction we had in mind, in the event of a refusal was the wrath of American mothers whose sons' lives would be placed in jeopardy.'[52]

Gray was authorized to assure de Valera that the United States had no intention of invading Ireland, though the taoiseach took the opportunity to complain at what he described as the 'sinister' remark made by Hickerson. At their meeting on 29 February Gray responded that it was a friendly warning from one official to another, 'as to what would probably happen if, as a result of his refusal to send away the Axis Legations, it later developed that information had reached the enemy which resulted in loss of American lives' – no more than that. De Valera insisted that his government had done all it could, but he could not guarantee the situation. Gray responded that this was precisely the problem: de Valera could not guarantee that information would not leak out. Accordingly, Gray said, 'you assume a grave moral responsibility for possible consequences' if a disaster did occur. In the course of what was a tense and at times acrimonious meeting, de Valera accused Gray of hostility to him personally and of trying to get Eire into the war since he arrived in Dublin. Gray vehemently denied this, though he acknowledged that he would have welcomed Eire's participation. De Valera took what Gray described as an isolationist position on the war and asserted that Ireland did not owe any gratitude for supplies sent by the United States or Britain, as they 'came about in the course of international trade', a remark that incensed Gray. Gray pointed out that Ireland was importing far more than it exported and that this was not normal trading. Nor would de Valera accept that Ireland could act like the United States prior to Pearl Harbor or follow the actions of some South American states who had broken off diplomatic relations with Germany without going to war. De Valera insisted that 'neither he nor the Irish people had been in any way responsible for the war, that they did not wish anyone on either side to lose his life and that they felt they had a right to live their own way and to remain withdrawn from the conflict'. Gray replied that while he could understand his reluctance to support the Allies in the past, he asked the taoiseach to accept that Eire would have suffered the same fate as other neutrals if it had not been for the 'protection of the Allied nations'. De Valera was not prepared to do so, responding that this claim was debatable. Gray then accused de Valera of not understanding the American point of view or its irritation that Eire was not concerned about the outcome, and de Valera seemed almost to accept this when he replied that 'neutral Ireland was in a much better position dispassionately to weigh the essential facts of the situation than were the peoples embroiled in the war'. According to Gray, the discussion ended with the two men shaking hands, but that de Valera did so 'with evident distaste'. In the period immediately after the meeting Gray noted a more isolationist tone in de Valera's pronouncements. He now emphasized the need to use the Irish language to resist anglicization and condemned the English language as a 'badge of servitude'.[53]

After receipt of the note on Monday 21 February de Valera had waited until Friday before approaching the leaders of the opposition parties. This reflected his usual contemptuous attitude to them on matters he considered the government's responsibility. In this case, as in others, he refused to cooperate with Fine Gael or discuss with them the nature of any reply to the United States. When the Fine Gael leadership asked de Valera to verify if the Allies threatened hostile action, de Valera responded that the rumours were a consequence of 'precautionary measures' taken by him in response to the note. It is remarkable that a government leader in a parliamentary democracy could receive what he considered a threatening request from a foreign power, mobilize his military and allow rumours to circulate, while taking four days to consult the opposition. De Valera also met leaders of the Labour party, who gave him their full support but who also wanted a prohibition on parliamentary questions dealing with sensitive topics such as Eire's relationship with the Allies. The leader of Clann na Talmhan, Michael Donnellan, was more belligerent, recommending that de Valera expel Allied diplomats if they had to remove the Axis legations.[54]

The Irish reply was de Valera's own, as his biographers show. The note is couched in terms of pained irritation, insisting in general terms that there was no espionage in Eire but that as a democratic state

Ireland had a right to determine its own policy. According to Frank Gallagher, who helped prepare the reply, an early draft was considered 'over apologetic' by him and some others of those present. Gallagher cited de Valera's response: 'to remember that we were balanced on a razor's edge and in the circumstances a note of apology might not do us much harm'. De Valera then went to Limerick to fulfil some commitments, taking the draft with him. During the weekend he attended a play put on by local schoolchildren about the persecution and torture experienced by Irish Catholics during the seventeenth century. De Valera was moved by this and when he returned to Dublin and to the draft, 'decided that no nation which had suffered as Ireland had should be too meek', and removed any hint of an apology. [55] The reply was leaked to the press a little later and in consequence the formal correspondence was published. The British thought that the leak originated with Fianna Fáil, though there was also a suggestion that it had come inadvertently from a Fine Gael TD. While it is not clear who leaked the information, the beneficiary was Fianna Fáil, which was able to take the high ground on defending Irish neutrality.

Gray wrote to Roosevelt in late March claiming that the American note had been a success. While Axis legation staff had not been withdrawn, Gray thought that intelligence cooperation would be enhanced and the partition issue sidelined. This was a far too optimistic assessment of the outcome. It is true that in March and April discussions took place between the Allies and Irish officials on improving intelligence cooperation, but there was little evidence that de Valera or Fianna Fáil were going to give up on the partition issue.[56]

Indeed, Brennan sought to mobilize Irish-American opinion against Gray and the State Department both over the note and more generally in respect of partition. Senator David Walsh read into the Congressional Record on 8 May 1944 a series of resolutions on Ireland from his constituents. These were traditional anti-partitionist positions, but included a demand not only that Irish neutrality be recognized but that Ireland be involved in any peace settlement at the end of the war. Hull challenged every item. He linked Walsh's statement directly to the American request, recounting in detail the support received in the United States for the contents of the note. Hull rejected as malicious the claim made by Walsh and indeed by the Irish government that the United States was going to use force against

Ireland and spelt out the American attitude to Ireland, implied in the note:

> The American government has at no time questioned Ireland's right to remain neutral, although it has doubted the wisdom of such a policy from the viewpoint of Ireland's own best interest. Nor has the American government even asked Ireland to break diplomatic relations with the Axis countries, although the American Government would naturally like to see such relations severed completely. If the Irish government considers its relations with Germany and Japan of such importance that diplomatic relations with those countries must be continued, maintenance of such relations through Irish representatives stationed in those countries would at least not constitute a direct danger to the lives of members of the American armed forces.

Hull was also dismissive of demands that the principles of the Atlantic Charter be applied to Ireland. The charter, he argued, was not just about rights but about obligations, adding that there was 'an obligation for each nation to demonstrate its capacity for stable and progressive government, to fulfil scrupulously its established duties to other nations', implying that Ireland had not fulfilled this criterion.[57]

Back in Ireland the *Irish Press* started a campaign against the note, Gray and the State Department, while in Washington Brennan was alerting friendly journalists to the conflict and blaming Gray for all the trouble. The *Irish Press* took the line in its 23 March editorial that Gray had misinformed the State Department as to conditions in Ireland and that the USA was behaving unreasonably in calling for the withdrawal of the Axis diplomats. Brennan pursued a similar line with the State Department and the American media. On one occasion Brennan was quoted as describing Gray as a dilettante with no diplomatic training who owed his post to the fact that he was related to Roosevelt. What Brennan wanted to get across, and this has been the view of most Irish historians since, was Gray's unsuitability for his job. Brennan also accused the State Department of ignorance on 29 March, claiming that American security officials were satisfied with the Irish situation. At a further meeting Brennan asked the State Department to issue a statement that 'Ireland was now co-operating with us in all essential matters', but this request was rejected on the grounds that Ireland had not asked for the withdrawal of the Axis diplomats. Brennan then threatened to publicize his claim that American security officials were satisfied with security in Ireland and that the State Department was unaware of the true situation. When Brennan said this Hickerson responded that if he did, the American reply would highlight that the request to withdraw the diplomats had been endorsed by the US military, including the joint chiefs of staff.[58] Whether rightly or wrongly, it is clear from State Department and presidential files that there was widespread agreement within the US military and political elites that the diplomats in Dublin should be withdrawn. When it was suggested to the State Department that Gray was acting on his own initiative or providing inaccurate reports, not only was he vigorously defended but department officials insisted that the note had widespread approval.[59] The Americans were dissatisfied with the Irish response, not with Gray, who was representing his country. That this dissatisfaction was not superficial is shown by the willingness of Roosevelt, Hull and the military chiefs to send another note expressing their disappointment. That this note was not in fact sent was due to the Irish willingness to upgrade their security cooperation in advance of D-Day and especially their acceptance that the country would be cut off from the continent until after the invasion.[60]

The source of Brennan's claims concerning American security officials was an OSS agent, Irvine 'Spike' Marlin, who had been educated in Ireland, stationed in Dublin and had married an Irishwoman. Walshe met Marlin with Colonel Bryan on 18 March and obviously approved of him, as he noted, 'we have felt in our dealings with him that he wants to be friendly towards this country'. Walshe seemed fearful that a further note would be sent by the United States which might contain new information on the dangers to Ireland. He seemed to be threatening a diplomatic breach if confidential information, which had been given to OSS by the Irish authorities, was publicly revealed. Marlin then suggested that the State Department might not be aware of the intelligence arrangements between the United States and Ireland, maintaining when pressed by Walshe that there was no tradition of cooperation in the United States between the State Department and the intelligence community. Marlin reinforced Irish prejudices against Gray in this conversation, certainly leaving Walshe with the impression that while OSS might have been

satisfied with intelligence arrangements, the State Department had
not known about them. As it happens this was unlikely, as OSS chief
William Donovan was close to Roosevelt and indeed provided a
briefing for him at the end of March that highlighted cooperation with
Ireland and also that Gray was in general aware of this cooperation.

Walshe met Marlin again the following day. The OSS man recommended that the Irish government publish their version of the situation and confidently predicted that Gray could not remain as
representative in Dublin if they did so. There is a clear connection
here with Brennan's campaign in the United States against Gray and
the State Department, which only started after Walshe's interview
with Marlin. The Irish government heard what it wanted to hear from
Marlin and used this confidential information to try to undermine
Gray and the American note.[61] Gray and Marlin had never seen eye to
eye on policy towards Ireland, but Gray's position was more representative of American policy and opinion than Marlin's. The information used by the Irish government originated with Marlin and it
may have been a mistake on their part to give it such prominence.
Gray quickly recognized Marlin's hand in the Irish strategy and must
have been gratified when Robert Stewart at the State Department
agreed that Marlin's 'connection with the Irish work seems to have
been unfortunate from the beginning'.[62] Nor were the Irish short of
resorting to a degree of intimidation. Gray believed the Irish authorities were trying to frighten him when they suggested extra police
protection; he refused on the grounds that there was no evidence of
animosity to himself or his staff and suggested that any tension would
be 'kept alive by designed agitation'. A little later his car was stopped
as it was travelling in excess of thirty miles per hour, the speed limit
in force for all cars on Irish roads imposed to conserve petrol. While
Gray acknowledged responsibility, he did note that he was using
American tyres and oil and there is a suggestion in a note to Walshe
that he had been set up.[63] The censors also carefully controlled the
way the continuing controversy was reported, stressing the Irish
position and limiting any discussion. One reporter interviewed a
number of people in Ireland immediately after the note and found
a considerable degree of understanding for the Americans and little
hostility to the request. The censors however refused to allow him to
send his copy out of the country, as the only position acceptable was

that 'the entire Irish people resented the affront to Irish neutrality'.
When the journalist remonstrated, he was told that if his information conflicted with the position taken by the government, then the
government's was the only acceptable one. The newspaperman also
complained that his phone was tapped. He developed a method of
getting copy out of the country, but when the Irish authorities discovered this, the police forced their way into his bedroom to question
him about a story that had been published in a British newspaper.[64]

Hardly had the first wave of controversy over the note subsided,
when another crisis loomed. In the House of Commons on 14 March
Churchill announced that Ireland would be isolated to prevent any
leakage of information prior to D-Day. Immediately after this,
Churchill wrote to the secretary of state for the dominions, Lord
Cranborne, insisting that 'there is no question of punishing the Irish
but only of preventing the German Embassy in Dublin from betraying
the movements of our armies. This will entail isolation measures.' He
followed this up with a note to Roosevelt that expanded on his
position. He wanted 'to keep them guessing for a while' but insisted
that 'all our actions will be taken from motives of self-preservation
and none from those of spite'. Nevertheless, the controls were strict,
including stopping all shipping to Spain and Portugal, grounding the
Irish airline and breaking all telephone and telegram communications
with Eire. While Walshe expressed some disquiet and not a little
hostility to Churchill's speech, in the following weeks Britain and
Ireland worked closely to ensure that no leakages took place. Walshe
went to London in early April and agreed a number of measures with
British and American officials to secure this objective. One outcome
of the London discussions was that Walshe agreed that an American
intelligence officer should be posted to Dublin to work with G2.
Perhaps the main reason a second and probably more forceful note
regarding the Axis legations was not sent was that Irish officials were
proving more forthcoming and cooperative with the United States
and Britain than had previously appeared.[65]

Walshe continued to insist that the problems between the United
States and Ireland could be attributed solely to Gray. Even before he
met Marlin on 18 March he was blaming Gray for the note on the
grounds that he 'misinformed his Government with regard to Irish
policy and conditions in this country, and was thereby primarily

responsible for what might have been a serious rupture in relations between Ireland and the United States'.[66] This was not a new position for Walshe. In October 1941 he had written a highly critical note to Brennan saying that Gray should be withdrawn from Dublin. Walshe had a rather peculiar view of how foreign diplomats should operate in Ireland, a view apparently shared by de Valera. Walsh wanted an Irish-American Catholic who would represent Ireland's view to the United States. Cudahy, who had been the US representative prior to Gray, 'was a success' according to Walshe, 'but was not left long enough to become a really reliable factor in our relations with America'. Walshe wanted a diplomat who would not criticize Irish policy if it conflicted with that of his own state. It is therefore not surprising that even after the war in Europe was over Walshe continued to highlight what he considered Gray's 'unfitness' for his post, advising Brennan to contact friendly politicians in Washington 'who would put an end to Gray's career'. There was a clear note of frustration in Walshe's correspondence with Brennan, however, as he also recognized that Ireland had become marginal to American concerns, though he did not admit this. Walshe bitterly complained that the State Department simply ignored Irish complaints, though this might have been an occasion for him to consider why that was so.[67] The problem for Ireland and for its diplomats was that, as Undersecretary of State Joseph Grew wrote to Gray, the Irish government had 'missed the boat' and American policy would be to 'adopt towards Ireland an attitude as frigidly indifferent as its government has seen fit to adopt towards the aspirations of the United Nations'. In effect, Grew was downgrading American representation in Dublin, refusing for example to appoint a press attaché. In these circumstances, Grew acidly commented, 'it would seem odd were we to send to the Legation an officer for the specific purpose of either ascertaining or attempting to influence public opinion' in Ireland.[68]

*

Once the Allies successfully invaded Europe in June 1944, Ireland receded from the centre of Anglo-American attention, though this did not prevent Irish representatives from feeling self-important on occasions. Brennan became excited towards the end of 1944 when the Americans approached the Irish to discuss landing rights for transatlantic air traffic. 'We realised,' he recalled in his memoirs, 'that

Ireland was now very important for the Americans.' De Valera wrote to Brennan emphasizing the importance of the negotiations for the Irish government. However, he warned Brennan to place political above economic considerations. Brennan was also to remember when taking decisions that 'territorially and culturally we belong rather to Europe than to the countries of the Western Hemisphere'. If Brennan or de Valera believed that Irish involvement in the aviation conference was bringing them back in from the cold, they were to be mistaken. Roosevelt wanted to assure Churchill that nothing had changed: 'We instructed Gray to make it clear to the Irish that signature of the agreement indicated no change whatsoever in our attitude toward Ireland any more than our signature of a similar agreement with Spain indicated any change in our attitude toward Franco.'[69]

The new secretary of state, Edward O. Stettinius, who had replaced Hull, agreed with Gray that the only interests the United States had in Ireland were 'trade and possibly air traffic and the continuing interest of avoiding involvement in the partition issue'. Stettinius went on to paint an alarming picture – from the Irish perspective – of the failure of relations between the two states. The United States continued to be unhappy with the Irish response regarding the Axis diplomats and war criminals, among other matters. While Stettinius was anxious to continue cordial relations with Ireland, the country would not have a place at the forthcoming peace conference, but more importantly Irish interests would have a much lower priority than those of the United Kingdom. Stettinius added insult to injury by commending the wartime policy of consultation with Britain before dealing with the Irish government, even over matters mainly to do with Ireland. On the crucial issue of partition, Stettinius affirmed it 'is not our affair', adding ominously:

> Whatever the situation may have been in the past, Ireland's atti-
> tude in the war has made it clearly inadvisable from the standpoint
> of American interests for us to urge Britain in the slightest to meet
> Irish demands. We will therefore resist to the utmost any pressure
> from any direction to bring us into the picture. Ireland certainly
> has no right to expect any different attitude on our part.[70]

At best American opinion by the end of 1944 was indifferent to Eire; but it was often hostile.

Roosevelt oscillated between these positions. On D-Day he replied to a resolution by the Ancient Order of Hibernians demanding an end to partition and the protection of Irish neutrality in a belligerent fashion, saying that for the good of 'American boys fighting a moral enemy' they had asked Eire to withdraw Axis diplomats, yet had been refused. Roosevelt's tone was bitter. It cannot have helped his humour that just before the presidential election of 1944 the United Irish Counties Committee had sent him a telegram asking if he agreed with Attlee's view that Ireland should not be at the peace table. If he did, the telegram threatened, this would be broadcast to Irish voters in the United States.[71] Roosevelt was nevertheless safely re-elected in November 1944 without the Irish issue surfacing. By the end of 1944 and early 1945 Roosevelt and the State Department were concerned with more pressing matters though at times Ireland did create some controversy. There was considerable tension between Gray and Walshe over possession of the German legation building as the war drew to a close, while other areas of conflict included the Irish positions on war criminals and whether they would hand over German ships if they docked at Irish ports. Over all of these issues de Valera and Walshe insisted on a very narrow interpretation of sovereignty and in some cases seemed to obstruct the Allies.[72]

By the time the war ended in Europe, Gray was ready to go home. He asked Byrnes, the new secretary of state, to replace him as soon as possible but remained in Dublin for another two years. There is no evidence that Gray was kept on in Dublin due to the influence of Eleanor Roosevelt; indeed, the evidence from the Gray papers, which includes the private correspondence between the Grays and Eleanor Roosevelt, is that Eleanor badly wanted them back in the United States after her husband's death and was looking forward to their return. The ill will of de Valera, Walshe and the Department for External Affairs made Gray's life uncomfortable in his final two years in Dublin and he was glad to return to the United States. Yet, as the war ended in Europe, animosities between nationalist Ireland and the Allies continued to make headlines.

De Valera's visit to Hempel outraged opinion in Europe and many in Ireland, while the republican mob that attacked Trinity College Dublin on 7 May, the same day that the German surrender was announced, did so because of alleged disrespect to the Irish flag. The original complaint was that the Irish tricolour had been flown below Allied flags on the flagpole, but the crowd then burnt a Union Jack after which the Trinity students attempted to burn the Irish flag. This led to a number of assaults on the college, at least one of which was led by future taoiseach, Charles Haughey. The riots that followed were directed against American, British and pro-British targets in Dublin, and the Irish government had to express its regret to the United States and United Kingdom representatives the following day. It was also reported that students at University College Galway in the west of Ireland had flown the swastika over the university building. Gray believed that police protection had been inadequate and also questioned the government's good faith. The riots were a very public and ugly expression of hostility to the Allied victory, but perhaps can be best understood in the context of continuing anti-British sentiment, which remained central to the Irish national consciousness. As Gray regretfully noted, the United States was now a target because of its refusal to support the Irish against the British. Gray's return to Washington in 1947 did not end the difficulties between Eire and the United States. The Irish government had created much of the tension and its legacy was to continue to affect relations between the two countries until the 1950s.

CONCLUSION: THE END
OF DE VALERA'S IRELAND?

When the war in Europe ended, it might be expected that the emergency would end as well. Indeed censorship was lifted soon after and imports recommenced slowly over the following year. However, the national emergency declared in 1939 was not rescinded until 1976 when a new emergency was declared as a result of the murder of British Ambassador Christopher Ewart Biggs. However, the war and some of its consequences continued to influence Ireland and its relationship with the outside world for some time after. De Valera warned his listeners in his reply to Churchill in May 1945 that though the war was over other threats remained. He hinted that hard times were ahead because of the uncertainty that the war had created. Irish diplomats and the Fianna Fáil elite were certainly concerned that Irish neutrality would be punished by the victorious Allies and went to considerable efforts to deflect any criticism. One backlash came when the Soviet Union vetoed Irish membership of the United Nations, and neither the British nor the Americans were prepared to invest much diplomatic capital in ensuring that Ireland received a seat. Frank Gallagher, the head of the Government Information Service, defended every aspect of Irish neutrality in an argument with Maffey in early August 1945. Gallagher's position was an extreme one: he asserted that the lack of bases in Eire had had no adverse effect on the Allied war effort, nor would availability have helped. Gallagher claimed that not a single Allied ship lost within 500 miles of the Irish coast would have been saved and the situation would have been the same if the entire island of Ireland had been independent and neutral.[1]

This was certainly not the view of the British or American commands who at various stages during the war had expressed the opinion that bases in Eire would help to reduce casualties. The British chiefs of staff suggested in March 1941 that 'the establishment of fighters in Southern and Eastern Eire might enable us to re-open the South-Western approaches to trade' as such fighters could have more readily intercepted German bombers flying from France to attack convoys in the Atlantic. In 1943 the United States joint chiefs of staff agreed that American lives would be saved if ports and airbases were available to the Allies in Eire.[2] De Valera never believed this and Joseph Walshe encouraged him in that view. Robert Menzies discovered this when he met de Valera in April 1941 to discuss the ports. He was shocked at de Valera's indifference to the war and his apparent ignorance of the strategic importance of Ireland. Menzies wrote that de Valera could not see why bases might be required and that he had found it necessary 'to explain to him the importance of air bases as a platform for fighting aircraft'.[3] An assessment by the Admiralty and the Royal Air Force at the end of the war concluded that Irish bases would have saved some 5,000 lives and 368 ships.[4] Moreover, Admiral Godt, chief of staff at U-boat operational control, confirmed when interrogated the importance of Eire to the submarine campaign. There is also evidence that the Germans were able to obtain intelligence from Eire at different stages of the war.[5] As a consequence of Irish neutrality Northern Ireland became vital. Not only did it it protect the north and north-westerly approaches to the Clyde and Liverpool, but by 1943 long-range aircraft were countering the U-boat threat in the North Atlantic.

This is not to say that Eire did not provide assistance to the Allies. As early as May 1941 Walshe concluded in a secret minute, 'We could not do more if we were in the war.' He listed the ways in which Eire was then assisting the British, including providing them with weather reports, routeing Axis communications through London and sharing intelligence and other information. Less specifically, Walshe noted that Eire was helping by exporting its surplus farm produce to Britain, though this would have been contested in London. More remarkable was his claim that 150,000 Irish nationals in the British forces and some 60,000 working in the factories were aiding the war effort. While this may have been true, it was certainly not a consequence of Irish government policy, except to the extent that the government regulated the movement of labour and men across the Irish Sea. Walshe went on to claim that Eire now had 400,000 men 'in military defence of two islands', a conclusion not really warranted by the evidence.[6] Ireland's help was acknowledged by MI5 and by the British government, though it was also recognized that it was always conditional. In early 1945 Lord Cranborne accepted that Eire had helped in 'unobtrusive ways' but went on to conclude that 'her general policy of neutrality, her refusal to grant us bases and to remove the Axis legations, and the unsatisfactory attitude over war criminals, puts her quite out of court'. De Valera's decision to extend his condolences when Hitler died only compounded the negative response to Irish neutrality.[7]

It is probable that Eire could have done more to support the Allies short of going to war. De Valera was fortunate that Ireland was distant from Germany and not placed under the pressure that Sweden and Switzerland had to deal with. In comparison with these democratic states Eire provided little direct support to the Axis but the question is rather whether it could have provided more assistance to the Allies. The answer from de Valera, Aiken and Walshe to this was no and many historians continue to accept this. However, there were occasions when Eire could have taken a more helpful attitude but did not do so. In February 1941, for example, MacEntee wanted de Valera to agree to the Ford Motor Company in Cork returning finished engines to Britain. Although this would not have directly affected Irish neutrality, de Valera rejected the proposal. During the trade discussions in 1940 Walshe admitted that the request for transhipment facilities was not contrary to the spirit of neutrality; indeed neutral Sweden had permitted Germany to move war materials and men across its territory on several occasions. What Britain asked for in 1940 was considerably less than Sweden provided, nor was it accompanied by any overt threat, as was the case with Germany. Providing transhipment facilities in 1940 would have caused difficulties for Eire, that is clear, but these facilities could have been provided at a later stage of the war without major consequences. Likewise, Eire could have provided manufacturing facilities without endangering its neutrality, depending on what was produced. Moreover, while it was certainly good strategy to proceed cautiously in 1940 and 1941, the same could not be said after 1942. Eire might have assumed a position of non-belligerence similar to that of Sweden in the Winter War between the Soviet Union and Finland. This was part of the package that Mac-

Donald offered in 1940 and even if it is agreed that de Valera could not have accepted such arrangements then, later moves towards a similar position could have brought considerable benefits to Eire. There is a case that the Allies would have benefited from Irish bases up to at least D-Day if not beyond that, yet the Irish government at no time sought to benefit from this recognition. Nor was de Valera prepared to expel the Axis legations or take a pro-Allied position on a number of occasions towards the end of the war. At best this was poor diplomacy, at worst it was myopic in the extreme. The Allies were winning the war by 1943, yet de Valera and his government continued to insist that Irish interests were best served by an absolutist version of Irish neutrality.[8]

The major defence of Irish neutrality has always been that it was in the national interest. National interest is difficult to calculate. Two things are important. The first is that it cannot be equated to party interest, or even the interests of the government. Secondly, it is rarely one thing. One policy objective might have a significant impact within a political system, but this is unlikely. It is often the case that when a particular objective has an overweening influence over policy then it is unobtainable, as was the ending of partition on the terms offered by de Valera. In Eire's case there were at least four issues that could be considered as serving the national interest. The first was maintaining Irish sovereignty, the second ending partition, the third guaranteeing that the Axis did not win the war and the fourth remaining on good terms with the Allies.

While Irish sovereignty was maintained, this was due to luck rather than any effective policy on the part of the Irish government. In the first place Eire was fortunate that it was close enough to Britain to receive its protection and that both states were democratic. As a result, while the prospect of Britain invading could never be entirely ruled out, it was always unlikely. Eire did remarkably little to ensure that Germany did not win the war. The government acted in public as if it did not care who won and hinted at times that there was no real difference between the two sides. Yet Germany was a continuing threat to Irish sovereignty. Hitler was contemptuous of neutrality in general and if the Nazis had won the war, the likelihood of any neutral state remaining independent seems very low indeed. Supporting Britain and the United States was the best possible way of defending

Irish sovereignty and though this did not necessitate joining the Allies it certainly implied a more positive response to Allied requests for assistance. It is quite understandable that de Valera and his government were reluctant to support Britain in the summer of 1940, as many observers had concluded that the British would be defeated. Yet circumstances changed, but Irish policy did not. By the summer of 1941 a more active policy on de Valera's part would have helped the Allied cause, and this was certainly the case after the United States entered the war in December 1941. The position taken by James Dillon in 1942 – to support the Allied cause without sending troops abroad – was the policy most likely to fulfil most if not all of the objectives of national policy enumerated above. Irish sovereignty would have been protected; the Allies would have received important assistance in defeating Hitler; Eire would have enhanced its relationship with its neighbours and friends. On the partition issue it is likely that involvement in the war would have provided the Irish government with improved diplomatic resources to pressurize the British on Northern Ireland. At the very least Eire would have been involved in the peace conference and the setting up of the United Nations, giving it a powerful influence at an early stage in the establishment of the post-war order. The failure to engage with the United States and Britain also left Catholics in Northern Ireland unprotected after the war, when Unionists could evade their responsibilities to their minority and use neutrality to dismiss Catholics and nationalists as unreliable and unpatriotic.

The major challenge to Irish neutrality during the Second World War is that it had little to do with national interest and everything to do with ideology. In February 1942 de Valera told Maffey that 'neutrality had become the religion of the country', and while this was clearly hyperbole it draws attention to how it was viewed by Fianna Fáil and a significant section of the population. In such circumstances neutrality cannot be understood as a diplomatic position or defended in terms of national interest; if so then it is open to change when national interest or diplomacy warrants it. A case can be made that in purely diplomatic terms or to serve the Irish national interest there were occasions when a reconsideration of policy was in order, yet this never occurred. It never did so because though neutrality was defended in diplomatic terms, the policy was metaphysical in content.

If seen in similar terms to religion it is unchanging and applied in all circumstances. This is what Irish neutrality has remained since the Second World War – an exercise in ideology and metaphysics, not a policy to direct the foreign relations of the state.

This can be seen in the period after the war itself. Eire remained isolated, withdrawing further into itself, hostile to Britain and alienated from the United States. David Gray left in 1947, much to the relief of de Valera and Fianna Fáil, but the problems he had faced in the country did not go away. The United States lost interest in Ireland as it forged its long-term European and global strategy in alliance with the United Kingdom. As Eire became more isolationist, the United States was experimenting with a new world order committed to free trade, democracy and European integration. Ireland remained distant from these trends until the 1960s. True, it participated in the Marshall Plan, but complained bitterly when it received a loan under the scheme rather than a grant. Irish officials contrasted this with Northern Ireland, which as part of the United Kingdom received grants. This, according to the Irish, cemented partition, and American policy was criticized in these terms. American officials were irritated by the Irish obsession with partition, believing it irrelevant in the wider European context. When the Irish minister for foreign affairs, Seán MacBride, threatened to refuse the loan, Paul Hoffman, the administrator of the Economic Co-operation Administration, retorted that it would be Ireland's funeral if it did so as there were other states that wanted the money. Ireland joined the OEEC, created to administer US aid to Europe, but its participation was nominal rather than active. When the United States put the Mutual Security Act in place in 1951 Ireland refused to accept aid under the scheme on the grounds that its neutrality was threatened but in fact because of anti-partitionism. According to a government statement, partition not only 'adversely affects the internal development of the Irish nation but dominates its approach to all question of external policy'. Nor did the country join NATO, despite its strong anti-communist tradition. Again partition was the ostensible reason for this, but Ireland's irrelevance to US policy can be seen in the lack of American interest in whether Ireland was a member or not. What is of interest is that although Ireland became a republic in 1949 and finally left the commonwealth, it continued along paths well established during the war.[9]

The negative impact of the Emergency and the Second World War continued well into the 1960s. Only then did it begin to fade, but it was not until the 1990s that the insidious influence of the policies, institutions and ideology of that era finally disappeared. Isolationism was the most prominent feature of the two decades after 1945. The country withdrew into itself, reinforcing the economic and social self-sufficiency that were the most marked features of the wartime period. This had devastating effects on Irish society. As a small agrarian state, Ireland could not provide for all of those born in the country, nor increasingly for those living there. Between 1945 and 1960 emigration accelerated, and though the worst was over by the early 1960s it never went away and returned again in the 1980s. The population declined during these decades to an all-time low, with over 500,000 people emigrating between 1946 and 1961. The majority of those who left were women, seeking escape from the increasingly dreary atmosphere of post-war Ireland. By the 1950s Ireland had both the lowest female labour force participation rate in Europe and the lowest marriage rate. Rural Ireland was devastated and this traditional society virtually collapsed under the strain of the exodus. There was a justified fear that Ireland was dying, but neither Fianna Fáil nor the other political parties could suggest a remedy. De Valera condemned emigration, suggesting on one occasion that there was enough work in the country for those who stayed, but this did not stop the flood.

This period also saw Ireland become a poor country. In comparative terms Ireland was not poor at the end of the Second World War; United Nations estimates at the end of the 1940s suggest that Ireland ranked eighth in the world in terms of per capita income, confirming other evidence from the 1930s. What is striking is that Ireland ranked alongside Belgium, the Netherlands and Denmark, and ahead of France, Austria and Finland. By the 1960s Ireland's per capita income was well behind most other states in Western Europe and especially Denmark, Austria and Finland. The reasons for this are complex but the following seem relevant. Many if not all states in Western Europe utilized Marshall Plan funding in an innovative fashion, whereas Ireland did not. Furthermore, most of these states formulated ambitious development plans during the 1950s that delivered growth and wealth. Virtually all of them accepted free trade and some also pursued European integration, both of which stimulated further growth. Ireland was unique in rejecting all of these paths. It remained protectionist throughout the 1950s, committed to agricultural exports to Britain and refusing to participate in the integration process at any stage. While the rest of Europe experienced a sustained boom, expanding employment opportunities and the beginnings of affluence, Ireland experienced a slump, massive depopulation and a widening income gap between it and other European states. By the time Ireland did decide to apply for membership of the EEC in 1961, and then only because the United Kingdom had opted to do so, GDP per head was only two-thirds of the European Community average and declining in real terms.[10] Economic nationalism had been central to Irish policy-making during the Emergency, indeed had been seen as a specific virtue by many in Fianna Fáil, and this did not change after 1945. De Valera knew little about the economy and gave no attention to the material needs of the population. The one innovative member of the cabinet, Seán Lemass, continued to support protection but even he was unable to push through the ambitious plans he had developed during wartime. Economic conservatism, special interests and nationalism condemned the Irish economy to slow growth and lack of innovation at a time when the opportunities for development in a wider world were numerous. For those who continued to live in Ireland, there were attractions. It was safe, stable and conservative, emphasizing traditional Catholic–nationalist values. It was a society largely unconcerned about the outside world, but perhaps irritated that the outside world did not take notice of it.

If conservatism characterized economic policy, continuity and consensus remained the main features of party politics. Fianna Fáil was the dominant party and de Valera continued as leader until 1959. The party's defeat in 1948 did not change this, as the inter-party coalition that replaced it was neither innovative nor original in policy terms. Fianna Fáil's defeat was probably a good thing for democracy, as the party had been in power for sixteen years and change was long overdue, but its influence on political life meant that no great trans-formation occurred. There were changes in emphasis, but this was due to personalities rather than any significant break with Fianna Fáil's consensus. Most governments after 1945 were short-lived and there was a degree of governmental instability, but there is little evidence that any of the alternative administrations had policies to address the changing circumstances that Ireland found itself in. Indeed, what is noticeable is a refusal to take part in the outside world and a reiteration of anti-partition rhetoric by all parties. When Fianna Fáil lost office in 1948 the party immediately mobilized an anti-partition campaign that was long on outrage but offered no way out of the problem. As late as July 1958, Aiken, then minister for external affairs, simply demanded of the British government that they unite the island on terms dictated by de Valera. According to Aiken, only de Valera could guarantee the acceptance of any arrangement between the two governments on unity and he would not remain in office indefinitely. British ministers were unimpressed, to say the least, confirming that while they might cooperate with Dublin to defeat the IRA, which was then engaged in a terrorist campaign against Northern Ireland, Britain had little interest in promoting a united Ireland. De Valera's influence was often negative; when in 1955 Lemass had attempted to refocus policy on Northern Ireland within Fianna Fáil to take account of Unionist opposition to Irish unity and provide a moderate alternative to republican fundamentalism, de Valera vetoed the proposals.[11] This failure to engage positively with Northern Ireland postponed the possibility of dealing with the problem in a realistic fashion. It was not until the 1960s that the Dublin government made a strategic shift in its policy and then it proved to be too late, as the return to violence in the region alienated both sides.

The illiberalism that was a feature of the wartime period continued. Censorship was applied with renewed vigour under pressure from Catholic activists. There was what has been described as a 'silent coup' by the secretive Knights of St Columbanus, who gained control of the Censorship Board, using their influence to dramatically increase the number of books banned. In 1954 alone the board banned over 1,000 books, whereas between 1930 and 1945 a total of 1,800 had been prohibited. This zealousness was apparent in all aspects of Irish life, with significant pressure to extend the power of Catholicism everywhere. Legislation and Supreme Court decisions frequently reflected the influence of the Church, a source of considerable anxiety to non-Catholic citizens. Furthermore, Ireland had no adoption law prior to 1952 because of Church opposition. When lay pressure eventually forced the government to act, the eventual legislation was only enacted after the powerful archbishop of Dublin,

John Charles McQuaid, was satisfied with its content. This Catholic and illiberal environment intimidated those who did not share the majoritarian ethos. There was social intimidation, but the state also joined in on one occasion, charging Alan Simpson with 'presenting for gain an indecent and profane performance' when he staged Tennessee Williams's *The Rose Tattoo* in 1957, invoking a two-hundred-year-old law to do so. That this intimidation was all-pervasive is demonstrated by the behaviour of Fianna Fáil TD Erskine Childers, later president of Ireland. He said privately to Seán MacEntee that Protestants believed they were being discriminated against in post-war Ireland, but in public at the very same time he affirmed that there was no discrimination.[12]

It is interesting to ask what would have happened if de Valera had retired in 1945 rather than 1959. Personality is important, and de Valera's continuing leadership after the war extended many of the negative and illiberal features of Irish society. Notwithstanding this, these features were also embedded in the society and a different leader would possibly have behaved much the same. Fine Gael was largely moribund for much of this period, often outdoing Fianna Fáil in presenting itself as the authentic voice of Catholic Ireland. Likewise, Clann na Poblachta, the short-lived republican party led by Seán MacBride, was simply Fianna Fáil mark two, drawing on the anger and frustration of republicans. Its claim to be radical was shallow, as the moderate Noël Browne discovered when MacBride withdrew support from him when the Catholic Church opposed his proposal to introduce free medical care for mothers and children. There was radical potential during the post-war years, but it was diffuse and confused. Radicalism was often equated with the violence of the republican movement and this alienated moderates such as Browne. Nor did the Labour party give much of a lead. Broken by the anti-communist split in 1944, it remained a conservative force in Irish politics until the late 1960s.

The main legacies of the Emergency were isolationism and lost opportunity. The roots of isolationism were well established by Fianna Fáil during the 1930s, and the wartime experience enhanced the policy's moral superiority. In consequence, policymakers in Ireland could not or would not see the challenge the new Europe provided or the opportunities which it offered. These were not all economic –

some were moral – but in all cases they were ignored and isolationism nearly led to the destruction of the society. De Valera's successor, Seán Lemass, retired in 1966 after only seven years as taoiseach, but his legacy was significant. His governments set in motion the modernization of Irish society and provided the impetus to dismantle most of what de Valera had put in place after 1932. Though Lemass was a product of the 1916 generation, his commitment to change during the 1960s was such that after him Irish society began to meet the challenges of delayed development, European integration and social change. This did not come easy, but the world of the Celtic Tiger is that of Lemass, not that of de Valera.

Leabharlanna Fhine Gall

Notes

Unless stated otherwise, all sources in this list of abbreviations are Irish. At the time of the Emergency what is now the Department of Foreign Affairs was known as the Department of External Affairs. Because of the way the archives are organized, DEA files from the 1940s appear in DFA file folders.

AARIR	American Association for the Recognition of the Irish Republic
AFIN	American Friends of Irish Neutrality
CAB	(British) Cabinet Office
DEA	Department of External Affairs
DF	Department of Finance
DFA	Department of Foreign Affairs
DH	Department of Health
DIC	Department of Industry and Commerce
DJ	Department of Justice
DO	(British) Dominions Office
DT	Department of the Taoiseach
FDRPL	Franklin Delano Roosevelt Presidential Library, USA
FO	(British) Foreign Office
ITGWU	Irish Transport and General Workers Union
ITUC	Irish Trade Union Congress
MA	Military Archives
MAF	(British) Ministry of Agriculture and Fisheries
NAI	National Archives of Ireland
NAUSA	National Archives of the United States of America
NLI	National Library of Ireland
PDDE	Parliamentary Debates Dáil Éireann
PDSE	Parliamentary Debates Seanad Éireann
PREM	(British) Prime Ministers' Office
PRO	(British) Public Records Office
UCC	University College Cork
UCDA	University College Dublin Archives
WUI	Workers Union of Ireland

1. CONDOLENCES ON HITLER'S DEATH

1 I have used 'Ireland' to refer to the twenty-six counties of the island of
   Ireland that seceded from the United Kingdom in 1922. Independent Ireland
   was originally known as the Irish Free State, but after 1937 as Eire or Ireland
   and after 1949 as the Republic of Ireland. I have used 'Eire' and 'Ireland'
   interchangeably where there is no risk of confusion.

2 O'Halpin, *Defending Ireland*, p. 152; for de Valera's remarks NLI Frank
   Gallagher Papers MS 18,375 (6); Gellner, *Plough, Sword and Book*, pp. 242–7;
   Overy, *Why the Allies Won*. Because we know the Allies won, we can fall into
   the trap of believing this was inevitable. However, as Overy insists, there were
   various times when other outcomes could have resulted.

3 O'Halpin, *Defending Ireland*, p. 152; PRO DO 121/85 for secret reports from
   Dublin, 1 September 1943. David Gray the American minister in Dublin also
   believed that Breen was an agent for the German legation NAUSA 841D/1323
   Gray to Hull, 18 January 1942. Breen is reputed to have fired the first shots in
   the Irish War of Independence when he and his colleagues brutally shot
   down two RIC men at Soloheadbeg. In the reward notice he is described as
   having a 'sulky bulldog appearance' and looking 'rather like a blacksmith
   coming from work'. For Breen's own romanticized view of his role in the
   struggle see Breen, *My Fight for Irish Freedom*.

4 Andrews, *Man of No Property*, p. 297; O'Halpin, *Defending Ireland*, p. 152.
   My father Brendan Girvin, a lifelong republican, continued to believe that the
   wrong side had lost the war. I was brought up with a strong respect for the
   nationalism and fighting qualities of the Third Reich. This was not unusual
   among republicans at the time and later, and also in evidence across Irish
   society.

5 PRO DO 35/1229/WX110/3 Maffey to London, 21 May 1945.

6 *New York Times*, 4 May 1945; *New York Herald Tribune*, 4 May 1945. Other
   reporting can be found in the *Washington Post* and *The Times* at the same
   time. The Irish Department of External Affairs has a file where many of these
   excerpts can be found: NAI DFA, P98.

7 *Sunday Independent*, 28 July 1946; Walsh, *Recollections of a Rebel* for his
   pro-Nazi sentiments; see also Hamilton, *The Speckled People*, for his father's
   continuing infatuation with Nazi Germany long after the war.

8 Cited in Keogh, 'Eamon de Valera and Hitler', p. 91 referring to review in
   Sunday Press, 6 November 1988.

9 There is a substantial literature on this topic. See Ellwood, *Rebuilding Europe*,
   for a useful summary of the literature and Rose, *What is Europe?*

10 For example, by 1961 when Ireland decided to apply for membership of the
   Common Market its per capita income was approximately two-thirds of the
   European average, whereas during the inter-war and immediate post-war
   periods income had been close to European averages. Girvin, *Union to Union*
   summarizes some of this discussion.

11 De Valera was president of the Executive Council 1932–7 and thereafter taoiseach. See Chapter Two for a discussion of changes in Ireland and the gaelicization of Irish political culture during the 1930s.

12 Brennan, *Ireland Standing Firm*. The original articles on which this book was based were published in the *Irish Press* in 1958.

13 NAUSA RG59 740.00116 Gray to Hull, 24 October 1944. I have been unable to ascertain from other sources if this was the case.

14 FDRPL Gray Papers draft letter prepared by Gray (no date but from context late 1945).

15 Both quotes are from Keogh, *Jews in Twentieth-Century Ireland*, p. 174.

16 Power, '*A Problem From Hell*' contains a critique of the United States.

17 PDDE 97 cc.2751–58, 19 July 1945; Bromage, *De Valera and the March of a Nation*, p. 284.

18 Murray, 'Obsessive Historian', pp. 40–1.

19 Hull, *Irish Secrets*, pp. 66–8, 73, 145–6, 156. Hull notes (p. 166) that 'the German Legation was involved in the active support of espionage operations in Ireland'.

20 De Valera to Robert Brennan, cited in Longford and O'Neill, *Eamon de Valera*, pp. 411–12.

21 Murray, 'Obsessive Historian', pp. 63, 40; O'Halpin, 'Historical revisit', pp. 389–94.

22 *Manchester Guardian*, 4 May 1945.

23 BBC broadcast cited in Gilbert, *Never Despair*, p. 12.

24 See for example the *Irish Press*, 14 and 15 May 1945; PRO DO 35/2089, Maffey correspondence, 2 August 1945.

25 FDRPL undated notes in Gray Papers Box 2, probably 1945 from context.

26 Walzer, *Just and Unjust Wars* discusses the right to be neutral but also the responsibility involved in this decision, pp. 234–50.

27 FDRPL Gray Papers Gray to Francis P. Matthews, 8 June 1945. The *Irish Press* in editorials and in reporting resumed its anti-partitionist policy during the course of August 1945.

28 Transcript of broadcast 16 May 1945 in Moynihan (ed.), *Speeches and Statements by Eamon de Valera*, pp. 470–6.

29 PRO DO 35/1229/WX110/3 'Broadcast by de Valera', 16 May 1945.

30 PRO DO 35/2088/WX101/104 report by Maffey of conversation with de Valera, 6 July 1945.

31 PDDE 97 cc.2729–37, 2744–47, 18 July 1945.

32 For a classic description of this see Cobban, *The Nation State and National Self-Determination*, pp. 245–309.

33 Bowman, *De Valera and the Ulster Question*, pp. 185–6.

34 PRO CP (46) 381 memorandum by the lord president of the council 'Eire and Northern Ireland', 16 October 1946. Morrison added that Unionists in the north would have to consider carefully the timing of when they might discuss partition, due to the more rapid birth rate of Northern Ireland Catholics.

35 Girvin, *Union to Union* pp. 176–80.

36 PDSE 30, cc.551–73, 26 July 1945; *Irish Independent*, 27 July 1945.

37 PRO FO 898/357 report on Irish position and Irish statement, 14 November 1944; Kochavi, 'Britain, the United States and Irish Neutrality', pp. 93–115.

38 PRO FO 898/357 'Top Secret "Casement" Meeting at Bush House', 11 January 1945, also note 22 January 1945. The debate in the House of Commons took place on 16 January 1945: 'Eire (War Criminals, Right of Asylum) cc.116–32.

39 PRO DO 35/1205 Machtig to Maffey, 20 December 1944; Foreign Office note on neutrality and asylum, 22 December 1944.

40 The extent to which a political motive might be invoked to refuse an extradition request under Article 40.4.1 of the Irish constitution is discussed in Hogan and Whyte, *The Irish Constitution*, pp. 879–86.

41 UCDA de Valera Papers P150/2553 de Valera to MacDonald, 22 May 1945; PRO PREM 8/1222 Herbert Morrison memorandum 'Eire and Northern Ireland', 16 October 1946, detailing conversation with de Valera, 12 September 1946; UCDA de Valera Papers P150/2582 Hempel to de Valera, 5 October 1946; PRO DO 35/1522 Maffey interview with de Valera, 12 October 1946; Dominion Office reply to Maffey, 15 October 1946.

42 NAI DEA P113. Rynne to assistant secretary with memorandum for taoiseach, 8 October 1946; revised memorandum, 10 October 1946; Brennan to Walshe, 4 February 1947.

43 For German opinion polls see Noelle and Neuman (eds), *The Germans*, pp. 202, 315; Robertson, *Crimes Against Humanity*.

44 Goldhagen, *Hitler's Willing Executioners*.

45 PRO DO 35/2088/WX101/104 Maffey report of conversation with de Valera, 6 July 1945; DO 35/2087/WX101/102 Maffey report of meeting with McQuaid, 4 July 1945.

46 PRO PREM 8/1222 memorandum from Herbert Morrison on conversation with de Valera, 12 September 1946, prepared for Atlee and circulated to the cabinet; DO 35/5205 report of conversation between British ambassador and de Valera, 29 September 1953.

47 NLI MS 22848 Shane Leslie Papers, O'Kelly to Leslie, 20 June 1955.

48 Barton, 'Relations between Westminster and Stormont', pp. 1–20; Lee, *Ireland 1912–1985*, pp. 301–2.

49 PRO PREM 8/1222 memorandum by Maffey, 3 August 1946; MacNeice, *Collected Poems*, pp. 202–3. The poem was written in 1942 at a time when the submarine threat to British shipping was at its most lethal.

2. THE MAKING OF DE VALERA'S IRELAND 1916–38

1 FDRPL PSF Box 3 'Ireland' Winant to Hull with copy of Menzies' memo on visit to Ireland April 1941.

2 FDRPL PSF 40 Cudahy to FDR, 27 October 1939.

3 NLI O'Brien Papers MS 13954 circular letter from Irish Neutrality League (1915); Girvin, *Union to Union*, pp. 36–53 discusses the impact of the First World War on Irish politics.

4 Bax, *Harpstrings and Confessions*.

5 Fitzpatrick, 'Donnchadh O'Briain'. I am grateful to Seán Fitzpatrick for providing me with a copy of this dissertation.

6 Brennan, *Ireland Standing Firm*, pp. 97–101; Skinner, *Politicians by Accident*; Ryan, *Unique Dictator*. The more recent tendency has been to debunk de Valera's role in Irish history and diminish his importance; see Coogan, *De Valera* for the most recent and comprehensive assessment. There are now signs of a more sensitive reappraisal of the man and his era: Doherty and Keogh (eds), *De Valera's Irelands* appeals for a more balanced evaluation while Mair, 'De Valera and Democracy' provides a judicious assessment.

7 Horgan, *Seán Lemass*, Farrell, *Seán Lemass* provide important insights into this politician.

8 This is not intended as a collective biography of Fianna Fáil but a summary of the shared origins of these men in the militant wing of Irish nationalism during the First World War. We still do not have biographies of most of them although some of the gaps are now being filled.

9 Kissane, *Explaining Irish Democracy*, pp. 1–8; Girvin, *Union to Union*, pp. 43–53; Garvin, 'Unenthusiastic Democrats'.

10 Hennessey, *Dividing Ireland*; Girvin, *Union to Union*, pp. 31–43.

11 Coogan, *De Valera*, pp. 96–9; Connolly, *Irish Public Opinion*; Laffan, *The Resurrection of Ireland*.

12 Miller, *Church, State and Nation*; Ward, *The Irish Constitutional Tradition*.

13 Girvin, 'The Life and Times of Sean O'Hegarty', pp. 80–5; Hart, *The IRA and its Enemies*, pp. 72–126.

14 Collins to McGarrity, 5 April 1922, cited in Cronin (ed.), *The McGarrity Papers*, pp. 116–17.

15 Bowman, *De Valera and the Ulster Question*, pp. 32–5; Hart, *The IRA and its Enemies*, pp. 273–92.

16 Garvin, *1922*; Coogan, *De Valera*, pp. 196ff; Girvin, 'The Life and Times of Séan O'Hegarty'.

17 *Irish Independent*, 18 March 1922. A slightly different version of this speech appears in Keogh, *Twentieth Century Ireland*, p. 5.

18 Cited in Coogan, *De Valera*, pp. 310–12, 348–54; NLI MS 17440 McGarrity Papers de Valera to McGarrity, 10 September 1922; Cronin (ed.), *The McGarrity Papers*, p. 133.

19 Regan, *The Irish Counter-Revolution*, pp. 101–62; Hirschman, *Shifting Involvements*.

20 De Vere White, *Kevin O'Higgins*, p. 153; O'Halpin, *Defending Ireland*, p. 54; Coogan, *De Valera*, pp. 354–5.

21 Brady, *Guardians of the Peace*; Girvin, *Between Two Worlds*; O'Halpin, *Defending Ireland*.

22 Both statements can be found in Dunphy, *The Making of Fianna Fáil Power*, p. 64.

23 De Valera to McGarrity, 11 March 1926 cited in Cronin (ed.), *The McGarrity Papers*, pp. 140–1.

24 Hanley, *The IRA*, pp. 113–14.

25 Moynihan, *Speeches and Statements*, pp. 133–43 for the La Scala speech; PDDE 22 c.1615, 21 March 1928. Horgan, S*eán Lemass*, pp. 55–8 reviews this issue in some detail and absolves Lemass of anti-democratic views at this time. PDDE 22 c.1615, 21 March 1928; Dáil debate, 14 October 1931 cited in Moynihan, *Speeches and Statements*, pp. 182–8.

26 O'Halpin, 'Parliamentary party discipline and tactics', p. 585.

27 Longford and O'Neill, *Eamon de Valera*, pp. 253–8; Coogan, *De Valera*, pp. 398–405.

28 UCDA Fianna Fáil Party Papers P176/443 minutes for 18 and 28 May 1928.

29 Andrews, *Man of no Property*, p. 90; Longford and O'Neill, *De* Valera, p. 253.

30 De Vere White, *Kevin O'Higgins*, pp. 240–1; English, *Armed Struggle*, p. 44.

31 Hanley, *The IRA*, pp. 119–20; Bowyer Bell, *The Secret Army*, pp. 94–5; Brady, *Guardians of the Peace*, pp. 149–50.

32 Coogan, *The IRA*, pp. 46–51 lists the number of violent incidents in 1926 alone.

33 PDDE 29, c.1562–1600, 8 May 1929.

34 Hanley, *The IRA*, pp. 120–5; Cronin, *The McGarrity Papers*, pp. 153–4.

35 See Regan, *The Irish Counter-Revolution* for a detailed assessment of Cumann na nGaedheal; for its success in foreign policy, see Fanning, Kennedy, Keogh and O'Halpin (eds), *Documents in Irish Foreign Policy*, especially Volumes II and III, which cover the period 1923–32.

36 UCDA Seán MacEntee Papers P67/453 letter to Fianna Fáil National Executive, 27 January 1936.

37 Girvin, *The Right in the Twentieth Century*, pp. 74–87.

38 Girvin, *From Union to Union*, pp. 63–105; Keogh, *Twentieth Century Ireland*, pp. 96–104; Keogh, 'The Constitutional Revolution', pp. 4–84.

39 Corkery, *Synge and Anglo-Irish Literature*, p. 19.

40 Kennedy, *Division and Consensus*, pp. 21–69.

41 NAI DT S1456 a–c for attitudes to First World War servicemen; Kennedy, *The Widening* Gulf, pp. 150–94; Barton, 'Northern Ireland, 1925–39', pp. 210–34.

42 See Girvin, *From Union to Union*, pp. 106–25; Cooney, *John Charles McQuaid*; Inglis, *Moral Monopoly* for assessments of this complex environment.

43 NAI DT S9637 'Cardinal MacRory: Privileges'; S9756 'Constitution'; Whyte, *Church and* State, pp. 24–62.

44 Allen, *Fianna Fáil and Irish Labour*, pp. 44–60; Clear, 'Women in de Valera's Ireland', pp. 104–14. See also Clear, *Women of the House* for a detailed assessment of women in Irish life during this period.

45 NAI DT S9880 'Women: Position Under Constitution' Walshe and Macardle letters; *Irish Press*, 11 and 17 May 1937; NAI DT S9287 'Women: Constitutional and Economic Position in Dáil Éireann'.

46 PRO DO 35/893 notes by Lord Devonshire of meeting with de Valera, 31 January 1939; DO 114/117, 7 November 1939 review of relations between Eire and the dominions.

47 PRO DO 114/117, 'British Commonwealth of Nations: Possible termination of Eire's membership', 7 November 1939; McMahon, *Republicans and Imperialists*, pp. 4–54.

48 UCDA Seán MacEntee Papers P67/179 MacEntee to his wife (undated but from context early 1938); P67/155 MacEntee to de Valera, 17 February 1938; PDDE 71 c.38, 27 April 1938.

49 PRO DO 35/893/5 notes of conversation with de Valera, 29 July 1938; note of conversation with de Valera, 4 October 1938; Devonshire note of meeting with de Valera, 1 February 1939.

50 UCDA Fianna Fáil Party Papers FF46, memo by Erskine Childers, 9 April 1934; FF790 general election report 1938 and election material for 1937 and 1938 elections.

51 PRO DO 35/895 note by Chamberlain of meeting with de Valera, 25 March 1939; note by Inskip of meeting with de Valera, 24 March 1939.

52 Bowyer Bell, *The Secret Army*, pp. 175–201; PRO DO 35/894/1 memorandum by Percieval Liesching, 5 July 1939; DO 35/893/6 report on incident, 19 January 1939; Mac Eoin, *The IRA in the Twilight Years*; NAI DEA A12 for further documentation.

53 Correspondence can be found in Cronin, *The McGarrity Papers*, pp. 170–2; NLI MS 22308 James L. O'Donovan Papers for Twomey correspondence.

54 PRO DO 35/893 Dulanty to secretary of state for fominions, 16 February 1939; Inskip note of meeting with Dulanty, 16 February 1939.

55 PRO DO 35/894 'Secret Report of Visit to Ireland' by Percival Liesching including meeting with Walshe, 30 June and 3 July 1939; DO 35/894/2 Home Office to Dominions Office, 1 September 1939; Dominions Office to Home Office, 12 October 1939.

56 *Prison Bars*, 11 March 1939; *Irish Press*, 12 December 1939. See also Behan, *Borstal Boy*.

57 McCormick was charged as James Richards, which was the assumed name he used in Britain.

58 The court case can be followed in the *Irish Press* 12–15 December 1939; I have also used *The Times* and the *Glasgow Herald* as cross-references. There is little difference in the reporting between Britain and Ireland.

59 NAI DEA A/113, 18 December 1939 note for secretary of the Department of External Affairs.

60 NAI DEA A113 report from Garda headquarters 15 December 1939 identifying both men.

61 I was told by a Cork republican that the individual who planted the bomb, whom I have met, believed that he and other participants had been set up by the IRA leadership and that the timing of the bombing had been deliberate. This was the reason why he had immediately left England despite orders to do otherwise. It is impossible to judge how reliable this information is after all this time, but its veracity cannot be entirely ruled out.

62 See letter to *Irish Times*, 1 February 1940, a copy of which is in NAI DT S11575A.

63 NAI DEA A113 draft instructions by taoiseach for Dulanty prepared by Walshe, 19 December 1939; de Valera to Eden, 24 January 1940.

64 NAUSA 841 D06/1236 Cudahy to Hull, 29 December 1939.

65 NAUSA 841 D00/1236 Kathleen Clarke, Fianna Fáil lord mayor of Dublin, to President Roosevelt, 1 February 1940; UCDA Fianna Fáil Party Papers P176/345 for Fianna Fáil national executive minutes, 6 November 1939.

66 PRO DO 130/12 Maffey to Machtig, 17 January 1940 on the meeting.

67 Longford and O'Neill, *De Valera*, pp. 359–60.

68 PRO DO 35/894/2 Maffey to London, 8 February 1940; NAUSA 840 D00/1241/2 for Welles's meeting with Lord Lothian, 3 February 1940; NLI MS 22,863 Shane Leslie Papers diary entry for 6 February 1940.

69 PRO DO 130/10, Maffey to London 8 February 1940; Note to Eden 16 February 1940.

3. NEUTRALITY IN THE PHONEY WAR

1 Canning, *British Policy towards Ireland*, pp. 241–7; *Irish Press*, 2 September 1939; *Irish Times*, 4 September 1939; *Cork Examiner*, 4 September 1939; *Kerry Champion*, 9 September 1939; *Wicklow People*, 9 September 1939; *Derry People*, 16 September 1939; *Derry Journal*, 4 September 1939; *Church of Ireland Gazette*, 15 September 1939.

2 PDDE 77 cc.1–18, 2 September 1939.

3 PDDE 77 cc.13–14, 2 September 1939; NLI Frank Gallagher Papers MS 18, 334 'Draft Note on Neutrality', September 1939; UCDA Desmond FitzGerald Papers P80/1117 heads of policy including notes by Desmond FitzGerald, September 1939.

4 UCDA Fianna Fáil Party Papers P176/345 Fianna Fáil National Executive minutes, 25 April 1938 where the National Executive approves of the agreement by both parties.

5 Hogan, *Election and Representation*, pp. 31–5. This comment is all the more important as Hogan had been a leading Fine Gael member and brother of the former Cumann na nGaedheal cabinet minister, Patrick Hogan.

6 UCDA Desmond FitzGerald Papers P80/1110 points for speakers 1943 and Fitzgerald notes, May 1944; PRO DO 114/117, 'British Commonwealth of Nations: Possible Termination of Eire's membership', 7 November 1939.

7 O'Longaigh, 'Preparing Law for an Emergency', pp. 36–47.

8 PDDE 77 cc.20–126, 2 September 1939 for exchanges.

9 PRO DO 35/894/1 note of conversations in Dublin, 5 July 1939.

10 UCDA Eamon de Valera Papers P150/2571 notes prepared by J. P. Walshe, 25 August 1939 for meeting with German minister; *Documents on German Foreign Policy Volume VIII*, pp. 241–2.

11 UCDA Eamon de Valera Papers P150/2571 'Visit of the Secretary of the Department of External Affairs to London', 6–10 September 1939.

12 UCDA Eamon de Valera Papers P150/2548, Chamberlain to de Valera, 19 September 1939; de Valera to Chamberlain, 22 September 1939; P150/2571, 'Visit of the Secretary of the Department of External Affairs to London', 6–10 September 1939.

13 PRO DO /130 'Discussion with Irish Ministers' Maffey to London, 4 October 1939; note of phone call from Walshe telling Maffey that a German submarine had been sighted in Dingle Bay.

14 Hull, *Irish Secrets*, pp. 66–9; Knowlson, *Damned to Fame*, pp. 297–8; Quinn, *Patrick Kavanagh*, pp. 119–29; UCDA Seán MacEntee Papers P67/210 MacEntee to Seamus O'Neill (no date but 1940 according to archivist).

15 NAI DEA 210/159 for some of the problems associated with repatriation; Milotte, *Communism in Modern Ireland*, pp. 182–8.

16 NLI MS 22,863 Shane Leslie Papers diaries 1914–44, 17 August 1939, 1, 3, 4, 7, 11, 14 September 1939, 19 October 1939. General Sir Hubert De La Pour Gough (1870–1963) is best known in Ireland for his role in the so-called Curragh Mutiny. While he identified closely with Ulster he was also a friend to moderate Irish causes throughout his life.

17 UCDA Eamon de Valera Papers P150/2574 Gough to de Valera, 29 October 1939; de Valera to Gough, 6 November 1939. Gough's introduction to de Valera seems to have been via the widow of Robert Erskine Childers, who had been executed by the Free State in 1922. Leslie, *The Irish Tangle For English Readers*, pp. 200–11.

18 UCDA Desmond FitzGerald Papers P80/1118C memorandum by Mulcahy, 14 September 1939 of meeting with de Valera, 13 September 1939.

19 UCDA Richard Mulcahy Papers P7A/110 'defence conference' note, 30 September 1939; 'Talk with Smith and Boland', 1 January 1940.

20 Fisk, *In Time of War*, p. 429 for details.

21 UCDA Dan Bryan Papers P71/29 'Notes on counter-intelligence' 1940; Fisk, *In Time of War*, pp. 104–27; Canning, *British Policy Towards Ireland*, pp. 254–60.

22 MA 'Memorandum on the Defence Forces', 23 August 1944.

23 UCDA Seán MacEntee Papers P67/195 Department of Finance memorandum, 16 January 1939; O'Halpin, *Defending Ireland*, pp. 133–42.

24 MA 'Memorandum on the Defence Forces', 23 August 1944.

25 MA 'General report on army 1st May 1940–30th September 1940', 24 October 1940.

26 O'Halpin, *Defending Ireland*, pp. 142–4.

27 MA S/103, 'General report on the army for the year 31st March 1940 to 1st April 1941', 31 May 1941.

28 PDDE 79 cc.42–118, 5 March 1940; Wylie (ed.), *European Neutrals and Non-Belligerents* for comparison.

29 NAUSA 841 D00/1237 Cudahy report to State Department, 10 January 1940; NAI DEA A12 memorandum, 15 March 1941 detailing meetings with various groups in New York.

30 NAI DJ JUS8/764 Garda report, February 1940.

31 Roche memorandum January 1939, cited in O'Longaigh, 'Preparing law for an emergency', p. 44.

32 NLI MS 27,176, Joe Clarke Papers correspondence, 16, 29 September 1939.

33 UCDA Fianna Fáil Party Papers F176/345 National Executive minute books, 6 November 1939 when concern was voiced at McGrath's hunger strike.

34 O'Longaigh, 'Emergency Law in Action', pp. 63–8.

35 *Irish Press* report on trial, 2 February 1940.

36 O'Longaigh, 'Emergency Law in Action', pp. 69–70; Horgan, *Lemass*, p. 108.

37 PRO DO 130/12 Maffey to Machtig, 13 July 1940.

38 PRO DO 130/12 Maffey to Machtig, 22 April 1940; NAI DEA A12 Boland to Dulanty, 11 May 1940; Dulanty to Walshe 18 June 1940.

39 NAI DT S11564A contains considerable details on these and other IRA attacks.

40 UCDA Frank Aiken Papers P104/3377 speech by Frank Aiken at Mullingar, 5 May 1940; Eamon de Valera Papers P150/2584, address by de Valera at Fianna Fáil Cavan County convention, February 1940; Erskine Childers at Fianna Fáil meeting Ballycolghan, County Longford reported in *Irish Press*, 22 January 1940; *Irish Independent*, 16 February 1940 for report of Traynor's speech; Moynihan, *Speeches and Statements*, pp. 423–4 for radio address by de Valera, 24 March 1940.

41 Hull, *Irish Secrets*, pp. 65–147 for the most authoritative assessment of this period. Stephan, *Spies in Ireland*, provides some interesting insights also.

42 PDDE 91 cc.600–6, 9 July 1943 statement by taoiseach.

43 NAI DT S12069 'IRA: proposed cessation of activities 1940' note, 9 September 1940 on de Valera's rejection; DEA A12, Gray to de Valera, 23 August 1940; Gray to Seán Fitzpatrick, 23 August 1940; DEA A8, copy of report by D. R. Kostal, 13 September 1940, apparently a decrypted copy. Interestingly the Department for External Affairs copy has this section vigorously underlined as it mentions the secretary of the Department of Industry and Commerce, who may have been Kostal's informant.

44 NAI DT S11896A 'Defence Conference' notes 30 May, 4 June 1940. The Defence Conferences were a minor political concession to the opposition and remained extremely restricted. Aiken refused to allow members to discuss the notes of previous meetings. Fisk, *In Time of War* pp. 160–1.

45 NLI MS 17,879, 'Pat Shannon'.

46 *Irish Times*, 20 June 1942 for a detailed report of the court case. The 'Hayes confession' was widely circulated by the IRA leadership; there is a copy in PRO DO 130/23. Coogan, after interviewing Hayes for his book on the IRA, believes the verdict is one of 'not proven', yet he provides little evidence to sustain such a charge. I share some of Coogan's doubts. The political and security atmosphere of 1941–2 camouflaged quite an amount and we still do not have access to many of the files that would help to resolve the question.

47 MA Dublin DDC/1240, note by Bryan, 2 October 1941; *Irish Independent*, 2 October 1941; PRO DO 130/23, Costar to Archer, 5 November 1941.

48 NAUSA 840 D001/193 Gray memorandum on Hayes' confession, 24 November 1941; 01/195, Gray to Hull 30 June 1942.

49 O'Longaigh, 'Emergency Law in Action', p. 68.

50 Adams, *Censorship*, pp. 240–3 for discussion. For general background on the censorship see Ó Drisceoil, *Censorship in Ireland*, pp. 1–2. NAI DT S6522 Moynihan to attorney general, 9 January 1934; memorandum by Department of Justice, 23 January 1934; Department of Justice to Moynihan, 21 March 1934. For further background on censorship see DJ H315/131, 2 May 1933.

51 NAI S11306, 16 November 1938; memorandum for government, 15 June 1939; UCDA Frank Aiken Papers P104/3429 'Censorship of war news, espionage etc in a neutral country during war', 7 March 1939 with additional notes.

52 UCDA Frank Aiken Papers P104/3456 memorandum 28 August 1939.

53 UCDA Frank Aiken Papers P104/3433 memorandum by Walshe, 18 September 1939; P104/3462 report on press censorship, 4 October 1939. Michael Knightly, the press censor, prepared these reports on a monthly basis.

54 UCDA Frank Aiken Papers P104/3433 Connolly to Aiken with memorandum for de Valera, 'The censorship of communications and the press', 23 September 1939. Connolly had been minister for posts and telegraphs and for lands in the first two Fianna Fáil governments before being appointed chairman of the Commissioners of Public Works.

55 UCDA Frank Aiken Papers P104/3466 no date but probably early 1940.

56 UCDA Frank Aiken Papers P104/3462 'Report on press censorship', 4 October 1939.

57 UCDA Frank Aiken Papers P104/3435 Connolly to Aiken, 17 October 1939.

58 UCDA Frank Aiken Papers P104/3436 Connolly to Aiken, 26 October 1939.

59 UCDA Frank Aiken Papers P104/3463 'Press censorship report', October 1939.

60 UCDA Frank Aiken Papers P104/3464 report for November, 1 December 1939; P104/3431, Dáil Report, 23 November 1939; P104/34663, which contains a sample of decisions by censor in November.

61 Ó Drisceoil, *Censorship in Ireland*, pp. 234–43.

62 UCDA Frank Aiken Papers P104/3464 report for November, 1 December 1939.

63 UCDA Frank Aiken Papers P104/3458 Connolly to Aiken, 20 December 1939 with memorandum dated 19 December 1939 from the chief telegram censor.

64 UCDA Frank Aiken Papers P104/3465 report for December 1939, 3 January 1940.

65 UCDA Frank Aiken Papers P104/3467 report for February, 9 March 1940.

66 NAI DT S11586, Frank Aiken 'Neutrality, censorship and democracy', 23 January 1940; MacEntee 'Memo regarding censorship', 6 February 1940; memorandum by Office of Controller of Censorship, 15 January 1940; cabinet decision on further legislation GC 2/134, 18 January 1940.

67 UCDA Frank Aiken Papers P140/3468 report for March, 5 April 1940

68 UCDA Frank Aiken Papers P104/3469 report for April, 6 May 1940.

69 UCDA Frank Aiken Papers P104/3470, 15 June 1940.

70 UCDA Frank Aiken Papers P104/3507 minutes of meeting in office of Frank Gallagher, Government Information Service, 12 March 1940 where instructions to press censor were agreed.

71 UCDA Frank Aiken Papers P104/3507 Coyne to Aiken, 14 March 1940; P104/3470, for decision on headline; PRO DO 35/1011/3 Bowen, notes on Eire, 31 July 1940 reporting conversation with Senator Crosbie (*sic*).

4. AN OFFER THAT COULD BE REFUSED: JUNE 1940

1 Hull, *Irish Secrets*, pp. 92–5; O'Halpin, *MI5 and Ireland*, pp. 52–3; UCDA Richard Mulcahy Papers P7A/210, 24 and 25 May 1940.

2 PRO DO 130/12, Maffey to London, 22 April 1940.

3 PRO DO 130/12 Maffey to London, 22 April 1940 postscript.

4 PRO DO 130/10 Maffey to Machtig, 10 May 1940.

5 Moynihan, *Speeches and Statements*, pp. 434–6. *Documents on German Foreign Policy Volume IX*, pp. 401–2, 422–4; Duggan, *Herr Hempel*, pp. 92–3.

6 PRO CAB 104/184 'Defence co-operation', which includes notes and minutes of meetings between Irish and British officials in May 1940; O'Halpin, 'British Intelligence, the Republican Movement and the IRA's German Links', pp. 108–31; O'Halpin, *MI5 and Ireland*, pp. 7, 21–2, 52–3; PRO DO 130/12 director of naval intelligence to Dublin, 18 May 1940 with enclosed report dated 15 May 1940.

7 De Valera thought that Ireland had a special relationship with the United States due to the large Irish-American population there, yet he never appreciated the priorities that the Roosevelt administration had in respect of the war.

8 Churchill to Roosevelt, 15 May 1940; Roosevelt to Churchill, 16 May 1940 in Kimball (ed.), *Churchill and Roosevelt I*, pp. 37–9. Although Roosevelt was cautious he added that he hoped that Churchill would continue to 'communicate with me in this way at any time', ending the letter 'the best of luck to you'. Churchill was surely encouraged by this response in particular, but also because Roosevelt valued such personal and intimate relationships with individuals.

9 Smith, *Hostage to Fortune*, pp. 429–30; FDRPL PSF 40 Gray to FDR, 16 May 1940; FDR to Gray 19 June 1940.

10 O' Halpin, *MI5 and Ireland*, pp. 22–3; O'Halpin, 'British Intelligence, the Republican Movement and the IRA's German Links', pp. 108–31.

11 Hull, *Irish Secrets*, pp. 89–95.

12 NAI DFA A3 'Cooperation with Britain in event of attack' (2/204) minutes of the first meeting between representatives of Eire and representatives of Dominions Office and service departments of United Kingdom, 23 May 1940. These are the minutes taken by the British at the time of the meeting. I have not been able to locate comparable information from the Irish side. MA Dublin EDP 1/4 'Operation Instructions: General Correspondence July–December 1940' note by General Dan McKenna on British forces and Irish army attitude to their quality, undated but from internal evidence written between 17 and 19 September 1940; Overy, *Why the Allies Won*, p. 13.

13 NAI DFA A3 'Cooperation with Britain in event of attack' (2/204). See also Fisk, *In Time of War*, pp. 149–89; Carroll, *Ireland in the War Years*, pp. 42–4.

14 NAI DFA A3 minutes of meeting, 24 May 1940; Carroll, *Ireland in the War Years*, pp. 41–4.

15 The information in this section is drawn from Carroll, *Ireland in the War Years*, pp. 43–4. Carroll has read the original version of Clarke's memoirs.

16 PRO PREM 3/130 'Eire (Possible Invasion) 1940–41' minutes of meeting between representatives of Dominions Office and service departments, 28 May 1940.

17 PRO PREM 3/130 Ismay to Churchill, 29 May 1940; Ismay to Churchill, 30 May 1940. Some of Ismay's alarm may have been prompted by a fairly lurid report from Antrobus of the United Kingdom's representative's office in Dublin, who wrote to Boland in External Affairs concerning information received from Dutch officers who claimed that the Germans had specific plans to attack Ireland, in NAI DFA A3, 1 June 1940. Gilbert, *The Churchill War Papers Volume II*, pp. 106–227.

18 PRO PREM 4/53/2 Halifax to Churchill, 24 May 1940; Canning, *British Policy towards Ireland*, pp. 262–75; Bowman, *De Valera and the Ulster Question*, pp. 216–27.

19 PRO DO 130/10 'Note in the Train', 3 June 1940 (read to lord president); see also PREM 4/53/2 '1940 Ireland'.

20 PRO PREM 4/53/2 Maffey to London, 11 June 1940. Interestingly, Maffey's assessment was echoed by that of German Minister Hempel, who also considered a German invasion would be disastrous for the Nazis. See *Documents on German Foreign Policy, Volume IX*, pp. 573–4, 601–3, 637–9.

21 Gilbert, *The Churchill War Papers Volume II* meeting of War Cabinet, 16 June 1940, pp. 342–3. See also discussion on French request to open armistice discussions with Germans, pp. 344–6.

22 The speech can be found in Gilbert, *The Churchill War Papers Volume II*, pp. 360–8.

23 PRO PREM 4/53/2 Churchill to Bevin, 18 June 1940.

24 Gilbert, *The Churchill War Papers Volume II*, pp. 379, 386.

25 Gilbert, *The Churchill War Papers Volume II*, pp. 390, 419.

26 PRO PREM 3/88/3 Churchill to Ismay, 30 June 1940.

27 Beer, *Modern British Politics*, pp. 212–16; PRO DO 114/117 note on 'enemy use of Eire as base for attack', 3 June 1940.

28 Gilbert, *The Churchill War Papers Volume II* meeting of war cabinet, 16 June 1940 pp. 342–3.

29 PRO PREM 3/131/2 Chamberlain to de Valera, 12 June 1940; Canning, *British Policy towards Ireland*, 266–74.

30 Gilbert, *The Churchill War Papers Volume II*, pp. 396–400 for details of policy, 15–21 June 1940.

31 Wylie, *European Neutrals and Non-Belligerents during the Second World War*, pp. 31–115 for a discussion of Belgium, Denmark and the Netherlands.

32 Bowman, *De Valera and the Ulster Question*, pp. 225–33; Canning, *British Policy towards Ireland*, pp. 275–81 for assessments of this offer.

33 PRO PREM 3/131/1 'Note of conversation between Mr de Valera and Mr MacDonald in Dublin on Monday June 17 1940'.

34 PRO PREM 4/53/2 '1940 Ireland' Bevin to Churchill, 18 June 1940; Churchill handwritten note on memorandum; Amery to Churchill, 18 June 1940; Londonderry to Churchill, 21 June 1940; Lord Rotherham to Churchill, 24 June 1940.

35 PRO PREM 3/131/1 'Note of talks between Mr de Valera and Mr MacDonald in Dublin on June 21 and June 22 1940'; NAI DT S11896A for notes on fifth meeting of Defence Conference, 19 June 1940.

36 PRO DO 130/12 Maffey to MacDonald with report of conversation with Gray, 24 June 1940.

37 NAI DFA A2 'Weekend developments in the war situation' by J. P. Walshe, no date but from internal evidence either late Sunday 23 or Monday 24 June 1940; PRO DO 130/12 Maffey to London reporting meeting with Walshe, 16 July 1940; Girvin, *From Union to Union* p. 119; Nolan, 'Joseph Walshe and the Management of Irish Foreign Policy'.

38 NAI DFA A2 'Britain's Inevitable Defeat', no date but from internal evidence late June 1940.

39 Gilbert, *The Churchill War Papers Volume II*, pp. 419–20; Orwell and Angus, *The Collected Essays, Journalism and Letters of George Orwell Volume II*, pp. 385–410; Best, *Churchill*, 169–82.

40 Fisk, *In Time of War*, pp. 215–16.

41 *Irish News*, 26 June 1940; *Irish Press*, 26 June 1940. The *Irish News* headlined this as a 'call to the nation'.

42 PRO DO 35/1011/3 Betjeman to Hodson, 21 June 1940. Betjeman described Walshe as minister for external affairs, but he was in fact secretary of the department. De Valera was both taoiseach and minister for external affairs 1932–48. This mistake was sometimes made by British officials.

43 PRO DO 35/1011/3 undated note on Hodson's letter (late June 1940); also internal correspondence 26–8 June 1940.

44 PRO CAB 123/96 Chamberlain memorandum for cabinet, 25 June 1940.

45 PRO PREM 3/131/1 'Note of conversation between Mr de Valera and Mr MacDonald', 26 June 1940.

46 PRO DO 35/1008/9 'Eire Defence: Protection of Eire by United Kingdom' MacDonald to London, 27 June 1940; London to MacDonald 27 June 1940; note on war cabinet meeting, 27 June 1940; Machtig to Cadogan on meeting with Kennedy, 27 June 1940.

47 Cited in Farrell, *Chairman or Chief*, p. 30.

48 PRO PREM 3/131/1 'Note of conversation by Mr MacDonald with Mr de Valera, Mr Aitken [*sic*] and Mr Lemass', 27 June 1940.

49 PRO CAB 123/96 de Valera to Chamberlain, 4 July 1940; Chamberlain to Ida Chamberlain, 7 July 1940, cited in Bowman, *De Valera and the Ulster Question*, p. 239.

50 NAI DFA P70 Dulanty to Walshe, 12 August 1942; 22 May 1941.

51 UCDA Richard Mulcahy Papers P7A/210, 5 July 1940 contains memoranda outlining various assessments of outcome.

5. NEUTRALITY IN PERILOUS TIMES

1 NAI DFA A9 Thomas to J. Connolly, 17 April 1940. The *People* was banned on 14 April for suggesting that Ireland could be used as a base for espionage. Orwell and Angus, *The Collected Essays, Journalism and Letters of George Orwell Volume II*, p. 390, diary entry for 2 June 1940.

2 UCDA Colonel Dan Bryan Papers P71/36, Archer to chief of staff, 10 July 1940; P71/30 note on counter-espionage, no date but probably mid-1940 from internal evidence; P71/33 'Matters affecting British and Irish relations', no date but likely to be late 1940 or early 1941.

3 NLI Frank Gallagher Papers MS 18375 (6).

4 PRO CAB 120/506 'Ireland' Churchill to Ismay, 7 July 1940; Maffey to London, 10 July 1940.

5 PRO PREM 3/129/2 Pim to Churchill 'General report on position in Ireland'; Fisk, *In Time of War*, pp. 142–3; DO 130/12 Maffey to London, 15 July 1940.

6 PRO PREM 3/129/2 'General Report on Position in Eire', 20 July 1940.

7 MA G2/2029 'Michael O'Donovan nom-de-plume Frank O'Connor', 26 June 1940.

8 PRO DO 130/12 Maffey to London, 1 July 1940; UCDA Frank Aiken Papers P104/372 for details of news censored.

9 NAI DFA A8 'Note on activities of Captain and Mrs Price', May 1940; PRO DO 130/12 Maffey to London, 16 July 1940.

10 O'Halpin, *MI5 and Ireland* pp. 20–1: O'Halpin, *Defending Ireland*, p. 189.

11 Hull, *Irish Secrets*, pp. 121–6.

12 PRO DO 130/12 Maffey to London with notes of conversation with Cosgrave, 11 July 1940; NAI DT S11896A minutes of Defence Conference, 9 July 1940; DO 130/12 London to Maffey, 4 July 1940.

13 PRO DO 130/12 Machtig to Maffey, 4 July 1940 with details of British thinking on policy towards Ireland. According to Machtig this letter had been read by the secretary of state, who agreed with its contents.

14 PRO DO 130/12, Maffey to Machtig, 11 July 1940.

15 PRO DO 130/12 Maffey to London, 15 July 1940.

16 Valiulis, 'The man they could never forgive'. This feeling was reciprocated by Fianna Fáil members; see Andrews, *Man of No Property*.

17 UCDA Eamon de Valera Papers P150/2597 Cosgrave to de Valera, 9 July 1940.

18 NAI DEA A2 memorandum for taoiseach, 11 July 1940.

19 UCDA Eamon de Valera Papers P150/2597 de Valera to Cosgrave, 13 July 1940; Cosgrave to de Valera, 16 July 1940.

20 UCDA Desmond FitzGerald Papers P80/1119(5) memorandum from Cosgrave, 15 November 1940.

21 PRO DO 130/12 Maffey to Machtig, 23 December 1940 on meeting with Cosgrave and Mulcahy.

22 UCDA Eamon de Valera Papers P150/2571 Walshe to de Valera with report of meeting with Maffey, 15 July 1940.

23 PRO DO 130/12 Maffey to London, 15 July 1940; Maffey meeting with de Valera note of conversation, 17 July 1940.

24 PRO DO 130/12 Granard to Caldecote, 12 August 1940; Barton to Caldecote, no date; Londonderry to Caldecote, 15 June 1940. See Kershaw, *Making Friends with Hitler*, for a critical assessment of Londonderry.

25 PRO DO 35/1008/9 Londonderry to Caldecote, 15 June 1940; Caldecote to Londonderry, 21 June 1940; Londonderry to Churchill, 22 June 1940; Churchill reply 21 June 1940.

26 PRO CAB 120/506 War Office to Downing Street, 20 July 1940.

27 NLI Shane Leslie Papers MS 22,863 typescript diaries 1914–44.

28 PRO DO 130/12 Maffey to Machtig, 15 July 1940.

29 NAI DFA A2, 15 July 1940; UCDA Eamon de Valera Papers P150/2571 Walshe memorandum for de Valera, 15 July 1940.

30 PRO DO 130/12, Maffey to London, 16 July 1940.

31 NAI DFA A2 Walshe memorandum for de Valera, 29 July 1940; note 25 July 1940, note 31 July 1940; DFA P48 Walshe to David Gray, 31 July 1940.

32 PRO CAB 21/881 'Eire' Stephenson to Cavendish Bentinck at the Foreign Office, 26 September 1940; reply with decision 1 October 1940; NAI DFA P48 Walshe to Gray, 31 July 1940.

33 NAI DFA A3 extract from letter to War Office; meeting between General Harrison, Maffey, de Valera, Aiken and Walshe, 1 July 1940.

34 MA 'Memorandum on the Defence Forces' Domhnaill Mac Cionnaith, 23 August 1944.

35 NAI DT S11896A Defence Conferences, 9 and 15 July 1940.

36 MA EDP 1/2 chief of staff to minister for defence, 6 June 1940.

37 MA EDP 1/4 general correspondence January to June 1940, 17 May 1940.

38 MA EDP 1/4 'Precautions re landing of arms', 11 May 1940; note by Aodh MacNeill, 23 May 1940, which describes the location of anti-aircraft guns around Dublin.

39 MA EDP 1/1 notes of meeting with taoiseach, 29 June 1940; second meeting on same day at 20.00 hours; Operational Order No. 2, 10 July 1940; Farrell, 'Professionalization and suicidal defence planning'.

40 NAI DFA A2 memo for taoiseach of meeting with Maffey, 29 July 1940; additional memorandum, 30 July 1940 and note added to memorandum, 31 July 1940.

41 MA EDP/1 GHQ operations orders and instructions: immediate necessity of inter-staff talks, no date but probably September or October 1940 from context.

42 MA EDP 1/4 operations instructions: general correspondence July–December 1940, 14 September 1940.

43 MA EDP 1/4 handwritten note by McKenna, no date but from file probably written 17–19 September 1940.

44 NAI DFA A8 decrypted messages from Kostal to London, 31 May 1940; 13 September 1940; PRO DO 130/12 Maffey to London on meeting with Walshe, 29 July 1940.

45 NAI DEA A8 report on Ireland Kostal to London decrypted, 13 September 1940.

46 UCDA Eamon de Valera Papers P150/2571 Walshe to de Valera, 19 August 1940; memorandum of discussion between secretaries of Department of External Affairs, Industry and Commerce, Supplies and Agriculture, 19 August 1940; Carroll, *Ireland in the War Years*, pp. 60–77.

47 NAI DFA A8 Liam Archer to Walshe, 26 September 1940 with report; NAI S11896A meeting, 4 September 1940 and subsequent for Aiken's non-committal view on the bombing.

48 Skidelski, *John Maynard Keynes*, pp. 46–175, which provides an intimate overview of Keynes' achievement.

49 PRO MAF 83/87 'Meeting with Irish butter representatives', 20 March 1940; Maffey to London, 20 March 1940; Eden to Woolton, 5 April 1940; Woolton to Eden, 10 April 1940; meeting at Dominions Office, 15 April 1940; memorandum in preparation for meeting with Irish ministers, 24 April 1940.

50 PRO MAF 83/87 minutes of meeting between Irish minister and Britain on trade, 30 April, 1, 2 and 4 May 1940; Meeting in Eden's room of British officials, 7 May 1940; Meeting with Irish officials at Dominions Office, 7 May 1940; Machtig note, 8 May 1940.

51 UCDA Eamon de Valera Papers 150/2571 Walshe to de Valera, 1 and 6 May 1940.

52 PRO MAF 83/87 Leydon to Brown, 17 May 1940; minute of meetings between

Irish and British officials, 28 May 1940; draft heads of agreement, 30 May 1940; Lloyd to Dulanty, 6 June 1940; minutes of meeting between representatives of Eire and United Kingdom, 30 May 1940.

53 PRO MAF 83/87 Lloyd to Machtig, 12 July 1940.

54 NAI DFA A2 Walshe to de Valera, 21 August 1940 reporting on discussion with Dulanty the previous night; DEA P25 Walshe to taoiseach, 21 and 23 August 1940; Dulanty to Dublin, 23 August 1940.

55 NAI DFA P25 British draft proposals, September 1940; remarks by Department of Finance, 7 September 1940; DEA 'Transhipment' 6 September 1940; DEA memorandum on general problems with agreement, 7 September 1940; memorandum on draft agreement prepared by secretaries of Agriculture, Supplies, Industry and Commerce, Finance and External Affairs, 19 September 1940.

56 NAI DFA P25 cabinet decision to reject British proposals, 24 September 1940; Leydon report, 15 October 1940; 21 October 1940 for new Irish proposals. PRO ADM116/5631 Machtig to Maffey, 23 October 1940 which contains secretary of state's view; DFA P25 Dulanty report of conversation with Lord Cranborne, 25 November 1940; note by Leydon, 31 December 1940.

57 PRO DO 35/1011/3 Hudson to Stephenson, 23 September 1940.

58 PRO DO 35/1011/3 'Opinion in Eire' by Miss Maxwell (MOI), no date but from internal evidence late August–early September 1940.

59 PRO DO 35/1011/3 Elizabeth Cameron (Bowen) 'Notes on Eire', 13 July 1940; 21 July 1940.

60 PRO FO 800/310 'Notes on Eire', 9 November 1940; Hodson to Stephenson, 10 June 1940; Stephenson to Hodson, 13 June 1940; Hodson to Stephenson, 25 June 1940.

61 PRO DO 35/1011/3 Betjeman to Hodson, 21 June 1940; the fairly positive reception for Betjeman's report at the Ministry of Information, 21 June 1940; 3 July 1940. See also joint meeting Ministry of Information and Dominions Office, 5 July 1940.

62 PRO DO 35/1011/3, 29 November 1940.

63 NAI DT S11896A, Defence Conference meeting, 6 November 1940.

64 MA EDP 1/2 Plan 2 Aodh O'Neill to McKenna, 13 November 1940; notes on conference held in Plans and Operation Branch, 21 November 1940; statement by chief of staff.

65 UCDA Fianna Fáil Party Papers P176/345 Fianna Fáil National Executive minutes of meeting, 11 November 1940.

66 NAI DFA A/82 Walshe to de Valera, 13 November 1940; 17 November 1940; PRO CAB 65/10 war cabinet meeting, 21 November 1940.

67 Gilbert, *The Churchill War Papers Volume II*, pp. 1042–9; Canning, *British Policy Towards Ireland*, p. 292; Fisk, *In Time of War*, pp. 286–90.

68 Gilbert, *The Churchill War Papers Volume II*, p. 1086.

69 Gilbert, *The Churchill War Papers Volume II*, pp. 1114–15; PRO DO 130/12 Maffey to Machtig, 19 November 1940.

70 Churchill to Roosevelt, 7 December 1940, in Kimball, *Churchill and Roosevelt I*, pp. 106–7.

71 Orwell and Angus, *The Collected Essays, Journalism and Letters of George Orwell Volume II*, diary entry for 14 March 1941, p. 438.

72 MA EDP 1/2 Plan 2 notes on conference, 21 November 1940.

73 MA memo prepared by Colonel O'Connell, 'German co-operation under GDP 2', 13 November 1940.

74 MA EDP 1/2 Plan 2 minutes of conference on GDP 2 held in taoiseach's office, 15 December 1940; minutes of conference held in Plans and Operations Branch, 15 December 1940; report 3 November 1940 and note 17 December 1940.

75 NAI DFA A21 memorandum by Walshe, 3 January 1941; note 6 January 1941; note 7 January 1941. Although de Valera refused entry to the additional staff in December, he accepted the right of the Germans to appoint them as long as they travelled from the United States 'by the ordinary way of travel', which of course involved landing in England. See Fisk, *In Time of* War, p. 251; Duggan, *Herr Hempel*, pp. 129–31.

76 NLI Shane Leslie Papers MS 22,863; NAI DT S11896A, Defence Conference meeting, 3 January 1941.

77 PRO CAB 120/506 Churchill to Ismay, 3 December 1940; Churchill to Wood, 5 December 1940; Cranborne to Churchill, 11 January 1941; Churchill to Cranborne, 17 January 1941; Churchill to Cranborne, 23 March 1941; FO 371/28889 war cabinet conference, 6 December 1940; PREM 3/131/4 Cranborne to Churchill, 2 February 1941; 'Memorandum on the defence forces, August 1944'; NAI DEA A2 memorandum, 29 March 1941; P203 memorandum, 22 May 1941.

78 PRO CAB 8/512 Bevin memorandum, 6 June 1941; meeting of Overseas Trading Committee to discuss Irish labour, 16 June 1941; Bevin to Churchill, 23 June 1941; Churchill approval, 27 June 1941.

79 MA S103 general report on the army, 31 May 1941; UCDA Frank Aiken Papers P104/3374, 9 July 1944.

80 Hull, *Irish Secrets*, pp. 144–95; Fisk, *In Time of War*, pp. 502–5.

6. THE (LOST) AMERICAN CARD: FDR, GRAY AND THE NEUTRALS 1938–41

1 NAUSA 841D01/181 Gray to Roosevelt, 16 May 1940.

2 NAUSA 841D01/181 Roosevelt to Gray, 7 June 1940.

3 NAUSA 841D01/181 Roosevelt to Gray, 7 June 1940; Churchill to Roosevelt, 5 May 1940; Roosevelt to Churchill, 16 May 1940; Roosevelt to Churchill, 13 August 1940 in Kimball, *Churchill and Roosevelt I*, pp. 37–59.

4 NAUSA 841D2222/24/14 Gray to Hull, 4 June 1940; Joseph C. Green note, 7 June 1940.

5 NAUSA 841D2222/24/14 Hull to Kennedy, 12 June 1940; Kennedy to Hull,

17 June 1940; Green note, 17 June 1940 concerning meeting with Donald Nelson, Chief of the Procurement Division of the Treasury; Hull to Gray, 20 June 1940.

6 NAUSA 841D2222/24/14 Gray to Hull, 18 June 1940; note 20 June 1940; memorandum on arms, 26 June 1940; Hull to acting secretary of war, 1 July 1940; Gray to Hull, 1 July 1940; Edgar P. Allen memorandum on decision to sell to Canada. There is a rather garbled version of this episode in Brennan, *Ireland Standing Firm*, pp. 32–5.

7 NAUSA 841D244/34/2 Irish request for destroyer, 19 July 1940; 841D244/34/3 Gray to Hull, 13 August 1940.

8 FDRPL PSF Box 40 Gray to FDR, 23 and 30 November 1940.

9 NAI DFA P35 copy of message to committee of American Association for the Recognition of the Irish Republic (AARIR) from de Valera, 12 November 1940; Coogan, *De Valera*, pp. 561, 575–6.

10 AFIN Papers St John's University New York Irish legation to AFIN, 9 June 1941. AFIN were critical of the Irish government and the legation for their weak support of the organization's efforts on behalf of Ireland and complained that the Irish had little appreciation of the American media or publicity. Minutes of Executive Council AFIN, 18 September 1941; NAI DFA P12/6 for legation correspondence with Dublin on the 1940 Democratic Convention, 22 and 24 1940.

11 Brennan, *Ireland Standing Firm*, pp. 26–30 for this period; de Valera's speech in *Irish Press*, 23 December 1940.

12 FDRPL Box 40 Gray to FDR, 4 February 1941; FDR to Gray, 6 March 1941.

13 Gilbert, *The Churchill War Papers Volume II*, pp. 144–5; Langer and Gleason, *The Undeclared War*, pp. 236, 272.

14 AFIN telegram sent to Willkie by O'Dwyer, 30 January 1941.

15 FDRPL PSF Box 40 Gray to Roosevelt, 4 February 1941; Nicholson, *The War Years 1939–1945*, pp. 142–3; FDRPL Gray Papers Gray to de Valera, 6 February 1941.

16 FDRPL Gray Papers memorandum of conversation, 22 January 1941 sent to de Valera, 6 February 1941. There are a number of Gray's memoranda for the State Department in the de Valera papers.

17 MA EDP 1/2 Plan 2 report of meeting in taoiseach's office, 15 December 1940; NAUSA 841D24/29 Gray to Hull, 24 February 1941.

18 NAUSA 841D24/29 Gray report of conversation with de Valera, 22 February 1941.

19 NAI DFA P35 'Visit of Mr Aiken to United States 1941' Walshe to Brennan, 24 February 1941; note of meeting between de Valera and Gray, 3 March 1941.

20 NAI DFA P35 Gray to Aiken, 28 February 1941; Gray to Eleanor Roosevelt, 28 February 1941; NLI Frank Gallagher Papers MS 18,334 Gray to Gallagher, 7 February 1941; Gallagher to Gray, 13 February 1941; Raymond, 'David Gray, The Aiken Mission'.

21 FDRPL Gray Papers Gray to de Valera, 6 February 1941.

22 NAUSA 841D24/29 Hull to Gray, 28 February 1941; Gray to Hull, 24 February 1941.

23 FDRLP Gray Papers personal note of conversation with de Valera, 26 February 1941.

24 FDRPL PSF Box 3 'Ireland' Donovan to the secretary of the Navy, 11 March 1941.

25 NAI DEA P35 notes dictated by Aiken after meeting with Donovan, 6 March 1941.

26 Boland statement cited in Fisk, *In Time of War*, p. 215; NAI DEA P12/6 Walshe to Brennan, 21 November 1940.

27 NAI DEA P35 Aiken meeting with Dr Salazar president of the council of ministers, 8 March 1941; Lintz, *Nazi Germany and Neutral Europe*, pp. 144–74.

28 NAUSA 740.0011/9664 Winant to Washington, DC, 6 April 1941 with report by Dominions Office, 28 March 1941 on Aiken in Lisbon.

29 NAUSA 841 D00/1306 Gray to Welles, 7 March 1941; FDRPL Gray Papers Gray to de Valera, 10 March 1941; 841D.00/1311 Gray to Hull, 20 June 1941; Dwyer, *Irish Neutrality and the USA*, pp. 85–121; PRO PREM 4/53/6 Lord Cranborne to Churchill for a similar view to that of Gray, 12 January 1941.

30 NAI DFA P35 'Attitude of the State Department towards us', 28 February 1941; DEA A12 copy of State Department letter to McGarrity, 8 March 1939.

31 However, the Irish government was slow to extend formal recognition to Israel because of its own sensitivities in respect of the Vatican. Keogh, ' "Making Aliya" '.

32 NAI DFA P35 'Attitude to the State Department', 28 February 1941.

33 In his memoirs Brennan confuses the date for these exchanges, placing it after the United States came into the war, *Ireland Standing* Firm, pp. 72–3; NAI DFA P35 'Appeal for Aid to Britain Signed by Sixty Prominent American Catholics', with notes on Brennan's activities in respect of the signatories, March 1941; Spellman was to act as an envoy for the president in 1942.

34 NAI DFA P35 'Anti-Irish Propaganda in the United States: Our Counter Propaganda', 28 February 1941; 'British Claims to Irish Ports', no date but from the internal evidence late February–early March 1941.

35 NAUSA 841 D0011/24/34 Winant to Hull, 13 March 1941 reporting on discussions with various British officials; UCDA Frank Aiken Papers P104/3479 for MacDermot's remarks and censorship.

36 *Irish Press*, 15 March 1941 reports Roosevelt's remarks on its front page: 'United States arms for Ireland?' NAI DFA P35, 15 March 1941 note on press conference and possible discourtesy; NAUSA 841 D00/24/35 Gray to Hull, 16 March 1941. It may also be a sign of Walshe's or de Valera's myopic views of the world that they expected the leader of a state with global interests to be well informed about Ireland.

37 NAUSA 841 D00/24/30 State Department memorandum on Aiken's visit to the United States prepared by the Division of European Affairs, 18 March 1941.

38 NAUSA 841 D00/24/57 note, 19 March 1941; NAUSA 841 D00/24/42 note by Welles on meeting with Aiken and Brennan, 20 March 1941.

39 NAUSA 740.0011/9530 memorandum of conversation between Welles, Aiken and Brennan, 20 March 1941.

40 NAI DFA P35 Brennan's report to Dublin on meeting with Welles, 21 March 1941.

41 NAI DFA P35 Brennan to Dublin with additional report of Aiken's meeting with Welles, 26 March 1941.

42 UCDA Frank Aiken Papers P104/ 3479 and P104/3573 for details of censorship. James Douglas (1887–1954) was a prominent Quaker and businessman who had been a member of the committee that drafted the 1922 Constitution.

43 NAUSA 841 D00/50/31 Gray to Hull, 27 March 1941.

44 NAUSA 841 D00/24/42 Acheson note on meeting with Aiken, 2 April 1941; 841 D00/24/45 Hull record of conversation with Aiken, 11 April 1941; Brennan, *Ireland Standing* Firm, pp. 50–1; NAI DFA P35 Brennan's report to Dublin on meeting with Acheson, 7 April 1941.

45 NAI DFA P35 Brennan to Dublin, 26 March 1941 which details Aiken's meetings in Washington as well as discussions with Irish-American organizations; Coogan, *De Valera*, p. 575.

46 Kimball, *Roosevelt and Churchill I*, p. 165; Langer and Gleason, *The Undeclared War* for more detailed discussion.

47 NAI DFA P35 Brennan to Dublin, 7 April 1941; 10 April 1941. The latter report is much more detailed but adds little of substance. There is no record of the meeting in the FDRPL files, but this was the practice with Roosevelt, who did not minute such meetings. UCDA Frank Aiken Papers P104/3585 contains Aiken's account of the visit and the exchange with Roosevelt.

48 FDRPL PPE 5643 FDR to de Valera, 15 April 1941, which is based on a draft prepared by Welles; OF 218, 15 April 1941 for another version; UCDA Frank Aiken Papers P104/3585 Aiken memorandum on American trip, 15 August 1941; Lindbergh, *The Wartime Journals of Charles A. Lindbergh*, pp. 477, 494–5; NAI DFA P35 Brennan's reports on meeting with Roosevelt, 7 April 1941; 10 April 1941; Brennan, *Ireland Standing Firm*, p. 47. When Brennan wrote these memoirs, Aiken was minister for external affairs in the government and it is unlikely that Brennan would have produced an unflattering description in the circumstances.

49 NAI DFA P35 Brennan to Dublin reporting meeting with Welles, 29 April 1941; Brennan to Dublin, 1 May 1941; Dublin to Washington, DC, 2 May 1941; DEA A24 Defence Conference meeting, 26 April 1941.

50 AFIN Papers contains a considerable number of these speeches and news reports on Aiken's trip to the United States.

51 Darryl Zanuck the film director complained to the Roosevelt White House about the Aiken trip: 'it is strange the United States would entertain or sponsor a foreign figure on an obvious propaganda trip'. FDRPL OF 218 'Ireland: Government of 1933–45' Stephen Early to General Robert C. Richardson, 20 May 1941; Zanuck letter, 14 May 1941.

52 Lindbergh, *The Wartime Journals of Charles A. Lindbergh*, pp. 477, 495; AFIN telegram to Eleanor Roosevelt, 16 May 1941.

53 Gallup, *The Gallup Poll Volume One*, p. 260. FDRPL OF 857 contains various opinion polls collected by Hadley Cantril for Roosevelt (see polls dated 23 October 1940, 11 December 1940 and 28 January 1941); Cantril, 'Public Opinion in flux', pp. 136–52; Dwyer, *Irish Neutrality and the USA*, p. 39.

54 AFIN Papers press release by O'Dwyer, 12 May 1941; report by James W. Walsh, 7 October 1941 on polling for Catholic Laymen's Committee for Peace.

55 FDRPL PSF Box 79, FDR to O'Connor, 19 May 1941; PSF 40 FDR to Gray, 21 August 1941.

56 FDRPL Box 40 Gray to FDR, 4 April 1941.

57 FDRPL Box 40 Gray to FDR, 22 April 1941; NAUSA 841 D0011/24/46 Gray to Hull, 8 April 1941; Hull to Gray, 9 April 1941.

58 FDRPL Gray Papers notes for conversation with de Valera, 26 April 1941; NAI DFA P35 copies of two memoranda for Irish government left by Gray with de Valera, 28 April 1941.

59 FDRPL Box 40 Gray to FDR, 7 May 1941; Longford and O'Neill, *Eamon de Valera*, pp. 381–2 where the impertinence claim is also made.

60 UCDA Frank Aiken Papers P104/3479 'Report for March 1941'; P104/3572 Coyne to Traynor, 23 May 1941. This file also contains details of what was censored.

7. NEUTRALITY, POLITICS AND PARTY IN THE EMERGENCY

1 PDDE 84 cc.1481–3, 3 April 1941; NAI DT S11586A, 'Neutrality, Censorship and Democracy', 23 January 1940.

2 PDSE 24 cc.2614, 4 December 1940.

3 PRO DO 130/28 Elizabeth Bowen, 'Notes on Eire', 9 February 1942; FDRPL PSF 40, Gray to Roosevelt, 1 and 27 January 1942; OF 218, Roosevelt reply to Brennan, 24 February 1942.

4 PDSE 24 cc.2614–16, 4 December 1940; PDDE 84 cc.1481–3, 3 April 1941.

5 PDSE cc.2607–8, 4 December 1940.

6 PDDE 85 c.1991, 18 February 1942.

7 PDDE 85 cc.1746–8, 4 February 1942.

8 PDDE 85 cc.1750–5, 4 February 1942; UCDA Frank Aiken Papers, P104/3479 'Report for March 1941', 19 May 1941.

9 PDDE 89 cc.503–9, 4 February 1943.

10 NAI DT S11306, 'Press censorship of election speeches', 15 February 1943. Frank Aiken Papers P104/3439 contains Aiken's telephone conversation with Senator Frank McDermott, 11 November 1940.

11 UCDA Fianna Fáil Party Papers P176/445 parliamentary party minutes, 20 March 1941.

12 UCDA Fianna Fáil Party Papers P176/445 National Executive minutes, 24 March 1941; parliamentary party minutes, 20 March and 20 November 1941.

13 PDDE 85 cc.2037–8, 4 March 1942.

14 NAI DIC E37/578 'Department of Supplies: record of activities'; Bradley, 'Speeding the plough', pp. 39–54.

15 NAI DFA 227/108 letter from Louie Bennett and others, no date but late 1942 from context.

16 NAI DT S13438A 'Necessitous Families', memorandum by Department of Local Government and Public Health, 6 March 1944; cabinet decision, 10 March 1944.

17 See Horgan, *Seán Lemass*, p. 98.

18 NAI DT S12886A memorandum by Department of Industry and Commerce on expenditure in United Kingdom/Ireland, 5 February 1941; McGall, 'The five-pound-a-week family'.

19 NAI DT S14005 'Memo on the relative cost of living of agricultural labourers and inhabitants of towns of different sizes', December 1940; DF F200/20/38, 17 November 1938 and 16 January 1939.

20 See NAI DT S12865 'Emigrants' for data.

21 Clear, *Women of the House*, pp. 62, 72.

22 Details can be found in NAI DIC E37/578 'History of Department of Supplies', which I consulted in the Department of Trade, Industry and Commerce; PDDE 85 cc.2047–50, 2055–7, 2146–214, 4 March 1942; UCDA Frank Aiken Papers P104/3441 for transcript of Denis Johnstone's broadcast, which includes a critique by Walshe, 3 December 1941.

23 UCDA Fianna Fáil Party Papers P176/445 parliamentary party minutes, 2 July 1942; PRO DO 130/28 Bowen 'Notes on Eire', 9 February 1942; DO 35/1228 report on visit to Dublin, 31 May 1943 by L. Cadbury.

24 NAUSA 840 D001/1339 Gray memorandum 'Political and economic conditions in Southern Ireland', 6 May 1942.

25 PDDE 88 cc.731–5, 15 July 1942.

26 O' Donoghue, 'Berlin's Irish War', p. 95.

27 PRO DO 130/28, 'Notes on Eire' by Elizabeth Bowen, 31 July 1942.

28 PRO DO 130/28 'Notes on Eire', 12 July 1942. See also Girvin, *Between Two Worlds*, pp. 134–40.

29 MA S/103/EDP/39/3 report for year 1 April 1941–31 March 1942.

30 NAI DT S11896A notes on Defence Conference, 30 May 1940; UCDA Fianna Fáil Papers P176/345 Fianna Fáil national executive minutes, motion by Seán Bonner, 6 May 1940, decision to postpone 27 May 1940 and 10 June 1940.

31 UCDA Eamon de Valera Papers P150/2597 Cosgrave to de Valera, 9 July 1940; Desmond FitzGerald Papers P80/119C memorandum by Cosgrave, 15 November 1940. Fisk, *In Time of* War, pp. 160–1 emphasizes the limited cooperation involved in the Defence Conference.

32 PDDE 86 c.450, 15 April 1942; 87, c.745, 2 June 1942.

33 PDDE 87 cc.2035–40, 30 June 1943.

34 PDDE 87 cc.2041–62, 30 June 1942; 88 cc.129–30, 7 July 1942.

35 PDDE 86 cc.445–6, 15 April 1942.

36 *Irish Times*, 24 August 1942.

37 Ó Drisceoil, 'Keeping the temperature down', pp. 177–9.

38 UCDA Seán MacEntee Papers P67/366 MacEntee to de Valera, 28 June 1943.

39 *Irish Times*, 24 August 1942.

40 PDDE 89 cc.1947–8, 14 April 1943.

41 See Ó Drisceoil, 'Keeping the temperature down'; PDDE 90 cc.94–9, 12 May 1943.

42 PDDE 89 cc.1955–8, 14 April 1943.

43 PRO DO 130/28 'Notes on Eire', 31 July 1942.

44 UCDA Desmond FitzGerald Papers P80/1109 'Heads of policy', January 1943; P80/1110, 'Points for speakers', January 1943.

45 PRO DO 130/128 'Notes on Eire', 20 February 1942 for further details.

46 UCDA Fianna Fáil Party Papers P176/444, 26 November 1942. See also criticism of government land policy expressed at meeting, 16 April 1942; Frank Aiken Papers P104/3486 and P104/3487 for reports on censorship during the first half of 1943.

47 Varley and Moser, 'Clann na Talmhan', pp. 39–43; Girvin, *Union to Union*, p. 265.

48 UCDA Seán MacEntee Papers P67/365 and P67/364 speech at Sligo Fianna Fáil convention, 29 May 1943. See also *Irish Independent*, 29 May 1943.

49 Milotte, *Communism in Ireland*, pp. 191–200.

50 UCDA Seán MacEntee Papers P67/362 election material 1943; P67/364 speech at Harolds Cross Bridge, 7 June 1943.

51 UCDA Seán MacEntee Papers P67/364 speech at Harolds Cross Bridge, 7 June 1943.

52 Ó Drisceoil, 'Keeping the temperature down', pp. 103–4.

53 UCDA Seán MacEntee Papers P67/363 Lemass to MacEntee, 10 June 1943.

54 PRO DO 121/85 report, 1 July 1943.

55 UCDA MacEntee Papers P67/366 MacEntee to de Valera, 28 June 1943.

56 Farrell, *Chairman or Chief*, p. 36–7.

57 UCDA Desmond FitzGerald Papers P80/1128 notes for speech by FitzGerald. See also *Irish Press* reporting late May 1943 for Fianna Fáil meetings; NLI Seán Milroy Papers MS 28–898, report 19 February 1942.

58 UCDA Seán MacEntee Papers P67/367 notes for election address, 1944.

59 *Irish Times* 'Eire's neutrality at stake', 2 March 1944; *Irish Press*, 'Taoiseach on value of party system: neutrality policy of whole people', 28 February 1944.

60 NAUSA 840 D001/250, Gray to State Department, 1 March 1944; MA S/103/ EDP/39/5 general report for year ending 31 March 1944, 18 April 1944; memorandum on the defence forces, August 1944. UCDA Frank Aiken Papers P104/ 3493–95 contains material on how censorship was used during the crisis.

61 UCDA Fianna Fáil Party Papers FF/439 parliamentary minutes, 3 November 1938; FF/440 parliamentary minutes, 8 April 1940.

62 NLI William O'Brien Papers MS 15684 for copy of speech.

63 UCDA Fianna Fáil Party Papers FF/793 'General election report 1944', 27 August 1944.

8. TO WAR: IRISH VOLUNTEERS IN THE BRITISH ARMED FORCES

1 FDRPL PSF Box 3 Robert Menzies, memorandum on visit to Northern Ireland and Eire, 3–5 April 1941; NAI DFA P81, 'Extent of Recruiting for British Forces' G2 memorandum January 1944; 'Recruiting from Ireland (26 Counties) for the British Forces', November 1945; PDDE 113 cc.1340–50, 10 December 1948.

2 Unless specifically referenced, these and other comments are based on the testimony of ex-servicemen and women who were interviewed by the Volunteers Project based in the History Department, University College Cork. Professor Geoff Roberts and I were the directors of this project, while Ms Tina Neylon carried out the interviews and has produced a summary of the individual tapes for use by researchers. Access to the archive can be obtained by contacting Professor Roberts.

3 *The Times*, 3 April 1946.

4 PRO DO 35/1230 note, 29 January 1946.

5 PRO DO 35/1228 Lemass conversation with Cadbury, 31 May 1943; letter from John Dulanty to the *Spectator*, 31 March 1944.

6 PRO DO 35/1230 contains much of the British correspondence on the volunteers, including a discussion on the number who volunteered from Ireland. FRDPL OF 218 'Ireland: Miscellaneous, 1943–5' telegram from United Irish Counties for Irish Freedom to Roosevelt, 30 October 1944.

7 *Belfast Telegraph*, 28 March 1944; PRO DO 35/1230/WX/32/1/140 'Service of Eire citizens in United Kingdom forces', which includes Brooke's speech and further estimates of numbers.

8 PRO DO 35/2089, Maffey to Machtig, 2 August 1945; DO 35/1230, N. E. Archer to R. R. Sedgwick, 15 November 1945.

9 NAUSA 841 D00/1346 report of conversation between E. L. Parker and F. Boland, 31 July 1942, sent to Washington, DC, 13 August 1942.

10 PRO DO 35/1230 note dated May 1945 on the use made by the Irish authorities of the volunteers since 1942; NAI DFA P81 memorandum by G2 Branch, 14 October 1943.

11 NAUSA 841D248/50/8–1044 memorandum of conversation between Aaron Brown, third secretary United States legation, and Ferguson, 5 or 6 August 1944; the *Boston Pilot* 26 May 1945.

12 PRO DO 35/1230 note on meeting in Dominions Office, May 1945.

13 *Irish Press*, 25 July 1945.

14 Northern Ireland Parliamentary Debates 23 c.1902, 4 September 1939 cited in Barton, 'Northern Ireland: the impact of war', p. 47; Churchill to Roosevelt, 11 April 1943 in Kimball (ed.), *Churchill and Roosevelt*, pp. 186–7.

15 PRO DO 35/1230 meeting at Dominions Offices, 30 November 1944.

16 See *Daily Telegraph*, 18 October 1944 for example of such a letter. PRO DO 35/1230 Costar to Sir John Stephenson, 1 December 1944.

17 PRO DO 35/1230 Machtig note, 4 December 1944; note by Lord Cranborne, 5 December 1944.

18 PRO DO 35/1230 note, 13 December 1944.

19 PRO DO 35/1230 Admiralty note, 7 January 1945; Air Ministry note, 7 January 1945.

20 PRO DO 35/1230 Costar to Mansergh, February 1945.

21 PRO DO 35/1230 Maffey note, 12 March 1945; Machtig to Cranborne, 16 March 1945; Cranborne note, 18 March 1945.

22 Letter to *The Times*, 26 March 1945 in which Ervine also points out that there were 78,000 people on the Irish unemployment register in January 1945 and cites various members of the Dáil to the effect that emigration to England had had beneficial affects for Ireland. It is not clear why he cites this evidence as it lends support to the view that there was a strong attraction in going to Britain for work at least if not to join the armed forces. FDRPL Gray Papers Gray to Ervine, 29 March 1945; Report in *Irish Times*, 25 July 1945.

23 Extract from travel diary, 24 July 1945 in Smith, *Hostage to Fortune*, p. 621.

24 PRO DO 35/1230 for correspondence.

25 PRO DO 35/1230 review of policy, March 1946; note, 25 February 1946; note in response to Lord Granard's letter, 29 January 1946.

26 Commonwealth Irish Association, *How Many? Irish Volunteers Served in His Majesty's Armed Forces in the War 1939–1946* by Henry Harrison and others (London, 9 April 1946); *Irish Independent* and *Irish Times*, 6 May 1946.

27 Dungan, *Distant Drums*, p. 104.

28 This account draws on interviews carried out for the Volunteers Project; McCarthy, *A Doctor's War*, p. 15.

29 NAI DFA 241/80. All citations are from this file unless noted otherwise.

30 UCDA Eamon de Valera Papers P150/2641 'Statement by Taoiseach, 2 April 1942'; *Irish Press*, 2 April 1942; NAI DFA 241/80 for additional material.

31 See Doherty, *Irish Men and Women in the Second World War*, pp. 21–6 for calculations.

32 These data have been calculated from Yvonne Therese McEwen MSc, FRSA, *Irish Volunteers and Volunteer Deaths in Irish Regiments 1939–1945* (University of Edinburgh, MSc research dissertation, 2003). I am indebted to

Ms McEwen for allowing me to read and cite her dissertation and for her advice on numerous aspects of this work.

33 NLI Shane Leslie Papers MS 22,863 Shane Leslie typescript diary.

34 Ó Drisceoil, *Censorship in Ireland*, pp. 171–9.

35 PRO DO 130/2 Maffey report to London on meeting with de Valera, 4 October 1939.

36 Volunteer Project Archives, University College Cork.

37 NAI DFA P81, which contains memoranda from G2 on recruitment to British armed forces and desertion from Irish armed forces.

38 Ó Drisceoil, *Censorship in Ireland*, pp. 163–5.

39 McEwen, 'Irish Volunteers and Volunteer Deaths', pp. 73–4.

40 Ó Drisceoil, *Censorship in Ireland*, pp. 111, 211; Volunteer Project Archives, University College Cork.

41 PDDE 97 cc.1879–1900, 4 July 1945; cc.1924–80, 5 July 1945; 98, cc.397–443, 18 October 1945. PRO DO 35/1230, 9 August 1945 contains newspaper reports on court cases in Eire of deserters who had fought for Britain.

42 Girvin, *From Union to Union*, pp. 109–10.

9. DIPLOMACY AS IDEOLOGY: NEUTRALITY JUNE 1941 TO AUGUST 1945

1 Cited in Jenkins, *Churchill*, p. 659.

2 NAUSA 841D2224/68 Gray to Hull, 1 July 1941; NAI DEA P12/6 Brennan to Walshe, 6 August 1941; UCDA Frank Aiken Papers P104/3482, 'Report for July 1941'.

3 Langer and Gleason, *The Undeclared War*, pp. 663–92; Kimball, *Forged in War*, pp. 94–102.

4 NAI DEA P12/6 Brennan to Walshe, 3 October 1941.

5 FDRPL PSF Box 40 Roosevelt to Gray, 21 August 1941.

6 NAUSA 841 D0024/70 statement prepared on Ireland for president, 21 July 1941; Gray meeting with de Valera, 18 July 1941; note dated 21 July 1941.

7 NAUSA 841 D0024/1317 Gray to Welles, 10 September 1941.

8 NAUSA 841 D0024/1317 Gray to Welles, 10 September 1941; 841 D0024/1318 Gray to Robert Burgess, 11 September 1941. Gray provided Walshe with a copy of these comments, who then responded in detail to Gray's views. NAI DFA P48 Walshe to Gray, 11 September 1941.

9 FDRPL PSF Box 40 Gray to Roosevelt, 12 September 1941.

10 FDRPL PSF Box 40 McRory to Gray, 20 October 1941; Gray to McRory 21 October 1941; NAI DFA P48 Joseph Walshe to Robert Brennan, 14 October 1941.

11 FDRPL PSF Box 40 Gray to Roosevelt, 21 October 1941. Gray also recommended that the United States should 'maintain good relations with the Irish people as opposed to the Irish government'; NAUSA 841 D0024/48/84, Gray to Welles, 3 November 1941. The evidence strongly suggests that

Brennan and Walshe in particular, but also de Valera, blamed Gray for the failure of the Aiken mission earlier in the year. See NAI DEA P48 Walshe to Brennan, 14 November 1941.

12 FDRPL PSF Box 40 Welles to Roosevelt, 14 November 1941; Irish legation aide-memoire, 15 October 1941; note from Brennan, 6 November 1941

13 NAUSA 841D48/75 Gray to State Department, 1 November 1941; 841D48/76 Hull to Gray, 15 November 1941; 841D48/78 Gray to Hull, 30 November 1941; 841D48/82 memorandum by State Department reporting Roosevelt's decision not to include Ireland in lend-lease.

14 Overy, *Why the Allies Won*, pp. 282–313 discusses the 'moral contest' in the struggle between the Allies and the Axis.

15 PRO PREM 3/131/7 Maffey note of conversation with Walshe, 14 March 1941.

16 FDRPL PSF40 Gray to Roosevelt, 17 December 1941.

17 Copy of Gray's statement can be found in NAI DEA P48, 18 December 1941. I have not been able to locate a published version of this in the main Irish newspapers.

18 De Valera's broadcasts on 14 and 25 December 1941 and his statement of 27 January 1942 can be found in Moynihan, *Speeches and Statements*, pp. 461–5.

19 FDRPL PSF Box 40, Gray to Roosevelt, 1 January 1942.

20 Longford and O'Neill, *Eamon de Valera*, pp. 392–5.

21 FDRPL PSF Box 40 Gray to Roosevelt, 27 January 1942; NLI Frank Gallagher Papers MS 18375, Dwyer, *Irish Neutrality and the USA*, pp. 139–59.

22 FDRPL PSF Box 40 Roosevelt to Marshall, 27 February 1942; State Department memorandum, 27 January 1942; Gray to Roosevelt, 27 January 1942.

23 FDRPL OF 218 'Ireland: Government of 1933–1945' Roosevelt to Brennan, 24 February 1942 in reply to Brennan's note of 6 February 1942.

24 FDRPL PSF Box 40 de Valera to Roosevelt, 20 April 1942; Roosevelt to Hull, 21 April 1942.

25 PRO CAB 120/506 'Eire' Churchill to foreign secretary, 5 February 1942; NAUSA 841 D0024/86 Winant to Hull, 11 February 1942.

26 NAUSA 841 D0024/90 Acheson to Stettinius, 23 February 1942.

27 FDRPL PSF Box 40 Gray to Roosevelt, 24 March 1942; Gray to Hull, 21 March 1942; McKenna to Gray, 19 March 1942; Gray to Hull, 23 March 1942.

28 FDRPL PSF Box 40 Gray to Roosevelt, 8 September 1942; 6 November 1942; 29 November 1942.

29 FDRPL PSF Box 40 Roosevelt to Gray, 16 September 1942; Nolan, 'Joseph Walshe', p. 196.

30 Nolan, 'Joseph Walshe', p. 209; NAUSA 841 D0024/1351 Welles to Gray, 2 October 1942; Gray memorandum on Ireland, 8 September 1942; statement by IRA Army Council, 31 August 1942; Report by Lieutenant Colonel Reynolds, US military attaché, 2 September 1942.

31 NAUSA 841 D0024/1351 Gray memo for State Department, 8 September 1942; 841 D0024/1344 Gray to Hull, 21 August 1942.

32 FDRPL PSF Box 40 Gray to Roosevelt, 6 November 1942.

33 FDRPL PSF Box 40 note by Gray, 9 November 1942; Maude Gray to Roosevelt, 28 November 1942.

34 Kimball, *Forged in War*, pp. 172–82 for the North African campaign.

35 FDRPL PSF Box 40 Gray memorandum 'Discussion of Anglo-Irish Problems at Ambassador Winant's Dinner', 28 November 1942; Gray to Roosevelt, 29 November 1942.

36 FDRPL PSF Box 40 Roosevelt to Gray, 18 December 1942; Gray to Roosevelt, 13 February 1943; NAUSA 841 D0024/1376 Gray to Welles, 12 February 1943; 841 D0024/1382 Gray to Welles, 27 February 1943. See also FDRPL PSF Box 40 Maffey to Machtig, 25 February 1943 complimenting Gray and emphasizing the effective cooperation between the two in Dublin.

37 PRO DO 35/2069 Maffey report of conversation with de Valera, 23 February 1943.

38 FDRPL PSF Box 40 Gray memorandum 'Discussion of Anglo-Irish Problems', 28 November 1942; PRO DO 35/2069 Maffey meeting with de Valera, 23 February 1943; NAUSA 841 D0024/1404 Gray to Welles, 15 March 1943; FDRPL Sumner Welles Papers Box 165 note on meeting with Brennan, 3 May 1943.

39 PRO DO 35/2077 Maffey report of meeting with de Valera, 13 October 1943; NAUSA 841 D001/211 Gray to State Department, 14 October 1943; 841 D001/215 Winant to Washington DC, 30 October 1943.

40 NAUSA 841D2222/5 memorandum from Hopkins to Hull, 13 April 1943; Churchill to Roosevelt, 11 April 1943 in Kimball (ed.), *Churchill and Roosevelt Volume II*, pp. 186–7; Roosevelt to Churchill, 19 April 1943, p. 192. See also correspondence at 841D2222/6 for some of the consequences.

41 Cooney, *John Charles McQuaid*, pp. 150–1.

42 PRO CAB 120/506 Churchill to Dominions secretary, 5 May 1943.

43 FDRPL PSF Box 40 Gray memorandum 'On recommendations for the adoption of a joint Anglo-American economic policy toward Eire shaped with reference to political considerations', 14 May 1943.

44 FDRPL PSF Box 40 Roosevelt to Hull, 15 June 1943; Hull to Roosevelt, 29 June 1943; Roosevelt to Admiral Leahy, 30 June 1943; Department of State memorandum to the president, 'Status of proposed approach to Ireland', 11 October 1943.

45 NAUSA 841 D001/209 Gray to Winant, 25 September 1943; Winant to Hull, 8 and 27 October 1943; 841 D01/204 Hull to Winant, 5 October 1943; 841 D01/209 Hull to Winant, 27 October 1943.

46 NAUSA 841 D001/206 Gray to Hull, 28 September 1943; Hull to Gray, 5 October 1943; 841 D001/213 Hull to Winant, 13 November 1943.

47 NAUSA 841 D001/217 Gray to Hull, 9 November 1943; 841 D01/220 Gray to Hull, 23 November 1943; 841 D01/224 Hull to Gray, 30 December 1943; 841 D01/225 Gray to Hull, 21 December 1943; Winant to Hull, 22 December 1943,

reporting on meeting with Eden; 841 D01/228 Hull draft for Roosevelt, 29 December 1943.

48 PRO CAB 120/506 Churchill to Dominions secretary, 2 February 1944; NAUSA 841 D001/235A Hull to Winant, 3 February 1944.

49 O'Halpin, *MI5 and Ireland*, pp. 66-7; 74-6; Dungan, *Distant Drums*, p. 119; O'Halpin, *Defending Ireland*, pp. 187-93; Quigley, *A US Spy in Ireland*, pp. 115-205.

50 NAUSA 841 D001/244 Gray to Hull, 21 February 1944; UCDA Eamon de Valera Papers P150/2658 de Valera annotations on American note, no date but presumably on or around 21 February.

51 NAUSA 841 D001/245 Gray to Hull, 23 February 1944; Cunningham, 'Ireland, Canada and the American Note', pp. 144-58.

52 NAUSA 841 D001/247 Gray to Hull, 24 February 1944; 841 D001/249 note by Hickerson on meeting with Brennan, 26 February 1944.

53 NAUSA 841 D001/280 Gray memorandum of conversation with de Valera, 29 February 1944.

54 UCDA Eamon de Valera Papers P150/2658 interviews with Fine Gael leadership, 25 February 1944; interview with Labour party members, 25 February 1944; telephone conversation with Donnellan, 26 February 1944; meeting with Donnellan, 28 February 1944; meeting with Norton and Davin, 29 February 1944.

55 NLI Frank Gallagher Papers MS 18375; Longford and O'Neill, *Eamon de Valera*, pp. 405-7.

56 FDRPL PSF Box 40 Gray to Roosevelt, 24 March 1944. See also OSS memorandum for the president, 30 March 1944 giving details of intelligence cooperation between the United States and Ireland.

57 FDRPL PSF Box 40 text of Hull's speech in memorandum for the president, 20 July 1944; NAUSA 841 D01/283, Gray to Hull, 18 March 1944.

58 NAUSA 841 D001/325A meeting with Brennan in State Department, 29 March 1944; 841 D01/343 memorandum of conversation with Robert Brennan in State Department, 21 April 1944. NAI DEA P48 includes copies of American newspaper reports explicitly citing Brennan as the source for these stories. It is evident that Brennan had sent these back to Dublin to demonstrate his impact.

59 NAUSA 841 D001/325A memorandum for Admiral Leahy, 31 March 1944 which summarizes the agreement reached on the note among the various military and civilian agencies in the United States; 841 D01/303 Hull to Gray, 30 March 1944; 841 D01/308 memorandum of conversation with Captain Lyle F. O'Rourke Army Air Corps in which Robert Stewart emphasizes the agreement among military and diplomatic circles on the threat posed by the Axis diplomats. At the same meeting Stewart openly and warmly supported Gray: 'we are aware that he is not popular with some of the Irish officials but that the reasons behind this have only increased our admiration for him'.

Stewart went on to praise Gray's courageous defence of his country in a difficult position.

60 O'Halpin, *MI5 and Ireland*, pp. 82–93.

61 UCDA Eamon de Valera Papers P150/2571 Walshe meeting with Marlin, 18 and 19 March 1944; Donovan's briefing for Roosevelt in FDRPL PSF Box 40, 30 March 1944.

62 FDRPL Gray Papers Box 7 Gray to Stewart, 23 June 1944; Stewart to Gray, 4 July 1944.

63 NAUSA 841 D001/271 Gray to State Department, 15 March 1944; NAI DEA P48 Gray to Boland, 14 March 1944; Gray to Boland, 29 March 1944.

64 NAUSA 841 D001/319 Brown to Washington, 24 March 1944; UCDA Frank Aiken Papers P104/3493 and 3494, which provide details of the censorship's tasks during the American note crisis during March and April.

65 PRO CAB 120/506 Churchill to Cranborne, 15 March 1944; Churchill to Roosevelt, 19 March 1944 in Kimball (ed.), *Churchill and Roosevelt Volume III*, pp. 57–8; UCDA Eamon de Valera Papers P150/2571 Walsh meeting with Maffey, 18 March 1944; Walsh note of meeting in London, 3 April 1944; NAUSA 841 D001/322 Gray to State Department, 5 April 1944; Winant to State Department, 5 April 1944; 841 D01/339A State Department to Winant, welcoming what was now seen to be Ireland's cooperative spirit, 7 April 1944.

66 Cited in Nolan, 'Joseph Walshe', p. 259, memorandum by Walsh, 16 March 1944.

67 NAI DFA P48 Walsh to Brennan, 14 October 1941; Walsh to Brennan, 11 June 1945.

68 FDRPL Gray Papers, Box 3 Grew to Gray, 4 May 1945; 29 March 1945; 30 April 1945.

69 UCDA Eamon de Valera Papers P150/2676 de Valera to Brennan, 14 October 1944; Brennan, *Ireland Stands Firm*, pp. 91–3; FDRPL PSF Box 40 Roosevelt to Churchill, 8 March 1945; Gray Papers Box 6 Stettinius to Gray, 6 January 1945 where he also insists there is no place for Ireland at a peace conference and that the civil aviation conference does not change policy in this respect.

70 FDRPL Gray Papers Box 6 Gray to Stettinius, 14 December 1944; Stettinius to Gray, 6 January 1944.

71 FDRPL OF 218 memorandum for president in reply to AOH resolution, 6 June 1944; telegram from United Irish Counties Committee to Roosevelt, 30 October 1944. I have not been able to find a reply to the AOH telegram.

72 FDRPL Gray Papers Box 2 correspondence with de Valera on repatriation of Germans during 1945 and 1946; Gray Box 3 Gray to Grew, 17 May 1945; Gray Papers Box 7 Gray to Walshe, 20 January 1945. Gray Papers Box 10 'the position of Eire (Ireland) today', 17 January 1945 is a highly critical assessment of future relations between the United States and Ireland.

CONCLUSION: THE END OF DE VALERA'S IRELAND?

1 PRO DO 35/2089 Maffey to Machtig, 2 August 1945.
2 PRO PREM 3/127/2 memorandum, 8 March 1941; Sloan, *The Geopolitics of Anglo-Irish Relations*, pp. 222–3.
3 FDRPL PSF Box 3 Report by Menzies on meeting in Dublin with de Valera, April 1941.
4 PRO DO 35/2089 'Use of Bases for Naval and Air Bases in Ireland', 17 June 1946.
5 Sloan, *The Geopolitics of Anglo-Irish Relations*, p. 227; Duggan, *Herr Hempel*, pp. 214–16.
6 NAI DEA A3 'Help given by Irish Government to the British in relation to the Actual Waging of the War', 24 May 1941.
7 PRO CAB 66/62 'Position of Southern Ireland', 21 February 1945.
8 Leitz, *Nazi Germany and Neutral Europe*, pp. 51–63.
9 Girvin, 'Did Ireland benefit from the Marshall Plan?' pp. 204–8.
10 Girvin, 'Did Ireland benefit from the Marshall Plan?' pp. 208–20. Johnson and Kennedy, 'The Two Economies in Ireland in the Twentieth Century' has detailed assessments.
11 Girvin, *From Union to Union*, pp. 176–80.
12 Girvin, *From Union to Union*, pp. 112–15. Whelan and Swift, *Spiked*, discloses unsavoury aspects of state–Church relations during the 1950s.

Bibliography

PRIMARY SOURCES

National Archives of Ireland Dublin

Department of the Taoiseach
Department of Finance
Department of Industry and Commerce
Department of Justice
Department of Foreign Affairs
Department of Health

University College Dublin Archives

Patrick McGilligan Papers
Seán MacEntee Papers
Desmond FitzGerald Papers
Richard Mulcahy Papers
Ernest Blythe Papers
Frank Aiken Papers
Eamon de Valera Papers
Cumann na nGaedheal Party Minutes
Fine Gael Party Minutes
Fianna Fáil Party Papers
Colonel Dan Bryan Papers

National Library of Ireland Dublin

Commission on Vocational Organisation:
    Evidence and Minutes to the Commission
Thomas Johnson Papers
Shane Leslie Papers
William O'Brien Papers
Frank Gallagher Papers
Briscoe Papers
James L. O'Donovan Papers

J. J. O'Connell Papers
Pat Shannon Papers
Joe Clarke Papers
M. J. McManus Papers
McGarrity Papers

Military Archives Cathal Brugha Barracks Dublin

General Reports on Army 1940–1945 (S/103)
Memorandum on the Defence Forces, August 1944
Various memoranda on defence plans during the Emergency (EDP)

Public Records Office Kew London

Prime Ministers' Office
Cabinet Office
Dominions Office
Foreign Office
Ministry of Agriculture and Fisheries

National Archives United States of America College Park Maryland

General Records of the State Department

Franklin Delano Roosevelt Presidential Library Hyde Park New York

Gray Papers
Presidential Papers
Sumner Welles Papers

Irish Business and Employers Confederation

Federation of Irish Manufacturers: Council Minute Books

PRINTED SOURCES

Adams, M. Censorship: The Irish Experience (Dublin, 1968)
Alapuro, R. and Allardt, E. 'The Lapua Movement: The Threat of Rightist Takeover in Finland 1930–32' in J. J. Linz and A. Stepan (eds) The Breakdown of Democratic Regimes: Europe (Baltimore, 1978), pp. 122–41
Allen, K. Fianna Fáil and Irish Labour 1926 to the Present (London, 1997)
Andrews, C. S. Man of No Property (Cork, 1982)
Augusteijn, J. (ed.) Ireland in the 1930s (Dublin, 1999)
Barrington, R. Health, Medicine and Politics in Ireland, 1900–1970 (Dublin, 1987)

Barton, B. 'Relations between Westminster and Stormont during the Attlee premiership', *Irish Political Studies*, 7 (1992), pp. 1–20

Barton, B. 'Northern Ireland: the impact of war, 1939–1945', in B. Girvin and G. Roberts, *Ireland and the Second World War*, pp. 47–75

Barton, B. 'Northern Ireland, 1925–39' in J. R. Hill (ed.) *A New History of Ireland: VII Ireland 1921–1984* (Oxford, 2003)

Bax, M. *Harpstrings and Confessions: Machine-Style Politics in the Irish Republic* (Assen, 1976)

Beer, S. H. *Modern British Politics* (London, 1965)

Behan, B. *Borstal Boy* (London, 1958)

Best, G. *Churchill: A Study* (London, 2001)

Bielenberg, A. and O'Mahony, P. 'An Expenditure estimate of Irish national income in 1907', *Economic and Social Review* 29: 2 (1998), pp. 107–32

Blanchard, J. *The Church in Contemporary Ireland* (Dublin, 1963)

Blanshard, P. *The Irish and Catholic Power* (London, 1954)

Böll, H. *Irish Journal* (New York, 1967)

Bowman, J. *De Valera and the Ulster Question 1917–1973* (Oxford, 1982)

Bowyer Bell, J. *The Secret Army* (London, 1972)

Bradley, D. G. 'Speeding the Plough: the Formation of the Federation of Rural Workers, 1944–1948', *Saothar* 11 (1986), pp. 39–54

Brady, C. *Guardians of the Peace* (Dublin, 1974)

Breen, D. *My Fight for Irish Freedom* (Dublin, 1924)

Brennan, R. *Ireland Standing Firm and Eamon de Valera: A Memoir* (Dublin, 2002)

Bromage, M. C. *De Valera and the March of a Nation* (New York, 1956)

Browne, N. *Against the Tide* (Dublin, 1986)

Canning, P. *British Policy towards Ireland 1921–1941* (Oxford, 1985)

Cantril, H. 'Public Opinion in flux', *American Academy of Political and Social Sciences* (March 1942), pp. 136–52

Carroll, J. *Ireland in the War Years* (Newton Abbot, 1975)

Chubb, B. *The Constitution and Constitutional Change in Ireland* (Dublin, 1978 revised edition)

Clark, C. *The Conditions of Economic Progress* (London, 1957, 3rd edition).

Clear, C. *Women of the House* (Dublin, 2000)

Clear, C. 'Women in de Valera's Ireland 1932–48: A Reappraisal' in G. Doherty and D. Keogh (eds) *De Valera's Irelands* (Cork, 2003), pp. 104–14

Clinton, W. D. 'The National Interest: Normative foundations', *Review of Politics* 48: 4 (1986), pp. 495–519

Coakley, J. 'Competing Conceptions of Legitimacy and the Creation of the New State', *Etudes Irlandaises* 20: 1. (1995), pp. 55–62

Cobban, A. *The Nation State and National Self-Determination* (London, 1969, revised edition)

Commission of Inquiry into Banking, Currency and Credit, *Reports* (Dublin, 1938)

Commission on Emigration and other Population Problems, *Reports* (Dublin, 1954)

Commission on Vocational Organisation, *Report* (Dublin, 1944)

Committee on the Constitution, *Report* (Dublin, 1967)

Connolly, T. R. *Irish Public Opinion and the Republican Movement 1916–1918* (MA thesis: University College Cork, 1995)

Conway, W. 'Marriage in Ireland: Church and State', *Irish Ecclesiastical Review* 5th Series, Volume 68 (1946), pp. 361–6

Coogan, T. P. *The IRA* (London, 1970)

Coogan, T. P. *De Valera: Long Fellow, Long Shadow* (London, 1993)

Cooney, J. *John Charles McQuaid: Ruler of Catholic Ireland* (Dublin, 1999)

Corkery, D. *Synge and Anglo-Irish Literature* (Cork, 1931)

Cronin, M. 'Defenders of the Nation? The GAA and Irish Nationalist Identity', *Irish Political Studies* 11 (1996), pp. 1–19

Cronin, M. 'The Blueshirt movement, 1932–5: Ireland's Fascists?', *Journal of Contemporary History* 30: 2 (1996), pp. 311–32

Cronin, M. *The Blueshirts and Irish Politics* (Dublin, 1997)

Cronin, S. (ed.) *The McGarrity Papers*, (Tralee, County Kerry, 1972)

Crotty, R. *Irish Agricultural Production* (Cork, 1966)

Cunningham, E. 'Ireland, Canada and the American Note' in D. Keogh and M. O'Driscoll, *Ireland in World War Two*, pp. 144–58

Daly, M. E. *Industrial Development and Irish National Identity 1922–1939* (Dublin, 1992)

De Valera, E. *National Discipline and the Majority Rule* (Dublin, 1936)

De Valera, E. *Ireland's Stand: Being a Selection of Speeches of Eamon de Valera During the War (1939–1945)* (Dublin, 1946)

De Vere White, T. *Kevin O'Higgins* (Tralee, County Kerry, 1966)

Deeny, J. *To Cure and to Care* (Dublin, 1989)

Delaney, E. 'State, politics and demography: the case of Irish emigration 1921–71', *Irish Political Studies* 13 (1998), pp. 25–50

Delaney, E. *Demography, State and Society: Irish Migration to Britain 1921–1971* (Liverpool, 2000)

Documents on German Foreign Policy Volume VIII Series D (London, 1954)

Documents on German Foreign Policy Volume IX Series D (London, 1956)

Documents on German Foreign Policy Volume X Series D (London, 1957)

Documents on German Foreign Policy Volume XI Series D (London, 1961)

Doherty, G and Keogh, D. (eds) *De Valera's Irelands* (Cork, 2002)

Doherty, R. *Irish Men and Women in the Second World War* (Dublin, 1999)

Duggan, J. P. *Herr Hempel at the German Legation in Dublin 1937–1945* (Dublin, 2003)

Dungan, M. *Distant Drums: Irish Soldiers in Foreign Armies* (Dublin, 1993)

Dunphy, R. *The Making of Fianna Fáil Power in Ireland 1923–1948* (Oxford, 1995)

Dwyer, T. Ryle *Irish Neutrality and the USA: 1939–1947* (Dublin, 1977)

Ellwood, D. W. *Rebuilding Europe* (London, 1992)

English, R. *Armed Struggle: A History of the IRA* (London, 2003)

Fanning, R., Kennedy, M., Keogh, D. and O'Halpin, E. (eds) *Documents on Irish Foreign Policy: Volume I 1919–1922* (Dublin, 1998)

Fanning, R., Kennedy, M., Keogh, D. and O'Halpin, E. (eds) *Documents on Irish Foreign Policy: Volume III 1926–1932* (Dublin, 2002)

Fanning, R. *The Irish Department of Finance 1922–1958* (Dublin, 1978)

Farrell, B. *Chairman or Chief? The Role of the Taoiseach in Irish Government* (Dublin, 1971)

Farrell, B. *The Founding of Dáil Eireann: Parliament and Nation-Building* (Dublin, 1971)

Farrell, B. *Seán Lemass* (Dublin, 1983)

Farrell, B. (ed.) *The Irish Parliamentary Tradition* (Dublin, 1975)

Farrell, B. (ed.) *De Valera's Constitution and Ours* (Dublin, 1988)

Farrell, T. 'Professionalization and suicidal defence planning by the Irish army, 1921–1941', *Journal of Strategic Studies* 21: 3 (1997), pp. 67–85

Fisk, R. *In Time of War: Ireland, Ulster and the Price of Neutrality 1939–45* (London, 1983)

FitzGerald, G. *All in a Life* (Dublin, 1991)

Fitzpatrick, S. 'Donnchadh O'Briain Requests and Representations: An Unceasing Life of Fidelity to Fianna Fáil' (MA thesis: Department of Modern History, University College Dublin 1994)

Freeman, T. W. 'Emigration from Rural Ireland', *Journal of the Statistical and Social Inquiry Society of Ireland*, 17 (1944–5), pp. 404–22

Gallagher, M. *Electoral Support for Irish Political Parties 1927–1973* (London, 1976)

Gallagher, M. 'The Pact general election of 1922', *Irish Historical Studies*, 21: 48 (1979), pp. 404–21

Gallagher, M. (ed.) *Irish Elections 1922–44: Results and Analysis* (Limerick, 1993)

Gallup, G. *The Gallup Poll: Public Opinion 1935–1971*, three volumes (New York, 1975)

Garvin, T. *The Evolution of Irish Nationalist Politics* (Dublin, 1981)

Garvin, T. *Nationalist Revolutionaries* (Oxford, 1987)

Garvin, T. 'Unenthusiastic Democrats: The Emergence of Irish Democracy' in R. J. Hill and M. Marsh (eds) *Modern Irish Democracy* (Dublin, 1993)

Garvin, T. *1922: The Birth of Irish Democracy* (Dublin, 1996)

Gaughan, J. A. *Thomas Johnson 1872–1963* (Dublin, 1980)

Gilbert, M. *Never Despair: Winston S. Churchill 1945–1965* (London, 1988)

Gilbert, M. (ed.) *The Churchill War Papers Volume I: At the Admiralty, September 1939-May 1940* (New York and London, 1993)

Gilbert, M. (ed.) *The Churchill War Papers Volume II: Never Surrender, May 1940–December 1940* (London, 1994)

Girvin, B. 'Nationalism, Democracy and Irish Political Culture' in B. Girvin and

R. Stürm (eds) *Politics and Society in Contemporary Ireland* (Aldershot, 1986), pp. 3–28

Girvin, B. *Between Two Worlds: Politics and Economy in Independent Ireland* (Dublin, 1989)

Girvin, B. *The Right in the Twentieth Century* (London, 1994a)

Girvin, B. 'The Act of Union, Nationalism and Religion: 1780–1850' in J. Elvert (ed.) *Nordirland in Geschichte und Gegenwart/Northern Ireland – Past and Present* (Stuttgart, 1994b)

Girvin, B. 'Irish Agricultural Policy, Economic Nationalism and the Possibility of Market Integration in Europe' in R. T. Griffiths and B. Girvin, *The Green Pool and the Origins of the Common Agricultural Policy* (London, 1995), pp. 239–59

Girvin, B. 'Irish Economic Development and the Politics of EEC Entry' in R. T. Griffiths and S. Ward, *Courting the Common Market* (London, 1996), pp. 247–62

Girvin, B. 'Political Culture, Political Independence and Economic Success in Ireland' in *Irish Political Studies* 12 (1997a), pp. 48–77

Girvin, B. 'Political independence and democratic consolidation' in M. Holmes and D. Holmes (eds) *Ireland and India: connections, comparisons and contrasts* (Dublin, 1997b), pp. 120–44

Girvin, B. 'The State and Vocational Education 1922–1960' in J. Logan (ed.) *The Teachers' Union: The TUI and its Forerunners* (Dublin, 1999), pp. 62–92

Girvin, B. 'Politics in wartime: governing, neutrality and elections', in B. Girvin and G. Roberts, *Ireland and the Second World War* (Dublin, 2000), pp. 24–46

Girvin, B. 'Nationalism, Catholicism and Democracy: Hogan's intellectual evolution' in D. Ó Corráin (ed.) *James Hogan: Revolutionary, Historian and Political Scientist* (Dublin, 2001), pp. 163–76

Girvin, B. *From Union to Union: Nationalism, Democracy and Religion in Ireland – Act of Union to EU* (Dublin, 2002)

Girvin, B. 'Did Ireland benefit from the Marshall Plan? Choice, strategy and the national interest in comparative context' in T. Geiger and M. Kennedy, (eds) *Ireland, Europe and the Marshall Plan* (Dublin, 2004), pp. 182–220.

Girvin, B. and Roberts, G. (eds) *Ireland and the Second World War: Politics, Society and Remembrance* (Dublin, 2000)

Girvin, K. 'The Life and times of Seán O'Hegarty (1881–1963)' (MPhil thesis: University College Cork, 2003)

Goldhagen, D. J. *Hitler's Willing Executioners: Ordinary Germans and the Holocaust* (London, 1996)

Goulding, G. M. *George Gavin Duffy 1882–1951: A Legal Biography* (Dublin, 1982)

Hamilton, H. *The Speckled People* (London, 2003)

Hanley, B., *The IRA 1926–1936* (Dublin, 2002)

Harkness, D. W. *The Restless Dominion* (London, 1969)

Hart, P. 'The Protestant Experience of Revolution in Southern Ireland' in
R. English and G. Walker, (eds) *Unionism in Modern Ireland* (Dublin, 1996),
pp. 81–98

Hart, P. *The IRA and Its Enemies: Violence and Community in Cork 1916–1923*
(Oxford, 1998)

Hartigan, M. 'Irish Emigration 1931–1961', (MA thesis: University College Cork,
1990)

Hennessey, T. *Dividing Ireland: World War I and Partition* (London, 1998)

Hindley, R. *The Death of the Irish Language: A qualified obituary* (London, 1990)

Hirschman, A. O. *Essays in Trespassing: Economic to Politics and Beyond*
(Cambridge, 1981)

Hirschman, A. O. *Shifting Involvements* (Oxford, 1982)

Hogan, G. 'Irish Nationalism as a Legal Ideology', *Studies*, 300 (1986),
pp. 528–38

Hogan, G. 'A Fresh Look at Tilson's Case', *Irish Jurist* 33 (1998), pp. 311–32

Hogan, G. and Whyte, G. *The Irish Constitution: J. M. Kelly* (Dublin, 1994, 3rd
edition)

Hogan, J. *Could Ireland Become Communist?* (Dublin, 1935)

Hogan, J. *Modern Democracy* (Cork, 1938)

Hogan, J. *Election and Representation* (Cork and Oxford, 1945)

Horgan, J. *Seán Lemass: The Enigmatic Patriot* (Dublin, 1997)

Horgan, J. *Noël Browne: Passionate Outsider* (Dublin, 2000)

Hull, M. *Irish Secrets: German Espionage in Wartime Ireland 1939–1945* (Dublin,
2003)

Inglis, T. *Moral Monopoly: The Rise and Fall of the Catholic Church in Modern
Ireland* (Dublin, 1998)

Jackson, P. 'Outside the Jurisdiction – Irishwomen Seeking Abortion' in
C. Curtin, P. Jackson and B. O'Connor (eds) *Gender in Irish Society* (Galway,
1987)

Jenkins, R. *Churchill* (London, 2001)

Johnson, D. and Kennedy, L. 'The Two Economies in Ireland in the Twentieth
Century' in J. R. Hill (ed.) *A New History of Ireland VII Ireland 1921–1984*
(Oxford, 2003), pp. 452–86

Jonas, M. *Isolationism in America: 1935–1941* (Ithaca, New York, 1966)

Judah, T. *Kosovo: War and Revenge* (London, 2000)

Kavanagh, P. *Collected Poems* (New York, 1964)

Kellas, J. G. *The Politics of Nationalism and Ethnicity* (London, 1998, 2nd
edition)

Kennedy, D. *The Widening Gulf: Northern Attitudes to the Independent Irish
State, 1919–49* (Belfast, 1988)

Kennedy, K., Giblin, T. and McHugh, D. *The Economic Development of Ireland
in the Twentieth Century* (London, 1988)

Kennedy, M. *Division and Consensus: The Politics of Cross-Border Relations in
Ireland, 1925–1969* (Dublin, 2000a)

Kennedy, M. (ed.) *Irish Foreign Policy, 1919–1966: From Independence to Internationalism* (Dublin, 2000b)

Keogh, D. 'The Constitutional Revolution: An Analysis of the Making of the Constitution' in Frank Litton (ed.) *The Constitution of Ireland 1937–1987* (Dublin, 1988), pp. 4–84

Keogh, D. 'Eamon de Valera and Hitler: An Examination of International Reaction to the Visit to the German Minister, May 1945', *Irish Studies in International Affairs*, 3: 1 (1989), pp. 69–92

Keogh, D. *Ireland and Europe 1919–1989* (Cork, 1990)

Keogh, D. *Twentieth Century Ireland: Nation and State* (Dublin, 1994)

Keogh, D. 'The Role of the Catholic Church in the Republic of Ireland 1922–1995' in Forum for Peace and Reconciliation, *Building Trust in Ireland* (Belfast, 1996), pp. 85–214

Keogh, D. *Jews in Twentieth-Century Ireland: Refugees, Anti-Semitism and the Holocaust* (Cork, 1998)

Keogh, D. '"Making Aliya": Irish Jews, the Irish State and Israel' in D. Keogh, F. O'Shea, and C. Quinlan, (eds) *Ireland: The Lost Decade in the 1950s* (Cork, 2004), pp. 252–72

Keogh, D. and O'Driscoll, F. 'Ireland' in T. Buchanan and M. Conway (eds) *Political Catholicism in Europe* (Oxford, 1996), pp. 275–300

Keogh, D. and O'Driscoll, M. (eds) *Ireland in World War Two: Neutrality and Survival* (Cork, 2004)

Kershaw, I. *Making Friends with Hitler: Lord Londonderry and the Roots of Appeasement* (London, 2004)

Kimball, W. F. (ed.) *Churchill and Roosevelt: The Complete Correspondence Volumes I–III* (Princeton, New Jersey, 1984)

Kimball, W. F., *Forged in War: Roosevelt, Churchill and the Second World War* (New York, 1997)

Kissane, B. 'The not-so-amazing case of Irish democracy', *Irish Political Studies* 10 (1995), pp. 43–68

Kissane, B. 'Majority rule and the stabilisation of democracy in the Irish Free State', *Irish Political Studies*, 13 (1998), pp. 1–24

Kissane, B. *Explaining Irish Democracy* (Dublin, 2002)

Knowlson, J. *Damned to Fame: the Life of Samuel Beckett* (London, 1996)

Kochavi, A. J. 'Britain, the United States and Irish Neutrality, 1944–5', *European History Quarterly* 25 (1995), pp. 93–115

Laffan, M. *The Resurrection of Ireland: The Sinn Féin Party 1916–1923* (Cambridge, 1999)

Langer, W. L. and Gleason, S. E. *The Challenge to Isolation: 1937–1940* (London, 1952)

Langer, W. L. and Gleason, S. E. *The Undeclared War: 1940–1941* (New York, 1953)

Larkin, E. *The Roman Catholic Church and the Creation of the Modern Irish State 1878–1886* (Dublin, 1975)

Lee, J. and O'Tuathaigh, G. *The Age of de Valera* (Dublin, 1982)

Lee, J. J. 'Aspects of Corporatist Thought in Ireland: The Commission on Vocational Organisation, 1939–43' in A. Cosgrave and D. McCartney (eds) *Studies in Irish History* (Dublin, 1979), pp. 324–46

Lee, J. J. *Ireland 1912–1985: Politics and Society* (Cambridge, 1989)

Leitz, C. *Nazi Germany and Neutral Europe during the Second World War* (Manchester, 2000)

Leslie, S. *The Irish Tangle for English Readers* (London, 1946)

Lindbergh, C. A. *The Wartime Journals of Charles A. Lindbergh* (New York, 1970)

Longford, Earl of and O'Neill, T. P. *Eamon De Valera* (London, 1970)

Mac Eoin, U. *The IRA in the Twilight Years, 1923–1948* (Dublin, 1997)

MacCarthy, A. *A Doctor's War* (Cork, 2005)

MacDermott, E. *Clann na Poblachta* (Cork, 1998)

MacNeice, L. *Collected Poems* (London, 1979)

Mair, P. *The Changing Irish Party System* (New York, 1987)

Mair, P. 'De Valera and Democracy' in T. Garvin, M. Manning and R. Sinnott (eds) *Dissecting Irish Politics: Essays in Honour of Brian Farrell* (Dublin, 2004), pp. 31–47

Manning, M. *The Blueshirts* (Dublin, 1970)

Manning, M. *James Dillon: A Biography* (Dublin, 1999)

Mansergh, N. *The Irish Free State* (London, 1934)

McCarthy, C. *Trade Unions in Ireland 1894–1960* (Dublin, 1977)

McCullagh, D. *A Makeshift Majority: The First Inter-Party Government, 1948–51* (Dublin, 1998)

McDowell, R. B. *The Irish Convention 1917–18* (London, 1970)

McGall, R. 'The five-pound-a-week family', *Standard*, Dublin, 28 July 1944

McGarry, F. (ed.) *Republicanism in Modern Ireland* (Dublin, 2003)

McInerney, M. 'The Gerry Boland Story', *Irish Times*, 11 October 1968

McKee, E. 'Church–State Relations and the Development of Irish Health Policy: The Mother and Child Scheme, 1944–53', *Irish Historical Studies*, 25: 98 (1986)

McMahon, D. *Republicans and Imperialists* (New Haven and London, 1984)

Miller D. W. *Church, State and Nation in Ireland 1898–1921* (Dublin, 1973)

Milotte, M. *Communism in Modern Ireland* (Dublin, 1984)

Milotte, M. *Banished Babies: The Secret History of Ireland's Baby Export Business* (Dublin, 1997)

Mjøset, L. *The Irish Economy in a Comparative Institutional Perspective* (Dublin, 1992)

Montague, J. *Collected Poems* (Oldcastle, County Meath, 1995)

Moss, W. *Political Parties in the Irish Free State* (New York, 1933)

Moynihan M. (ed.) *Speeches and Statements by Eamon De Valera 1917–73* (Dublin, 1980)

Murphy, G. 'The Politics of Economic Realignment, Ireland 1948–1964' (PhD thesis: Dublin City University, 1996)

Murray, P. 'Obsessive Historian: Eamon de Valera and the Policing of his Reputation' in *Proceedings of the Royal Irish Academy*, Volume 101C (2001), pp. 37–65

Murray, P. *Oracles of God, The Roman Catholic Church and Irish Politics, 1922–37* (Dublin, 1999)

Newman, J. *Studies in Political Morality* (Dublin and London, 1962)

Nicholson, H. *The War Years 1939–1945* (New York, 1967)

Noelle, E. and Neumann, E. P. (eds) *The Germans: Public Opinion Polls 1947–1966* (Westport, Connecticut, 1967)

Nolan, A. 'Joseph Walshe and the Management of Irish Foreign Policy 1922–1946' (PhD thesis: University College Cork, 1997)

Ó Buachalla, S. *Education Policy in Twentieth Century Ireland* (Dublin, 1988)

Ó Corráin, D. (ed.) *James Hogan: Revolutionary, Historian and Political Scientist* (Dublin, 2000)

Ó Drisceoil, D. *Censorship in Ireland 1939–1945* (Cork, 1996)

Ó Gráda, C. *Ireland: A New Economic History* (Oxford, 1994)

Ó Gráda, C. *A Rocky Road: The Irish Economy since the 1920s* (Manchester, 1997)

O'Brien, C. C. *God Land: Reflections on Religion and Nationalism* (Cambridge, Massachusetts, 1988)

O'Brien, C. C. *Memoir: My Life and Themes* (Dublin, 1998)

O'Brien, J. A. 'The Vanishing Irish' in John A. O'Brien (ed.) *The Vanishing Irish: The Enigma of the Modern World* (New York, 1953)

O'Connor, E. *A Labour History of Ireland* (Dublin, 1992)

O' Donoghue, D. 'Berlin's Irish War', in D. Keogh and M. O'Driscoll (eds) *Ireland in World War Two* (Cork, 2004), pp. 93–106

O'Halpin, E. 'Parliamentary party discipline and tactics: the Fianna Fáil archives 1926–32', *Irish Historical Studies* 30: 120 (1997), pp. 581–90

O'Halpin, E. 'Historical Revisit: Dorothy Macardle, The Irish Republic (1937)', *Irish Historical Studies* 31:123 (May 1999) pp. 389–94

O'Halpin, E. *Defending Ireland: The Irish State and its Enemies Since 1922* (Oxford, 1999)

O'Halpin, E. 'British Intelligence, the Republican Movement and the IRA's German Links, 1935–45' in F. McGarry (ed.) *Republicanism in Modern Ireland* (Dublin, 2003a), pp. 108–31

O'Halpin, E. (ed.) *MI5 and Ireland, 1939–1945: The Official History* (Dublin, 2003b)

O'Leary, C. 'Professor Lee's Ireland' (Unpublished manuscript in author's possession)

O'Leary, D. *Vocationalism and Social Catholicism in Twentieth Century Ireland* (Dublin, 1999)

O'Leary, E. 'The Irish National Teachers' Organisation and the Marriage Bar for Women National Teachers, 1933–1958', *Saothar* 12 (1987), pp. 47–52

O'Longaigh, S. 'Preparing Law for an Emergency, 1938–1939' and 'Emergency

Law in Action, 1939–1945' in D. Keogh and M. O'Driscoll (eds) *Ireland in World War Two: Neutrality and Survival* (Cork, 2004), pp. 36–47 and 63–80

Orwell, S. and Angus, I. (eds) *The Collected Essays, Journalism and Letters of George Orwell Volumes I–IV* (Harmondsworth, Middlesex, 1970)

Overy, R. *Why the Allies Won* (London, 1995)

Pašeta, S. *Before the Revolution: Nationalism, Social Change and Ireland's Catholic Élite, 1879–1922* (Cork, 1999)

Power, S. *'A Problem From Hell' America and the Age of Genocide* (New York, 2002)

Prager, J. *Building Democracy in Ireland* (Cambridge, 1986)

Quigley, M. S. *A US Spy in Ireland* (Dublin, 1999)

Quinn, A., *Patrick Kavanagh* (Dublin, 2003)

Rafter, K. *The Clann: The Story of Clann na Poblachta* (Cork, 1996)

Raymond, R. J. 'David Gray, the Aiken Mission and Irish Neutrality, 1940–41', *Diplomatic History* 9 (Winter 1985), pp. 55–71

Regan, J. M. 'The Politics of Reaction: the dynamics of treatyite government and policy, 1922–33', *Irish Historical Studies* 30: 120 (1997)

Regan, J. M. *The Irish Counter-Revolution 1921–1936* (Dublin, 1999)

Roberts, G. 'The British Offer to End Partition, June 1940', *History Ireland* 9: 1 (2001), pp. 5–6

Robertson, G. *Crimes Against Humanity: The Struggle for Global Justice* (London, 1999)

Rose, R. *What is Europe?* (London, 1996)

Rosenberg, J. L. 'The 1941 Mission of Frank Aiken to the United States: An American Perspective', *Irish Historical Studies*, 22: 88 (1980), pp. 162–77

Ryan, D. *Unique Dictator – A Study of Eamon de Valera* (London, 1936)

Rynne, S. *Father John Hayes, Leader of Muintir na Tíre* (Dublin, 1960)

Schmitt, D. *The Irony of Irish Democracy: The Impact of Political Culture on Administration and Democratic Political Development in Ireland* (London and Toronto, 1973)

Sinnnott, R. *Irish Voters Decide* (Manchester, 1995)

Skidelski, R. *John Maynard Keynes: Fighting for Britain 1937–1946* (London, 2000)

Skinner, L. C. *Politicians by Accident* (Dublin, 1946)

Sloan, G. R. *The Geopolitics of Anglo-Irish Relations in the Twentieth Century* (London, 1997)

Smith, A. *Hostage to Fortune: The Letters of Joseph P. Kennedy* (New York, 2001)

Smith, M. 'The Title An Taoiseach in the 1937 Constitution', *Irish Political Studies* 10 (1995), pp. 179–84

Stepan, A. 'Religion, Democracy and the "Twin Tolerations"', *Journal of Democracy* 11: 1 (October 2000), pp. 37–57

Stephan, E. *Spies in Ireland* (London, 1963)

Titley, B. *Church, State and the Control of Schools in Ireland, 1900–1944* (Kingston and Montreal, 1983)

United Nations European Commission for Europe, *Economic Survey of Europe in 1951* (Geneva, 1952)

Valiulis, M. G. ' "The Man They Could Never Forgive" – The View of the Opposition: Eamon de Valera and the Civil War' in J P. O'Carroll, and J. A. Murphy (eds) *De Valera and His Times* (Cork, 1983), pp. 92–100

Valiulis, M. G. *Almost a Rebellion: the Irish Army Mutiny of 1924* (Cork, 1985)

Varley, T. 'Farmers against nationalists: the rise and fall of Clann na Talmhan' in R. Gillespie and G. Moran (eds) *Galway: History and Society* (Dublin, 1995)

Varley, T. and Moser, P. 'Clann na Talmhan: Ireland's last Farmers' Party', *History Ireland* (Summer 1995), pp. 39–43

Walker, B. *Dancing to History's Time: History, Myth and Politics in Ireland* (Belfast, 1996)

Walsh, J. J. *Recollections of a Rebel* (Tralee, County Kerry, 1944)

Walzer, M. *Just and Unjust Wars* (New York, 1977, 2nd edition 1992)

Ward, A. J. *The Irish Constitutional Tradition* (Dublin, 1994)

Ward, C. 'Ireland' in H. Mol (ed.) *Western Religion: A Country by Country Sociological Inquiry* (The Hague, 1972)

Whelan, G, with Swift, C. *Spiked: Church–State Intrigue and 'The Rose Tattoo'* (Dublin, 2002)

White, J. *Minority Report: The Protestant Community in the Irish Republic* (Dublin, 1975)

Whyte, J. H. *Dáil Deputies* (Dublin, 1965)

Whyte, J. H. *Church and State in Modern Ireland 1923–1970* (Dublin, 1971)

Whyte, J. H. 'Ireland: Politics without social bases' in R. Rose (ed.) *Electoral Behaviour: A Comparative Handbook* (New York, 1974), pp. 619–51

Whyte, J. H. *Catholics in Western Europe* (Dublin, 1981)

Wolf, J. B. ' "Withholding Their Due": The Dispute Between Ireland and Great Britain Over Unemployment Insurance Payments To Conditionally Landed Irish Wartime Volunteer Workers', *Saothar* 21 (1996), pp. 39–45

Woodberry, R. D. and Shah, T. S. 'The Pioneering Protestants' in *Journal of Democracy* 15: 2 (April 2004), pp. 47–61

Wylie, N. (ed.) *European Neutrals and Non-Belligerents during the Second World War* (Cambridge, 2002)

Index

Index

Picture Credits

1, 2, 3, 4, 7, 14, 15, 17, 23, 33 – copyright © Examiner Publications

5, 13 – copyright © Getty Images

6, 10, 18, 19, 20, 21, 22, 24, 25 – Irish Military Archives

8, 9, 31 – National Library of Wales, Illingworth, copyright © Solo Syndication/
Associated Newspapers

30 – David Lowe, University of Kent, Solo Syndication/Associated Newspapers

11, 12, 16, 26, 27, 28, 29 – *Dublin Opinion*, copyright © National Library of Ireland

32 – copyright © *Irish Times*

Visit **www.panmacmillan.com** to read more about all our books and to buy them. You will also find features, author interviews and news of any author events, and you can sign up for e-newsletters so that you're always first to hear about our new releases.

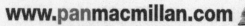

www.panmacmillan.com

GIFT SELECTOR
YOUR ACCOUNT
WISH LIST
WAITING LIST

| HOME | ABOUT US | IMPRINTS | TRADE/MEDIA | CONTACT US | ADVANCED SEARCH | SEARCH | GO |

| BOOK CATEGORIES | WHAT'S NEW | AUTHORS/ILLUSTRATORS | BESTSELLERS | READING GROUPS |

Coming Soon...

Reading Groups

Competitions
Feeling Lucky?

Extracts
Sneak Previews

Interviews

Events
Meet Our Stars

Reviews
What The Critics Say

News & Awards

Editor's Choice
What We're Reading

© 2005 PAN MACMILLAN   ACCESSIBILITY   HELP   TERMS & CONDITIONS   PRIVACY POLICY   SEND PAGE TO A FRIEND